EFFICIENT RENT-SEEKING

CHRONICLE OF AN INTELLECTUAL QUAGMIRE

EFFICIENT RENT-SEEKING

CHRONICLE OF AN INTELLECTUAL QUAGMIRE

edited by

Alan A. Lockard

Center for the Study of Public Choice
George Mason University

and

Gordon Tullock

James M. Buchanan Center for Political Economy
George Mason University

KLUWER ACADEMIC PUBLISHERS
Boston / Dordrecht / London

Distributors for North, Central and South America:
Kluwer Academic Publishers
101 Philip Drive
Assinippi Park
Norwell, Massachusetts 02061 USA
Telephone (781) 871-6600
Fax (781) 871-6528
E-Mail <kluwer@wkap.com>

Distributors for all other countries:
Kluwer Academic Publishers Group
Distribution Centre
Post Office Box 322
3300 AH Dordrecht, THE NETHERLANDS
Telephone 31 78 6392 392
Fax 31 78 6546 474
E-Mail <services@wkap.nl>

Electronic Services <http://www.wkap.nl>

Library of Congress Cataloging-in-Publication Data

Efficient rent seeking : chronicle of an intellectual quagmire / edited by Alan A. Lockard and Gordon Tullock.
p. cm.
A collection of 36 articles previously published in scholarly journals, many in the 1990's and from Public Choice.
Includes bibliographical references and index.
ISBN 0-7923-7242-5 (alk. paper)
1. Rent (Economic theory) I. Lockard, Alan A. II. Tullock, Gordon.

HB401 .E37 2000
333.01'2—dc21 00-051989

Printed on acid-free paper
Printed in the United States of America

TABLE OF CONTENTS

Acknowledgements

We wish to thank the following for permission to reprint:

Chapter 10	Reprinted by permission of the Trustees of the University of Illinois, the copyright owner.
Chapter 12	Reprinted from *Journal of Political Economy* by permission of The University of Chicago Press, the copyright owner.
Chapter 17	Reprinted from *The Economic Journal*, 101, 1522-1534, copyright (1991) by permission of The Royal Economic Society.
Chapter 21	Reprinted from *Journal of Institutional and Theoretical Economics* 149/3 by permission of the author.
Chapter 22	Reprinted from *Economic Letters* 1, Kyung Hwan Baik, "Effort Levels in Contests: The Public-Good Prize Case," 363-67, copyright (1993), with permission of Elsevier Science.
Chapter 24	Reprinted from *European Journal of Political Economy* 10, Shmuel Nitzan, "Modelling Rent-Seeking Contests," 41-60, copyright (1994), with permission of Elsevier Science.
Chapter 26	Originally published in *Games and Economic Behavior*, Vol. 7, 406-427, copyright (1994) by Academic Press, reprinted by permission of the publisher.
Chapter 29	Reprinted from *Economic Letters* 56, Peter Kooreman and Lambert Schoonbeek, "The Specification of the Probability Functions in Tullock's Rent-Seeking Contest," 59-61, copyright (1997), with permission from Elsevier Science.
Chapter 33	Reprinted from *Public Finance Review,* Vol. 27, No. 5, William F. Shughart II, "The Reformer's Dilemma," 561-565, copyright (1999) by Sage Publications, Inc., reprinted by permission of Sage Publications, Inc.
Chapter 34	Reprinted from *The Economic Journal* 109, by permission of The Royal Economic Society.

The copyright for the articles which originally appeared in *Public Choice* are held by Kluwer.

Introduction

Some time ago I accidentally stumbled on a paradox. I stumbled on it in the context of rent seeking, but with time I realized it has wider implications. Specifically where ever there is competitive entry into a profit-making situation then it would appear to fit my model. My model is interesting because there is no real equilibrium.

The conditions come right out of elementary economic theory. It is assumed that the competitors make investments and the likelihood of success depends on the size of those investments. There is only one prize, which is different from our ordinary economy, but in other aspects it seems perfectly normal. The resources invested are subject to declining marginal returns and indeed that is why the problem arises.

In my model the declining returns are shown in the way they normally are in elementary economics. This seems reasonable although perhaps too regular for the real world. Roughly speaking each investor has a possibility of success proportional to the square root of his or her investment and inversely proportional to the square roots of his competitor's investment. Since the model is given completely in the first essay contained here I will not go further. Unfortunately it leads to paradoxical conclusions. Further, although the matter is entirely theory and in the real world things may be more complicated, the paradox seems to be quite general. In other words it raises questions about the market, which so far have not been solved. Speaking for myself I have faith and think that Capitalism will survive, but I would like to understand how the model fails.

This volume is essentially an exercise in intellectual history. After the original article was published various people wrote in with apparent solutions. In my role as editor I published them and as the author I responded. Since I am enthusiast for markets my role was an unfortunate one. I kept saying that their solutions were wrong and hence that there were problems in the market. I must admit that they did find difficulties with my work, which I acknowledge, but on the whole my paradox stood up.

With time the attacks on my article became more complex and eventually there was a fall off of interest. The present situation is that this particular difficulty has not been completely cleared up, but we know a lot more about it. The purpose of this collection is firstly to revive interest and secondly to present an interesting intellectual history of a most involved problem in economic theory. I expect both theorists and historians to be interested although to tell the truth I do not imagine enough will be interested so we will make the New York Times best-seller list. Indeed I doubt that the printing costs will be covered by sales. It's an intellectual contribution, and although it is in economics is not an economic project.

We have two editors, one (myself) holds a special chair in both the law school and the Center for the Study of Public Choice. The other is a graduate student. Those among my readers who are accustomed to academic culture will immediately realize how labor was divided between us. I had the idea and he did the work.

-Gordon Tullock

EFFICIENT RENT SEEKING

Gordon Tullock

MOST of the papers in this volume* implicitly or explicitly assume that rent-seeking activity discounts the entire rent to be derived. Unfortunately, this is not necessarily true; the reality is much more complicated. The problem here is that the average cost and marginal cost are not necessarily identical.

This is surprising because in competitive equilibrium the average cost and marginal cost are equal and rent seeking is usually a competitive industry. If marginal cost is continuously rising, then marginal and average cost will be different.[1] In the ordinary industry the average cost curve of an individual enterprise is usually U-shaped, with economies of scale in the early range and diseconomies of scale in the latter range. In equilibrium, the companies will be operating at the bottom of this cost curve, and therefore average and marginal costs will be equated.

A second and much more important reason for the equality of marginal and average cost is that if there is some resource used in production of anything produced under continuously rising costs, then the owners of that resource will charge the marginal cost. People engaged in manufacturing (or whatever activity with which we are dealing) will face a cost that incorporates these rents of the original factor owners. Thus, the assumption that the costs are constant over scale is suitable for practical use.

Unfortunately, both these reasons are of dubious validity in the cause of rent seeking. First, there seem to be no particular economies of scale. As far as we can see, for example, such monster industries as big oil and the natural gas producers do not do as well in dealing with the government as do little oil or, in the gas case, householders. In general, it would appear that there is no range of increasing returns in rent seeking. However, this is admittedly an empirical problem and one for which, at the moment, we have little data. It is, in any event, dangerous to assume that the curves are all U-shaped and competition will adjust us to the minimum point of these curves.

---

* Tullock here refers to the original volume this article was published in, *Toward a Theory of the Rent-Seeking Society,* rather than this work. Ed.

[1] This is obviously also true if marginal cost is continuously falling.

This is particularly so, since there is no obvious reason why all rent seekers should have identical efficiencies.

The second and more important reason why we can normally assume that supply curves are, in the long run, flat is that if they are continuously rising, factor owners can generally achieve the full rent by selling their factors at their marginal value; hence, the enterprises face essentially flat supply prices. Unfortunately, this has only a limited application in rent seeking. Suppose, for example, that we organize a lobby in Washington for the purpose of raising the price of milk and are unsuccessful. We cannot simply transfer our collection of contacts, influences, past bribes, and so forth to the steel manufacturers' lobby. In general, our investments are too specialized, and, in many cases, they are matters of very particular and detailed good will to a specific organization. It is true that we could sell the steel lobby our lobbyists with their connections and perhaps our mailing list. But presumably all these things have been bought by us at their proper cost. Our investment has not been paid, but there is nothing left to transfer.

Similarly, the individual lobbyist spends much time cultivating congressmen and government officials and learning the ins and outs of government regulations. There is no way he can simply transfer these contacts, connections, and knowledge to a younger colleague if he wishes to change his line of business. The younger colleague must start at the bottom and work his way up. Thus, it seems likely that in most rent-seeking cases, the supply curve slants up and to the right from its very beginning. This means that rent-seeking activities are very likely to have different marginal and average costs, even if we can find an equilibrium.

It might seem that with continuously upward sloping supply curves and a competitive industry, there would be no equilibrium. This turns out not to be true, although the equilibrium is of a somewhat unusual nature. The analytical tools required to deal with it are drawn more from game theory than from classical economics.

In my article, "On the Efficient Organization of Trials,"[2] I introduced a game that I thought had much resemblance to a court trial, or, indeed, to any other two-party conflict. In its simplest form, we assume two parties who are participating in a lottery under somewhat unusual rules. Each is permitted to buy as many lottery tickets as he wishes at one dollar each, the lottery tickets are put in a drum, one is pulled out, and whoever owns that ticket wins the prize. Thus, the probability of success for A is shown in equation (1), because the number of lottery tickets he hold is amount A and the total number in the drum is $A + B$.

---

[2] Gordon Tullock, "On the Efficient Organization of Trials," Kyklos 28 (1975): 745-762.

$$P_A = \frac{A}{A + B} \tag{1}$$

In the previously cited article, I pointed out that this model could be generalized by making various modifications in it, and it is my purpose now to generalize it radically.[3]

Let us assume, then, that a wealthy eccentric has put up $100 as a prize for the special lottery between *A* and *B*. Note that the amount spent on lottery tickets is retained by the lottery, not added onto the prize. This makes the game equivalent to rent seeking, where resources are also wasted.

How much should each invest? It is obvious that the answer to this question, from the standpoint of each party, depends on what he thinks the other will do. Here, and throughout the rest of this paper, I am going to use a rather special assumption about individual knowledge. I am going to assume that if there is a correct solution for individual strategy, then each player will assume that the other parties can also figure out what that correct solution is. In other words, if the correct strategy in this game were to play $50, each party would assume that the other was playing $50 and would only buy fifty tickets for himself, if that were the optimal amount under those circumstances.

As a matter of fact, the optimal strategy in this game is not to buy $50.00 worth of tickets but to buy $25.00. As a very simple explanation, suppose that I have bought $25.00 and you have bought $50.00. I have a one in three chance of getting the $100.00 and you have a two in three chance., Thus, the present value of my investment is $33.33 and the present value of yours is $66.66, or, for this particular case, an equal percentage gain. Suppose, however, that you decided to reduce your purchases to $40.00 and I stayed at $25.00, This saves you $10.00 on your investment, but it lowers your present value of expectancy to only $61.53 and you are about $5.00 better off. Of course, I have gained from your reduction, too.

You could continue reducing your bet with profit until you also reached $25.00. For example, if you lowered your purchase from $26.00 to $25.00, the present value of your investment would fall from $50.98 to $50.00, and you would save $1.00 in investment. Going beyond $25.00, however, would cost you money. If you lowered it to $24.00, you would reduce the value of your investment by $1.02 and only save $1.00. It is assumed, of course, that I keep my purchase at $25.00.

I suppose it is obvious from what I have said already that $25.00 is equilibrium for both, that is, departure from it costs either one something. It is not true, however, that if the other party has made a mistake, I maximize

---

[3] For a previous generalization of the model and an application to arms races, see Gordon Tullock, *The Social Dilemma: The Economics of War and Revolution* (Blacksburg, Va.: Center for Study of Public Choice, 1974), pp. 87-125.

my returns by paying \$25.00. For example, if the other party has put up \$50.00 and I pay \$24.00 instead of \$25.00, I save \$1.00 in my investment but reduce my expectancy by only \$0.90. My optimal investment, in fact, is \$17.00. However, if we assume a game in which each party knows what the other party has invested and then adjusts his investment accordingly, the ultimate outcome must be at approximately \$25.00 for each party.[4] The game is clearly a profitable one to play, and, in fact, it will impress the average economist as rather improbable. However, it is a case in which inframarginal profits are made, although we are in marginal balance. At first glance, most people feel that the appropriate bet is \$50.00, but that is bringing the total return into equality with the total cost rather than equating the margins.

To repeat, this line of reasoning depends on the assumption that the individuals can figure out the correct strategy, if there is a correct strategy, and that they assume that the other people will be able to figure it out, also. It is similar to the problem that started John von Neumann on the invention of game theory, and I think it is not too irrational a set of assumptions if we assume the kind of problem that rent seeking raises.

But there is no reason why the odds in our game should be simple linear function of contributions. For example, they could be an exponential function, as in equation (2):

$$P_A = \frac{A^r}{A^r + B^r} \tag{2}$$

There are, of course, many other functions that could be substituted, but in this paper we will stick to exponentials.

It is also possible for more than two people to play, in which case we would have equation (3):

$$P_A = \frac{A^r}{A^r + B^r, \ldots, n^r} \tag{3}$$

The individuals need not receive the same return on their investment. Indeed, in many cases we would hope that the situation is biased. For example, we hope that the likelihood of passing a civil service examination is not simply a function of the amount of time spent cramming, but that other types of merit are also important. This would be shown in our equations by some kind of

---

[4] It would make no difference in the reasoning here, or in any of the following work, if there were an insurance company always willing to buy a bid at its true actuarial value. For example, if you had put in \$25.00 and the other party had also put in \$25.00, it would give you \$50.00 for it, and if you had put in \$26.00 and the other party \$25.00, it would give you \$50.98. But rent seeking normally involves risk, and hence I have kept the examples in the risky form.

bias in which one party receives more lottery tickets for his money than another.

We will begin by changing the shape of the marginal cost curve and the number of people playing, and leave bias until later. Table 6.1 shows the individual equilibrium payments by players of the game, with varying exponents (which means varying marginal cost structures) and varying numbers of players. Table 6.2 shows the total amount paid by all of the players, if they al play the equilibrium strategy.

I have drawn lines dividing these two tables into zones I, II, and III. Let us temporarily confine ourselves to discussing zone I. This is the zone in which the equilibrium price summed over all players leads to a payment equal to or less than the total price. In other words, these are the games in which expectancy of the players, if they all play, would be positive. Although we will start with these games, as we shall see below there are cases in which we may be compelled to play games in zones II and III where the expectancy is negative.

If we look at zone I, it is immediately obvious that the individual payments go down as the number of players rises, but the total amount paid rises. In a way, what is happening here is that a monopoly profit is being competed away. Note, however, when the exponent is one-third or one-half, even in the limit there is profit of $66.66 or $50.00 to the players taken as a whole. Thus, some profit remains. With the cost curve slanting steeply upward, these results are to some extent counterintuitive. One might assume that with a positive return on investment, it will always be sensible for more players to enter, thereby driving down the profits. In this case, however, each

TABLE 6.1
Individual Investments
(N - person, No Bias, with Exponent)

	Number of Players				
Exponent	2	4		10	15
1/3	8.33	6.25		3.00	2.07
1/2	12.50	9.37	I	4.50	3.11
1	25.00	18.75		9.00	6.22
2	50.00	37.50		18.00	12.44
3	75.00	56.25	II	27.00	18.67
5	125.00	93.75		45.00	31.11
8	200.00	150.00		72.00	49.78
12	300.00	225.00		108.00	74.67
			III		

TABLE 6.2
Sum of Investments
(N - person, No Bias, with Exponent)

Exponent	2	4	10		15	Limit
	Number of Players					
1/3	16.66	25.00	30.00		31.05	33.30
1/2	25.00	37.40	45.00	I	46.65	50.00
1	50.00	75.00	90.00		93.30	100.00
2	100.00	150.00	180.00		186.60	200.00
3	150.00	225.00	270.00	II	280.05	300.00
5	250.00	375.00	450.00		466.65	500.00
8	400.00	600.00	720.00		746.70	800.00
12	600.00	900.00	1,080.00		1,120.05	1,200.00
				III		

additional players lowers the payments of all the preceding players and his own, and the limit as the number of players goes to infinity turns out to be one where that infinity of players has, at least in expectancy terms, sizable profits.

Throughout the table, in zones I, II, and III, individual payments go down as we move from left to right, and total payments rise. We can deduce a policy implication from this, although it is a policy implication to which many people may object on moral grounds. It would appear that if one is going to distribute rents, nepotism is a good thing because it reduces the number of players and, therefore, the total investment. This is one of the classical arguments for hereditary monarchies. By reducing the number of candidates for an extremely rent-rich job to one, you eliminate such rent-seeking activities as civil war, assassination, and so forth. Of course, there are costs here. If we reduce the number of people who may compete for a given job, you may eliminate the best candidate or even the best two thousand candidates., This cost must be offset against the reduction in rent-seeking costs.

On the other hand, many cases of rent seeking are not ones in which we care particularly who gets the rent. In such matters as government appointments where there are large incomes from illegal sources, pressure groups obtaining special aid from the government, and so on, we would prefer that there be no rent at all, and, if there must be rent, it does not make much difference to whom it goes. In these cases, clearly, measures to reduce rent seeking are unambiguous gains. Thus, if Mayor Richard Daley had confined all of the more lucrative appointments to his close relatives, the social savings might have been considerable.

If we go down the table, the numbers also steadily rise. Looking at two players, for example, from an exponent of one-third, which represents an extremely steeply rising cost curve, to an exponent of two, which is much flatter, we get a sixfold increase in the individual and total payments. This also suggests a policy conclusion. On the whole, it would be desirable to establish institutions so that the marginal cost is very steeply rising. For example, civil servants' examinations should be, as far as possible, designed so that the return on cramming is low, or, putting it another way, so that the marginal cost of improving one's grade is rapidly rising. Similarly, it is better if the political appointments of the corrupt governments are made quickly and rather arbitrarily, so that not so many resources are invested in rent seeking.

Once again, however, there is a cost. It may be hard to design civil service examinations so that they are difficult to prepare for and yet make efficient selections.[5] Here again, if we are dealing with appointments to jobs that we would rather not have exist, the achievement of profits through political manipulations and the like, there is no particular loss in moving down our table. Thus, laws that make it more expensive or more difficult to influence the government—such as the campaign contribution laws—may have considerable net gain by making the rise in marginal cost steeper. There is a considerable expense involved, however. The actual restrictions placed on campaign contributions are designed in a highly asymmetrical manner, so that they increase the cost for some potential lobbyists and not for others. Whether there is a net social gain from this process is hard to say.

So much for zone I; let us now turn to zones II and III. In zone II, the sum of the payments made by the individual players is greater than the prize; in other words, it is a negative-sum game instead of a positive-sum game as in zone I. In zone III, the individual players make payments that are higher than the prize. It might seem obvious that no one would play games of this sort, but, unfortunately, this is not true.

Before von Neumann began his work on the theory of games, students of probability divided gambling situations into two categories: pure chance and games of strategy. We may take two simple examples. If Smith flips a coin and Jones calls the outcome, we have a game of pure chance, provided only that Smith does not have enough skill actually to control the coin. This is so even if the coin is not a fair one, although Jones might not properly calculate the odds under those circumstances. In this game, the

---

[5] There is another solution, which is to put the civil service salary at the same level as equivalent private salaries. Under these circumstances, there would be no rent seeking. Given the political power of civil servants, however, I doubt that this would be possible.

properly calculated, but mathematical, odds are fifty-fifty, and there is no great problem.

Consider, however, a very similar game, in which Smith chooses which side of the coin will be up and covers it with his hand until Jones calls either heads or tails. The coin is then uncovered, and if Jones has properly called the bet, Smith pays him; if he has not, Jones pays Smith. This is a game of strategy. The early writers in this case reasoned that there was no proper solution to the game, because if there were a proper solution, both parties could figure it out. Thus, for example, if the proper thing for Smith to do was to play heads, he would know that Jones would know that this was the proper thing to do; hence, the proper thing for Smith to do would be to play tails. Of course, if the proper thing is to play tails, then Jones will also know that; therefore, the proper thing to do is to play heads. It will be seen that his is an example of the paradox of the liar.

The early students of probability argued that in circumstances like these there was no proper solution and referred to it as a game of strategy, which was roughly equivalent to throwing up their hands. In games of this sort, von Neumann discovered that there might be (not necessarily was, but might be) a solution. In the particular case of coin matching, there is no simple solution, but in many real-world situations there could be a strategy for Smith that he would still retain even though Jones could figure it out and make the best reply.

If there was such a strategy, it was called a saddle point. Von Neumann also pointed out that one should consider not only pure strategies but also mixed strategies. Further, in zero-sum games there is always some mixed strategy that has a saddle point. This proof can also be extended to differential games, which are the kind of games we are now discussing, but unfortunately, it applies only to zero-sum games, and our games are not zero-sum.[6]

A broader concept of equilibrium was developed by Nash, but unfortunately the games in zones II and III have a very pronounced discontinuity at 0. In consequence, there is no Nash equilibrium. These games have neither dominant pure strategies, saddle points, nor dominant mixed strategies. They are games of strategies in the older sense of the word, games for which we can offer no solution.

Let us here reexamine the idea of a solution in order to make this clear. If there is such a solution, anyone can compute it. Thus, Smith must choose his strategy knowing that Jones will know what he is going to do. Similarly, Jones must choose knowing that Smith will be able to predict accurately what he will do. There is no law of nature that says all games will

---

[6] Except, of course, for those games which lie along the boundary between zone I and zone II,

have solutions of this sort, and these, unfortunately, are in a category that do not.

For a simple example, consider the game shown on Table 6.1 in which there are two players. Smith and Jones again, and assume that the exponent on the cost function is 3. The individual payment is shown as $75, and the result of the two players putting up $75 is that they will jointly pay $150 for $100. Each is paying $75 for a fifty-fifty chance on $50, which appears to be stupid.

However, let us run through the line of reasoning that may lead the two parties to a $75 investment. Suppose, for example, that we start with both parties at $50. Smith raises to $51. With the exponent of three, the increase in the probability that he will win is worth more than $1—in fact, considerably more. If Jones counters, he also gains more than $1 by his investment. By a series of small steps of this sort, each one of which is a profitable investment, the two parties will eventually reach $75, at which point there is no motive for either one to raise or lower his bid by any small amount. They are in marginal adjustment, even though the total conditions are very obviously not satisfied.

But what of the total conditions? For example, suppose that Jones decides not to play. Obviously, his withdrawal means that Smith is guaranteed success, and, indeed, he will probably regret that he has $75 down rather than $1, but, still, he is going to make a fairly good profit on his investment.

Here we are back in the trap of the coin-matching games. If the best thing to do, the rational strategy, in this game is not to play, then obviously the sensible thing to do is to put in $1. On the other hand, if the rational strategy is to play, and one can anticipate the other party will figure that out, too, so that he will invest, then the rational thing to do is to stay out, because you are going to end up with parties investing at $75. There is no stable solution.

Games like this occur many times in the real world. Poker, as it is actually played, is an example, and most real-world negotiations are also examples of this sort of thing; in the case of poker, there is no social waste, because the parties are presumably deriving entertainment from the game. Negotiations, although they always involve at least some waste, may involve fairly small amounts because the waste involved in strategic maneuvering may be more than compensated by the transfer of information that my permit achievement of a superior outcome. But in our game this is not possible, In the real world there may be some such effect that partially offsets the waste of the rent seeking. In most rent-seeking cases, however, it is clear that this offset is only partial, and in many cases of rent seeking the activity from which, the rent will be derived is, in and of itself, of negative social value. Under these circumstances, not only do we have the waste of rent seeking, we also have the net social waste imposed by the rent itself.

In the real world, the solution to rent seeking is rather apt to end up at $75 in our particular case instead of at zero, because normally the game does not permit bets, once placed, to be withdrawn. In other words, the sunk costs are truly sunk; you cannot withdraw your bid. For example, If I decide to cram for an examination or invest a certain amount of money in a lobby in Washington that is intended to increase the salaries of people studying public choice, once the money is spent, I cannot get it back. If it turns out that I am in this kind of competitive game, the sunk-cost aspect of the existing investment means that I will continue making further investments in competition with other people studying of the examination or in hiring lobbyists. In a way, the fact that there is an optimal amount—that even with the previous costs all sunk we will not go beyond $75 in the particular example we are now using –is encouraging. Although sunk costs are truly sunk, there is still a limit to the amount that will be invested in the game.

Note that this game has a possible precommitment strategy.[7] If one of the parties can get his $75 in first and make it clear that it will not be withdrawn, the sensible policy for the second party is to play zero; hence, the party who precommits makes, on this particular game, a profit of $25.

Unfortunately, this analysis, although true, is not very helpful. It simply means that there is another precommitment game played. We would have to investigate the parameters of that game, as well as the parameters of the game shown in tables 6.1 and 6.2, and determine the sum of the resources invested in both. Offhand, it would appear that most precommitment games would be extremely expensive because it is necessary to make large investments on very little information. You must be willing to move before other people, and this means moving when you are badly informed.[8] But, in any event, this precommitment game would have some set of parameters, and, if we investigate them and then combine them with the parameters of the game that you precommit, we would obtain the total cost. I doubt that this would turn out to be a low amount of social waste.

The situation is even more bizarre in zone III. Here the equilibrium involves each of the players' investing more than the total prize offered. It is perhaps sensible to reemphasize the meaning of the payments shown in table 6.1 They are the payments that would be reached if all parties, properly calculating what the others would do, made minor adjustments in their bids

---

[7] Thomas C. Schelling, *The Strategy of Conflict* (Cambridge, Mass.: Harvard University Press, 1960).

[8] As an amusing sidelight on this problem, a referee of an earlier draft of this paper objected to my above paragraph on the ground that the first party should not put in $75 but some smaller number closer to $55 that would be enough to bar the other party. Note, however, that if one paused to figure out the actual optimal number, the other party would get in first with his $75.

and finally reached the situation where they stopped in proper marginal adjustment. They are not in total equilibrium, of course.

Once again, the simple rule—do not play such games—is not correct, because if it were the correct rule, then anyone who violated it could make large profits. Consider a particular game invented by Geoffrey Brennan, which is the limit of table 6.1 as the exponent is raised to infinity. In this game, $100 is put up and will be sold to the highest bidder, but all the bids are retained, that is, when you put in a bid, you cannot reduce it. Under these circumstances, no one would put in an initial bid of more than $100, but it is not at all obvious what one *should* put in. Further, assume that the bids, once made, cannot be withdrawn but can be raised. Under these circumstances, there is no equilibrium maximum bid. In other words, it is always sensible to increase your bid above its present level if less than $100 will make you the highest bidder. The dangers are obvious, but it is also obvious that refusal to play the game is not an equilibrium strategy, because of the paradox of the liar mentioned above.

In games in zones II and III, formal theory can say little. Clearly, these are areas where the ability to guess what other people will do, interpret facial expressions, and so on, pays off very highly. They are also areas where it is particularly likely that very large wastes will be incurred by society as a whole. Unfortunately, it seems likely that rent seeking is apt to lead to these areas in some cases.

Obviously, as a good social policy, we should try to avoid having games that are likely to lead to this kind of waste. Again, we should try to arrange that the payoff to further investment in resources is comparatively low, or , in other words, that the cost curve points sharply upward.

One way to lower the social costs is to introduce bias into the selection process. Note that we normally refer to bias as a bad thing, but one could be biased in the direction of the correct decision. For example, a civil service exam might be so designed that it is very likely to pick out people who have the necessary natural traits and is very hard to prepare for. This would be bias in favor of the appropriate traits, but it would be a desirable thing. Similarly, we would like to have court proceedings biased in such a way that whoever is on the right side need not make very large investments in order to win, and if this is true, the people on the wrong side will not make very large investments either, because they do not pay.

On the other hand, bias can be something which, at least morally, is incorrect. We referred above to Mayor Daley's appointments of his relatives, and this would be a kind of bias. In that particular case, presumably bias would reduce total rent seeking and not lower the functional efficiency of the government of Chicago, but there are many cases where this kind of bias *would* lower efficiency.

TABLE 6.3
Individual Investments
(2-Party, Bias, Exponent)

	Bias				
Exponent	2	4		10	15
1	22.22	16.00		8.30	5.90
2	44.44	32.00	I	16.53	11.72
3	66.67	48.00		24.79	17.58
5	111.11	80.00	II	41.32	29.30
8	177.78	128.00		66.12	46.88
12	266.67	192.00		99.17	70.31
			III		

Bias, it will be seen, is rather similar to the restriction on the number of players we have discussed above. Instead of totally cutting off some players, we differentially weigh the players. For example, assume that player *A* is given five times as many coupons for his one-dollar investment as are the other players. This would bias the game in his favor, although not to the extreme of prohibiting others from buying tickets. This kind of bias, once again, is rather similar to designing your examination to select natural traits. If player *A* can, with one hour of cramming, increase his probably score on a civil service exam as much as can player *B* with five hours of cramming, then the system is biased in favor of *A*, and we would anticipate that the total cost of rent seeking would go down.

Let us now turn to table 6.3. In this table, we have only two parties competing because the situation is mathematically complex and, in any event, having more than two parties would require a three-dimensional diagram. Along the top is the degree of bias toward one player, which is measured here simply in the number of tickets he gets per dollar, it being assumed that the less-advantaged player gets one ticket per dollar. We have omitted the lower exponents of table 6.1, because it is immediately obvious that bias very sharply reduces total rent seeking.

Table 6.4 is the sum over both players of all the payments shows in table 6.3, and, in this case, they always just double the figures in table 6.3.

It turns out that, using our simple mathematical apparatus, both players—the one who is favored by the bias and the one who is not—make the same investment. This is a little counterintuitive, but not very, since most of us do not have very strong intuitions on these matters. In any event, it may simply be an artifact of the particular mathematical formalism we have chosen.

TABLE 6.4
Sum of Investments
(2-Party, Bias, Exponent)

	Bias				
Exponent	2	4		10	15
1	44.44	32.00		16.60	11.80
2	88.88	64.00	I	30.06	23.44
3	133.34	96.00		49.58	35.16
5	222.22	160.00	II	82.64	58.60
8	355.56	256.00		132.24	93.76
12	533.34	384.00		198.34	140.62
			III		

It will be noted immediately that zone I is much larger in this case than in the unbiased cases of tables 6.1 and 6.2. Indeed, even with an exponent of 8—which means an extremely flat cost curve—a bias of 15 leads to the game still being in zone I. Thus, such bias does pay off heavily in reducing rent seeking.

It is also true that this kind of bias, in general, is easier to arrange by socially desirable techniques than the earlier suggestions made to reduce rent seeking. Once again, designing personnel selection procedures so that they select the best man at relatively low cost to him is an example. Another would be some kind of policy selection process that was heavily biased in favor of efficient, or "right," policies. Both these techniques, if we could design them, would have large payoffs, not only in reducing rent-seeking activity but also in increasing efficiency of government in general. Thus, it seems to me that introducing this rather special kind of bias into rent seeking would be desirable in many areas, even if we ignore the rent-seeking savings.

However, for many rent-seeking activities, it is admittedly very hard to find a way to introduce bias at all or to introduce bias in a way that leads to better outcomes. Once again, if we assume that Mayor Daley does not restrict his appointments to his relatives but simply gives relatives a differential advantage, depending on how close they are to him, we have a bias system that will reduce rent seeking. However, it will not lead to outcomes in any way superior. Similarly, the restrictions placed on campaign contributions and other methods of attempting to influence government policy are biased in the sense that they are heavier burdens for some people than for others, and it is not clear whether this bias will lead to policy choices superior to those obtained without it. Thus, the only gain is the possibility of reduction in total rent seeking.

Thus ends our preliminary investigation of rent seeking and ways to reduce its social cost. When I have discussed the problem with colleagues, I have found that the intellectually fascinating problem of zones II and III tends to dominate the discussion. This is, indeed, intellectually very interesting, but the real problem we face is the attempt to lower the cost of rent seeking, and this will normally move us into zone I. Thus, I hope that the result of this paper is not mathematical examination of the admittedly fascinating intellectual problems of zones II and III, but practical investigation of methods to lower the cost of rent seeking.

APPENDIX TO CHAPTER 6

Mathematical Appendix, or Labor Saving Calculation Methods

When I first began working on this paper, I discovered that the equations that would have to be solved were higher-order equations, and therefore, simply assigned to my graduate assistant, William J. Hunter, the job of approximating the results by using a pocket calculator. He promptly discovered the rather astonishing regularity of column 1, which implied that it would not be all that difficult to solve the equations even if they were higher order. Before I had had time to do anything other than shudder vaguely about the problem, however, I went to lunch with my colleague, Nicolaus Tideman, told him the problem, and he solved it on a napkin. This gave us the equation for tables 6.1 and 6.2 Having discovered this simple algorithm, when we wanted to prepare tables 6.3 and 6.4, once again we asked Tideman, and he obliged with equal speed. The equations used are:

$$P_A = R\frac{N-1}{N^2} \qquad \text{(Tables 6.1, 6.2)}$$

$$P_A = R\frac{b}{(b+1)^2} \qquad \text{(Tables 6. 3, 6.4)}$$

Where
P_A = equilibrium investment
R = exponent, or the determinant of steepness of the supply curve.
N = number of players, and
b = bias weight

Long-run equilibrium and total expenditures in rent-seeking

WILLIAM J. CORCORAN*

1. Introduction

The lure of excess profits or rents associated with monopoly power gives rise to expenditures to obtain these rents. Competitive rent-seeking behavior is recognized as a factor which must be included among the wastes associated with monopoly power (Tullock, 1967; Posner, 1975).[1] The expenditures are aimed at transferring wealth rather than its creation, and the use of resources to obtain this transfer is a loss to society. How important rent-seeking is as a part of the total monopolistic waste hinges on the size of the total expenditures induced by a given level of excess profits.

Posner (1975) and Becker (1968) assert that total expenditures in the rent-seeking process will just equal the value of the rents to be gained although neither is specific about how this result would occur. This hypothesis has been adopted by those writing about rent-seeking and, more recently, it appears to have attained the status of an axiom (Foster, 1981). If rent-seeking could fit within the perfectly competitive model one would expect – in the long run – the equality of total expenditures and total revenues. The analogy with perfect competition, however, is not accurate. One difference is that the expenditures in rent-seeking are made to influence the probability of winning, not to cover the cost of production. Another is that in the case of one payoff only one competitor wins and obtains a positive return on his investment, the rest lose everything. Tullock (1980) shows that in a simple two-player lottery each player will maximize his expected value by investing one-quarter of the payoff at stake, not one-half, where total expenditures would equal the payoff. He goes on to show that the total expenditures can be greater, equal, or less than the payoff; the

* Thanks are due to Gordon Karels and several anonymous referees for valuable comments leading to substantial improvements in this paper.

Economics Program, University of Nebraska, Omaha, NE 68182.

result depends upon the number of players and the marginal cost of influencing the probability of winning. Thus, it cannot be assumed, as first thought, that a given rental payoff will give rise to wasteful expenditures of equal value.

Upon further consideration, however, it can be seen that Tullock's model, as portrayed, pertains to the short-run. Each solution for total expenditures is for a given number of players which is analogous to the short-run solution in perfect competition for a given number of firms. Presumably, the assertion that total expenditures equals the payoff is made with a long-run perspective in mind, since it is in the long-run that the perfectly competitive model has this property.

This paper will incorporate long-run considerations into Tullock's model of the competitive process with the object of reconsidering the total expenditures attracted by a given payoff. First the shortrun results will be reviewed.

2. Short-run

In the model used by Tullock competitors attempt to maximize their expected net present value, V, which is given by:

$$V_A = \frac{a^r}{a^r + b^r} Pe^{-\varrho t} - a \tag{1}$$

where a and b are expenditures by players A and B; P, the payoff at time t; ϱ the player's discount rate and $a^r/(a^r + b^r)$ is a generalized probability function where r reflects the ease of affecting the probability of winning. As r increases the marginal cost decreases. The probability function is considered within a lottery framework, where a and b can, for example, be the number of one dollar tickets being purchased to obtain the payoff. In the simplest case where r equals one, the probability of winning by player A is equal to the ratio of the number of tickets he purchased to the total number of tickets purchased, i.e., $a/a + b)$. If the number of players involved were increased, c, d, etc., would be added to the denominator, as appropriate.

To determine the expenditure by each player a Cournot reaction process is employed, whereby equation (1) is differentiated and the derivative set equal to zero. This results in a Cournot-Nash equilibrium solution whereby each of n competitors spends

$$a = \frac{(n\text{-}1)r}{n^2} Pe^{-\varrho t} \tag{2}$$

It is clear that since each player spends an equal amount, the solution is symmetric, the probability of their winning is the same, i.e., l/n. Multiplying (2) by n gives the total expenditure in rent-seeking by all players

$$T = \frac{(n\text{-}1)r}{n} P e^{-\varrho t} \tag{3}$$

This last equation provides the basis for Tullock's short-run policy recommendations for minimizing total expenditures or total waste in rent-seeking. First, it is desirable to minimize the number of players involved in rent-seeking activity. This results in a lower value for the term $(n\text{-}1)/n$. Total expenditures would be zero where the number of players is held to one.[2] In this regard Tullock remarks that 'nepotism is a good thing.' Second, the marginal cost of affecting the probability of winning should be steeply rising. Total expenditures vary directly with the value of r, that is, inversely with marginal cost. It can be added for the short-run, that total expenditures also vary inversely with the opportunity cost rate of discount, ϱ. Thus policies which increase the opportunity cost (for instance, delay receipt of the payoff) will reduce total expenditures.

3. Long-run

The crucial consideration for determining the long-run solution is the possibility of entry and exit in the rent-seeking process. Players considering entry or exit will take into account the alternative uses of their funds. This opportunity cost will be measured by the rate of return which incorporates a separation in time between expenditures and receipts. If the rate of return obtainable on other projects is less than that offered by the rent-seeking option then players will enter; if greater, players will exit.

The expected rate of return, π, to each competitor in the lottery is a function of the ratio of the expected payoff and individual expenditures; thus

$$e^{\pi t} = \frac{P/n}{(n\text{-}1)rPe^{-\varrho t}/n^2} \tag{4}$$

or

$$\pi = \varrho + \frac{1}{t} \ln \frac{n}{(n\text{-}1)r} \tag{5}$$

Players will enter until $\pi = \varrho$ which occurs when

$$\ln \frac{n}{(n-1)r} = 0 \tag{6}$$

or

$$n = \frac{r}{r-1} \tag{7}$$

An alternative approach to long-run equilibrium must be taken where the payoff is received as soon as expenditures are made, i.e., $t = 0$ in equations (2) and (3). In this case, rather than focusing on the profit rate which will be infinite, a decision to enter will consider the existence of positive profits as given by

$$P/n - a = P\frac{n + r - nr}{n^2}. \tag{8}$$

Entry will occur until this falls to 0 which happens when

$$n = \frac{r}{r-1} \tag{9}$$

the same result as (7). If $r \leq 1$, entry is unbounded; this is akin to the results expected in industries with persisting decreasing returns to scale.[3]

Substituting (7) into the equation for total expenditures (3) we obtain

$$T = Pe^{-\varrho t} \tag{10}$$

which indicates that in long-run equilibrium the total expenditures by all competitors in the rent-seeking process will equal the payoff discounted by the opportunity cost rate of return.

The results of (10) show that if long-run equilibrium can be attained, the r-value, a measure of the marginal cost of influencing the chances of success, falls out of consideration. Consequently, it would be incorrect to conclude that an increase in the marginal costs will lower total expenditures in rent-seeking (Tullock, 1980). As r decreases (as marginal costs increase) we can see from equation (2) that individual expenditures decrease. We can also see from equation (5), however, that the expected rate of return to each competitor increases, or from equation (8) that profits increase which induces entry.[4] The resulting increase in the number of competitors exactly offsets the decline in individual expenditures so the total expenditure remains constant. Therefore, as equation (10) indicates, T is invariant with respect to r.

An obvious question concerns the length of time to achieve long-run equilibrium. It includes both the time for information of a rent-seeking opportunity to become available,[5] and the time necessary to make the appropriate expenditures. The latter is usually the sole consideration in perfect competition where the long-run is determined by the length of time it takes to vary all inputs. In some situations, as in the case of a lottery, these expenditures could be made within a relatively brief period and the time for information to transpire would then be of central importance. There will certainly be sufficient time for both to take place where similar rent-seeking opportunities occur at regular intervals. The long-run can also exist, however, for a one-time never-to-be-repeated payoff when prior knowledge is widespread and expenditures can be made with little delay.

4. Implications and summary

The objective of this paper is to investigate the assertion that a given rent payoff gives rise to an equal value of total expenditure. An analogy with perfect competition suggests a long-run perspective, which would allow the number of players to vary. Accordingly, a game theoretic model of the competitive process where competitors anticipate rival reactions and expend resources to increase their probability of winning is extended to include entry. Long-run equilibrium occurs when the incentive for entry is dissipated, i.e., expected profits equal 0 or the expected rate of return equals the opportunity cost discount rate. When this occurs total expenditure in rent-seeking is found to equal the payoff as in the standard competitive case.

How does this result affect Tullock's policy recommendations? His first finding that total expenditures in rent-seeking can be minimized by holding the number of players down remains intact. Essentially, this requirement restricts entry and as a result maintains the short-run conditions indicated by equations (2) and (3) for a given number of firms. His second recommendation, that of increasing the marginal cost of improving a player's probability of winning must, however, be qualified. If the long-run equilibrium is attained total expenditures will equal the payoff regardless of the marginal cost. If the marginal cost is such that the long-run equilibrium is unbounded, there exists a continuous incentive for new entry. It is possible that total expenditures will increase as entry mounts, but this cannot be determined. A policy of increasing the marginal cost will work, however, if carried out in conjunction with a restriction on entry. In this case the short-run results still apply. Finally, an additional policy recommendation can be deduced. From equation (10) total rent-seeking expenditures will be reduced if the opportunity cost discount rate of return is increased. This may be achieved by such actions as increasing the lag between rent-seeking expenditures and the associated payoff, or unfettering alternative productive investments (reduced taxes, deregulation, etc.). Both result in a larger discount of the payoff.

The results support the concern with rent-seeking behavior. It indicates that in the long-run each opportunity for rent – a transfer of wealth – displaces an opportunity for the creation of value which will be equal to or greater than the rent payoff. It will be greater, of course, where the investment alternative cannot capture the full social gain.[6]

NOTES

1. Competition as used here refers to rivalrous behavior which implies that a degree of influence can be exerted by each participant in determining the outcome; this is markedly different from perfect competition, where each is powerless to affect the price (see McNulty, 1968).
2. When n equals 1, n-1 equals zero; at the other extreme, as n becomes very large the $$\lim_{n \to \infty} \frac{n-1}{n} = 1$$
3. See, for example, Varian (1978: 60).
4. The variation of profits with r can be determined by taking the derivative, d/dr $(P(n+r-nr)/n^2)$. This result in $P(1\text{-}n)/n^2$, which indicates a negative relationship between profits and r, the marginal cost, for $n>1$.
5. More exactly, it involves the time for the number of players necessary to obtain equilibrium to be informed.
6. This would occur where an innovator could not capture the total consumer's surplus of a newly introduced product.

Long-run equilibrium and total expenditures in rent-seeking: A comment

GORDON TULLOCK*

Although Corcoran is mathematically right, I believe his comment is not very helpful. In order to discuss the matter in some detail, I have reproduced here Table 1 from my 'Efficient Rent-Seeking.'[1] This shows the equilibrium investment of each individual, different numbers of individuals playing the game (*n*), and differing values of *r*. Table 2, also reproduced (ibid.), shows the total investment.

Corcoran assumes that in a dynamic process the profits would be exhausted, i.e., that people would enter or leave until such time as there was no profit in doing so. In his equation 7, he calculates the number of entrants necessary to meet this condition. I have no complaints about his algebra, but as I shall point out below, equation 7 is not very helpful.

In terms of Tables 1 and 2, if individuals are able to enter, they have an incentive to enter as long as the value in Table 1, for the appropriate values

Table 1. Individual investments (N-person, no bias, with exponent)

	Number of players				
Exponent	2	4	10		15
1/3	8.33	6.25	3.00		2.07
1/2	12.50	9.37	4.50	I	3.11
1	25.00	18.75	9.00		6.22
2	50.00	37.50	18.00		12.44
3	75.00	56.25	27.00		18.67
5	125.00	93.75	45.00	II	31.11
8	200.00	150.00	72.00		49.78
12	300.00	225.00	108.00		74.67
		III			

* Department of Economics, George Mason University, Fairfax, VA 22030.

1. 'Efficient rent-seeking,' in *Toward a theory of the rent-seeking society*, edited by James M. Buchanan, Robert D. Tollison, and Gordon Tullock, 1980, pp. 97–112. College Station: Texas A&M University Press.

Table 2. Sum of investments (N-person, no bias, with exponent)

	Number of players					
Exponent	2	4	10	15		Limit
1/3	16.66	25.00	30.00	31.05		33.30
1/2	25.00	37.40	45.00	46.65	I	50.00
1	50.00	75.00	90.00	93.30		100.00
2	100.00	150.00	80.00	186.60		200.00
3	150.00	225.00	270.00	280.05		300.00
5	250.00	375.00	450.00	465.65	II	500.00
8	400.00	600.00	720.00	746.70		800.00
12	600.00	900.00	1,080.00	1,120.05		1,200.00
			III			

of n and r, is less than $\frac{1}{n}$. For any given value of r, the total return to rent-seeking with equilibrium entry, is 1 (the 'prize') minus the total investment (the value in Table 2 at the given value of r and the last value of n for which total investment is ≤ 1. It may be noted that the total return to rent-seeking is not generally zero. Consider first situations in which r is less than 1. Corcoran says 'If $r \leq 1$ entry is unbounded.' (The solution to equation 7 is a negative number of people.) In this case it is clear that the profits are not exhausted, as can be seen from my Table 2. If r is one-third, then even if an infinite number of people choose to play, only one-third of the profits will be exhausted.

Turn next to the case where r is between 1 and 2. It is in this case that I think Corcoran makes what contribution his article does make. If, for example, r is 1.5 then n is 3, and it does seem to me quite likely that entry would proceed until such time as three people had entered, at which point profits would be exhausted. Suppose, however, that r is 1.6. Then n is 2 2/3. But the number of entrants must be an integer.

If only two people have entered there are profits for that collectivity of two, whereas a third entrant will guarantee for himself and his predecessors net losses. It is also not possible for two people to enter in full, and the third person to put in only two-thirds as much as they have because it would be a losing bet for the third person.

When $r > 2$, all solutions lie with some number between 1 and 2 playing the game. Thus, entry would cease with one entrant, who would have positive profits.

For the benefit of those who have not read my original article, it will be noted that there are lines in Table 2 dividing the parameter space into categories 1, 2, and 3. Categories 2 and 3 raise the problem that it doesn't seem sensible to play these games but, on the other hand, refraining from playing them guarantees very large profits to the one person who does play. Thus there is another game in the precommitment stage, in which the parties attempt to make the first commitment so that no one else will enter. This other game must be investigated, and it seems to me that the major value of Corcoran's paper is in laying out some of the framework in which this precommitment game would be played.

It should be kept in mind that although an economist is annoyed to discover opportunities for true profit in a competitive economy, that is merely an intellectual problem. The real problem of rent-seeking is the waste of resources. We don't want the rent-seeking cost to work out to the same as the benefit. We would much prefer that the benefit come at zero rent-seeking cost, and if that is not possible that the cost at least be low.

So much for Corcoran. I should like to take this opportunity to clear up some loose ends on the original article on which he comments. Turning back to Tables 1 and 2, in the article, 'Efficient Rent-Seeking,' I said that in zones 2 and 3, as shown on the figure, 'There is no stable solution (page 103). I was more correct than I realized. I had made only a partial check of the second order conditions and it turns out that for the bulk of the numbers in zones 2 and 3, specifically those where $r<\frac{n}{n-2}$, the second-order conditions for mutual maximization are not met. Thus we really should have had zones 2, 3, and 4, but what I have said about zones 2 and 3 would remain true respect to 2, 3, and 4.

Although it makes no practical difference in the outcome, it may be of some interest to explain how I came to make this mistake. Because of the way in which our research proceeded, I began by establishing that all of the two-person equilibria were stable. There were a few tests of individual outcomes in other areas, but unfortunately I chose, in order to simplify my work, those in which the exponent was 1. Thus the area of instability was missed.

With respect to Tables 3 and 4, having to do with two persons, biased processes, there are corrections of two sorts that must be mentioned. First, due to an error in the calculation procedure, the numbers are correct only if the column headings are reinterpreted as b_r, rather than b. For the second-order conditions to be satisfied the bias factor must be between $\frac{r-1}{r+1}$ and its reciprocal. Thus, bias has an even greater impact in reducing rent-seeking than I suggested.

But although in this case the failure to check the second order conditions thoroughly turned out to be irrelevant, I certainly don't believe we could always count on that. To repeat the advice which you hear so often but which is unfortunately frequently disregarded, always check the second order conditions.

Efficient rents 1

Rent-seeking behavior in the long-run

WILLIAM J. CORCORAN
GORDON V. KARELS*
Department of Economics, The University of Nebraska, Omaha, NB 68182-0048

1. Introduction

The original work on rent-seeking conjectured that rent-seeking expenditures would completely dissipate the rent sought (Posner, 1975; Becker, 1968). Presently it appears to be accepted as a fundamental tenet in spite of the lack of knowledge of how such a result would come about (Demsetz, 1976; Foster, 1981). Tullock (1980) using a game-theoretic approach with a Cournot-Nash (C-N) response function showed that total expenditures can be greater than, equal to, or less than the rent payoff depending on the number of players and the marginal cost of influencing the probability of winning. Corcoran (1983) extended Tullock's model to a long-run setting, i.e., free entry, and found that under these conditions rents will be dissipated. Tullock (1983) agreed in part, but still maintained that where marginal costs were rapidly falling or rising throughout, Corcoran's long-run solution does not pertain.

The models employed by Corcoran and Tullock assume the probability of winning with an expenditure of 'a' is given by:[1]

$$Pr(a) = \frac{a^r}{a^r + b^r} \tag{1}$$

where 'b' is the expenditure of the other player and 'r' reflects the marginal cost of influencing the probability of winning. The expected profit with an expenditure of 'a' is then given by:

$$E\,[\pi(a)] = \frac{a^r}{a^r + b^r} X - a \tag{2}$$

where X is the value of rents.[2]

* The usual disclaimer applies. The authors are grateful to Gordon Tullock for helpful comments and suggestions.

The C–N equilibrium solution to the maximization of expected profits yields:

$$a = \frac{n-1}{n^2} rX \tag{3}$$

where n is the number of players.

Since each player is assumed identical this solution holds for all players. The amount of money expended to capture the rents will simply be the number of players times the value of 'a' from equation (3). This was the basic equation used by Tullock when he noted that whether or not rents were dissipated depended upon the values of n and r.

Corcoran, building on Tullock's work, assumed entry would continue until profits are reduced to zero for each firm. He then proceeded to solve for the long-run equilibrium number of players by setting equation (2) equal to zero and substituting equation (3). This yields:

$$n = \frac{r}{r-1} \tag{4}$$

From this equation we can see the difficulties that Tullock raises with Corcoran's result. He points out that when $r \leq 1$, the equilibrium number of players would be negative and that rents are not exhausted even with an infinite number of players. Corcoran noted that in this case entry was unbounded with the situation analogous to production under strictly decreasing returns in a competitive industry. In that case each firm ends up producing an infinitesimal output level with a profit positive level and an infinite number of firms in the industry.

A second difficulty is the equilibrium number of players is not necessarily integer valued when r is greater than one. For example, when r is equal to 1.6, the solution value for n is 2.6. By solving equation (4) for r we can find the values of r that are consistent with an integer number of players. That is:

$$r = \frac{n}{n-1}. \tag{5}$$

A third problem pointed out by Tullock is that if the solution is not integer valued, one firm could make positive profits but a potential entrant would be dissuaded by anticipated losses upon entry. For example, if $r = 3$, then $n = 1.5$ and one player alone would make expected profits but the two together would have expected losses under the C-N solution. Tullock suggested that the rent-seeking game for such a case would shift to a 'precommitment stage' in which parties anticipate other entrants and possibly make a commitment whereby no one else is willing to enter.

A fourth problem arises in terms of the validity of the C–N solution for certain values of r greater than one. If for instance, $r = 3$ and $n = 2$ then each player would bet \$75 according to equation (2). Total expenditures would be \$150 in a game where the payoff is only \$100. Each player has an expected loss of \$25 with such a bet.

Tullock (1980) addresses this problem by stating that in such cases no Nash equilibrium exists and there is no stable solution to the game. For example, if both players were to bet \$50 (with $r = 3$) then it would be profitable for one to increase his bet to \$51. Tullock then points out that it then becomes marginally profitable for the other player to also increase his bet to \$51. The betting would increase in this manner to \$75.

From a long-run standpoint a player must consider alternative earnings possibilities of the rent-seeking expenditures. Thus, in the case just cited where it is marginally profitable (expected losses fall by more than \$1) to match the \$51 bet, it is also a strategy that yields negative expected profits as a whole. The question is whether or not a player will choose a strategy which guarantees expected losses. If we require all players to consider the alternative of a zero loss with a zero bet then it must be the case that the value of expenditures in rent-seeking by all participants can never exceed the prize.

One obvious implication of the assumption of no strategies that yield expected losses is, as stated, the fact that expenditures could never exceed the value of rents. This result appears counterintuitive because of the competitive nature of rent-seeking activity. A similar result exists, however, in the competitive sealed bid auction for prizes of uncertain value. Wilson (1977) showed that the winning bid for such an item (all other bids returned) approaches the true value of the item from below. This implies that no overbidding occurs even when the true value is not known, because each participant plays a strategy of avoiding the 'winners curse' problem of only winning those tracts where values have been overestimated. One implication of these models as pointed out by Capen, Clapp and Campbell (1971) is that the optimal bid of a firm should decrease, not increase, in the face of increased competition.

Having set out some of the basic problems with the long-run solution to rent-seeking behavior, the remainder of the paper addresses possible solutions. In the next section we look at the game where $r \leq 1$. We then explore the more complex case where $r > 1$ and look at several definitions of long-run competition. The last section summarizes our findings. We point out at this stage that all numerical examples utilized in the paper assume a payoff of \$100.

2. Values of r less than or equal to one

When r takes on a value of one or less the C-N solution has several interesting characteristics. First, no matter how many competitors there are, no firm ever incurs an expected loss. This is important in the long-run, as entry would always be invited with such an incentive.

Second, it will always pay for each player to split its bets, assuming the other firm maintains its current bet. Both of these statements are illustrated in Table 1. First, assume $r = .5$ and $n = 2$. Then the optimal bet for each player is $12.50 with expected profits of $37.50 each. Suppose one of the players decides to submit two bets with total profits being the combined value of the individual profits. This is equivalent to having $n = 3$, with an optimal bet of $11.11. The resulting expected profit per bet is $22.22. Since one of the players owns two of the bets, his overall expected profit is $44.44, which exceeds his profit when there were just two bets. Notice also that the player making just one bet now has an incentive to split his bet. The optimal bet of each is now $9.375 with profits of $31.25 by splitting the bet versus the $22.22 without. Table 1 also presents two other r values which yield the same result.

Table 1. Optimal bets and associated expected profits for selected values of r and n

r	n	Optimal bet	Expected profit
.5	2	12.50	37.50
.5	3	11.11	22.22
.5	4	9.375	15.625
.5	10	4.50	5.50
.5	50	.98	1.02
.5	100	.495	.505
.5	1000	.0004995	.0995005
.75	2	18.75	31.25
.75	3	16.67	16.67
.75	4	14.0675	10.9375
.75	10	6.75	3.25
.75	50	1.47	.53
.75	100	.7425	.2575
.75	1000	.074925	.0025075
1	2	25	25
1	3	22.22	11.11
1	4	18.75	6.25
1	10	9.00	1.00
1	50	1.96	.04
1	100	.99	.01
1	1000	.0999	.0001

As can be seen from the above example, each firm, in the long run, has an incentive to keep splitting bets. The number of bets submitted *(n)* must eventually go to infinity and the optimal bet approaches zero. Note from Table 1 that the expected profit on each bet is still positive even when *n* is very large (1000). This is analagous to the output-plant size decision of the competitive price-taking firm under strictly decreasing returns. Long-run adjustment always results in a smallei plant size.

The reason for this result has to do with the behavior of the probability of winning function specified in equation (1). It can be shown that when $r \leq 1$, the function is strictly concave which implies that the probability of winning increases at a decreasing rate as the bet '*a*' increases.[3] Therefore, the biggest incremental change in the probability of winning occurs close to $a = 0$ and, hence, each player is driven to bet near that level.

As an example of splitting one's bets, consider the efforts of a lobbyist in attempting to persuade a senator to vote a given way on a bill. The effort could involve meeting with the senator once and spending an hour of time explaining the issue or the alternative strategy of meeting several times and reminding the senator of the critical issues involved. If the marginal impact of the meeting is greatest for the initial minutes of contact ($r \leq 1$) then the strategy of meeting several times will yield the highest overall probability of influencing the senator. It is in this general sense we refer to the concept of splitting the bet.

Tullock has pointed out that in the cases where $r < 1$ the value of expenditures by all participants is less than the payoff and, hence, not all rents are dissipated in the long-run. While this is not disputed, note that the game itself is not very meaningful, as the bet is infinitesimally small and the number of players is infinite.

One possible solution to this degeneration of the game is to impose a minimum bet on all participants. For each player the problem is to maximize expected profits as before but now subject to a minimum value on an individual bet.[4]

The solution to this problem is as follows:

(1) If the value from the C–N solution is greater than, or equal to, the minimum bet, the C–N solution is the optimal bet.
(2) If the value from the C-N solution is less than, or equal to, the minimum bet, the minimum bet is the optimal value.

Such a restriction on the game is illustrated in Table 2 for several values of *r* and *n*. In the first example where $r = .5$ and the minimum bet is \$1, each player must bet the minimum when there are 50 or more players (actually 49 or more players forces a minimum bid). With fifty players each bidding one dollar, each player still expects to make \$1 of profit. Thus, to an outside player there are positive expected profits to be made through entry.[5] These profits exist until 100 players are in the game. At that point all rent is dissipated and no entry is invited.

For the case where $r = 1$ with a minimum bet again of \$1 we get the long-run equilibrium solution of 100 players each submitting the minimum bet. By examining Table 2 it should become apparent that all the rent will be dissipated if the size of the payoff is integer divisible by the minimum bet. The final example in Table 2, where $r = .5$ and a minimum bet of \$0.99 yields positive expected profits with 101 players and negative profits with 102 players. That last player would not enter as there is no bet that will give positive expected profits to all players.[6]

Generally most rent-seeking activities do not have minimum bet requirements.[7] A part of rent-seeking activity which closely parallels that of the minimum bet requirement, however, is transactions costs. An example occurs in the mail-in sweepstakes lottery. In such a case, instead of a minimum bet requirement there is a fixed entry fee - the cost of postage, stationary and the entrant's time cost. Before mailing in the entry, assuming profit maximization, the probability of winning times the payoff would have to exceed the cost of entry. An interesting article by Selby and Beranek

Table 2. Optimal bets and associated expected profits for selected values of *r* and *n* with a minimum bid constraint

r	n	Cournot-Nash solution	Minimum bet	Optimal bid	Expected profit
.5	2	12.50	\$1	12.50	37.50
.5	10	4.50	1	4.50	5.50
.5	25	1.92	1	1.92	2.08
.5	50	.98	1	1	1
.5	75	.657	1	1	.33
.5	100	.495	1	1	0
.5	110	.492	1	1	–.09
1	2	25	1	25	25
1	10	9	1	9	1.00
1	25	3.84	1	3.84	.16
1	50	1.96	1	1.96	.04
1	75	1.315	1	1.315	.0178
1	100	.99	1	1.00	0
.5	2	12.50	.99	12.50	37.50
.5	10	4.50	.99	4.50	5.50
.5	25	1.92	.99	1.92	2.08
.5	50	.98	.99	.99	1.01
.5	100	.495	.99	.99	.01
.5	101	.4902	.99	.99	.000099
.5	102	.4852	.99	.99	–.0096

(1981) provides an analysis with regards to sweepstakes contests. Their estimate of the transactions costs of entry into a sweepstakes lottery (direct and indirect) amounted to \$.20, which was little more than the price of a postage stamp at that time.

If we assume utility maximization instead of profit maximization then we would need to include in the payoff the pleasure received from the gamble. Under such a model individuals may play even if the expected payoff is less than the entry fee because of the utility generated by the game itself.

3. Values of *r* greater than one

This section of the paper addresses Tullock's main concern with Corcoran's original article, i.e., the behavior of players in a dynamic lottery where the *r* value is greater than one. His concern focuses on the point where existing players would make profits but an entrant will cause expected losses for all. This suggests a precommitment stage where existing players consider their bets with the intent of deterring further entry.

The long-run is understood to mean a game that could be replayed continually under the postulated conditions. With a given number of players already in the game, they would want to bet in a manner which guarantees non-negative expected profits for themselves (existing players are referred to as incumbents henceforth) and insuring only negative profits to a potential entrant. We define such a bet as a 'pre-emptory' bet.

It can be shown that a range of pre-emptory bets exists for different values of *r* and *n*. Assuming that all incumbents place equal bets (follow the same strategy) the range of pre-emptory bets is determined as follows: First, because each incumbent must receive non-negative expected profits, the upper end of the range is determined by dividing the payoff by the number of incumbents. Thus, with two incumbents the maximum pre-emptory bet, independent of the value of *r*, is \$50; with three incumbents \$33.33; etc. Second, the low end of these bets is determined by the point below which positive profits can be made by an entrant. Within the range it is also the point of maximum expected profit for the incumbents. Although, the low end declines as the number of incumbents increases, it does so at a slower rate than the upper end.[8] At some point it becomes impossible for the incumbents to eliminate positive profit opportunities for a potential entrant while ensuring positive expected profits for themselves, i.e., the upper end and the lower end are equal. This suggests an equilibrium number of incumbents.

To illustrate this, consider the range of pre-emptory bets for an *r*-value of 1.4 in Table 3. With two incumbents this range is \$33.51 to \$50. With eight incumbents it narrows to \$12.45 to \$12.50. At nine a bet of \$11.11 by each player dissipates total rents - the maximum bet - but \$11.44 is the

Table 3. Range of pre-emptory investments (Cournot-Nash solution in parentheses)

Exponent (r-value)	Number of players 1	2	3	4	5	6	7	8	9	10	11	12	13	14	15	28	29
1.1	100.00 – 73.74	50.00 – 39.27 (27.50)	33.33 – 27.07 (24.44)	25.00 – 20.92 (20.63)	20.00 – 17.08 (17.60)	16.67 – 14.47 (15.28)	14.29 – 12.58 (13.47)	12.50 – 11.14 (12.03)	11.11 10.01 (10.86)	10.00 9.10 (9.90)	9.09 8.34 (9.09)	8.33 – 7.70 (8.40)	7.69 – 7.17	7.14 – 6.70	6.67 – 6.29	3.571 – 3.565	3.448 – 3.453
1.2	100.00 – 67.73	50.00 – 35.77 (30.00)	33.33 – 25.52 (26.67)	25.00 – 20.08 (22.50)	20.00 – 16.67 (19.20)	16.67 – 14.32 (16.67)	14.29 – 12.60 (14.69)	12.50 – 11.27	11.11 – 10.22	10.00 – 9.35	9.09 – 8.64	8.33 – 8.04	7.69 – 7.52	7.14 – 7.07	6.67 – 6.68		
1.3	100.00 – 58.27	50.00 – 34.19 (32.50)	33.33 – 25.03 (28.89)	25.00 – 20.06 (24.38)	20.00 – 16.90 (20.80)	16.67 – 14.69	14.29 – 13.05	12.50 – 11.77	11.11 – 10.75	10.00 – 9.92	9.09 – 9.22						
1.4	100.00 – 54.98	50.00 – 33.51 (35.00)	33.33 – 25.09 (31.11)	25.00 – 20.43 (26.25)	20.00 – 17.42	16.67 – 15.29	14.29 – 13.70	12.50 – 12.45	11.11 – 11.44								
1.5	100.00 – 52.92	50.00 – 33.34 (37.50)	33.33 – 25.44 (33.33)	25.00 – 21.00	20.00 – 18.10	16.67 – 16.03	14.29 – 14.46										
1.6	100.00 – 51.61	50.00 – 33.47 (40.00)	33.33 – 25.98 (35.55)	25.00 – 21.70	20.00 – 18.88	16.67 – 16.85											
1.8	100.00 – 50.32	50.00 – 34.24 (45.00)	33.33 – 27.33 (40.00)	25.00 – 23.30	20.00 – 20.58												

2.0	100.00 – 50.00	50.00 – 35.36 (50.00)	33.33 – 28.87 (44.44)	25.00 – 25.00	20.00 – 22.37
2.5	100.00 – 51.02	50.00 – 38.67 (62.50)	33.33 – 32.88	25.00 – 29.31	
3.0	100.00 – 52.92	50.00 – 42.00 (75.00)	33.33 – 36.69		
4.0	100.00 – 56.99	50.00 – 47.93 (100.00)	33.33 – 43.31		
5.0	100.00 – 60.63	50.00 – 52.79			
6.0	100.00 – 63.73	50.00 – 56.78			

minimum necessary to insure negative profits for a potential entrant. Thus, to keep out potential entrants each player would have to be willing to accept an expected loss or suffer expected losses due to their entry. This choice is not viable in the long-run, and players will exit.

A similar result occurs where incumbents settle at the C–N solution. For example at $r = 1.4$ in Table 3 the C–N solution for four players is \$26.25 which is larger than the maximum pre-emptory bet. The resulting negative expected profits implies that the number of players must be less than four in the long-run.

It can also be seen in Table 3 that the maximum number of incumbents for a positive range of pre-emptory bets declines as the r-value increases. For example, at $r = 1.4$ the maximum number is eight and declines to two when $r = 3.0$. Note also that the minimum pre-emptory bet first declines as the r-value increases, and then increases. For one player the minimum is 50.00 at an r-value of 2.0.

4. Hit and run competition

We are interested in determining the long-run equilibrium solution. Consider first where players will enter as long as positive expected profits exist for placing a bet. We denote this usual profit incentive as 'hit and run' competition. Incumbents, or those looking at the game in a 'precommittal' sense, can thus prevent this hit and run competition by bidding in the pre-emptory range.

Within the pre-emptory range an infinite number of solutions exists. Two of these were considered. One is the C–N solution given by equation (3) which may come about because of internal competition. As indicated the C–N solution will only be admissible if it results in non-negative expected profits, i.e., when it falls within the pre-emptory range. A given number of players cannot be sustained if the C–N solution is above the upper end of the range, and exiting will occur. There also exists the possibility that the C–N solution can lie below the pre-emptory range. Where this occurs entry will take place because of positive expected profit opportunities. Eventually, as the number of players increases, the C–N solution for incumbents will move within the pre-emptory range and eliminate the positive profit incentive for entrants. Thus for $r = 1.1$ in Table 3, between 5 and 11 players are viable in the long-run when they place a C–N bet.

The second long-run solution considers players recognizing their mutual interdependence and colluding to maximize profits. This is the solution to the original Cournot problem suggested by Chamberlin (1962). The collusion solution would be at the lower end of the pre-emptory range where incumbents can maximize their expected profits while deterring hit and run

Table 4. Sum of individual investments at equilibrium (hit and run entry, incumbents collude)

	Number of players														
Exponent (*r*-value)	1	2	3	4	5	6	7	8	9	10	11	12	13	14	...	28
1.1	73.74	78.54	81.51	83.68	85.40	86.82	88.06	89.12	90.09	91.00	91.74	92.40	93.21	93.80	99.82	
1.2	63.73	71.54	76.56	80.32	83.35	85.92	88.20	90.16	91.98	93.50	95.04	96.48	97.76	98.98		
1.3	58.27	68.38	75.09	80.24	84.50	88.14	91.35	94.16	96.75	99.20						
1.4	54.98	67.02	75.27	81.72	87.10	91.74	95.90	99.60								
1.5	52.92	66.68	76.32	84.00	90.05	96.18										
1.6	51.61	66.94	77.94	86.80	94.40											
1.8	50.32	68.48	81.99	93.20												
2.0	50.00	70.72	86.61	100.00												
2.5	51.02	77.34	98.94													
3.0	52.92	84.00														
4.0	56.99	95.86														
5.0	60.63															
6.0	63.73															

entrants through expected losses. Thus for $r = 1.4$ in Table 3, 5 incumbents would each bet \$17.42, the low end of the pre-emptory range. It may be possible, however, for the number of incumbents to be too large to exclude potential entrants. This occurs, for example, with nine incumbents when $r = 1.4$. A bid of \$11.11 per player yields zero expected profits for the incumbents, while a larger bet of \$11.45 is necessary to exclude hit and run competition. Exit would have to occur until there were eight players in the game.

Hit and run competition allows multiple equilibria in the number of incumbents both when they collude and when they settle at the C–N solution. Total expenditure will vary accordingly. Table 4 provides aggregate expenditures for the hit and run competition long-run equilibrium where incumbents collude and Table 5, where incumbents bet at the C–N solution.

In Table 4 aggregate expenditures range from a minimum of \$50 for 1 player at an r-value of 2.0 to a maximum of \$100, the value of the payoff. For solutions where at least two incumbents exist, the minimum is \$66.68 at the r-value 1.5. It can be seen that the greater the number of players the greater the dissipation of rents. For example, at $r = 1.2$ one player bets \$63.73 while 14 players in aggregate bet \$98.18. Finally, for a given number of players aggregate expenditures increase with the r-values although for six or less players they first decline. For three players aggregate expenditures fall from \$81.51 at an r-value of 1.1 to \$75.09 at $r = 1.3$ and thereafter increase to \$98.84 at $r = 2.5$.

In Table 5 showing aggregate expenditures when players settle at the C–N solution a smaller range of players make up possible equilibria than in the collusion case. This occurs because of the additional constraint that the C–N solution must fall within the pre-emptory range. Here again, aggregate expenditures increase as the number of players increases and as the r-value increases.[9] At each value of n and r the C–N solution which assumes competitive behavior, dissipates more of the payoff than the collusion solution.

5. Hardball competition

Another type of competitive response in a precommittal or long-run sense can be explored. We denote this response as 'hardball' competition. In hardball competition it is assumed entry will occur so long as a player can be accommodated (positive expected profit opportunities exist with him in the game) even though it may mean incurring short-run expected losses.

Entry occurs in this hardball case because the potential entrant recognizes that he can impose expected losses on the incumbents through his entry. The incumbents are then forced to revise their bets to insure non-negative ex-

Table 5. Sum of individual investments at equilibrium (hit and run entry, incumbents at Cournot-Nash solution)

	Number of players										
Exponent (*r*-value)	1	2	3	4	5	6	7	8	9	10	11
1.1	73.74[a]				88.00	91.68	94.29	96.24	97.74	99.00	100.00
1.2	63.73[a]		80.01	90.00	96.00	100.00					
1.3	58.27[a]		86.67	97.52							
1.4	54.98[a]	70.00	93.33								
1.5	52.92[a]	75.00	100.00								
1.6	51.61[a]	80.00									
1.8	50.32[a]	90.00									
2.0	50.00[a]	100.00									
2.5	51.02[a]										
3.0	52.92[a]										
4.0	56.99[a]										
5.0	60.63[a]										
6.0	63.73[a]										

[a] Cournot-Nash solution not applicable to one player; minimum investment for maximum expected profit is indicated.

pected profits. For the pre-emptory ranges given in Table 3 it can be shown that, given that incumbents maintain their existing bets, a potential entrant can impose expected losses on them and himself if he enters.[10] Further, the greater the expected profits of the incumbents the smaller the expected losses of an entrant. Such a situation gives an entrant some bargaining leverage over the incumbents. To forestall such entry completely, the incumbents would have to place a zero-expected profits bet, the maximum of the pre-emptory range.

If incumbents accommodate the hardball entrant the revised bets could be either the C–N bet or, if it can be arranged, the collusion bet. With either, however, more hardball entry will be invited. The number of players increases until, as in the hit and run case, the minimum bet of the pre-emptory range yields negative expected profits. Entry of players beyond this point would guarantee expected losses for all, and as a result the numbers cannot be sustained. Thus, an equilibrium number of players exist where the lower end of the pre-emptory range equals the upper end of the range. This number can easily be determined for the different r-values in Table 3. For instance, with $r = 1.1$, the hardball equilibrium would have 28 players; with $r = 1.5$, 6 players; with $r = 2.0$, 4 players; etc. For r-values larger than 4, only one player can be sustained.

The total expenditures by r-value under hit and run and hardball competition are given in Table 6. From this it can be seen that hardball competition tends towards a larger number of competitors and a greater tendency to dissipate the payoff. Aggregate expenditures (where more than one incumbent exists) range from \$75 for two players at the C–N solution and an r-value of 1.5 (from \$84 for two colluding players at an r-value of 3.0) to \$100. Aggregate expenditures for most cases exceed \$90. The C–N solution results in less aggregate expenditure (marginally greater for r-values 1.1 and 1.2) than the collusion solution. This may appear surprising but not so when one considers that a given number of players colluding provides more profits at each r-value and thus a greater potential for entry than the C–N solution.

One further consideration is that resources may be expended to participate in the bidding process, i.e., transactions costs. Examples of this include: information gathering, and organizing and maintaining a cartel. The direct effect of these transactions costs is to reduce by an equal amount the expected payoff of the incumbent players and, correspondingly, it will also reduce the maximum – zero expected profits – bid, which is the upper end of the pre-emptory range. Since long-run equilibrium occurs where the upper and lower ends of the pre-emptory range are equal, the existence of transactions costs implies that total expenditures in the process of rent-seeking will be reduced by the amount of transactions costs.

The analysis of the effect of transactions costs suggests a policy recom-

Table 6. Sum of individual investments at equilibrium (hardball entry)

Exponent (r-value)	Number of players: 1	2	3	4	5	6	7	8	9	10	11	12	13	14	. . .	28
1.1											100.00[a]					98.82[b]
1.2						100.00[a]								98.98[b]		
1.3				97.52[a]						99.2[b]						
1.4			93.33[a]					99.60[b]								
1.5		75.00[a]				96.18[b]										
1.6		80.00[a]			94.40[b]											
1.8		90.00[a]		93.20[b]												
2.0		100.00[a]		100.00[a]												
2.5	51.02[a]		98.64[b]													
3.0	52.92[a]	84.00[b]														
4.0	56.99[a]	95.86[b]														
5.0	60.63[a, b]															
6.0	63.73[a, b]															

[a] Incumbents at Cournot-Nash solution. For one player minimum investment is shown.
[b] Incumbents collude.

mendation to reduce resource use in rent-seeking. If a lump sum licensing arrangement can be applied to the participants of a rent-seeking process it will displace by an equal amount for each player the resources used in actual rent-seeking. And, therefore, total expenditures in rent-seeking will be less by the total expenditures on the license.

6. Summary and implications

We have analyzed long-run behavior in rent-seeking under several conditions and behavioral hypotheses. The question of interest is whether or not the long-run expenditures will exactly equal the value of the rents. Our results depend on the type of competitive response which is assumed to exist in the long-run and on the r-value governing the probability of winning.

For the case where the r-value is less than or equal to one, Tullock has pointed out that aggregate expenditures will always be less than the value of the game. The long-run solution, however, results in each firm submitting an infinitesimal bid – not a very realistic solution. We showed that when a minimum bet requirement is imposed, the number of players is determined in the long-run, and all rents will be dissipated if the minimum bet is integer divisible into the payoff. If not, aggregate expenditures depend upon the size of the minimum bet relative to the total payoff; however, the tendency towards complete dissipation of expected profits still exists.

For r-values greater than one we looked at entry under hit and run and hardball competition. Under hit and run competition entry occurs if the potential entrant can make positive expected profit. In the long-run this suggests that incumbents make their bets to pre-empt potential competition. We found a range of possible pre-emptory bets. Using this range we considered the Cournot-Nash and the collusion solutions. For both cases the hit and run entry assumption allows various numbers of incumbents to be a stable equilibrium. For high r-values, however, only one player can exist. Aggregate expenditures under both kinds of solutions dissipate the greater part but not all of the available rents. As the number of players is increased greater dissipation of the rents results.

Hardball competition was defined as entry occurring so long as accommodation could be forced by imposing expected losses on the incumbents if accommodation and resulting expected profits for the entrant are not obtained. This would require the potential entrant to be willing to absorb a short-run loss. If this type of entry is carried out, the number of players increases to the point where the minimum pre-emptory bid yields a negative expected profit for the players. The number of players will thus depend upon the r-value. The rents will always be very nearly dissipated in hardball competition whether the incumbents collude or settle at the C–N solution initially.

These results assume the payoff is known with certainty and is treated as if the game is continually replayed. Since all players were assumed identical, the long-run results could also be considered the solution where each possible player has time to consider alternatives and signal 'precommittal' behavior.

It is perhaps interesting that the results concerning hardball competition are similar in nature to those obtained in the monopoly analysis of Baumol, Panzar and Willig (1982) on potential competition. They find that the presence of potential competition dissipates monopoly profits under certainty and non-increasing average costs. This is very similar to our findings that rents are nearly dissipated with the potential for entry if the entrant would be willing to accept short-run losses.

Given the social objective to minimize the expenditure of resources in rent-seeking the following are implied by our results:

1. Disallowing any type of entry and minimizing the number of players will hold down the aggregate expenditure of resources. Further reductions will be obtained if collusion is encouraged allowing players to place the minimum bet to maximize expected profits.
2. If entry cannot be disallowed then regulate against hardball competition whereby entrants incur short-run expected losses to gain accommodation by incumbents. Here again collusion is preferable, not only because it results in minimum expenditures by each incumbent but also because the C–N solution is unstable at low numbers of players for certain r-values and hit and run entry will result.
3. If hardball entry cannot be prevented then encouraging competition among the incumbents with a likely C–N solution appears to be marginally preferable to allowing collusion.
4. Application of a lump sum cost as a condition for participating in the rent-seeking process, e.g., a license, will reduce the total expenditure in rent-seeking by an equal amount.

NOTES

1. For the sake of simplicity here and throughout the paper, the probability of winning is expressed assuming only two players. This assumption does not change our results and more players can be accommodated by changing the term b^r to $\sum_{i=1}^{n-1} b_i^r$ where $n-1$ is the number of opponents.
2. Corcoran used the discounted value of rents given by Xe^{-pt} for his long-run analysis. His long-run solution assumed entry as long as the rate of return exceeded the discount rate,

p. In the simpler case where the payoff is received immediately upon placing the bet, entry would occur so long as profits are positive. The main results of the analysis are unchanged with the simplifying assumption.

3. The probability of winning with a bet of 'a' is assumed to have the explicit form:

$$F(a) = \frac{a^r}{a^r + \sum_{i=1}^{n-1} b_i^r}$$

$F'' < 0$ is a sufficient condition for F to be strictly concave in 'a.' Performing the differentiation and simplifying yields:

$$F'' < 0 \text{ if}$$
$$a^{-1}(r-1) < 2\,[ra^{r-1}(a^r + b^r)^{-1}].$$

Assuming $a, b > 0$ then $r \leq 1$ is a sufficient condition for this. Concavity of F also assures that the second-order condition of the C–N solution is satisfied.

4. Mathematically we can set up this constrained maximization problem with the following Lagrange function

$$L = F(a)\,X - a + \lambda(Z - a)$$

where X is the value of the payoff
a is the bet
Z is the minimum bet
$F(a)$ is the probability of winning
and λ is the unknown Lagrange multiplier.

With $F(a)$ defined as $a^r/(a^r + b^r)$ with $r \leq 1$ the objective function will be strictly concave and with the associated linear constraint the Kuhn-Tucker sufficient conditions are:

1. $F'(a)\,X\text{-}1\text{-}\lambda \leq 0,\ a(F'(a)\,X\text{-}1\text{-}\lambda) = 0,\ a \geq 0$
2. $Z\text{-}a \geq 0,\ \lambda(Z\text{-}a) = 0 \lambda \geq 0$

where all expressions are evaluated at the solution value of λ and a. We know that 'a' will always be positive so we have two possible cases.
First, $\lambda = 0$ which means the constraint is not binding. Making use of this information in equation (1) above yields

$$F'(a)\,X\text{-}1 = 0$$

which is the usual condition for the Cournot-Nash and yields

$$a = \frac{n-1}{n^2} rX.$$

The second case is where $\lambda > 0$ so the constraint is binding. With both a and λ positive equation (2) above gives us:

$$(Z - a) = 0$$

or

$$a = Z.$$

Thus, the optimal bet is the minimum bet when the constraint is binding in the Cournot-Nash equilibrium.

5. There is as illustrated earlier, an incentive for those already in the game to submit another bet and increase expected earnings. In either case the total number of bets rises so long as expected profits are still positive.
6. One could make the argument that players would always be constrained in the betting by the smallest unit of currency. In the U.S., one cent becomes the constraint and since one is divisible into every payoff, all rents would be dissipated.
7. One exception is the sealed bid auctioning of public lands for mineral leases. In these auctions, the government has a reservation price on each tract although the reservation price is not known prior to the submission of bids. If the maximium bid falls short of the reservation price, the tract is retained by the government for auctioning at a later date. In these auctions only the winning firm's bid is retained and thus the effect is somewhat different in that it is to insure that all rents cannot be captured by the bidder.
8. We can solve for the incumbents minimum pre-emptory bet to maximize profits from equations

$$1)\ E\ [\ (a)] = \frac{a^r}{a^r + \sum_{i=1}^{n-1} b_i^r}\, X - a = 0$$

and

$$2)\ E'[\ (a)] = 0$$

This insures that the entrant's optimal bet can at best attain zero expected profits. The solution for each incumbent's bet is:

$$b = \frac{r-1}{r} x / [n(r-1)]^{1/r}$$

9. This can also be determined by multiplying equation (30) by n.
10. For example, the optimal bet by an entrant (derived from 1) and 2) in note 8) is $(r\text{-}1)X/r$. When entry occurs the expected value of an incumbent betting for maximum expected profits while preventing hit and run entry, is negative.

Efficient rents 2

Free entry and efficient rent seeking

RICHARD S. HIGGINS
Federal Trade Commission

WILLIAM F. SHUGHART II
ROBERT D. TOLLISON*
Center for Study of Public Choice, George Mason University, Fairfax, VA 22030

1. Introduction

This paper concerns rent seeking and the extent to which rents are dissipated under various circumstances. Gordon Tullock's (1967) insight that expenditures made to capture an artificially created transfer represent a social waste suggested that the cost to the economy of monopoly and regulation is greater than the simple Harberger (1954) deadweight loss. Indeed, under Tullock's original formulation and in the extensions of his work by Krueger (1974) and Posner (1975), rents are exactly dissipated at the social level ($1 is spent to capture $1), so that the total welfare loss from such activities is equal to the Harberger triangle plus the rectangle of monopoly profits.

More recent contributions have identified instances of imperfect rent dissipation. Rogerson (1982) finds that rent dissipation will be incomplete when rent seekers face differential start-up costs or in situations where a monopoly franchise is reassigned periodically in such a way as to give advantage to the incumbent monopolist. Hillman and Katz (1984) obtain similar results when rent seekers exhibit risk aversion and the value of the transfer is 'large.' Lastly, using a model in which rent seekers know the correct strategy (if it exists), but where the probability of obtaining a transfer is not a linear function of rent-seeking expenditures, Tullock (1980) finds situations of either underbidding or overbidding. We shall have more to say about Tullock's analysis in Section 2 below.

While the importance of these results to the measurement of the social cost of monopoly and regulation is transparent, there is a curious aspect to most of the models in the literature on rent seeking. Both the value of the transfer and the number of rent seekers are normally fixed. The latter assumption removes from consideration the method by which rents are dissipated where entry is possible. Indeed, since monopoly rights are assigned in these models either by a pure lottery or by award to the highest bidder

* We have benefitted from comments by James Buchanan, Gerard Butters, Robert Mackay, Gordon Tullock, and two anonymous referees. Remaining errors are our own.

among a predetermined number of contestants, an important antecedent question is left unanswered: What determines the equilibrium number of rent seekers?

In this paper, we investigate the degree of rent dissipation when the number of active rent seekers is endogenous. Building upon Tullock's (1980) model, we show that in a market where the award is based on 'effort,' entry fees are nonrefundable, and contestants are risk neutral, there exists a symmetric mixed-strategy zero-profit equilibrium. This result implies that all rents are dissipated (expectationally), and that the expected number of active rent seekers depends on the value of the rents to be appropriated, among other things. Moreover, we are able to demonstrate that under-, over-, or exact dissipation of the monopoly rents is possible depending on the actual number of active rent seekers. On average, however, rents are completely dissipated.

This paper is organized as follows. Section 2 provides a summary of Tullock's model, introducing along the way the key elements in our analysis. Our model is presented in Section 3, and Section 4 contains some concluding remarks.

2. A critique of the Tullock model

Consider the static monopoly depicted in Figure 1. A competitive industry with constant long-run marginal costs (LMC) equal to P_c is costlessly transformed into monopoly. Output falls from Q_c to Q_m as a result, and market price rises to P_m. In the standard analysis, the welfare loss is represented by the triangle ABC, and the rectangle of monopoly profits, P_mABP_c, is treated as a pure transfer from consumers to the monopolist.

Tullock's (1967) insight was that any resources spent to capture P_mABP_c were also part of the social cost of monopoly. Posner's (1975) example is instructive on this point. Suppose that 10 bidders vie for a transfer worth \$100,000. If the bids are nonrefundable and all contestants are risk neutral, each will offer \$10,000 for the right to be the monopolist. At the social level, the monopoly returns are exactly dissipated – \$100,000 is spent to capture \$100,000. The welfare cost of the monopoly is thus equal to the area of the trapezoid, P_mACP_c.

Tullock (1980) subsequently proposed a model in which results other than exact dissipation of rents are possible.[1] In the model, N participants seek a prize, L. The probability of winning is assumed to be

$$p_i = X_i^R / \sum_{j=1}^{N} X_j^R,$$

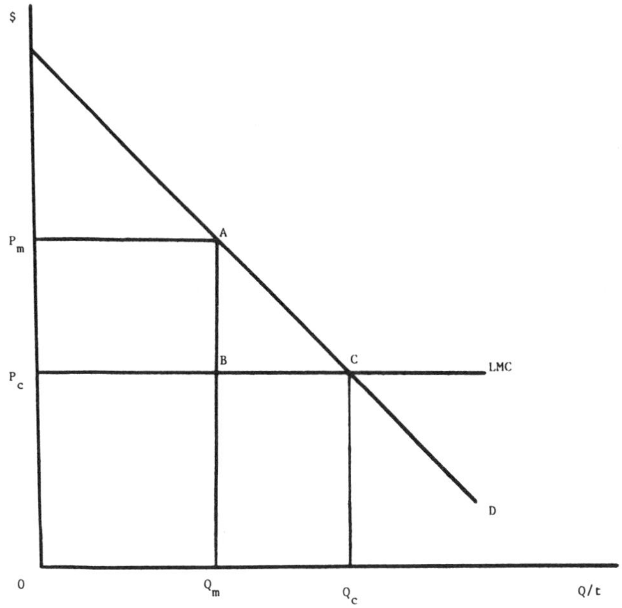

Figure 1.

where X_i is the amount bid by individual *i* and the value of the exponent, *R*, denotes possible marginal cost structures confronting the participants. (The higher is *R*, the easier it is for contestants to raise their probability of winning at the margin.) Tullock assumes further that if a correct individual strategy exists, each participant knows it and plays with the presumption that the other parties can discover the same solution. Given these circumstances, each individual chooses the bid, X_i^*, that maximizes $LP_i - X_i$. The joint solution of these *N* marginal conditions is

$$X_i^* = R(N-1)L/N^2.$$

Thus, Tullock shows that, depending on *N* and *R*, the players will spend in the aggregate more or less than *L*. Actually, however, the value of *R* drives the entire result. In the case of two participants, for example, overbidding occurs whenever *R* exceeds two. Indeed, with two players and $R > 2$, *each* of the bids will be greater than the value of the prize.

We can illuminate the relationship between *R* and *N* further by extending Tullock's model to allow entry of participants until there is zero profit from playing the game, that is, until all rents are dissipated. Zero profit occurs when $NX_i^* = L$. Solving this expression for *N* yields

$$N^* = R/(R-1).$$

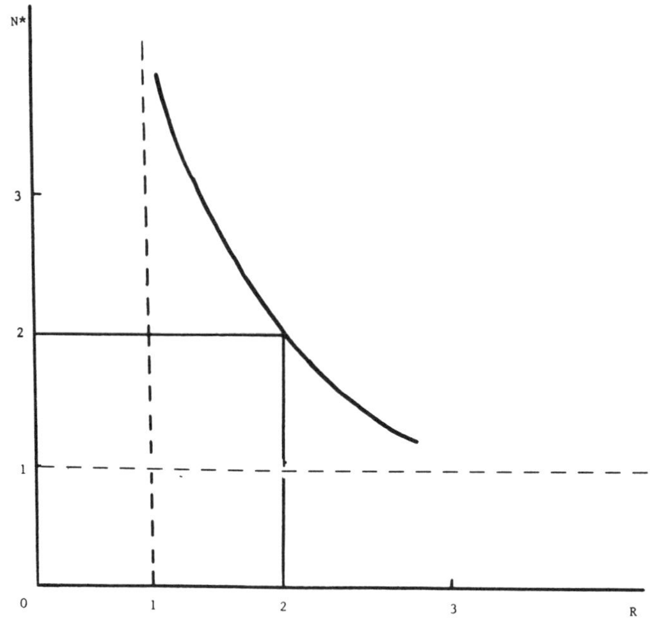

Figure 2.

Note, first, that N^* is independent of L. This suggests that for a given R, the same number of people will play the game when the prize is \$1 as will participate when the prize is \$100,000. Second, when $R = 1$, underbidding obtains with any finite N; it requires an infinite number of players to dissipate all rents. Third, as R increases from 1, N falls asymptotically to unity. (These relations are depicted in Figure 2.) In short, R must lie on the interval (1, 2) for the zero-profit result to make sense. Only if we are willing to assert $1 < R < 2$ is there an optimal N that dissipates all rents.

Extending Tullock's model by allowing for entry, we find that all rents are dissipated, but only under such restrictive conditions that we are led to ask, why does the probability of winning the game have the particular form assumed by Tullock? Moreover, within that structure, what determines R? In what follows, we offer a more general specification of the competition for rents.

3. Free entry and rent dissipation

In our model there are N potential rent seekers.[2] Each of them has two decisions to make. Each first decides whether or not to compete for the monopoly right. Each of the $m(\leq N)$ active rent seekers then chooses a level of effort to maximize the expected value of securing rents, given the efforts of other active participants.[3] In contrast to existing models in the literature, we let the expected number of active rent seekers be defined by a zero-profit condition.[4] The *actual* number of active players may under- or overdissipate rents, but *ex ante* and on average, rents are exactly dissipated when the players exhibit risk neutrality. We first describe how the rents are assigned among the active rent seekers, and then we analyze potential rent seekers' decisions concerning whether to participate actively.

It is useful to think of our model of rent assignment in terms of the 'comparative hearings' conducted by the Federal Communications Commission (FCC) in granting a radio or television license. We suppose the license to be worth L, and individuals expend effort U_i to qualify for the franchise.[5] They invest in market research, program development, lobbying activities, and so forth. The effort costs $C(U_i)$, assumed to be identical for all contestants. We also suppose, however, that the FCC's decision-making process is subject to error. Perhaps there is some room for (unbiased) discretion, the effort of applicants can be observed only imperfectly, or in the case that several applicants supply equal effort, the winner is chosen at random. Thus, the FCC looks at the vector of efforts $(U_1, U_2, \ldots, U_m)$ and grants the license to the applicant supplying the highest level of effort, subject to the error element. Each contestant's measured effort (relevant effort) is thus $W_i = U_i + E_i$, the true effort plus a random variable. We assume that the E_i are independently distributed with zero mean and constant variance.

First, consider the case of two contestants. The license will be awarded to applicant 1 when $U_1 + E_1 > U_2 + E_2$, or when $U_1 - U_2 + E_1 > E_2$. Thus, the probability of winning for applicant 1 is given by

$$P_w^I (U_1, U_2) \equiv \int_{-\infty}^{\infty} \theta(E_1) \int_{-\infty}^{V_1} \theta^1(E_2) dE_2 dE_1, \tag{1}$$

where $V_1 = U_1 - U_2 + E_1$.

We now use the Nash condition to define equilibrium. Applicant 1 chooses the level of effort, U_1, that maximizes

$$LP_w^1(U_1, U_2) - C(U_1)$$

holding U_2 constant, and applicant 2 optimizes over the symmetric problem.

The marginal conditions are

$$L(\partial P_w^1/\partial U_1) - C'(U_1) = 0, \text{ and} \tag{2a}$$

$$L(\partial P_w^2/\partial U_2) - C'(U_2) = 0, \tag{2b}$$

where the $C'(\cdot)$ represent each contestant's marginal cost of effort. Using the definition in (1), the two first-order conditions become

$$L \int_{-\infty}^{\infty} \theta(E_1)\,\theta(U_1 - U_2 + E_1)\,dE_1 - C'(U_1) = 0, \text{ and} \tag{3a}$$

$$L \int_{-\infty}^{\infty} \theta(E_2)\,\theta(U_2 - U_1 + E_2)\,dE_2 - C'(U_2) = 0. \tag{3b}$$

These relations give reaction functions that in equilibrium define equal efforts U_1^* and U_2^* described by

$$L \int_{-\infty}^{\infty} \theta^2(E)\,dE - C'(U^*) = 0. \tag{4}$$

Equation (4) is obtained by exploiting the symmetry properties of the problem, noting that $\theta(U_1 - U_2 + E_1)$ and $\theta(U_2 - U_1 + E_2)$ are in equilibrium equal to $\theta(E_1)$ and $\theta(E_2)$, respectively, since $U_1^* = U_2^*$.

Equation (4) suggests that equilibrium effort depends on the value of the license, L, on the steepness of marginal costs, and on the nature of the error distribution, specifically the 'mean density' (see, e.g., Nalebuff and Stiglitz, 1983). In particular, the applicants will each expend a greater level of effort the more valuable the prize and the less rapidly marginal costs rise with effort. (If marginal costs are constant, there is no optimal effort.)

In order to examine the relationship between total rents and total rent-seeking effort, we must specify the functions more completely. Suppose that E follows a uniform distribution on the interval $[-D/2, D/2]$ and that $C(U) = a + (b/2)U^2$. Equation (4) is now

$$L(1/D) - bU^* = 0,$$

which implies that $U^* = L/bD$. Total rents are, of course, L, and from the cost function aggregate rent-seeking expenditures are $2[a + (b/2)(L/bD)^2]$. The net gains are therefore $L - [2a + (L^2/bD^2)]$. Note that the more error there is in the decision-making process, the lower the effort and hence the lower the cost. In the extreme case where effort does not count, the competition reduces to a pure lottery with fixed entry cost, a. Here the net gain is $L - 2a$.

We next generalize to m applicants. In the special case outlined above where each of m applicants incurs costs of $C(U) = a + (b/2)U^2$ and the distribution of decision-making errors is uniform on $[-D/2, D/2]$, the optimal individual effort is $U^* = L/bD$.[6] Effort is, therefore, independent of m when the E_i are uniformly distributed. Although this is clearly a special case, we retain the uniform distribution because it greatly facilitates the analysis of rent seekers' prior decisions whether to be active participants.

For each number of active participants greater than one there is an expected profit given by $L/m - [a + (b/2)(L/bD)^2] \equiv E\pi(m)$. When $m = 0$, profit is zero, and when $m = 1$, there is really no contest so profit is $L - a$.

As m varies from 2 to N, $E\pi(m)$ declines at a constant rate equal to $C(U^*)$.[7] Depending on the parameters of the model, $E\pi$ may be negative beyond some particular value of m. And finally, since m assumes only integer values, there may be no value of m for which $E\pi$ is exactly zero. In the latter case there will be some particular value of m, say m^0, at which $E\pi(m^0)>0$ and $E\pi(m^0+1)<0$.

To model the N potential rent seekers' participation decisions, we make some simplifying assumptions. First, we assume that all rent seekers announce simultaneously their decisions to play or not to play. The fixed cost component, a, is incurred when a rent seeker decides to be active, and a decision to be active is binding. That is, the rent seeker must pay an entry fee equal to a to be an active participant, which would be forfeited if the entrant were to withdraw. The rent seekers do not decide on their optimal levels of effort at the time they commit to active participation. They choose the appropriate levels of effort only after they know how many other active participants there are.[8]

As Tullock (1980: 105–109) has emphasized, because expected profit is in general negative for some number of active participants less than N, there is no symmetric pure strategy equilibrium in our entry game. He refers to this problem as the 'paradox of the liar.' We resolve the paradox by allowing our rent seekers to choose mixed strategies.

Furthermore, since effort is independent of m in our example based on the uniform error distribution, expected net return over the variable cost of effort may be negative beyond some number of active players. Under these circumstances, players minimize losses by dropping out according to an optimal mixed strategy, forfeiting the fixed entry fee. To avoid complicating the analysis of the initial entry decision we assume that expected profit (net of variable cost) from the contest is nonnegative for all $m \leq N$.[9]

Each of the N rent seekers chooses to participate actively with probability p_i. The expected value of actively seeking rents is found by weighting $E\pi(m)$ by the probability that only $m-1$ other rent seekers will actively participate, summing these terms, and multiplying by p_i. In the symmetric mixed-strategy equilibrium the expected value of being an active rent seeker must be zero for each rent seeker. And, each player's choice of p_i, given the probabilities of the others, must simultaneously maximize the expected values for each player, which equal zero.

In the present case, there is a straightforward way to find equilibrium p. We know that the individual expected gain must equal the individual expected cost. Expected cost is $p\{C^*[1-(1-p)^{N-1}]+a(1-p)^{N-1}\} = p\{a+(b/2)U^{*2}[1-(1-p)^{N-1}]\}$.[10] Expected gain for the individual is $L[1-(1-p)^N]/N$. That is, expected gain is total gains, L, times the probability that at least one rent seeker becomes active, all divided by the total number of rent seekers. Thus,

$$L[1-(1-p)^N]/N = p\{a+(b/2)U^{*2}[1-(1-p)^{N-1}]\}. \tag{5}$$

When N is large, (5) is simply $L/N = pC^*$, and $p^* = L/NC^*$, provided L/NC^* is not greater than 1. When $L/NC^* > 1$, the equilibrium strategy is for all N rent seekers to contest actively for the monopoly rents.

When the N rent seekers choose probability p^* so that there is zero expected profit from engaging in rent seeking, rents are fully dissipated *ex ante*. *Ex post* – that is, after a realization from the binomial distribution of active participants – profit from engaging in the contest may be positive or negative depending on the particular realization. On average, the actual number of active contestants equals the expected number, Np^*, and expected return over the cost of effort in the contest will just equal the fixed cost. For other realizations of active contestants, expected net return from the contest may exceed sunk cost (underdissipation of rents) or be less than sunk cost (overdissipation).

We conclude by noting the relationship between the average number of active rent seekers and the other parameters of the model. Specifically,

$$\begin{aligned} Np^* &= N(L/NC^*) \\ &= L/[a+(b/2)(L/bD)^2]. \end{aligned} \tag{6}$$

From (6) we determine that $\partial Np^*/\partial a < 0$ and $\partial Np^*/\partial D > 0$. Thus, assuming that $p^* < 1$ to begin with (i.e., $L-a > 0$ and $L/m - C^* < 0$ for all m beyond $m^0 \leq N$), there are fewer active rent seekers the higher the entry fee, and more active rent seekers the greater the role of chance in assigning rents. Moreover, we see from (6) that the expected number of active rent seekers is independent of the size of the pool of potential rent seekers. Of course, in general when effort varies with the number of active rent seekers, this result is unlikely.

The relationship between the expected number of active rent seekers and the size of the prize is surprisingly ambiguous. A higher prize induces two opposing responses. For a given level of effort, a higher L increases the expected gain from being an active rent seekers. However, since a higher L induces greater effort the cost of active participation is also raised, and the overall effect of increasing L on the probability of actively seeking rents is ambiguous. Specifically, when the variable cost of effort exceeds the fixed entry fee, an increase in the size of the prize induces less active participation. Finally, when the error in the decision-making process is very large, that is, $D \rightarrow \infty$, the 'hearing' reduces to a pure lottery, and effort becomes irrelevant. In this case $Np^* = L/a$ (when $L/a < N$), and an increase in the size of the prize unambiguously increases active participation.

4. Concluding remarks

In the competition for a monopoly right in which the number of bidders is fixed, Tullock and others have found the value of the resources spent in the aggregate to capture the transfer to be sometimes less than and sometimes greater than the value of the monopoly. We think this approach to be incomplete since it leaves unanswered the question of what determines the number of individuals who will vie for the right to be the monopolist. It is unsatisfactory to imagine, for example, that the franchisor sets the number of contestants. One could then foresee that rent seeking would arise to influence the permissible number of bidders, and this merely moves the rent-seeking dissipation question one step back.

Our approach has been to extend these models in two ways. First, for a given number of active rent seekers, the monopoly right is granted according to the contest model developed by Nalebuff and Stiglitz (1983). This model clearly reveals that overdissipation of monopoly rents generally occurs only when there is some fixed cost of effort – or what amounts to the same thing, when active participation requires a nonrefundable entry fee. According to the contest model of granting rents, the extent to which rents are dissipated depends positively on the number of active rent seekers.

Second, since expected profit in the contest is generally negative beyond some number of contestants less then the potential number of contestants, we construct an economic model of the entry decision. To avoid Tullock's 'paradox of the liar' – the absence of a symmetric pure-strategy equilibrium – our potential rent seekers adopt mixed entry strategies. We show that there is a symmetric mixed-strategy zero-profit equilibrium in which each of N potential rent seekers actively engages in the rent-seeking contest with probability p. Thus, the actual number of active rent seekers is a draw from the binomial distribution with parameters N and p. For the expected number of contestants, Np, rents are exactly and fully dissipated. Over- and underdissipation of monopoly rents are possible, but only *ex post*.

The implications of our analysis are straightforward. First, when there are no restrictions on the number of individuals who may vie for the right to capture an artificially created transfer, entry will occur, and resources will be spent up to the point where the expected net value of the transfer is zero. Such competition leads to exact dissipation of the present value of the flow of rents associated with the transfer, and in static terms, makes the social cost of the monopoly equal to the value of the Tullock trapezoid. Second, even if entry is limited, overbidding for the franchise will in general not occur, the value of the Tullock trapezoid sets an upper limit on the social cost of monopoly.

The result that rents are fully dissipated depends critically on the assumption of risk neutrality. While we have not analyzed the case of risk aversion completely, several predictions about the characteristics of equilibrium appear straightforward. First, if the marginal contestant is risk averse, then setting net expected utility equal to zero implies that in the limit the monetary value of the rents will not be fully dissipated. Moreover, the extent to which rents are dissipated will be less the greater the degree of risk aversion, the smaller the value of the appropriable rents relative to initial wealth, and the higher the fixed cost of entry (see Hillman and Katz, 1984: 107). Second, the extent of rent dissipation will also depend on the assumptions made concerning the supply of rent seekers and their risk aversion distribution. For example, there may be a large enough pool of potential rent seekers with zero risk aversion that the equilibrium number of active rent seekers will all be risk neutral. In this case all rent will be dissipated expectationally. Third, and most importantly, with risk aversion as with risk neutrality, overdissipation will not be observed *ex ante*.

Finally, the theory of rent seeking, as exposited here and elsewhere, puts considerable pressure on the argument that monopoly promotes a transfer of wealth from consumers to owners of monopoly firms (Comanor and Smiley, 1975). As Posner (1975: 821) observed, rent seeking implies that monopoly profits are dissipated, not transferred. This argument is correct as far as it goes. Only it does not go far enough, and it would carry us well beyond the scope of this paper to present a careful analysis of the impact of rent seeking on the level and distribution of wealth. Suffice it to say here that the effect of rent seeking on the level and distribution of wealth will be a function of the mechanism used to assign rents in a society, attitudes toward risk, comparative advantages in rent seeking, and so on (Higgins and Tollison, 1984).

NOTES

1. In a recent paper, Corcoran (1984) raises several of the same points about Tullock's analysis which we independently noted, and which are set out in the remainder of Section 2. He suggests, for example, that bidders will enter until in the long run the expected payoff from playing the game is just equal to the return realizable from alternative investments, and that in equilibrium, the number of contestants depends only upon the value of the parameter, R, which in Tullock's model represents the structure of marginal costs facing the participants. Corcoran goes on to state, correctly, that aggregate rent-seeking expenditures will in the long run be invariant with respect to R. What Corcoran fails to note (and what Tullock, 1984, shows suspicion of, but does not fully demonstrate in his comment) is that for the zero-profit result to make sense, R must be restricted to the interval (1, 2). Where we differ from Corcoran is in our development of a more general approach to the question of rent dissipation under conditions of free entry (see Section 3).

2. The number of potential rent seekers is fixed in our model. We do not analyze the decision to be among the pool of potential rent seekers.
3. Thus, our rent-seeking model is analogous to Shubik's (1959) game-theoretic model of oligopoly in which firms in-being are distinguished from active competitors.
4. The major exception is Corcoran (1984); see note 1. One may question whether equilibrium is the appropriate restriction to apply to the problem of rent seeking for a known monopoly right. Consider Frank Knight's example of the California gold rush. Overinvestment occurred in that case because no one entrant could possibly determine how many others would attempt to stake claims. Admittedly, our model requires that all players have this type of information, but we think that the assumption is justifiable on the ground that it permits us to derive testable implications about the determinants of rent-seeking activity.
5. If the license is perfectly durable, L reflects the discounted value of the flow of rents in perpetuity. On the other hand, if there is some positive probability that the rents will be expropriated in the future, this will reduce the present value of the license. The exact nature of the license right in this regard is immaterial to our results.
6. When there are m rent seekers, individual i wins when $W_i > W_j$ for all $j \neq i$, that is, when $U_i - U_j + E_i > E_j$ for all $j \neq i$. If we assume that the errors are distributed independently, the probability that player i wins given E_i is

$$\prod_{j \neq i} \int_{-\infty}^{V_i} g(X_j)\, dX_j, \tag{a}$$

where $V_i = U_i - U_j + E_i$. To get the probability that i is successful, we integrate (a) over E_i and obtain

$$\int_{-\infty}^{\infty} [\prod_{j \neq i} \int_{-\infty}^{V_i} g(X_j)\, dX_j] g(X_i)\, dX_i \equiv P(U_1, \ldots, U_i, \ldots, U_m). \tag{b}$$

The partial derivative of $P(U)$ with respect to U_i evaluated at the symmetric solution is

$$(m-1) \int_{-\infty}^{\infty} g^2(X) G^{m-2}(X)\, dX. \tag{c}$$

Thus, the marginal condition in the symmetric case when g is the uniform density over $[-D/2, D/2]$ is

$$L(1/D) - bU^* = 0. \tag{d}$$

7. Obviously, if U^* were not independent of m, $E\pi$ would depend on m in a more complex way.
8. Alternatively, we might have supposed the N rent seekers to make a joint effort and entry decision. We have not worked through the implications of such a model.
9. The drop-out decision would have to be modeled in the same way as the initial decision to enter. The drop-out game would be played repeatedly until the expected return to effort in the contest was nonnegative for the remaining players. Thus, for all m for which expected net return over variable cost would be negative, $E\pi$ will be limited to the loss of fixed cost.
10. Expected cost is not simply pC^* because when there is only one active participant, no effort needs to be expended. The probability that a particular individual incurs only cost a is $(1-p)^{N-1}$. The probability that a particular individual is not the only active rent seeker and thereby incurs cost C^* is $1-(1-p)^{N-1}$.

Efficient rents 3
Back to the bog

GORDON TULLOCK
Center for Study of Public Choice, George Mason University, Fairfax, VA

My role in connection with the efficient rent-seeking model (Tullock 1980) is, I think, a rather ill-omened one. I began the discussion by inventing a model with an apparent paradox. The market doesn't clear even with free entry and competition. There have been a number of efforts to deal with this problem (Corcoran, 1984; I commented on it in the same issue, pp. 95-98). (1985) Corcoran and Karels and Higgins, Shughart, and Tollison (1985) are further efforts to solve the problem.

It is my unfortunate role, having discovered this particular intellectual swamp, to frustrate efforts to get out by pushing people back in. I first invent a difficult problem and then when people try to solve it, I say that their solutions are either wrong or at least incomplete. I should therefore say, that I do think that the work of Corcoran, Karels, Tollison, Shughart, and Higgins, has indeed made progress toward a solution even if they have not finally solved the problem.

Corcoran and Karels come close to solving the original problem provided we keep the framework of efficient rent-seeking rigid and unchanging. The problem is that there is one assumption in that initial framework which I now realize was unduly restrictive.

It is a usual practice among economists, when we observe a number of people engaging in the same kind of competitive activity to assume that they all behave the same. The reason for this is partly that they face the same problem and we would assume they reach the same conclusion, but I think even more importantly, that an assumption that they do not behave in the same manner means that you have to explain why some of them carry out one policy and some another.[1] In the particular case of efficient rent-seeking, it is in general, more profitable to violate this rule. You will make more money if you do not make the same bid as your colleagues.

Before going further, I should frankly confess that I have no solution to this problem. It appears once again to be a case of the paradox of the liar. If one deviates from the pattern, he makes a profit, if all follow his example, they lose. The sensible behavior for an individual is not sensible unless the other people are doing something else. If this gives the reader a headache, I can only recommend Tylenol.

Let me take an obvious example from Corcoran and Karels (1985: 234 f.) Table 3. Suppose that we are in the area of increasing marginal efficiency, specifically the exponent or *r* value is 1.5. If seven people are playing, he puts the minimum preclusive bid at \$14.29.[2] Suppose that one of the players instead of putting in \$14.29 puts in \$14.39, while the other six stick to the \$14.29. As a result, he acquires an expectancy equivalent to \$14.41. The \$.10 additional investment has paid off with \$.12. Each other player loses \$.02.

The reason that this would occur is I suppose fairly obvious whenever *r* is greater than 1. This is the area of increasing marginal returns and hence the return on additional marginal units will always be greater. Many equilibria in which all of the people are assumed to make the same investment will be subject to this problem. Indeed, in many cases, a complete outsider entering and making a large bid can gain. For example, consider eight people playing with r 1.3 and each putting in \$12.50. This is of course spending \$12.50 to buy an expectancy of \$12.50. Suppose that a ninth party arrives and puts in \$25.00. His expectancy is \$26.14. The expectancy of the original eight has of course gone down sharply.

I realize that the problems that this will generate. Once again, we seem to be in a situation in which there is no rational way of playing the game. If nine players each put in \$25.00, the result is disastrous.

One way of dealing with this problem of course, if for individuals to attempt to put in individually preclusive bets before anyone else enters. The outcome of such preclusive bets is shown in the left column of Table 5, of Corcoran and Karels (p. 239). The problems here are first, the one that I mentioned in my original article (1980) which is that it leads to a previous game to be first. There is however, a second problem here which is that is we look at real-life rent-seeking activity, it is a little hard to see what the equivalent of making that single large initial investment is. A lobbyist can hardly simultaneously provide Congressmen with twenty two dinners and five blondes. In corrupt societies where cash is used, this problem of course, if less severe.

When we have an exponent less than 1, i.e., when they're declining returns to scale, Corcoran and Karels essentially depend on the fact that there will, in practice, be a least feasible bid. I have no quarrels with this, but I should point out that there is here a problem analogous to the problem we have discussed above which makes calculation at least difficult. Look at their Table 1 (p. 230) and consider the first line. Suppose that one of the two people who are placing a bet instead of placing a bet of \$12.50, places one of \$12.00. He of course does not have an even chance of winning, so his expected return is not \$50.00, but \$49.49. His expected profit is \$37.49, instead of \$37.50. But his percent return on capital is better. If he had put in \$12.50, he would have received a profit three times his initial capital. If he puts in \$12.00, he receives a profit 3.12 times his original capital. Of course the other player, the one who still put in his $12.50, does better than he would had the first player also put in $12.50. Specifically, he makes an additional expected $.51. This is however, only a return of 3.04 times his capital. The explanation, of course, is that here we are in an area of declining marginal returns.

Naturally I am not claiming that I have solved the problem. What I have done is make it more difficult. Let us now turn to Higgins, Shughart, and Tollison. The first thing to be said, is that all of the problems mentioned above apply here also. When playing one of their stochastic strategies, it will normally not be rational to play the same amount as the others are doing.[3] It is also subject to the problem that a single large preclusive bet normally dominates their stochastic procedure. But once again, the high profitability of such a preclusive bet means that there would be a previous game to obtain such preclusion.

The basic point of the Higgins, Shughart, and Tollison paper is to arrange through stochastic methods that all of the players receive a normal return on their capital (as most economic work, this is shown as zero profit) by stochastic means. There are occasional situations in which the number of players for the zero profit condition is an integer. More commonly however, it is not and their stochastic model is designed to deal with this much more numerous category. Unfortunately, there is here a defect. The mathematical expression that they use has the ingenious characteristic that the same (zero is usual) profit is made by playing every time, by playing their stochastic procedure, or by transferring ones capital to some other normally profitable activity. If however, one of their players, instead of playing stochastically, chooses to play every time, he will achieve a normal return on his strategy, the other players will suffer losses.

The reason is clear, although a little involved. When I put my bid in, whether I do it because Higgins, Shughart and Tollison's stochastic process tells me I should at this time, or for some other reason, that stochastic process followed by the other players gives me an expectancy of exactly normal profits. If I play continuously, I will get normal profits, But since I am not playing the stochastic model, I am entering more often than I should and am inflicting a negative cost on others. Every time that I play when by the stochastic model I shouldn't, I lower the profits of the other players.

In general, in this kind of efficient rent-seeking model, an individual player imposes external costs on others. The Higgins, Shugart and Tollison model guarantees that these external costs are evenly distributed and balanced by profits. A single player who deviates by playing more often injures the other players.

Now it should be pointed out that there's no strong motive for a player to do this. It is true he will be able to invest more capital in an activity which gives a normal return, and he might drive some of the other players out in which event he would begin making positive profits. The latter possibility of course brings us into the extremely complex area of preditary competition and I don't want to go through that very lengthy argument. I do presume my readers are already familiar with it. Suffice it to say that it does not seem as if this would be a long-run way of obtaining profits.

The other problem here is not that once the Higgins, Shughart and Tollison equilibrium stochastic process has reached equilibrium someone may deviate, but that is very hard to see how you would get there to begin with. Clearly they are not talking about a carefully calculated conspiracy among all the players, because if there is such a conspiracy, there are far more profitable strategies to play. Their equilibrium would have to be obtained by players who simply find out over time that this is the appropriate strategy. Unfortunately, there seems no path by which they can do so.

As an example illustrating the problem, suppose that we have a situation in which seven players, if they all made the same and optimal bid regularly, would make a positive profit, whereas eight players, if they all made the same and equal bid would lose. We start with eight players. All of them are losing, but one of them who has read Higgins, Shughart, and Tollison calculates the efficient stochastic strategy and begins following it.

There will now be two different kinds of games. Firstly, those games in which this player, after consulting his table of random numbers, plays. In those games there will be eight players and all of them will lose. The second set are the ones in which he does not play, there are seven players, and all of them gain or at least lose less. By his behavior, he has benefited the others for at least some of the games while in all the games in which he plays, he loses as much as before. If a second player began following the same policy once again, the players who were not playing stochastically, would do better than those who were.

Note, there's nothing in this which indicates that anybody will actually make a positive profit. It is just that the non-stochastic players will more often have a profit in a particular play than the stochastic players and these profits will on the average, be larger. Thus there is no way for the players by simple experimenting with different stochastic procedures to reach the Higgins, Shughart, and Tollison equilibrium.

As I said before, my role in this controversy is to watch people trying to get out of the swamp and then push them back in. Clearly, my role is not a constructive one, but nevertheless, I feel it is necessary. On the other hand, it seems to me that if the work of Corcoran, Carroll, Higgins, Shughart, and Tollison has not gotten us out of the swamp, it has at least moved us to a place where the mud is less deep. I don't know much more about the geography of the swamp but the prospect that we can find a bit of dry land somewhere has improved.

NOTES

1. The so called Hawk-Dove literature, helps to provide an explanation for this kind of behavior under some circumstances. Unfortunately, it is not applicable to the subject of this comment.
2. This involves rounding. There are seven players and 7 x 14.29 is of course lightly more than $100 but the matter is unimportant for the example.
3. I recently saw a propaganda movie about the Chinese communes. It was made several years ago, and would not be permitted in present day China, but I saw it in Philadelphia. In one sequence each of the Commune children was encouraged to work faster than the others.

The design of rent-seeking competitions

ROBERT MICHAELS
Department of Economics, California State University, Fullerton, CA 92634

Abstract

In the standard Tullock model of rent-seeking as a noncooperative game, aggregate expenditures by seekers can equal, exceed, or fall short of total rents depending on what is assumed about the number of seekers and the marginal return to a seeker's investment. If the supply of an input into the rent-seeking process is controlled by a politician who receives payment from seekers for it, the indeterminacy of the process becomes a less serious problem. He supplies it and designs the rent-seeking game to maximize his wealth. The author derives expressions for the number of seekers and the marginal return parameter which maximize the politician's wealth in one-input and two-input rent-seeking processes.

1. Introduction

As models of rent-seeking behavior have grown in generality, our problems in deriving and interpreting their predictions have grown apace. The initial statements by Tullock (1967) and Posner (1975) assumed competition among risk-neutral seekers for a monopoly right, constant supply prices of all inputs used in obtaining a monopoly, and a probability of success by a seeker proportional to his investment relative to the investments of others. Under these circumstances, it was claimed that aggregate resources invested by seekers would be equal to the value of the rent, and that on average the seekers of monopolies would earn a competitive return on their investments.

The theoretical result on total dissipation of rents is quite fragile. If seekers are risk-averse and maximize expected utility, total resources invested in rent-seeking will typically be less than total rents. (Hillman and Katz, 1984). Moreover, the degree of dissipation is highly dependent on the concept of equilibrium which is assumed, and on the assumed proportionality of the odds of winning to the relative size of one's contribution (Tullock, 1980a; Michaels 1986a). If the odds increase nonlinearly with the relative size of a

*The author thanks Robert Ayanian, Bruce Benson, Walter Hettich, Richard Ruppert, Gordon Tullock, and David Wong for their helpful comments. An earlier draft of this paper was read at the 1986 Meeting of the Public Choice Society.

player's contribution then a symmetric, noncooperative equilibrium among risk-neutral players, if it exists, may be characterized by total investments which are either less than or greater than total rents. Attempts to get around this awkward result by imposing a long-run equilibrium on the system have thus far been unsatisfactory (Corcoran, 1984; Corcoran and Karels, 1985; Higgins, Shughart and Tollison, 1985; Tullock, 1984 and 1985).

In this paper, I propose a different approach to the problem. It is related to the previous literature by the general form of the game which the seekers play. It is new in that it attempts to impose a structured equilibrium through the addition of institutional detail. The neglect of this detail is a curious omission in the received literature, particularly when one considers the orientation of its major authors.[1] The critical detail is that a rent-seeking process is not exogenously imposed. Rather, it is designed and implemented through a political process in which rational individuals interact.

I envision a rent-seeking process as one in which the parameters of the relationship between the amount invested by a player and his odds of winning are set by a politician. The politician, who might be either a dictator or a competitor, designs the process to maximize his own wealth subject to election constraints. The link between rent-seeking expenditures and the politician's wealth lies in the fact that the politician in office is a monopoly supplier of a primary input ('influence') which is of importance in determining the winner of a rent-seeking competition.

A moment's thought about estimates of monopoly rents in regulated industries suggests a major problem. Looking at Posner's (1975: 818) summary of economists' estimates of these rents, the implied dollar values in individual cases are astronomical, even more so when capitalized and aggregated. If politicians dispense the rights to such tremendous amounts of wealth, why do they manage to capture so little of it for themselves? Attempts to quantify the rents due to regulation and identify its beneficiaries (e.g., Moore, 1978) have never to my knowledge imputed a dollar gain to those officials responsible for enabling others to compete for such gains. While we frequently speak of regulations as constrained in form and quantity by the need to create and maintain coalitions of beneficiaries (Peltzman, 1976), it remains hard to understand why a politician receives such minimal rewards for an effort into which he provides an essential input. The model of this paper, suitably extended, should shed light on the problem.

In the next section of the paper, I present the basic model, a summary of results in the received literature, and an extension in which the politician monopolizes the sole input into rent-seeking. Section 3 gives some results for the case in which the seeker must use a politically supplied input in conjunction with one which is purchased in the market. Section 4 discusses the many margins along which rent-seeking competitions may be designed, and offers conclusions and suggestions for further research.

2. A single-input model

Following Tullock (1980a) at the start, assume there are N seekers, each of whom is identical save for the amount of rent-seeking capital, K_i, which he has accumulated. N. is determined exogenously. Tullock's model assumes that K_i is identically equal to rent-seeking expenditure. The probability p_i that applicant i will be successful is given by:

$$p_i = \frac{K_i^r}{\sum_{j=1}^{N} K_j^r}. \tag{1}$$

The opportunity in question is assumed to offer wealth of W to the winner with certainty. Following Tullock, I assume a symmetric, noncooperative equilibrium. Each player holds a zero conjectural variation about the others, i.e., assumes that they will not make any response to a change in his investment.

The major paradoxes of that equilibrium are by now well known. In a two-player game the sum of investments will equal W only if r equals 2. As the number of players approaches infinity, the sum of their investments approaches W only if the exponent is unity. With a lower exponent than 2 in the two-player case, or a lower exponent than 1 in the infinite-player case, aggregate investment falls short of W. Reversing the inequalities on the exponents leads to aggregate investment in excess of W. For sufficiently high exponents in games with a finite number of players, an individual's investment can exceed W.

2.1 *A simple formulation of the appropriability problem*

In Tullock's model, the disposition of rent-seeking expenditures is unspecified.[2] In this section, I propose a simple alternative. Assume that a monopoly politician sets the parameters of the rent-seeking operation in such a way that he maximizes his residual income from the expenditures made by seekers. Let us assume that a seeker will only be accredited, i.e., have the right to enter the lottery, if he has paid a certain amount F to agents other than the politician. F is the fixed charge of filling out an application, producing records, retaining an attorney, etc. It is assumed independent of the prior status of the seeker and the amount he will subsequently invest. It is determined exogenously. Investment after the fixed charge takes the form of bribes given to the politician. Assume that the rent-seeking process then takes the form of a Tullock lottery, where the bribes are capital.

If the politician can set the parameters of the process to maximize his returns, the strategy seems clear. He will set things up so that his returns are maximized subject to no seeker spending more than his own expected returns. If he can find a strategy that exhausts the rents (see below), he will want N = 2, since this maximizes the difference between W and NF. (I am assuming that if there is only one applicant no bribe is necessary.) All he need do to exhaust expected rents is to set r appropriately. Let K be the amount spent by an optimizing seeker. Adapting the formula from Tullock (1980a: 112), rents will be exhausted in the symmetric equilibrium where $pW - K = 0$ for the representative seeker. Where N is controllable at 2, we have:

$$\frac{(K-F)^r}{2\,(K-F)^r} W - \frac{1}{4} rW = 0, \tag{2}$$

and the r which exhausts all rents in seeker expenditures while maximizing the politician's bribe income equals 2. If N is not reducible to 2, r should be set according to:

$$\frac{(K-F)^r}{N(K-F)^r} W - \frac{N-1}{N^2} rW = 0, \tag{3}$$

which yields

$$r = \frac{N}{N-1}\,. \tag{4}$$

Throughout I am assuming that the optimal total investment for a seeker exceeds F.

2.2 *Some consequences of the formulation*

A politician who can set r (or, better yet, r and N) will certainly have an incentive to set it at a level which maximizes his takeout from the lottery. Why will he not set an r which overdissipates the rents? If entrants can anticipate that the game will be played to a symmetric Cournot-Nash equilibrium, as Tullock hypothesizes, they should also be able to predict N, and thus rationally decide whether to enter the game or not. The anomalous outcome, in which it pays one seeker to enter after each has calculated a negative expected return if all of them enter (Tullock, 1985) depends too strongly on unstated assumptions about the possibilities for negotiation among players and the possibility of reconsideration of a decision not to enter. With no institutions specified, it is hard to evaluate the potential importance of such an anomaly.

There seems to be an easier way around the anomaly in any case. A politician who persistently offers unprofitable rent-seeking opportunities will lose the support of seekers and be replaced by one who offers profitable opportunities. If institutions permit the anomalous outcome of one seeker purchasing the opportunity for a dollar after all the others have rationally dropped out because r is excessive, our politician is clearly not maximizing his wealth. More fundamentally, if it is so easy to set up a scheme in which seekers systematically bankrupt themselves in attempts to get rich, the private sector would have invented it a long time ago. It is hard to view most seekers as the equivalent of those risk preferrers who are already served quite adequately by the privately-organized gambling industry[3] (Friedman, 1981).

The problems of unexploited profit or indeterminacy vanish from the rent-seeking model as soon as we assume a residual claimant, much as they vanish in ordinary models of markets. The apparent paradoxes of the rent-seeking model cease to exist when it is placed in a simple institutional setting. Even this simplest of models yields some predictions. First, it explains why there will frequently be barriers whose effect is to limit the number of potential seekers (a cable-TV franchise applicant must typically show prior financial stability; only a municipal utility can compete for a primary allocation of inexpensive power produced at a federal hydroelectric site). Second, if N and r are given, a politician will have an incentive to attempt to cut F. The less that is exhausted in paperwork and legal fees, the more that is available for a politician to appropriate.

The model also sheds some light on the structure of rent-seeking contests in which divisibility if feasible over time or space or subsets of the contest. If there are no fixed costs of seeking, and capital markets are perfect, a politician should be indifferent as to whether he sets up a single once-and-for-all contest for the rent or whether he sets up a periodic auction. The existence of rent-seeking costs which are not appropriable by the politician should bias the process to one of long-term contracting, which is frequently observed (Landes and Posner, 1975; Michaels, 1979). If the fixed costs of negotiating for contracts between private parties are sufficiently lower than those of bidding for a government contract, more rents can be gained by a politician who names only a primary contractor and gives that contractor discretion as to subcontractors.[4]

Finally, there is little reason in this model to make the process biased. The politician's prime interest is that the largest possible amount accrue to him, regardless of source. As is clear from the results in Tullock (1980a), for a given bias parameter (possibly one given by another law), it is generally possible to set up the contest so that rents are still dissipated in payments to the politician. There is little discernible gain to be made by setting up an obviously biased lottery, even if it is legal to do so.

3. A multiple-input model

3.1 *The seeker's demands for inputs*

Consider another stylized rent-seeking process. A commission of unbribable bureaucrats will transfer wealth of W to the winner of a Tullock lottery. The parameters of the lottery are set by a monopoly politician. Assume for the time being that there is no fixed charge to enter the competition. Rent-seeking capital acquired by seeker A, K_A, originates according to a linear homogeneous production function:

$$K_A = F(X_A, Y_A) \tag{5}$$

where X_A and Y_A are inputs, F_1, F_2, and F_{12} are positive, and F_{11} and F_{22} are negative.[5] Input X is supplied by the politician, who is its only supplier. He acts as a rational monopolist and sets a price of P_X. Input Y is available on the market at a fixed price P_y.

The important points can most easily be derived if we restrict ourselves to a model with two seekers, A and B. The probability of player A winning is given by:

$$P_A = \frac{K_A^r}{K_A^r + K_b^r} \tag{6}$$

The exponent is set exogenously and is assumed to be sufficiently low that each player reaps nonnegative expected returns in the symmetric Cournot equilibrium. Player A chooses X_A and Y_A to maximize

$$\Pi_A = p_A W - P_x X_A - P_y Y_A \tag{7}$$

subject to (6) and a similar expression for K_B. Differentiating, we have:

$$\frac{\partial \Pi}{\partial X_A} = W \frac{\left[\begin{array}{l} (K_A^r + K_B^r)\, r K_A^{r-1} \dfrac{\partial K_A}{\partial X_A} - K_A^r\, r\, K_A^{r-1} \dfrac{\partial K_A}{\partial X_A} \\ + r\, K_B^{r-1} \dfrac{\partial K_B}{\partial X_B} \dfrac{\partial X_B}{\partial X_A} + \dfrac{\partial K_B}{\partial Y_B} \dfrac{\partial Y_B}{\partial X_A} \end{array} \right]}{(K_A^r + K_B^r)^2} - P_X = 0, \tag{8}$$

and a symmetric expression for $\dfrac{\partial \Pi}{\partial Y_A}$. The final parenthesized terms in the numerator are conjectural variations. In the Cournot-Nash model, they are assumed to be zero for all players and inputs. In the symmetric equilibrium,

$K_A = K_B$. After simplification, A's demands for X and Y are implicitly given by:

$$\frac{\partial K_A}{\partial X_A} - \left(\frac{4K_A}{Wr}\right) P_X = 0$$
$$\frac{\partial K_A}{\partial Y_A} - \left(\frac{4K_A}{Wr}\right) P_Y = 0. \tag{9}$$

In the N-seeker case, Tullock's (1980a: 112) result generalizes to:

$$\frac{\partial K_A}{\partial X_A} - \frac{N^2 K_A}{(N-1)Wr} P_X = 0$$
$$\frac{\partial K_A}{\partial Y_A} - \frac{N^2 K_A}{(N-1)Wr} P_Y = 0 \tag{10}$$

The individual seeker's total expenditure is independent of the prices of the inputs in the symmetric equilibrium. We have:

$$X_A P_X + Y_A P_Y = \frac{(N-1)Wr}{N^2 K_A}\left(X\frac{\partial K_A}{\partial X_A} + Y\frac{\partial K_A}{\partial Y_A}\right) \tag{11}$$
$$= \frac{(N-1)\,Wr}{N^2}$$

by Euler's theorem. With two or more seekers, expenditure by the individual decreases as N increases. The sum of all individual expenditures increases with N, but at a decreasing rate.

3.2 *The optimum number of seekers*

Under constant returns to scale, total expenditures by seekers on each input will increase as the number of seekers increases. Total expenditure by each seeker will be $\frac{N-1}{N^2}$ Wr. Now assume as before that a nonrecoverable fixed payment F must be made by a seeker to someone other than the suppliers of X and Y. Without this payment, he cannot credibly produce his rent-seeking capital. $\frac{N-1}{N^2}$ Wr – F will then be spent on X and Y by the seeker. In the symmetric equilibrium, everyone's total expenditure on capital will fall by F, and the probability of an individual winning will remain the same as before.

Facing an exogenously determined F, the politician wishes to set N which maximizes the difference between aggregate rent-seeking expenditures and aggregate fixed costs. This yields the largest pool of wealth from which he can extract payment for X. Total expenditure by N seekers is given by:

$$XP_x + YP_y + NF = \frac{N-1}{N} Wr, \tag{12}$$

where X and Y are total purchases of inputs. Assuming continuity of N, the problem is:

$$\max_{(N)} \frac{(N-1)}{N} Wr - NF, \tag{13}$$

whose solution is:

$$N^* = \sqrt{\frac{Wr}{F}}. \tag{14}$$

The optimal number of seekers to allow increases with the size of total rents and the size of the Tullock exponent. It varies inversely with the fixed charge which must be paid to outsiders.

3.3 *Properties of the input demands*

To simplify the algebra, assume that N has been determined exogenously and that F is zero. Since an optimizing seeker's total expenditure is fixed, his remaining task is to allocate it efficiently between X and Y, given their prices. His problem is a familiar one:

$$\max_{(X_A, Y_A)} K_A (X_A, Y_A) \tag{15}$$

subject to:

$$X_A p_X + Y_A P_Y = \frac{N-1}{N^2} Wr. \tag{16}$$

setting up a lagrangian, L, and differentiating:

$$\frac{\partial L}{\partial X_A} = \frac{K_A}{X_A} - \lambda P_X = 0$$

$$\frac{\partial L}{\partial Y_A} = \frac{K_A}{Y_A} - \lambda P_Y = 0 \qquad (17)$$

$$\frac{\partial L}{\partial} = -X_A P_X - Y_A P_Y + \frac{N-1}{N^2} Wr = 0$$

where λ is the lagrange multiplier. Comparative static differentiation straightforwardly yields $\frac{dX_A}{dP_X} < 0$, $\frac{dX_A}{dW} > 0$, $\frac{dX_A}{dr} > 0$, and $\frac{dX_A}{dN} < 0$, assuming continuity of N. In the absence of further data, $\frac{dY_A}{dP_X}$ appears to be of ambiguous sign. If the politician-supplier of X_A is a monopolist, however, he will operate where the elasticity of demand for it exceeds unity. With total expenditure fixed, this implies $\frac{dY_A}{dP_X} > 0$.

The aggregate problem for the seekers can be handled in an analogous manner. As a group, they maximize total capital produced, and it is then distributed equally among the seekers. Using unsubscripted variables to name aggregate quantities, we can derive $\frac{dX}{dP_X} < 0$, $\frac{dY}{dP_X} > 0$, $\frac{dX}{dW} > 0$, $\frac{dX}{dr} > 0$, and $\frac{dX}{dN} > 0$, again in the absence of a fixed entry charge.

3.4 *Elasticities of the derived demands*

In the Tullock lottery, a participant's spending on inputs to produce rent-seeking capital is fixed and, if the number of participants is predetermined, aggregate expenditure on that capital is constant. This is equivalent to fixing the elasticity of demand for capital at unity, both for the individual rent-seeker and in the aggregate. By assumption, input Y is available to rent-seekers at a fixed price. Under constant returns to scale, the elasticity of derived demand for politically supplied input X is:

$$\eta_{xx} = k + (1-k)\sigma, \qquad (18)$$

(Ferguson 1969, Hicks 1970), where k is the share of X in total cost and σ is the elasticity of substitution. The cross-elasticity of demand for Y with respect to the price of X is:

$$\eta_{xy} = k(\sigma - 1). \tag{19}$$

A nondiscriminating monopolist politician whose marginal cost of producing X is constant at C will price his output to seekers at:

$$P^* = C/(1 - \frac{1}{\eta_{xx}}). \tag{20}$$

Among other things, this implies a higher markup of price over marginal cost as σ increases, provided that $\sigma > 1/2(1-k)$. The markup will increase or decrease with the share of X in total cost as σ exceeds or falls short of unity. This is, of course, the Hicksian rule that being 'unimportant' (low k) only makes demand for an input more elastic if 'consumers' (whose elasticity = 1 in this model) can substitute more easily than producers.

3.5 *Competing politicians*

The question of the return to politicians in the long run is properly the subject of another paper (Michaels, 1986b). Any results depend on what is assumed about the process of political competition and how long the rents from a given competitive episode are expected to last. The price of a politically supplied input falls to its cost of production in only a minor subset of duopoly models. If rents are long-lived, e.g. from a franchise of indeterminate length, then competition must take the form of a single bidding process. On some arguments (e.g., Demsetz, 1968), this single process may be sufficient to remove the monopoly rents which a true monopolist would otherwise make.

As noted in the introduction, a model of full dissipation of rents on rent-seeking resources carries with it major empirical difficulties. Firstly, the gains to be made from monopolization (regulation) are strikingly large. Why do most politicians in democracies seem to capture so little of the rents which they could put up for grabs? (And why is so much politically lucrative activity unregulated?) One possible argument in favor of a hypothesis of effective competition in democracies is that the governing classes in dictatorships tend to live better relative to the rest of the population than is the case in democracies. Until we can better identify and measure exactly what the politician supplies to rent-seekers (and its production cost), we can only make conjectures.

In my argument, a determinate solution to the rent-seeking problem becomes even more distant, even with monopoly politicians, since the relative shares of any created rents become a matter to be determined by a mix of competition, legislation, and bargaining. The monopoly politician can extract a premium over production cost for the input he supplies. This is a pure transfer unless there is a preliminary rent-seeking competition to become a monopoly politician (Tullock, 1980b). If the price of the politician's input is driven down to marginal cost, resource waste in the Tullock model will increase, since total spending by seekers is a constant.[6]

4. Conclusions

Any theory of rent-seeking must ultimately be a theory of institutions. The model of this paper is an attempt to outline some of the options which might define the attributes of those political institutions in which resources are dissipated by those competing for the right to supernormal returns. The Tullock lottery as originally conceived operates in an institutional void. The probability mechanism, the exponent, the bias parameter (if any), and the symmetric Cournot-Nash solution are all imposed on the model from above. Here I have asked about what might happen if a monopoly politician can set certain parameters of a Tullock lottery.

In this model, the politician earns income by selling an input into the rent-seeking process. He wishes to maximize his gains. Adding the assumptions of fixed costs and rational expectations over repetitive lotteries by seekers explains why the politician will attempt to limit the number of seekers and why the exponents will be set a level which does not overdissipate rents. Adding assumptions about the nature and degree of political competition would clearly enrich the model. Doing so might help to predict those activities in which the government will seek out and set up rent-seeking competitions, the amounts of rents which will go up for competition, and the frequency with which competition for a given rent will occur.

At a deeper level, the model of this paper may yield insights into the forms actually taken by legislation. If the politician faces a derived demand for those inputs which he supplies, he will have an incentive to parameterize the production function for rent-seeking capital in such a way as to maximize his gains. The most obvious possibility is to be a dictator, i.e., to supply the only input into the rent-seeking process, and thereby expropriate all of the rents. If the production function for rent-seeking capital depends on joint use of political and market inputs, the legislation which defines the competition can do so by defining such parameters of the production function as cost shares and the elasticity of substitution.

The model might also be of use in understanding bureaucratic and related administrative processes. What will be the differences between those rent-seeking competitions which originate in profit-maximizing politics and those which originate in budget-maximizing bureaucracy? What if the passage of legislation which sets up a rent-seeking competition requires a coalition between legislators and bureaucrats? Clearly those pieces of legislation such as the Administrative Procedures Act, which partially define the fixed costs of rent-seeking, should properly be treated as endogenous. Finally, whence comes the typical bias in favor of the incumbent in repetitive rent-seeking competitions?

NOTES

1. One notable exception is Congleton (1984), who shows that under certain assumptions less will be invested by a seeker attempting to obtain a right to rents from a committee than by a seeker attempting to obtain such a right from a single administrator.
2. Tullock (1980a: 99) models the process as one in which a 'wealthy eccentric' offers a fixed amount of cash as a lottery prize. The organizer is assumed to be sufficiently wealthy or sufficiently eccentric that he will not exercise his power to amass a staggering amount of wealth by setting N and r appropriately.
3. Tullock's statement (1980a: 107) that long-run negative-sum games exist in poker and certain unspecified negotiations is unconvincing. The former, as he acknowledges, is a consumption good (and there are some who make a living for themselves by winning consistently). Negotiators who persistently engage in the latter, even if acting as the agents of others, will face the survival problems outlined in the text above.
4. One possible argument against long-term and consolidated arrangements comes to mind. A politician might announce a value of r which exhausts rents from seekers, collect the bribes, and then announce that he was raising r and would offer seekers the chance to bid additional amounts. One method of establishing a reputation as one who does not do this is to subdivide opportunities to provide an adequate demonstration of honesty. Another is to administer several classes of opportunities (e.g., a legislator typically sits on more than one committee) and thus establish consistency.
5. Fisher (1985) argues the unlikelihood of constant returns to scale in a production function for obtaining monopolies. Here, however, we have a production function for obtaining lottery tickets, rather than for gaining a monopoly with certainty.
6. The question of dissipation by precocious investment is itself an extremely difficult empirical matter. The opportunities that will be put up for rent-seeking may arise at random and not be amenable to diversification of investments (e.g., inventions and human capital). The full dissipation result will then probably hold only under highly specific assumptions about capital market equilibrium.

Rent-seeking with non-identical players

RICHARD J. ALLARD
Department of Economics, Queen Mary College, Mile End Road, London E1 4NS

Introduction

Recent discussion of rent-seeking games (see Tullock, 1980 and 1985; Corcoran and Karels, 1985; Higgins, Hughart and Tollison, 1985; Appelbaum and Katz, 1986) has largely involved identical players and been mainly concerned with the extent of under or over dissipation of rents, although Tullock has commented at some length on the 'intellectual mire' arising from possible non-existence of a Cournot-Nash equilibrium when there are increasing returns to rent-seeking expenditures. There has been very little comment on the more prevalent problem of multiple equilibria, though the credibility of any equilibrium depends on all the players recognising it as unique. Furthermore, given the rarity with which players are in practise observed to be identical, it is surprising that there has been no follow up to Tullock's (1980) discussion of the effect of differential advantages (which he referred to as bias), even though the very notion of an n player game implies an ordering if there are more than n potential competitors, which in turn implies some differences amongst players.

The primary objects of this paper are thus to consider why we might expect differential rent-seeking abilities between players, and to examine their role in determining whether a unique equilibrium exists and in the consequential extent of the dissipation of rents, though most attention is paid to the question of uniqueness because of its logical primacy. The formal analysis is confined to a single stage one-off game, though it is recognised that stronger uniqueness results might be obtained by introducing suitable intermediate stages or by viewing the game as one component in a more general super-game. The model is essentially that of Tullock (1980), and the basic form of this model, with no differentials between players, is set out and analysed in the next section. The impact of differentials on the existence of multiple equilibria is considered in Section 3, whilst in Section 4 bounded rationality is used to justify the analysis of models with differentiated players.

2. The basic symmetrical model

I use the model presented by Tullock (1980) where, in a competition amongst n players to capture a rent (s) the ith player incurs expenditure x_i and secures a probability of winning given by

$$p_i = x_i^r / \sum_1^n x_j^r$$

This can be explicitly recast in the form of a lottery in which the ith player uses x_i to produce q_i lottery tickets by setting

$$q_i = x_i^r \text{ or } x_i = q_i^a$$

where $a = 1/r$. Writing

$$Q^* = \sum_1^n q_i \text{ and } Q_i = Q^* - q_i$$

so that Q_i is production of lottery tickets by firms other than the ith, expected profits (E) for firm i are given by

$$E = \frac{q}{Q + q} - q^a \tag{2.1}$$

where we have set $s = 1$ (essentially measuring x in units of s), and have dropped the i subscripts. Since we will be looking for Cournot-Nash equilibria, Q is treated as fixed to give the first-order conditions

$$aq^{a-1} = Q/(Q+q)^2 \tag{2.2}$$

It is convenient to re-express these equations in terms of the ratio

$$v = q/Q$$

to give expected profits

$$E = \frac{v}{1+v} - v^a Q^a \tag{2.3}$$

and the first-order condition[1]

$$rv/(1+v)^2 = v^a Q^a = x \tag{2.4}$$

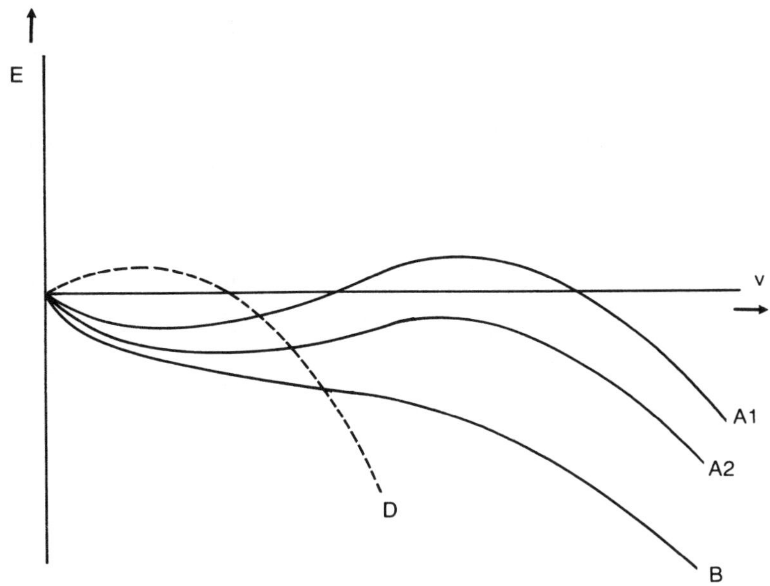

Figure 1.

Before examining the symmetric n-player game, we note that with increasing returns to expenditures on rent-seeking ($r > 1$), equation 2.4 (or 2.2) will not always have a solution. The graph of E against v from equation 2.3 (which might be called a residual profit curve) can display the 3 forms illustrated in Figure 1[2], depending on the values of Q and r. Type A1 has an internal maximum with positive profits, type A2 an internal local maximum at which profits are negative, and type B has no stationary point (for positive v). It can be shown that type A1 occurs when[1]

$$Qr^r(r-1)^{-(r-1)} < 1 \tag{2.5}$$

(requiring lower values of Q and r), whilst to avoid type B (where there is no solution to equation 2.4) requires

$$Qr^r(r-1)^{-(r-1)} < 2^{-2r}(r+1)^{r+1} \tag{2.6}$$

To ensure that with type A we have a maxima rather than a minima, we also require

$$v > (r-1)/(r+1) \tag{2.7}$$

When equation (2.6) is satisfied, we can substitute (2.4) into (2.3) to give the maximum expected profit as

$$E = \frac{v}{1+v} - \frac{rv}{(1+v)^2} \tag{2.8}$$

With decreasing returns to rent-seeking expenditures ($r < 1$), the expected profits curve always follows the concave form shown as D in Figure 1, so that there is a unique solution to the first-order condition, which will always be a maximum with positive expected profits.

For a symmetric n-player Cournot-Nash equilibrium the solutions are familiar. We must have $v = 1/(n-1)$, so that equation 2.4 gives

$$x = r(n-1)/n^2 \tag{2.9}$$

For a maximum we need to impose condition (2.7) which becomes

$$n < 2r/(r-1) \text{ or } r < n/(n-2) \tag{2.10}$$

and for a positive profit outcome, which is a necessary condition for a Cournot-Nash equilibrium where players have the option of setting $x = 0$, equation 2.8 gives the condition[3]

$$r < 1/(n-1) \tag{2.11}$$

In terms of achieving a unique Cournot-Nash equilibrium to this single stage one-off game, we can identify four problems, the first and last of which involve no Cournot-Nash equilibrium whilst the middle two involve multiple equilibria.

1. As stressed by Tullock (1980), n-players might find themselves drawn into a competition even though (2.11) does not hold. Having started they are unable to withdraw their bids and therefore move to the internal maximum at which they have an expected loss.

The other problems arise when the number of competitors is not predetermined.

2. If, for example, everyone knows that only $n = 2$ satisfies (2.11) but there are 5 potential players, how are 2 participants to be chosen? Assuming no pre-match collusion, a solution requires a natural ordering so that, in general, if there is to be an n person game all potential competitors know the identity of the 'top' n players who will therefore actually participate. Despite the frequent explicit assumption of symmetry as between players, some ordering assumption must also be implicit in most models.

3. Even with an ordering, there will for any value of r often be several values of n which give rise to a Cournot-Nash equilibrium.[4] Thus if 3, 4 and 5 person games are possible, how do players 4 and 5 decide whether to enter, and how do players 1, 2 and 3 know whether to allow for the entry of 4 and 5?
4. If player 1 alone were allowed to pre-commit, then with $r > 1$ it would very often pay him to choose the pre-emptive stake which would make it unprofitable for any subsequent players to enter.[5] Without pre-commitment, such a pre-emptive outcome cannot be a Cournot-Nash equilibrium, but might either player 1 or some of the others still take the possibility of such an outcome into account?

Failure to resolve problems 2 and 3 might be the reason why players find themselves facing problem 1. As indicated above, problem 2 can be overcome by the assumption of an ordering, whilst it is not impossible to introduce stages into the game in such a way that problems 3 and 4 are resolved. However, we will stick to a single-stage game and in the next section investigate the extent to which cost differentials between players (which are also the obvious source of any ordering) might effect problem 3. The possible way out of the problems via mixed strategies (as suggested by Higgins, Shughart and Tollison (1985)) is not pursued since they do not give rise to plausible solutions to non-constant sum games (see, for example, Shubik, 1982: 249–251). For the rest of the paper, problem 4 is removed by ignoring the possibility of pre-emption.

3. Cost differentials

As discussed in Section 4, there are likely to be (perhaps substantial) differences between players with respect to the cost effectiveness of rent-seeking activities. Within the current model these can be introduced in a number of ways. Using a more general formula for the number of lottery tickets

$$q = b(x-c)^r - k \tag{3.1}$$

k and c respectively represent required initial outlays of tickets or expenditures (in the normal case where they are positive they are equivalent to fixed costs, whilst if negative they represent 'head starts'), and $b > 1$ indicates greater efficiency at the margin. However, increases in r have an ambiguous effect, reflecting lower efficiency for $(x-c) < 1$ but higher efficiency for $(x-c) > 1$. Although Tullock (1980) allows for variations in b, this is with only two players, and the most analytically convenient approach is to set $k = 0$, $b = 1$ and allow variations in c. Equation (2.3) becomes

$$E = \frac{v}{1+v} - v^a Q^a - c \tag{3.2}$$

whilst the expression (2.8) for maximum expected profits becomes

$$E = \frac{v}{1-v} - \frac{rv}{(1+v)^2} - c \tag{3.3}$$

The first-order conditions (2.2) and (2.4) remain unchanged. Thus the benefits of differentiation are obtained at minimum analytical sacrifice, but similar qualitative results would be obtained from other means of allowing for differentials.

To investigate the possible equilibria, we designate a closed n player Cournot-Nash equilibrium (in which all players operate at their internal (local) maximum) as CN(n), and the corresponding output of lottery tickets as $\bar{Q}(n)$. Let F(n) be the expected profit (E_n) of the nth player in CN(n), and G(n) be the maximum profit which the nth player could achieve by entering a CN(n – 1) whilst incumbents maintain output at $\bar{Q}(n-1)$. (For type A2 curves [Figure 1] this is taken at the internal maximum whilst for type B, G is undefined.) Using F* and G* to denote the corresponding functions when players have identical costs with c = 0, then setting v = 1/(n – 1) in 2.8 gives

$$F^*(n) = \frac{1}{n}\left(1 - \frac{r(n-1)}{n}\right) \tag{3.4}$$

whilst, when it exists, G* is given by substituting the value of v which solves[6]

$$v^{1-a}(1+v)^{-2} = (n-2)(n-1)^{a-2} \tag{3.5}$$

into (from 2.8)

$$G^*(n) = \frac{v}{1+v} - \frac{rv}{(1+v)^2} \tag{3.6}$$

Values of F* and G* corresponding to selected values of r and n are given in Table 1 and illustrated (for r = 1.2) in Figure 2. For comparison, the table also gives the expenditures (x) at CN(n).

For CN(n) to remain a Cournot-Nash equilibrium when the number of active competitors is no longer pre-determined requires F(n) > 0 whilst G(n + 1) < 0 (the n player equilibrium is profitable whilst the corresponding level of output $\bar{Q}(n)$ makes it unprofitable for the $(n+1)^{th}$ player to enter). Thus with c = 0 for all players, we see from Table 1 that for r = 1.3 there are equilibria at n = 3 and n = 4; for r = 1.1 at n = 3, 4 and 5; and for r = 1.2 at values

Table 1. Profit levels and expenditures when c = 0 (× 1000)

r		n									
		3	4	5	6	..	10	11	..	20	21
	F*	44	6	−8							
1.3	G*	12	–	–							
	x	289	244	208							
	F*	67	25	8	0						
1.2	G*	36	−6	–	–						
	x	267	225	192	167						
	F*	89	44	24	14	..	1	0			
1.1	G*	61	13	1	–	..	–	–			
	x	244	206	176	153	..	99	91			
	F*	133	81	56	42	..	19	17	..	7.3	6.8
0.9	G*	110	55	35	26	..	12	11	..	5.4	5.1
	x	200	169	144	125	..	81	74	..	43	41
	F*	178	119	88	69	..	37	33	..	16.7	15.9
0.7	G*	160	97	71	56	..	31	28	..	15.2	14.5
	x	156	131	112	97	..	63	58	..	33	32

x is expenditure and F* is profit in n player equilibrium, G* is profit for entrant into (n − 1) player equilibrium (− indicates no internal optimum). All values are multiplied by 1000 relative to formuli in text.

of n from 5 to 11. For CN(n) to be a unique equilibrium also requires that $F(n+1) < 0$ (thus disqualifying CN(n + 1) because of negative profits) and that $G(n) > 0$ (disqualifying CN(n − 1) because entry is not deterred). Thus the condition is that F(n) and G(n) are positive whilst F(n + 1) and G(n + 1) are negative.

When $c \neq 0$, then

$$F(n) = F^*(n) - c_n \text{ and } G(n) = G^*(n) - c_n$$

Drawing in an illustrative c_n curve in Figure 2 (since $c_i < c_j$ for $i < j$, so that firm 1 has the lowest fixed costs, the curve is rising), it is evident that $F(n) > 0$ only if $F^*(n)$ is above c_n (and similarly for G(n)). Thus the condition for a unique equilibrium is that both F* and G* intersect the c curve between the same two adjacent integers, as in Figure 2 – CN(3) is a unique equilibrium. Whilst in broad terms it is evident that there is more chance of getting a unique equilibrium with a steeper c curve and, to a lesser extent, with a higher c curve, the discrete nature of the criterion leads to 'arbitrary' results. Thus with the

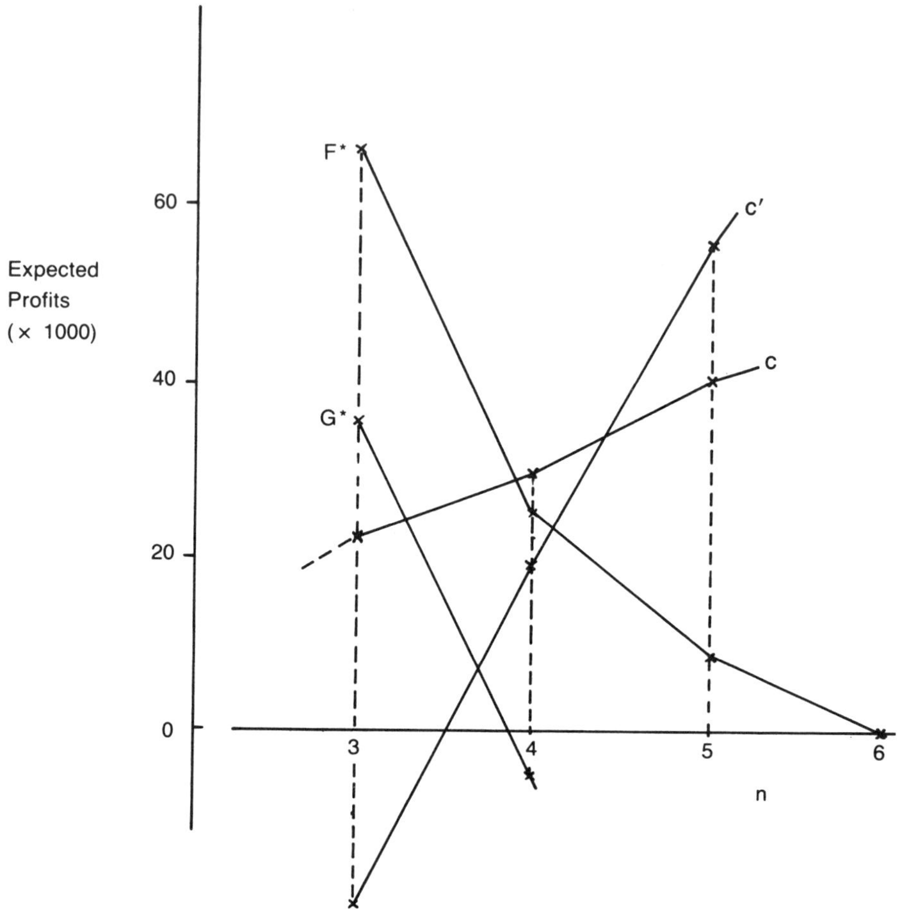

Figure 2.

steeper curve c′, both CN(3) and CN(4) are possible equilibria. Again in very loose terms, if the horizontal distance between where the F and G curves intersect the c curve is 0.5, the chance that the cuts will fall between adjacent integers is the same as that they will straddle an integer, so that there is an evens change of getting a unique equilibrium. For $r > 1$, inspection of the upper-portions of Table 1 show that the difference between c_n and c_{n+1} required to achieve this horizontal difference varies from around 0.01 to 0.05, and represents from around 5% up to over 20% of the level of expenditures, x. Thus compared with the extensive multiple equilibria when $c = 0$, plausible cost differences of this magnitude, whilst they cannot in general guarantee a unique equilibrium, do give reasonable prospects of uniqueness and at worst lead to double equilibria.

With decreasing returns to expenditures on rent-seeking ($r < 1$), it is well known that in the simple Tullock model ($c = 0$) there is no finite equilibrium number of players. This is because the marginal cost of producing lottery tickets tends to zero with q so that it is always worth a new player entering even if only at infinitesimal scale (curve D in Figure 1). Thus to secure any equilibrium, fixed costs of entry (c) must be strictly positive, but in all other respects the analysis is exactly the same as for $r > 1$. Some illustrative values for $r = 0.9$ and 0.7 are given in the lower part of Table 1, and following the same rough procedure as in the preceding paragraph, the difference between c_n and c_{n+1} required to achieve a horizontal difference between the points at which G* and F* intersects c of at least 0.5 varies between 0 and 0.03, representing between 0% and 22% of the level of expenditures (x).

When c is constant (identical players), then for any value of r (provided $c > 0$ for $r < 1$) the largest value of n for which F(n) is positive will generally have F(n) close to zero, and only be different from zero because of the integer nature of n. With differences in c, this rule only applies to the nth player whilst the intra marginal players may have substantial positive expected profits, so that the total expenditures on rent-seeking will be less than the rent, with the extent of under dissipation tending to increase as the differences in c increase.

4. Differentials between players and bounded rationality

Whilst the existence of differentials in rent-seeking abilities conform with our every day experience, it is sometimes argued that if such profitable differentials now exist, they represent rents arising from an earlier round of rent-seeking activity. This would have two implications, the first being that since differentials are the product of rent-seeking, a full rent-seeking analysis should use initial conditions which pre-date any differences and therefore assume uniform abilities. The second is that the sum of expenditures on acquiring the current rents should not be limited to those in the current competition, but should also include those aimed at acquiring an advantageous starting point for the current competition. Thus the use of differential abilities to argue for under-dissipation of rents would be invalid, since we should be taking the analysis back to the point where no such differentials exist.

Whilst it is clearly true that economic agents take some account of future rounds of the never-ending competition when determining current activity, the extent to which they do so is in particular limited by bounded rationality. Thus, back in the 1950s when licenses to operate commercial television stations in the U.K. were first issued, it is just not plausible to argue that potential bidders would take proper account of all the contingencies that might effect the impact of their winning a 1950s-license on their prospects in any comparable competition in the 1990s. To do so would have required them to list the sort of licenses that might come to exist (along with subjective probabilities for each), to estimate the expected rents to be obtained from each, and to assess the impact on the chances of winning such licenses of having held a 1950s-license. Even if they could have carried out the exercise in full, it would not have been worth their while.

To argue that future contingencies are not perfectly evaluated is not to go to the other extreme and suggest they are totally unforeseen, but to the extent they are unforeseen, the relevant attributes which players bring to the competition are in essence randomly distributed by fate. There is no way in which they would have been competed for in the past, since they were not known to be of value, but once they have been dealt out, and are seen to differ as between players, they will effect the outcome of the game and the way it is played. Provided at least some of the advantages in the current competition were unforeseen, there exist differentials as between players independently of any previous rent-seeking activity. The introduction of differences as between players is therefore not an artificial mechanism designed to help overcome a nasty dilemma, but is far more realistic on both theoretical and empirical grounds than the assumption that all players are identical. Consequentially, since differences tend to lead to reduced expenditures, we may generally expect rents to be under-dissipated.

4. Concluding remarks

This paper has investigated the extent to which differences as between players can resolve the indeterminate nature of many rent-seeking games. These differences might be limited to a generally accepted ordering amongst players so that in considering n person games all potential players will know which are the leading n players who should therefore participate. Within the Tullock model analysed here this still leaves as indeterminate those games with multiple equilibria. The number of equilibria is reduced when the differences between players, and the resulting ordering, are associated with differences in the effectiveness of rent-seeking activity. However, whilst we have shown that fairly modest differences can be guaranteed to lead to either a unique or dual equilibria, there is in general no way of ensuring a unique equilibria. Thus dual equilibria can exist even with substantial cost differences, and with smaller differences there may be more extensive multiple equilibria. Along with situations in which a single player might choose a 'pre-emptive' level of expenditure (which generally implies non Cournot-Nash equilibria, and which case has not been considered here), a satisfactory equilibrium solution to one of these multiple equilibria games would seem to require it to be reformulated as a multistage game.

With players given the option not to participate, equilibria cannot involve over full dissipation of rents and, with differences in rent-seeking abilities, will generally lead to only partial dissipation, and hence to positive expected profits from rent-seeking activity. Because of bounded rationality these profits are unlikely to have been (fully) competed away in some previous competition. Bounded rationality also justifies the assumption of differences between players at the initiation of rent-seeking activity, and indeed makes it a far more acceptable assumption than that players are identical.

Finally, it is worth noting that this analysis into rent-seeking behaviour (like all such analyses) is essentially the same as that into 'profit-seeking' behaviour – as far as the players are concerned there is no distinction. In particular, it applies to competition for market power by means of innovation. The only distinction arises through the social values of the resulting expenditures, from which we decide the extent to which the expenditures (and hence the factors that determine their level) should be encouraged or discouraged.

Notes

1. A note setting out the mathematical derivations of equations 2.4 to 2.7 is available from the author.
2. The model proposed by Higgins, Shughart and Tollison (1985) will generally lead to the same range of possible curves (A1, A2 and B), so that in qualitative terms their analysis is relevant to the model used here.
3. The negative profits in Tullock (1980: Table 6.1) correspond to cases where players find themselves without the option of setting $x = 0$, although as Tullock himself points out (1984) some of the entries also correspond to joint minima rather than joint maxima and should therefore be omitted. The negative profits which underlie some of the 'underestimates of rent-seeking' in Table 1 of Appelbaum and Katz (1986) arise partly from the fact that all groups in society are explicitly forced to contribute to the value of the rent, and partly from the (implicit) assumption that they must all subsequently participate in the competition.
4. This point is elucidated above in Section 3, and is also evident from Table 3 of Corcoran and Karels (1985).
5. Corcoran and Karels (1985) also raise the possibility of several players combining to pre-empt further entry – thus n-players collude and jointly decide the output of lottery tickets required to deter entry by the $(n+1)$th player (C-K operate in terms of expenditures rather than lottery tickets – see their Table 3). When there are increasing returns ($r > 1$), the most efficient way of achieving this pre-emption is that the incumbents should assign (presumably on the basis of a preliminary lottery) the whole output to a single one of their members, rather than assigning output equally amongst themselves.
6. As a potential entrant, player n faces the output from CN(n – 1) which was designated $\bar{Q}(n-1)$. From (2.9), the level of expenditure by each of the $(n-1)$ players is

   $$x = r(n-2)/(n-1)^2$$

   Now

$$[\bar{Q}(n-1)]^a = [(n-1).q]^a = (n-1)^a .x$$

and substituting this value for Q^a in (2.4) gives (3.5).

Equilibrium Conditions for Efficient Rent Seeking: The Nash-Cournot Solution

David L. Cleeton

Tullock presents a model of the rent-seeking behavior of risk-neutral individuals. This model has sparked the interest of a number of researchers[1] and the literature has expanded Tullock's model in a variety of directions. This article sets out the original problem in the formal framework of a Nash-Cournot game. While only part of Tullock's original article looks at rent seeking in the Nash-Cournot framework, this framework is a useful way to summarize the analysis of rent-seeking behavior. I will show that many of the problems addressed by other authors can be seen more clearly when one works through the detailed results of Tullock's model using the Nash-Cournot equilibrium concept.[2] I will also show the pedagogical value of using this unifying framework to study rent-seeking behavior, and I will present an important result concerning the possibility of overdissipation as stated in Tullock's original model.

THE MODEL

I formalize the problem as follows: let K be the present value of the monopoly rent that N identical, risk-neutral individuals are attempting to obtain, $N \geq 2$. I will assume that the probability for individual i of obtaining the rent K can be represented as a function of the individual's investment in securing K and the total investments of all individuals. This probability is given by $P_i = [\, I_i^R \,/\, \Sigma I_i^R \,]$ where I_i is the expenditure on rent seeking by individual i, R is a parameter inversely related to the slope of the marginal cost curve associated with investment in acquiring the monopoly, $R > 0$, and $\Sigma I_i^R = I_1^R + I_2^R + \ldots + I_N^R$. Risk-neutral rent seekers attempt to maximize the expected value of their rent-seeking behavior or:

(1) $$\text{Max (with respect to } I_i) \ V_i = P_i K - I_i.$$

Using a Nash-Cournot equilibrium concept, the individual assumes that the choices of investments for all other individuals are given when maximizing V_i. With this assumption, the first-order condition for each individual is given by:

(2) $$dV_i / dI_i = (dP_i / dI_i) K - 1 = 0$$
$$\text{where } dP_i / dI_i = [RI_i^{R-1} (\Sigma I_i^R) - RI_i^{R-1} I_i^R] / [\Sigma I_i^R]^2.$$

Equation (2) has the usual marginal interpretation where each individual's expected value is maximized when the expected marginal revenue, $E [MR_i] = (dP_i / dI_i) K$, is equated to the expected marginal cost, $E [MC_i] = 1$, all in terms of dollars of investment in rent seeking. Each dollar spent on rent seeking represents a constant marginal cost of \$1, and the expected marginal revenue from this investment depends on the value of the parameter R.

Since all the I_i's are identical let $I_i = I$. Substituting this into (2) and simplifying, noting that with $I_i = I$, $P_i = 1 / N$ for all i, we obtain:

$$dV_i / dI_i = [RI^{2R-1} (N - 1) / N^2 I^{2R}] K - 1 = 0 \text{ or}$$

(3) $$dV_i / dI_i = [R (N - 1) K / N^2 I] - 1 = 0.$$

Solving for the optimum, I^*, we obtain Tullock's result:

(4) $$I^* = [RK (N - 1) / N^2].$$

Each of the rent seekers invests I^* and obtains an equal probability of $(1 / N)$ of receiving the rent K. The rent-seeking ratio, C, gives the proportion of the rent K that is dissipated by the aggregate investments of all individuals and is given by:

(5) $$C = \Sigma I^*_i / K = NI^* / K = R(N - 1) / N.$$

As Tullock noted, the rent-seeking ratio has a limiting value of R as N approaches infinity. Furthermore, in this case the monopoly rent is fully dissipated when R has a value of $+1$.

I would like to show that the structure of the problem places further restriction on the value of R and, therefore, the value of the rent-seeking ratio C. Let us first examine the second-order condition that must hold for the maximization problem given in (1). The second-order condition is given by:

(6) $$d^2V_i / dI_i^2 = (d^2P_i / dI_i^2) K < 0.$$

The differentiation of (2) and the result that $I^* = I_i$ lead to the following:

(7) $$d^2V_i / dI_i^2 = [(R - 1) N^2 - 2RN] / [R (N - 1) K] < 0.$$

Rewriting (7) in terms of R, we find that the second-order condition holds if $R < [N / (N - 2)]$.[3] We can obtain another bound on R by noting that individuals would be unwilling to invest in rent-seeking behavior unless the expected value were nonnegative. In terms of my notation, I require $V (I^*) \geq 0$, and this represents a rational participation rule for the individuals. The substitution of (4) into (1) results in $V (I^*) = (K / N) - [RK (N - 1) / N^2]$ or $V (I^*) = [KN - RK(N - 1)] / N^2 \geq 0$. Simplifying this inequality, we obtain the condition:[4]

$$R \leq N / (N - 1). \tag{8}$$

If (8) holds, I can show that the second-order condition must also be satisfied. I assumed $R > 0$, which implies that $(N + 2R) > (N + R)$. (8) requires that $RN \leq (N + R)$. Thus, if $RN \leq (N + R)$, and $(N + 2R) > (N + R)$, then $(N + 2R) > RN$, which is sufficient for the second-order condition to hold. Thus, if $R \leq [N / (N - 1)]$ and $R > 0$, we will satisfy both the nonnegativity condition in (8) and insure that the second-order condition in (7) holds. A rational participation rule as required in (8) insures the second-order condition given in (7) and guarantees an equilibrium in the Nash-Cournot framework. Thus, the following condition is sufficient for a Nash-Cournot equilibrium:

$$0 < R \leq N / (N - 1). \tag{9}$$

Combining the results from (5) and (9), we see that bounds on the rent-seeking ratio are:

$$0 < R \leq N / (N - 1) \text{ and } C = [R (N - 1) / N] \text{ imply}$$

$$0 < C = [R (N - 1)] / N \leq 1. \tag{10}$$

Equation (10) clarifies the question of the overdissipation of the rent, $C > +1$. Overdissipation of the rent implies a violation of the rational participation rule, that is, $C > +1$ implies that $[R (N - 1) / N] > +1$ or $R > [N / (N - 1)]$, but this leads to a negative expected value of participation in rent seeking.

Table 1 summarizes the restrictions that are placed on R and C as functions of the number of rent seekers (N), that is, given N, only the stated range of values for R and the resulting range of values for C will be consistent with a Nash-Cournot equilibrium.

Table 1

RANGES OF VALUES FOR *R* AND *C* GIVEN *N*

	$0<R\leq N/(N-1)$	$0<C\leq 1$
$N = 2$	$0<R\leq 2$	$0<C\leq 1$
$N = 3$	$0<R\leq 3/2$	$0<C\leq 1$
$N = 4$	$0<R\leq 4/3$	$0<C\leq 1$
$N\to\infty$	$0<R\leq 1$	$0<C\leq 1$

If we view the number of rent seekers (N) as exogenous, the rent-seeking ratio (C) becomes a simple function of the parameter R, where $C = [R (N - 1) / N]$ and where the domain of the function is limited to $0 < R \leq [N / (N - 1)]$ and the range is $0 < C \leq 1$.

A family of rays, one ray for each value of N, relating the rent-seeking ratio and the parameter R result. These are illustrated in the Chart.

Chart.

THE RENT-SEEKING RATIO (*C*) AS A FUNCTION OF THE COST PARAMETER (*R*)

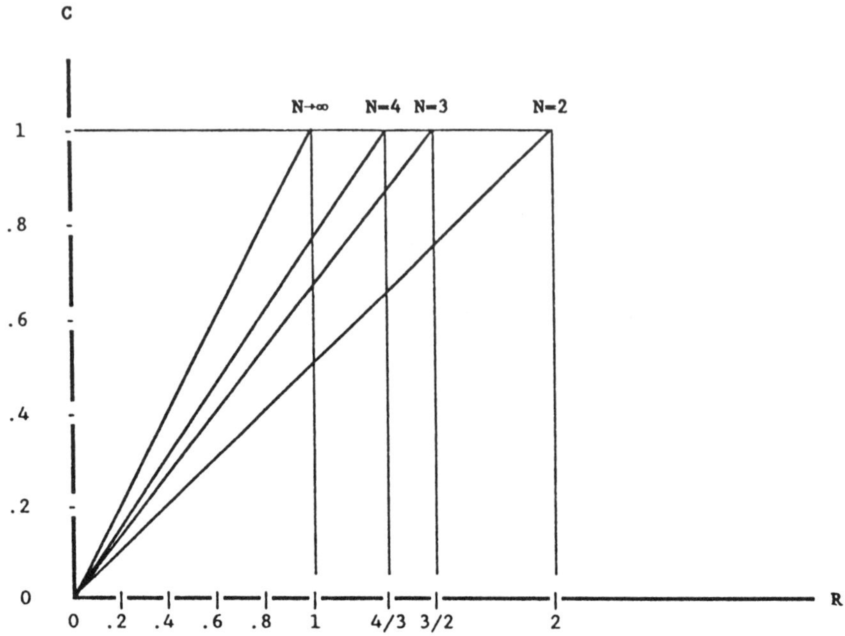

These families of rays are instructive in demonstrating the results of Tullock's model. Holding the number of rent seekers constant, we find that as the parameter R increases, in Tullock's interpretation, this corresponds to a less steeply sloped marginal cost function for rent seeking, the rent-seeking ratio increases, that is, more of the monopoly rent is dissipated by rent seeking. For a given R, the rent-seeking ratio increases at a decreasing rate with the number of rent seekers.[5]

Thus, if the number of rent seekers is fixed exogenously, it is possible, given the fixed technology of rent-seeking behavior as summarized by the parameter R, to obtain an equilibrium in the Nash-Cournot framework where all of the rent is not fully dissipated. One should keep in mind that the solution concept employed here rules out any strategic behavior on the part of the rent seekers.

We can easily extend the model to allow N to be endogenous and determined by entry and exit motives. That is, we should allow the existence of positive equilibrium profits, which occurs when the rent-seeking ratio is less than +1, to motivate new entrants into the rent-seeking game.

Let us consider the dynamics of rent seeking when there are initially only two rent seekers ($N = 2$). I have shown that with $N = 2$, a Nash-Cournot equilibrium exists only if $0 < R \leq 2$. Consider the case where $R = 2$. Here each party invests $I^* = [RK (N - 1) / N^2] = (1/2) K$ and expects to receive $V(I^*) = [(1/N)K - I^*] = (1/2)K - (1/2)K = 0$. The rent-seeking ratio is $C = [R(N-1)/N] = [NI^*/K] = 1$. We have an equilibrium where rent seeking has fully dissipated the monopoly rent, the expected return has been driven to 0 for both rent seekers, and, therefore, no other rent seekers are motivated to enter. If R were less than 2, we would have $I^* = [RK/4] < [(1/2)K]$, $V(I^*) = [(1/2)K - I^*] > 0$ and $C = R/2 < 1$. Here the monopoly rent would not be fully dissipated and each rent seeker would expect a positive return. Would this motivate entry on the part of another party?

If R is fixed and a third party entered, the expected return to each rent seeker would become $V(I^*) = [KN - RK(N-1)]/N^2$. With $N = 3$ for $V(I^*) > 0$, we must have $[3K - 2RK] > 0$, which requires $R < 3/2$. Thus, no entry would occur if R was in the range $3/2 \leq R = 2$. If we refer back to the Chart, we can see that along the $N = 2$ ray a value of R less than 3/2 is inconsistent with a Nash-Cournot equilibrium, if entry is allowed. We can drop a vertical line from the upper endpoint of the $N = 3$ ray down to the $N = 2$ ray and remove the lower portion of the $N = 2$ line. Using similar logic, we can rule out all values of $R < 4/3$ as being inconsistent with a three-person equilibrium, that is, if $N = 3$ and $R < 4/3$ then a fourth person would be motivated to enter the rent-seeking competition. The driving force behind the result that free entry and exit does not necessarily lead to complete dissipation of the entire amount of the rent is the noncontinuous nature of the variable N.[6] A similar situation would arise in a Nash-Cournot model of production where firms attempt to maximize their profit by the choice of output, given the output of other firms and a fixed market demand. Given the production technology and the fixed total demand for the product, the Nash-Cournot equilibrium for N firms may result in positive profits for each firm, but the entry of another firm would produce negative profits for each of the $N + 1$ firms. Thus, it is the noncontinuous nature of the variable N, and not the lack of competitive entry and exit motives, that can produce a Nash-Cournot equilibrium with positive profits for all participants.

One could, of course, argue that the individuals who do not participate in the rent-seeking behavior when positive equilibrium profits exist will have an incentive to pay a current participant for the right to replace him in the rent-seeking game. Such competition for entry would be expected to produce payments to current participants or represent an opportunity cost to the current participants if they choose not to take the payment, which would drive the expected profits of all individuals to 0. Thus, even in the case where N is not a continuous variable, a second level of competition for entry rights may bring into play rent-seeking behavior that will fully dissipate all rents.

Just as the entry motive rules out certain combinations of N and R as equilibria, so would exit motives. In fact, I have already incorporated these into the model. For example, if we started with $N = 3$ and $R = 3/2$, we would have an equilibrium with no motives for entry or exit. If, however, R were to increase above 3/2, the expected return for the three rent seekers would become negative and induce exit. It was this logic that gave the upper limits on the allowable range of R for any given N.

Summing up the effect of making N endogenous through entry and exit motives for rent seeking, Table 2 gives the values of R, N, and C that are consistent with Nash-Cournot equilibria when N is endogenous.

Table 2

EQUILIBRIUM VALUES FOR *N* AND *C* GIVEN *R*

Domain of R	Endogenous Equilibrium Value for N	Range of Rent-Seeking Ratio $C = R(N-1)/N$
3/2 to 2	2	3/4 to 1 [$C = R/2$]
4/3 to 3/2	3	8/9 to 1 [$C = 2R/3$]
5/4 to 4/3	4	15/16 to 1 [$C = 3R/4$]
$(N+1)/N$ to $N/(N-1)$	N	$(N^2-1)/N^2$ to 1 [$C = R(N-1)/N$]
0 to 1	$N \to \infty$	0 to 1 [$C = R$]

Thus, the endogeneity of N, through entry and exit motives, gives the following equilibrium values for N (the number of rent seekers) and C (the rent seeking ratio):

(11) If $0 < R \leq 1$, then N will approach infinity, and $C = R$;

(12) If $1 < R \leq 2$, then $[1/(R-1)] < N \leq [R/(R-1)]$, and $C = [R(N-1)/N]$.

For example, if $R = 1.8$ then $N > (10/8)$ and $N \leq (18/8)$ so $N = 2$ and $C = 0.9$ or if $R = 1.11$ then $N > 9.09 = (1/.11)$ and $N \leq 10.09 = (1.11/.11)$ so $N = 10$ and $C = 0.999$.

SUMMARY

My model has confirmed many of Tullock's insights into the behavior of rent seekers. In particular, I have shown that when the number of rent seekers is exogenous, their maximizing behavior places upper and lower bounds on the acceptable equilibrium values of the rent-seeking ratio and upper and lower bounds on the parameter R that will be consistent with a Nash-Cournot equilibrium. Tullock's statement that $0 < R \leq 1$ and $C = R$ is shown to hold when N approaches infinity. When N is not infinite, the acceptable bounds on R and C are derived.

If we allow N, the number of rent seekers, to be endogenous and determined by entry and exit motives, we find that the exogenous value of the parameter R determines N, the number of rent seekers, and C, the rent-seeking ratio, in a one-to-one fashion and makes the equilibrium value of C unique for a given R. C is a function only of R and no longer a function of both R and N. Thus, the steepness of the marginal cost curve facing rent seekers will determine in a unique fashion both the equilibrium number of rent seekers and the equilibrium rent-seeking ratio.

Finally, as I noted, the noncontinuous nature of the variable N, the number of rent seekers, may serve to obscure a secondary level of rent-seeking competition. If the technology of primary rent seeking, that is, the observed direct investment costs by individuals to obtain a monopoly rent, leads to a Nash-Cournot equilibrium characterized by positive expected profits on the part of the active bidders, an incentive will exist for the nonbidders to compete among themselves to induce at least one of the active bidders to trade places with them. This secondary level of rent-seeking competition may not be observed in the market[7] but would represent an opportunity cost or entry cost that would drive the expected profit to 0 and dissipate fully the available rent.

Appendix

Derivation of the first-order condition:

(1) Max (with respect to I_i) $V_i = P_i K - I_i$ where $P_i = [\, I_i^R / \Sigma I_i^R \,]$

$$dV_i / dI_i = [\,(RI_i^{R-1}(\Sigma I_i^R) - RI_i^{R-1} I_i^R) / (\Sigma I_i^R)^2\,] \cdot K - 1 = 0.$$

Given $I_i = I$:

$$\begin{aligned} dV_i / dI_i &= [\,(RI^{R-1} NI^R - RI^{R-1} I^R) / (NI^R)^2\,] \cdot K - 1 = 0 \\ &= [\, RI^{2R-1} (N - 1) / N^2 I^{2R} \,] \cdot K - 1 = 0 \\ &= [R (N - 1) K / N^2 I\,] - 1 = 0. \end{aligned}$$

Solving for the optimum, I^*, we obtain: $I^* = R (N - 1) K/N^2$.
This is Equation (4) in the text.

Derivation of the second-order condition:

$$d^2V_i / dI_i^2 = \{\,[\, R (R - 1)\, I_i^{R-2} (\Sigma I_i^R) + R^2 I_i^{R-1} I_i^{R-1} - R (2R - 1)\, I_i^{2R-2} \,] \cdot (\Sigma I_i^R)^2 - 2RI_i^{R-1} \cdot (\Sigma I_i^R) \cdot [\, RI_i^{R-1} (\Sigma I^R) - RI_i^{2R-1} \,]\,\} / \{\,[\,(\Sigma I_i^R)^4\,] / K\,\}.$$

Given $I_i = I$, we can simplify to obtain:

$$\begin{aligned} d^2V_i / dI_i^2 &= \{\,[\, R (R - 1) N - R (R - 1) \,] N^2 I^{4R-2} - 2RNI^{4R-2} [\, RN - R \,]\,\} / [\, N^4 I^{4R} / K \,] \\ &= [\,(R - 1) N^2 - 2RN \,] / [\, R (N - 1) K \,] = [\, RN^2 - N^2 - 2RN \,] / [\, R (N - 1) K \,] \\ &= [\, N (RN - N - 2R) \,] / [\, R (N - 1) K \,] = [\, R (N^2 - 2N) / R (N - 1) K \,] - [\, N^2 / R (N - 1) K \,] \\ &= [\, N (N - 2) / (N - 1) K \,] - [\, N^2 / R (N - 1) K \,] < 0, \end{aligned}$$

which we can rewrite as:

$N(N-2)/(N-1)K < N^2/R(N-1)K \leftrightarrow R < N^2(N-1)K/N(N-2)(N-1)K \leftrightarrow R < N/(N-2)$.

Thus, the second-order condition is $d^2V_i/dI_i^2 < 0 \leftrightarrow R < N/(N-2)$. This is Equation (7) in the test.

The rational participation rule is given by:

$$V_i(I^*) = P_i \cdot K - I^* = [I^{*R}/\Sigma I^{*R}] \cdot K - I^* = [I^{*R}/NI^{*R}] \cdot K - I^* \geq 0$$
$$= [1/N] \cdot K - I^* = [K/N] - [R(N-1)K/N^2] \geq 0.$$

or

$$V_i(I^*) = [K/N] - [R(N-1)K/N^2] \geq 0 \leftrightarrow K/N \geq [R(N-1)K/N^2]$$

When we solve for R, we obtain:

$$R \leq KN^2/[N(N-1)K] = N/(N-1).$$

Thus, $V_i(I^*) \geq 0 \leftrightarrow R \leq N/(N-1)$. This is Equation (8) in the text.

NOTES

*I would like to thank Joseph Jadlow, David Schap, Gordon Tullock, and a referee from *The Quarterly Review of Economics and Business* for helpful comments on this topic.

1. See Corcoran [1], Corcoran and Karels [2], Higgins, Shughart, and Tollison [4], Hillman and Katz [5], Jadow [6], Rogerson [7], and Tullock [9, 10] for various specifications of the model. For an alternative model, which argues that rents may be dissipated in the form of nonprice competition, see Gifford [3].

2. Other game theoretic solutions to the rent-seeking problem can be found in those articles cited in note 1. While some of these formulations extend outside of the Nash-Cournot equilibrium framework, they all begin their modeling by using the Nash-Cournot solution as the point of departure.

3. Tullock [9], p. 97, reports that the second-order conditions are *not* met when $R < N/(N-2)$. His statement is incorrect, and the inequality should be reversed.

4. Corcoran [1] and Corcoran and Karels [2] attempt to rationalize a similar result based on a zero expected profit condition that is driven by entry and exit. The result obtained here is independent of the number of rent seekers and depends only on a rational participation rule for risk-neutral individuals.

5. These results can be derived directly from partial differentiation of the equation $C = R(N-1)/N$. Holding N fixed, C increases with R at a fixed rate equal to $(N-1)/N$. Holding R fixed, C increases with N at a decreasing rate. The cross partial is positive.

6. The solutions proposed by Corcoran and Karels [2] to obtain a rent-seeking ratio equal to $+1$, such as bet splitting and so-called preemptory betting, depend on strategic behavior on the part of individuals and, thus, do not fit into the Nash-Cournot equilibrium framework.

7. Whether these secondary rent-seeking costs are observed depends on whether the incumbents in the primary rent-seeking competition actually sell their "participation rights" or simply treat the value of those rights as an opportunity cost of remaining in the primary rent-seeking competition.

Conflict and rent-seeking success functions: Ratio vs. difference models of relative success*

JACK HIRSHLEIFER

Department of Economics, University of California, Los Angeles, CA 90024-1477

Abstract. The rent-seeking competitions studied by economists fall within a much broader category of conflict interactions that also includes military combats, election campaigns, industrial disputes, lawsuits, and sibling rivalries. In the rent-seeking literature, each party's success p_i (which can be interpreted either as the probability of victory or as the proportion of the prize won) has usually been taken to be a function of the *ratio* of the respective resource commitments. Alternatively, however, p_i may instead be a function of the *difference* between the parties' commitments to the contest. The Contest Success Function (CSF) for the difference form is a logistic curve in which, as is consistent with military experience, increasing returns apply up to an inflection point at equal resource commitments. A crucial flaw of the traditional ratio model is that neither one-sided submission nor two-sided peace between the parties can ever occur as a Cournot equilibrium. In contrast, both of these outcomes are entirely consistent with a model in which success is a function of the difference between the parties' resource commitments.

1. Introduction

Following the seminal contributions of Gordon Tullock (1967, 1980), a number of papers[1] have explored various aspects of rent-seeking competitions. In such contests, each of N players invests effort C_i ($i = 1, \ldots, N$) in the hope of gaining a prize of value V. Existing analyses have mainly explored the nature of equilibrium with varying numbers of contestants, the central issue addressed being whether or not under- or over-dissipation of rents will occur.

The fundamental notion of competitions in which relative success is a function of the parties' respective resource commitments applies far beyond the rent-seeking context. Military combats, election campaigns, industrial struggles (strikes and lockouts), legal conflicts (lawsuits), and even rivalries among siblings or between spouses within the family all fall under this heading. Owing perhaps to failure to perceive these wider implications, the papers in the rent-seeking literature generally do not adopt a *general-equilibrium* approach which would make explicit provision for the alternative productive or consumptive

* In preparing successive drafts of this paper I have benefited from suggestions and comments from Michele Boldrin, Avinash Dixit, Arye L. Hillman, David Hirshleifer, Eric S. Maskin, David Levine, Eric Rasmusen, John G. Riley, Russell Roberts, and Leo K. Simon.

uses of resources employed in rent-seeking competitions. Also, what is very important, a general-equilibrium model would typically make the value of the prize an endogenous variable rather than an exogenously given parameter. I have attempted to provide such a general-equilibrium analysis in Hirshleifer (1988).

This note has a more limited aim, however. My main purpose is to point out that Tullock's basic equation for success in rent-seeking competition represents only one of two canonical families of possibilities, the second and at least equally interesting family having been totally ignored in the existing literature. Specifically, in Tullock's formula each party's success is a function of the *ratios* of the respective efforts or inputs C_i. As will be shown, a number of significantly different results are obtained when, alternatively, relative success is determined by the *differences* among the inputs. I will also be allowing for possibly different prize valuations $V_i \neq V_j$.[2]

2. Contest success functions

For $N=2$ players, in Tullock's basic model the proportionate outcomes p_i depend in a simple way upon the contest inputs or efforts C_i:

$$p_1/p_2 = (C_1/C_2)^m \tag{1}$$

Here each p_i may be interpreted either as the party's respective *probability of success* in a discrete either-or competition or else as the *proportionate share* of the prize won in a continuous-outcome contest. Since $p_1 + p_2 = 1$, equation (1) is equivalent to:

$$p_i = \frac{C_1^m}{C_1^m + C_2^m} \tag{2}$$

For given C_2, this may be called the Contest Success Function (CSF) for player #1; the CSF for the other player is defined correspondingly. (I have implicitly been assuming that the two sides' resources have equal effectiveness in the contest. More generally, it would be possible to adjust each side's C_i by an effectiveness coefficient; this straightforward generalization will be omitted here.)

The effect of the "mass effect parameter" m upon the shape of player #1's Contest Success Function is displayed in Figure 1, in which player #2's resource input has been arbitrarily fixed at $C_2 = 100$. Regardless of the level of m, we see that $p_1 = p_2 = .5$ when $C_1 = C_2$. If $m \leq 1$, diminishing returns to competitive effort hold throughout. But for $m > 1$, an initial range of increasing returns exists instead. More specifically, taking the second derivative in the usual way, the inflection point along the CSF of player #1 is determined by the condition:

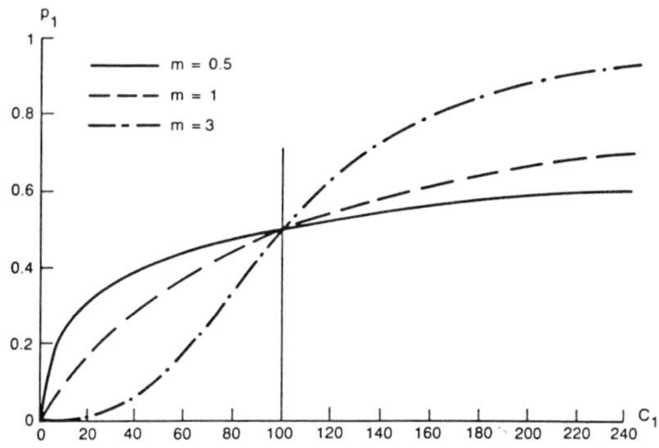

Figure 1. Contest success function: Ratio form

$$\frac{C_1}{C_2} = \left(\frac{m-1}{m+1}\right)^{1/m} \tag{3a}$$

or, equivalently,

$$p_1 = (m-1)/2m \tag{3b}$$

Since m cannot meaningfully be zero or negative we see that, for given C_2, there is a point of inflection in the positive range of C_1 only if $m > 1$.[3]

While it is often plausible to assume that contest power is a function of the *ratio* of the forces or efforts committed, this is by no means the only possibly valid functional relation. Nor are all the implications of the ratio form always reasonable. One implication, for example, is that a side investing zero effort must lose everything so long as the opponent commits any finite amount of resources at all, however small, to the struggle. When, alternatively, the outcome is assumed to be a function of the *difference* between the two sides' efforts, a player can have some chance or share of success even without committing resources to the contest. In struggles between nations, for example, one side may surrender rather than resist. While the hope may sometimes be to appease the aggressor, it might make sense to surrender to a totally unappeasable opponent if the submitting nation does not expect to lose absolutely everything by giving up the struggle. And this is reasonable, since in general it will be costly for the victor, even in the absence of resistance, to locate and extract all the possible spoils.

There is one other factor to consider, namely, the location of the inflection point of the CSF. When it comes to military interactions, ''God is on the side of the larger battalions.'' There is an enormous gain when your side's forces increase from just a little smaller than the enemy's to just a little larger.[4] This implies that the range of increasing returns to player #1's commitment C_1 extends up to $C_1 = C_2$, or equivalently up to $p_1 = p_2$.[5] But, we have seen, when the ratio form of the CSF is used, increasing returns, if present at all (that is, if $m > 1$), can only hold up to some $C_1 < C_2$.

Postulating that contest success depends upon the *difference* between the resource commitments, the required conditions – that $C_1 = 0$ need not imply $p_1 = 0$, and that the inflection point occurs at $C_1 = C_2$ – are met by the *logistic* family of curves:

$$p_1 = \frac{1}{1+\exp\{k(C_2-C_1)\}} \tag{4}$$

where p_2 is defined correspondingly. (As is logically required $p_1 + p_2 = 1$.) In particular, when $C_1 = 0$ player #1 still retains a share of success $p_1 = 1/(1 + \exp\{kC_2\})$. Figure 2 shows several CSF curves for varying k, where k is the "mass effect parameter" applicable to the logistic function.

In a military context we might expect the *ratio form* of the Contest Success Function to be applicable when clashes take place under close to "idealized" conditions such as: an undifferentiated battlefield, full information, and unflagging weapons effectiveness. In contrast, the *difference form* tends to apply where there are sanctuaries and refuges, where information is imperfect, and where the victorious player is subject to fatigue and distraction. Given such "imperfections of the combat market," the defeated side need not lose absolutely everything. (For the sake of concreteness I have been using military metaphors and examples, but analogous statements can evidently be made about non-military struggles – e.g., lawsuits or political campaigns or rent-seeking competitions.)

The generalization of equation (2) for any number of players N was provided in Tullock's initial paper. For the ith contestant, the probability of success becomes:

$$p_i = \frac{C_i^m}{C_1^m + C_2^m + \ldots + C_N^m} = \frac{C_i^m}{\Sigma_j C_j^m} \tag{5}$$

Of course, the p_i's sum to unity.

Employing the difference (logistic) form instead, the corresponding generalization of equation (4) is:

$$p_i = \frac{\exp\{kC_i\}}{\Sigma_j \exp\{kC_j\}} \tag{6}$$

It is evident from the form of the last fraction on the right that, as required, the sum of these p_i's will also be unity.[6]

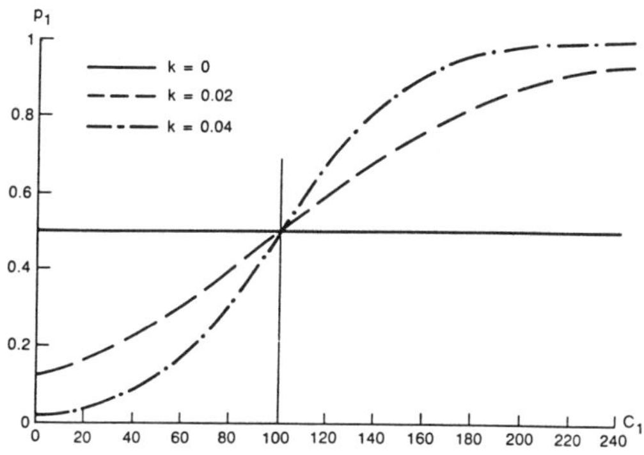

Figure 2. Contest success function: Difference (logistic) form

To illustrate, if N = 3 and i = 1, equation (6) becomes:

$$p_1 = \frac{1}{1 + \exp\{k(C_2 - C_1)\} + \exp\{k(C_3 - C_1)\}} \qquad (6a)$$

Both (5) and (6) fall within the more general category of *logit* functions.[7]

3. Symmetrical Nash-Cournot equilibrium

As has been mentioned, when the ratio form of the CSF applies each side will surely always commit some resources to the contest. If peace is defined by the condition $C_1 = C_2 = 0$, then peace can never occur as a Cournot equilibrium under the traditional ratio model!

The demonstration is simple. Side #1 will be seeking to maximize its "profit":

$$Y_1 = Vp_1 - C_1 \qquad (7)$$

where V is the given value of the prize and p_1 is determined as in equation (2). A similar equation holds of course for player #2. Suppose momentarily it were the case that $C_1 = C_2 = 0$, the parties sharing the prize equally without fighting. Then, assuming only that $V > 0$, under the Cournot assumption either player would be motivated to defect, since even the smallest finite commitment of resources makes the defector's relative success jump from 50% to 100%. In effect, the marginal profitability of i's contest contribution is infinite when $C_i = 0$.

In contrast, when the logistic Contest Success Function applies, two-sided peace may easily hold as a stable Cournot solution. Since the player who defects from $C_1 = C_2 = 0$ does not get the benefit of a discrete jump from 50% to 100% success, there is a finite marginal gain to be balanced against the marginal cost of contest effort.[8]

Numerical Example 1

Player #1 seeks to maximize his profit as in equation (7), with p_1 defined by the logistic CSF equation (4) above. If $C_2 = 0$, then finding the derivative in the usual way leads to:

$$\frac{k \exp\{-kC_1\}}{(1+\exp\{-kC_1\})^2} = \frac{1}{V}$$

For $C_1 = 0$ to be a solution, we must have $V = 4/k$. By symmetry, an analogous equation will hold for player #2. So if, for example, $k = .04$ and $V = 100$, then (as claimed) $C_1 = C_2 = 0$ will indeed be a Cournot equilibrium. In this equilibrium $p_1 = p_2 = .5$ so that the parties each have profit of 50.

4. Asymmetrical equilibrium

What about the possibility of *one-sided submission* rather than two-sided peace? This means that player #1 (say) chooses $C_1 > 0$ while player #2 sets $C_2 = 0$. For such an outcome, some kind of asymmetry must be introduced – in the parties' valuations of the prize, in the effectiveness of their respective contest efforts, or possibly in the costs of such efforts. But regardless of any such asymmetries, under the ratio model one-sided submission as a Cournot equilibrium can no more occur than could two-sided peace!

We need look only at asymmetries due to inequalities in valuations of the prize. Specifically, suppose $V_1 > V_2$, suggesting that there might be a Cournot equilibrium with $C_1 > 0$ while $C_2 = 0$. Using the profit equation (7) for player #1, and equation (2) for the Contest Success Function in ratio form, the first-order condition is:

$$\frac{\partial Y_1}{\partial C_1} = \frac{V_1^m C_1^{m-1}(C_2^m)}{(C_1^m + C_2^m)^2} - 1 = 0 \tag{8}$$

Evidently, whenever $C_2 = 0$ the marginal profit of contest effort to player #1 is always negative. So under the ratio form of the CSF, it will never be possible to have an asymmetrical contest outcome with one party having zero and the other having positive commitment of resources.

For the difference form (logistic CSF), however, the asymmetrical outcomes are quite different. First of all, taking the partial derivatives of the respective Contest Success Functions leads to:

$$\frac{\partial p_1}{\partial C_1} = \frac{\text{kexp}\,\{k(C_1 + C_2)\}}{(\exp\{kC_1\} + \exp\{kC_2\})^2} = \frac{\partial p_2}{\partial C_2} \tag{9}$$

This possibly surprising proposition states that at any pair of C_1, C_2 choices, the partial derivatives (the "marginal products" of the respective contest efforts) are always the same for both sides. It follows immediately that, if the valuations V_1 and V_2 are unequal, it is impossible to simultaneously satisfy (as the respective first-order conditions for a profit maximum would require):

$$\frac{\partial p_1}{\partial C_1} = 1/V_1 \quad \text{and} \quad \frac{\partial p_2}{\partial C_2} = 1/V_2 \tag{10}$$

Thus, when the difference form of the CSF applies, there cannot be an *interior* asymmetrical Nash-Cournot solution. (Whereas, we have just seen, using the ratio form there cannot be a *corner* asymmetrical solution.)

This impossibility theorem for the difference form is somewhat too strong, since it is an artifact of the assumption implicit in equation (7) that the Marginal Cost of contest effort is constant. If the Marginal Cost of contest effort is rising, equations (10) might be satisfied so as to permit an interior Nash-Cournot equilibrium. More generally, with rising Marginal Cost there could be either a corner or an interior asymmetrical solution, depending upon the numerical parameters and the exact functional form.[9]

Assuming for simplicity that Marginal Cost is constant as in equation (7), the Reaction Curves RC_1 and RC_2 associated with the logistic CSF are parallel straight lines of 45° slope, up to a point of discontinuity. More specifically, in the continuous range the Reaction Curve equations are:[10]

$$\begin{aligned} C_1 &= C_2 + A_1, \text{ where } A_1 = (2/k)\cosh^{-1}\{.5\text{sqrt}(kV_1)\} \\ C_2 &= C_1 + A_2, \text{ where } A_2 = (2/k)\cosh^{-1}\{.5\text{sqrt}(kV_2)\} \end{aligned} \tag{11}$$

The discontinuities fall into three distinct patterns – depending upon the relative positions of the points C_i^0, C_i', and C_i'' as sketched in Figures 3 through 5 – each leading to a particular class of Cournot solution.

The pattern of Reaction Curves RC_1 and RC_2 pictured in Figure 3 represents the "strong asymmetry" case, which stems from a relatively large difference $V_1 - V_2$ between the parties' valuations of the prize. Here RC_2, the Reaction Curve for the lower-valuing player, rises as C_1 increases – but only

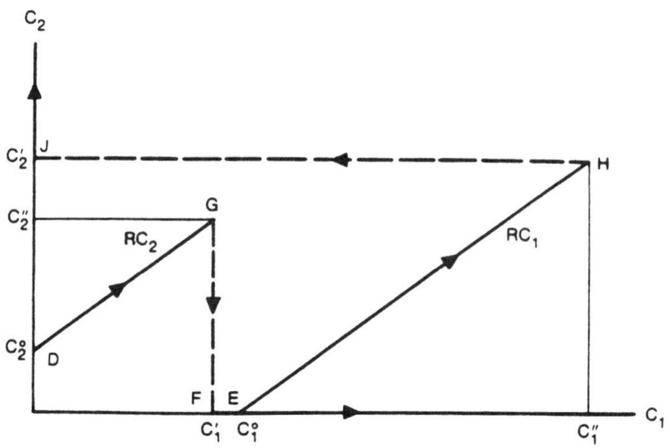

Figure 3. Logistic reaction curves: Strong asymmetry

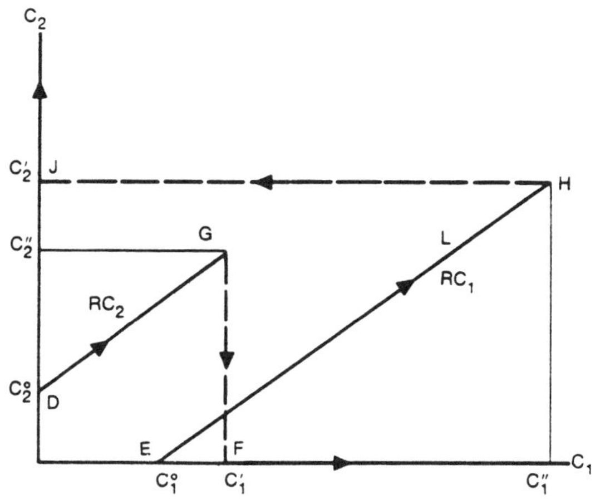

Figure 4. Logistic reaction curves: Moderate asymmetry

up to point G where the opponent's effort has reached a certain critical value C_1'. At G, player #2's optimum drops off discretely to $C_2 = 0$ (point F), and of course remains at zero for all higher values of C_1. (The explanation is that, given a logistic CSF, the lower-valuing player can always take home *some* profit by investing zero effort. Hence doing so always remains a viable alternative, and eventually becomes more advantageous than trying to keep up with very large contest efforts on the part of his higher-valuing opponent.) If, as in Figure 3, $C_1' < C_1^0$ – that is, point F is to the left of point E, the latter being the point where the higher valuing player's Reaction Curve RC_1 intercepts the horizontal axis – then the Nash-Cournot equilibrium is at E, where (C_1, C_2)

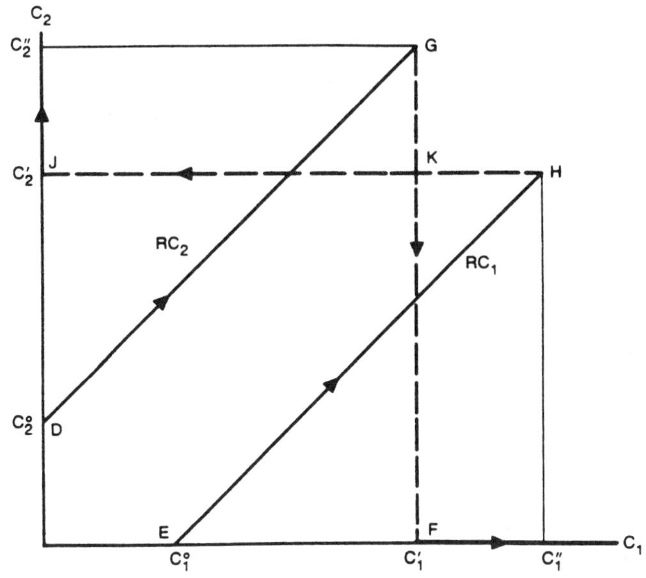

Figure 5. Logistic reaction curves: Symmetry or near-symmetry

$= (C_1^0, 0)$. It is easy to verify that, at point E, each player's effort is a *best response* to the opponent's choice. This solution represents one-sided submission: the lower-valuing player has abandoned the struggle.

Numerical Example 2

Once again each player seeks to maximize his profit $Y_i = Vp_i - C_i$, where p_i is defined by equation (4) above. Let the required asymmetry be in the valuations of the prize, where specifically $V_1 = 400$ and $V_2 = 100$. Assuming $k = .04$, the Reaction Curves are as pictured in Figure 3, with $C_1^0 = A_1 = 65.848$ and $C_2^0 = A_2 = 0$. If the higher-valuing player #1 takes $C_2 = 0$ as given, his profit-maximizing solution C_1 equals $A_1 = 65.848$ (point E). Turning to player #2, with $C_1 = 65.848$ taken as given the profit-maximizing[11] C_2 is indeed $C_2 = 0$.

The expectations on each side as to the other party's behavior being mutually consistent, this is a Cournot equilibrium. The associated shares are $p_1 = .933$, and $p_2 = .067$, and the profits are $Y_1 = 307.4$ and $Y_2 = 6.699$. Note that the higher-valuing player does *disproportionately* better: not only is his prize worth more, but he fights harder for it.

Figure 4 illustrates a "moderate asymmetry" pattern. Here, the difference between V_1 and V_2 being smaller, point E (the horizontal intercept of RC_1) lies to the left of point F (at the discontinuity along RC_2). In consequence, point

E, where player #2 unilaterally submits, is no longer a Cournot equilibrium. (That is, player #2 will no longer choose $C_2 = 0$ as his best response to player #1's choice of $C_1 = C_1^0 = A_1$.) As the prize valuations V_1 and V_2 approach equality, finally, the "symmetrical or near-symmetrical" pattern of Figure 5 is obtained. Here also, it will be evident, unilateral submission will not occur. The actual solutions for both the Figure 4 and the Figure 5 patterns involve mixed strategies on one or both sides,[12] but the specifics of these solutions are not of immediate concern to us.

As the next step, it would be natural to ask whether the ratio versus the difference forms of the Contest Succes Function lead to correspondingly different outcomes in terms of the Stackelberg or other asymmetrical solution concepts. I will not, however, be pursuing these implications here.

5. Conclusion

In analyzing rent-seeking or other conflict competitions, models allowing relative success to respond continuously to changes in contest commitments have heretofore assumed that success must be a function of the *ratio* of the parties' resource commitments. However, this assumption is inconsistent with the observation that two-sided peace or one-sided submission do sometimes occur in the world. When relative success is postulated to stem instead from the *numerical difference* between the respective contest inputs, a Contest Success Function taking the form of a logistic equation is derived. Two-sided peaceful outcomes emerge in Cournot equilibrium when the "mass effect parameter" of the logistic CSF curve is sufficiently low. One-sided submission can also occur when there is a large disparity between the parties' valuation of the prize. As these valuations approach equality, the logistic CSF leads to mixed-strategy Cournot equilibria.

Notes

1. See, e.g., Hillman and Katz (1984), Corcoran and Karels (1985), Higgins, Shughart and Tollison (1985), Appelbaum and Katz (1986), Allard (1988), Hillman and Samet (1987).
2. A recent paper of Hillman and Riley (1988) makes use of still another family of contest payoff functions, in which – in contrast with the sharing rules analyzed here – the entire prize, as in an auction, goes to the high bidder. Their paper also allows for differing prize valuations.
3. In the standard Lanchester equations of military combat (Lanchester, 1916 (1956); Brackney, 1959), the outcome is also assumed to depend upon the *ratio* of the forces committed. But for Lanchester the battle result is always fully deterministic, in the sense that the side with larger forces (adjusted for fighting effectiveness) is 100% certain to win. This makes the CSF a step function, which jumps from $p_1 = 0$ to $p_1 = 1$ when $C_1 = C_2$. So Lanchester's formula can be regarded as the limiting case of equation (2) as the mass effect parameter m goes to infinity.

The same holds also for the auction-style payoffs in Hillman and Riley (1988).

4. As seen in the previous footnote, the Lanchester equations of combat take this to the extreme. The larger force is 100% certain of victory; the smaller force has no chance at all.
5. Compare T.N. Dupuy's study of diminishing returns in combat interactions between Allied and German forces in World War II (Dupuy, 1987: Ch. 11). Dupuy's curves generally show the inflection point displaced slightly from the "equal forces, equal success" point, owing (on his interpretation) to the superior unit effectiveness of the German army.
6. I thank David Levine and Michele Boldrin who independently discovered this generalization of the logistic Contest Success Function.
7. The definition of the logit in this context is:

$$p_i = \frac{f(C_i)}{\Sigma_j f(C_j)}$$

Using only the general properties of logit functions, Dixit (1987) obtained some important qualitative results for "strategic" (non-Nash) behavior in asymmetrical contests.

8. For the analogous result in a general-equilibrium context, see Hirshleifer (1988, Part B).
9. Dixit (1987) appears to assume, incorrectly, that all logit functions do lead to an interior Nash-Cournot asymmetrical equilibrium.
10. Player #1 maximizes $Y_1 = p_1 V_1 - C_1$ where p_1 is given by:

$$p_1 = 1/(1 + \exp\{k(C_2 - C_1)\}) \equiv 1/D \text{ (writing D for the denominator)}$$

For given C_2, the first-order condition $dY_1/dC_1 = 0$ is:

$$V_1\,(dp_1/dC_1) \equiv kV_1 \exp\{k(C_2 - C_1)\}/D^2 = 1$$

Rearranging and taking square roots leads to:

$$\text{sqrt}(kV_1) = \exp\{(-k/2)(C_2 - C_1)\} + \exp\{(k/2)(C_2 - C_1)\}$$

Since $\cosh x \equiv .5\{\exp(x) + \exp(-x)\} \equiv \cosh(-x)$, we can write:

$$.5\,\text{sqrt}\,(kV_1) = \cosh\{-(k/2)(C_2 - C_1)\} \equiv \cosh\{(k/2)(C_2 - C_1)\}$$

Thus: $(k/2)(C_2 - C_1) = \cosh^{-1}\{.5\,\text{sqrt}\,(kV_1)\}$.

11. As suggested by the preceding discussion, this optimum is not at a smooth maximum (zero first derivative). Instead, player #2's profit function has a negative first derivative throughout, leading him to cut back effort until the limit of zero is reached.
12. The key feature guaranteeing existence of a Nash-Cournot equilibrium is that the payoff functions are continuous, even though the Reaction Curves have discontinuities. See Debreu (1952) and Glicksberg (1952). I thank Eric S. Maskin for this point.

Rationing and Rent Dissipation in the Presence of Heterogeneous Individuals

Wing Suen

University of Chicago

This paper discusses the implications of rationing by waiting when consumers have different time costs and personal valuations. The joint distribution function of time costs and personal valuations is used to characterize market equilibrium. It is argued that, under certain conditions, an increase in the variance of time costs will reduce the dissipation of rent. Furthermore, it is shown that introducing a secondary market for a rationed good does not necessarily improve welfare because total surplus under rationing by waiting depends more on the variance than on the level of time costs and personal valuations. The model is also used to discuss other institutions that involve rent-seeking activities, such as the patent system and import quotas.

When the price of a good is set below its market-clearing level, the divergence between the marginal value of the good and its price constitutes a nonexclusive income that people are willing to spend resources to capture. The ways in which resources are spent depend on the criteria of competition. For instance, under a price control, one common criterion of allocation is "first come, first served," and people will spend time waiting in order to obtain the good (Barzel 1974). In another example, innovators compete by spending interest income in premature innovations or by overspending in research to obtain patents (Barzel 1968; Dasgupta and Stiglitz 1980). It has also been argued that valuable rights are obtained from the government through

I have benefited from discussions with Yoram Barzel and Nick Pealy. Thanks are also due to Doug Allen, Keith Leffler, and a referee for their comments on earlier drafts of this paper. This paper is a revised version of chap. 5 of my dissertation (Suen 1988).

various forms of rent-seeking behavior (Tullock 1967; Krueger 1974; Posner 1975). What factors determine how valuable rights or commodities are allocated to heterogeneous individuals under nonprice competition?

In this paper, I shall analyze the problem of nonprice methods of rationing when consumers have different valuations for the rationed good and different costs of competing for it. Nonprice methods of allocation will result in the dissipation of rent since (1) goods do not necessarily go to the highest-valuing users and (2) competition for the rationed good involves the expenditure of real resources rather than the transfer of wealth. Earlier discussions of the problem (e.g., Barzel 1968; Posner 1975) usually assume implicitly that competitors are identical. Consequently, it is argued that competition will transform all rents into social costs, while at the same time the efficiency loss due to misallocation is largely ignored. When individuals are heterogeneous, rents will be fully dissipated only at the margin. Inframarginal consumers (i.e., those whose valuations for the good are higher than their full costs) will still be able to accrue differential rents. The fact that rents will not be fully dissipated in a model of heterogeneous competitors has been recognized by Barzel (1974), Rogerson (1982), Fisher (1985), and others. Here I shall show that, under certain conditions, the *greater* the differences in people's costs of competing for a rationed good, the *smaller* will be the extent of rent dissipation. In the light of this comparative statics result, I shall also discuss the relative merits of some institutions that involve rent-seeking activities.

The analysis in this paper is related to the literature on efficient rent seeking (e.g., Tullock 1980; Gardner 1987). I argue that the magnitude of the welfare loss due to rent-seeking behavior depends more on the variance than on the mean level of people's costs of seeking rent.[1] To facilitate exposition, the formal model used is a model of rationing by waiting, but applications to other contexts will also be discussed. The rationing model here is different from the models of Tobin (1952), Barro and Romer (1987), and Sah (1987) because they do not consider individuals' efforts to compete for a rationed good. The model is closest to that of Holt and Sherman (1982), although they have not analyzed the variance in people's waiting costs. De Vany (1976) and Carlton (1983) have discussed rationing models in which firms internalize the costs of waiting. My model is complementary to theirs in that it helps suggest how such costs may be reduced.

[1] The proposition here is different from the notion that welfare loss is smaller the smaller is the supply elasticity. A large variance in rent-seeking costs does not imply a highly inelastic supply of rent-seeking activities. The former is a global property about the supply curve while the latter is a local property (see also Suen 1988).

I. Time Costs, Personal Valuations, and Market Equilibrium

This section develops a simple model of rent seeking in which competition takes the form of rationing by waiting. Suppose that each individual can purchase one unit[2] of a rationed good, q, at a price, p, which is controlled at a level below the market-clearing price. Since quantity demanded exceeds quantity supplied at that price, waiting is necessary to obtain the good. A person's net valuation for the good will therefore depend on, among other things, the time it takes to get the good and his or her cost of time. To derive an expression for the net personal valuation for a rationed good, define the following indirect utility function for individual i:

$$U^*(q, w, y^F) = \max_{x,l} \{U(q, x, l) | x + wl \leq y^F\}, \tag{1}$$

where q is the amount of the rationed good consumed, w is the wage rate, y^F is full income, l is the amount of leisure, and x represents all other goods (whose price is normalized to one). For notational convenience, subscripts for individual have been suppressed. It should be borne in mind that individuals may have different wages, incomes, and utility functions. If the individual must spend an amount of time t (to be determined later) to obtain one unit of q, full income will change from $y + wT$ to $y + w(T - t)$.[3] The individual's net valuation for q can therefore be defined implicitly by this relationship:

$$U^*(0, w, y + wT) = U^*(1, w, y + w(T - t) - Z(y, w, t)). \tag{2}$$

In words, Z is the maximum amount of money that can be taken away from the individual who gets the rationed good and leave him as well off as without the good; that is, Z is the compensating variation of the rationed good.

The structure of equation (2) assumes that there is no direct utility associated with waiting. This implies that the net personal valuation Z can be written as

$$Z(y, w, t) = \theta(y, w) - tw. \tag{3}$$

Here θ may be interpreted as the gross personal valuation of the rationed good. The separability between θ and t is important in a model of heterogeneous consumers. People have different nonwage

[2] Under a price control, since the value of a good is greater than its money price, people will tend to buy the largest amount that is allowed. This largest amount may be defined as the unit of the good. Thus, even for goods that are divisible, the assumption of a discrete zero-one choice is reasonable.

[3] The criteria of competition may be multidimensional. For example, whether one is granted a valuable right may depend both on legal expenditures and on campaign contributions. In that case, t is interpreted as a combined score on the various dimensions, and w is the minimum per unit cost of achieving that score.

incomes, wage rates, and utility functions, but in equilibrium the amount of waiting time is the same for everybody.[4] With separability, it is possible to summarize consumer heterogeneity by just considering the joint distribution of gross values and time costs.[5]

Since each consumer purchases either one unit of the rationed good or none,[6] the market demand for the rationed good is equal to the number of consumers with $Z \geq p$ or, equivalently,

$$\theta \geq p + tw. \tag{4}$$

If the joint distribution of θ and w across individuals is represented by the density function $f(\theta, w)$, the market demand function is given by

$$D(p, t) = \int_{-\infty}^{\infty} \int_{p+tw}^{\infty} f(\theta, w)\, d\theta\, dw. \tag{5}$$

With the price of the good being fixed at p and competition occurring on the basis of one's willingness to wait, the length of the queue will adjust so that, in equilibrium, there will be a market-clearing waiting time t^* for which no one has an incentive to join or leave the queue. Quantity demanded at p and t^* will be equal to the available supply of the good, Q. That is,

$$Q = D(p, t^*(p, Q)). \tag{6}$$

If all individuals had the same gross valuation and the same time cost (say, θ_0 and w_0), the market-clearing waiting time would be given by

$$t^* = \frac{\theta_0 - p}{w_0}. \tag{7}$$

A waiting time less than (7) would not be an equilibrium because every consumer would rather wait longer and have the good than go without it, thus lengthening the waiting time. Equation (7) shows the extreme case in which the social surplus from the good would be completely eliminated by waiting. When consumers are heterogeneous, however, inframarginal consumers will have $\theta - t^*w > p$, thus retaining some surplus. The next section will discuss the relationship between the amount of surplus from the rationed good and the degree of heterogeneity across consumers.

[4] This is demonstrated in Barzel (1974). The statement is logically equivalent to the standard result of a single price in the market. See eq. (6).

[5] Barzel (1974) and Holt and Sherman (1982) assume that θ is a fixed function of w, so that it is unnecessary to consider their joint distribution. In a population of heterogeneous consumers, θ will be dependent on, but not determined by, w because y and other utility function parameters will also differ across individuals.

[6] As long as the number of units purchased is independent of one's wage rate, it is possible to treat a person who buys n units as n separate individuals. The analysis will go through by a suitable reinterpretation of the distribution of individual characteristics.

II. Rent Dissipation and Consumer Heterogeneity

The total social value of a good under a certain allocation mechanism can be defined as quantity times the conditional expectation of net personal valuation, given that the consumers satisfy that criterion of allocation. Under a price mechanism, if the market-clearing price is p^*, the total value is

$$V_1 = QE(\theta \mid \theta \geq p^*). \tag{8a}$$

On the other hand, the total value of a rationed good is equal to

$$V_2 = QE(\theta - t^*w \mid \theta - t^*w \geq p). \tag{8b}$$

Since V_1 is the maximum achievable social value of the good, $V_1 - V_2$ measures the welfare loss or the dissipation of rent under rationing by waiting.[7]

The condition for a rationing equilibrium requires that, at the margin, the net gain from a rationed commodity be equal to the time cost of acquiring it. Inframarginal consumers, whose gross personal valuations are greater than their time costs, are able to retain some rents. One might expect that the total surplus or differential rents under rationing by waiting will increase as consumers become more heterogeneous. This conjecture turns out to be correct provided *inframarginal* consumers have lower average wage rates than *marginal* consumers, because in such a case an increase in the variance in wage rates will imply a lower level of wage rates for inframarginal consumers, thereby reducing the welfare loss due to waiting.

To show the relationship between the variance in wage rates and the total surplus under rationing by waiting, let $w = \overline{w} + \sigma_w \epsilon$ and let $g(\theta, \epsilon)$ be the joint density function of θ and ϵ. Then equation (8b) can be rewritten as

$$V_2 = \int_{-\infty}^{\infty} \int_{p + t^*(\overline{w} + \sigma_w \epsilon)}^{\infty} [\theta - t^*(\overline{w} + \sigma_w \epsilon)] g(\theta, \epsilon)\, d\theta\, d\epsilon. \tag{9}$$

When we take the derivative of equation (9) and use the transformation $f(\theta, w) = g(\theta, (w - \overline{w})/\sigma_w)/\sigma_w$, the result is

$$\begin{aligned} \frac{\partial V_2}{\partial \sigma_w} = &- \int_w \left(t^* \frac{w - \overline{w}}{\sigma_w} + w \frac{\partial t^*}{\partial \sigma_w} \right) p \hat{f}\, dw \\ &- \int_w \int_\theta \left(t^* \frac{w - \overline{w}}{\sigma_w} + w \frac{\partial t^*}{\partial \sigma_w} \right) f\, d\theta\, dw, \end{aligned} \tag{10a}$$

[7] This is a more appropriate measure of rent dissipation than total waiting costs because it also includes the welfare loss due to misallocation.

where $\int_w$ stands for $\int_{-\infty}^{\infty}$, $\int_\theta$ stands for $\int_{p+t^*w}^{\infty}$, $\hat{f} = f(p + t^*w, w)$, and $f = f(\theta, w)$. If one differentiates the market-clearing condition with respect to σ_w, the first integral in (10a) can be seen to be identically zero. Moreover, $\partial t^*/\partial\sigma_w = -t^* \int_w (w - \overline{w}) \hat{f}\, dw / \sigma_w \int_w \hat{f}\, dw$. Making this substitution into the second term yields

$$\frac{\partial V_2}{\partial \sigma_w} = \frac{-t^*}{\sigma_w \int_w w\hat{f}\, dw} \left[\int_w \int_\theta (w - \overline{w}) f\, d\theta\, dw \int_w w\hat{f}\, dw \right.$$

$$\left. - \int_w \int_\theta wf\, d\theta\, dw \int_w (w - \overline{w}) \hat{f}\, dw \right]$$

$$= \frac{-t^*\overline{w} \int_w \hat{f}\, dw}{\sigma_w \int_w w\hat{f}\, dw} \left(\int_w \int_\theta f\, d\theta\, dw \int_w w \frac{\hat{f}}{\int_w \hat{f}\, dw}\, dw \right. \tag{10b}$$

$$\left. - \int_w \int_\theta wf\, d\theta\, dw \right)$$

$$= \frac{t^*\overline{w}}{\sigma_w} \frac{\partial t^*}{\partial p} [QE(w|Z = p) - QE(w|Z \geq p)].$$

Therefore, $\partial V_2/\partial\sigma_w$ is positive if and only if $E(w|Z \geq p)$ is less than $E(w|Z = p)$. In general, the value of these conditional expectations will depend on the entire distribution of θ and w. There are, however, two conditions either one of which is sufficient to ensure that $E(w|Z \geq p) < E(w|Z = p)$: (1) θ and w are independent or negatively correlated or (2) θ is the same to all individuals. If either of these conditions is met, inframarginal consumers will have a lower average wage than marginal consumers. Then an increase in the variance in wage rates will increase total surplus or reduce rent dissipation under rationing by waiting.[8]

The conclusion above may be useful in understanding an aspect of the patent system. The patent is traditionally conceived as "the right to an invention" (i.e., the rationed commodity). It is argued that under imperfect information innovators will compete by inventing prematurely or by overspending in research (i.e., waiting), thus dissipating the value of the innovation (see Barzel 1968; Dasgupta and Stiglitz 1980). Kitch (1977), on the other hand, suggests that the patent should more appropriately be viewed as "the right to invent," which serves to *constrain* the rush to capture the returns from an invention. His discussion of the prospect function of the patent system is not complete, however, because the argument can be pushed one step back: competition for the right to invent will result in dissipating behavior. Since the rights are not explicitly priced, both sys-

[8] If θ and w are positively correlated but the covariance between θ and Z is negative, the proposition will still be true.

tems will result in complete dissipation if innovators were homogeneous. The relevant question is, Which system will result in *less* dissipation when innovators are not homogeneous?

Since a patent is salable once it is granted, its value (i.e., θ) will be the same to all individuals. The result in this section therefore implies that dissipation will be smaller the greater is the *variance* in the costs of achieving the patent. It seems reasonable to suggest that when the patentable standard is set at an early stage of the innovative process (patent as the right to invent), the variance in the costs of achieving the patent will be relatively large because the costs will depend on many idiosyncratic factors such as the distribution of talents and luck. On the other hand, the variance in the costs of achieving the patent is expected to be relatively small if a finished invention is required (patent as the right to an invention) because the production of a finished invention usually involves a more systematic, long-term plan and the influence of luck is diminished.[9] It is therefore expected that a patent system that grants patents at the early stage of the innovative process will result in a smaller dissipation of rent.

III. Effects of a Secondary Market

The implications of the endogeneity of waiting time and the degree of heterogeneity in time costs are often overlooked. To emphasize their importance, I shall consider in this section the effects of introducing a secondary market for a rationed commodity. A secondary market ensures that highest-valuing users will obtain the rationed good in the secondary market, while lowest-wage people will wait for the rationed good in the primary market. It is as if the average personal valuation for the good had increased and the average time cost had decreased with the introduction of the secondary market. However, it is not necessarily true that total surplus from the rationed good will increase as a result. Since waiting time is endogenous, an increase in average value or a decrease in average cost will encourage people to wait longer. At the margin, rents must be fully dissipated. The amount of rents that is retained depends on the *differences* in people's time costs and personal valuations, not on their *levels*. It is possible (say, because the variance in wage rates among low-wage individuals is sufficiently small compared with the overall variance) that introducing a secondary market will increase the welfare cost of a rationing system.[10]

Consider a simple example of rationing equilibrium. To focus on

[9] The argument here is a stochastic counterpart to LeChatelier's principle, which says that long-run cost curves are more elastic than short-run cost curves.

[10] Cheung (1974) argues that if consumers are allowed to hire "waiters" to wait on their behalf, the dissipation of rent will be reduced because people who are standing in line will have lower time costs. However, if everybody is allowed to hire waiters, the

the effect of the variance in time costs among low-wage individuals, assume that θ and w are independent and let $f(\theta, w) = g(\theta)h(w)$, where

$$g(\theta) = 1/2 \quad \text{for } 0 < \theta \leq 2, \tag{11a}$$

$$h(w) = \begin{cases} 1/2 & \text{for } 0 < w \leq 1, \\ 1/2s & \text{for } 1 < w \leq s + 1. \end{cases} \tag{11b}$$

If $s = 1$, (11) is a uniform distribution. As s increases, the overall wage variance increases while the wage variance in the low-wage group remains unchanged.

In the absence of a secondary market and under the assumption that the price of the good is fixed at $p = 0$ with quantity $Q = 1/4$, the equilibrium waiting time t^* is characterized by

$$\int_0^{s+1} \int_{t^*w}^{2} g(\theta)h(w)\, d\theta\, dw = 1/4. \tag{12}$$

This gives

$$t^* = \frac{6}{s + 3}. \tag{13}$$

Total surplus can be computed as

$$\begin{aligned} V_2 &= \int_0^{s+1} \int_{t^*w}^{2} (\theta - t^*w)g(\theta)h(w)\, d\theta\, dw \\ &= \frac{2s^2 + 3s + 3}{2(s + 3)^2}. \end{aligned} \tag{14}$$

Note that $\partial V_2/\partial s > 0$, which is consistent with the previous result that, when θ and w are independent, an increase in the degree of heterogeneity in time costs will increase total surplus.

On the other hand, consider the nature of equilibrium when a secondary market exists. If $\hat{p}$ is the equilibrium price of the good in the secondary market and $\hat{t}$ is the equilibrium waiting time in the primary market, people who consume the rationed good must have $\theta \geq \hat{p}$ and people who wait in line must have $w\hat{t} \leq \hat{p}$. Both markets must clear. Therefore,

$$\int_{\hat{p}}^{2} g(\theta)\, d\theta = \int_0^{\hat{p}/\hat{t}} h(w)\, dw = 1/4. \tag{15}$$

Solving for $\hat{p}$ and $\hat{t}$, we get

$$\hat{p} = 3/2, \tag{16a}$$

$$\hat{t} = 3. \tag{16b}$$

---

waiting line will get longer. The market for waiting service has the same effects as a secondary market for the rationed commodity.

Comparing t^* and $\hat{t}$, we can see that waiting time is longer when a secondary market is introduced.

Total surplus from the good in the presence of a secondary market is equal to

$$V_3 = \int_{3/2}^{2} \theta g(\theta)\, d\theta - \int_{0}^{1/2} 3wh(w)\, dw \\ = 1/4. \tag{17}$$

Comparing the total benefits with and without the secondary market, we get

$$V_2 - V_3 = \frac{3(s+1)(s-1)}{4(s+3)^2} > (<)\ 0 \quad \text{if and only if } s > (<)\ 1. \tag{18}$$

When s is large, the variance in time costs of the low-wage group is small relative to that of the overall population. The small variance means that little surplus can be retained if it is the low-wage people who wait, as is the case when there is a secondary market. The welfare loss due to rationing by waiting increases as a result.[11]

The example above casts doubt on the notion that increased flexibility in contractual arrangements under price control would always reduce the welfare cost. When property rights are not well defined, some restrictions on behavior may be socially beneficial because they may help limit the extent to which wasteful competition takes place. It is often argued that if ration coupons are resalable, both coupon recipients and people who buy the coupons can be made better off because of mutual benefits from exchange.[12] This suggestion is correct if people cannot spend resources to obtain the coupons. However, the issuing of coupons to individuals is often based on criteria that are alterable at a cost. For example, if coupons are issued to the "poor," people will have less incentive to earn money income so that rents will be partially dissipated. When resale is permitted, the value of the coupons to recipients will increase, and the disincentive to earn money income also increases. Similarly, if import quotas are made transferable, the incentive to obtain them through more intensive

[11] Another application is the cost of litigation. Legal disputes arise when property rights are not clearly defined. As litigating parties attempt to capture some portion of the nonexclusive income, rents are being dissipated through costly litigation. It is plausible that the difference in legal abilities between litigating parties themselves is greater than that of their attorneys because lawyers receive more or less similar training. Thus, while lawyers may be more efficient litigants than their clients, litigating costs may increase when both contending parties can hire lawyers.

[12] See, e.g., Alchian and Allen (1983) and Hirshleifer (1988). For a different view, see Tobin (1952) and Sah (1987). The analyses of Tobin and Sah have not taken into account the effect of endogenous rent seeking.

rent-seeking activities will increase as well. If the costs of these rent-seeking activities increase by an amount greater than the gains from trade, the social costs of the rationing system will be higher with the introduction of a secondary market.

IV. Summary

In this paper I have discussed the implications of rationing by waiting when consumers have different time costs and personal valuations. I argue that a greater degree of consumer heterogeneity will reduce the dissipation of rent if inframarginal consumers have lower average time costs than marginal consumers. Since it is the variance rather than the mean level of time costs and personal valuations that matters, it is shown that the introduction of a secondary market for a rationed good does not necessarily reduce the welfare loss due to rationing. Throughout the discussion, it has been assumed that information is imperfect. People who want to obtain a good have to actually spend time waiting in line to establish their priority. Rent dissipation is not complete because people with initial advantages earn differential rents. In Fudenberg et al. (1983) and Harris and Vickers (1985), it is shown that under perfect information the slightest differences in initial advantages will eliminate all dissipation. While the conclusions in this paper are not as strong as theirs, they may be more useful in the comparison of the costs of rent-seeking activities under different institutions.

Efficient rent-seeking under varying cost structures

CHRIS PAUL
AL WILHITE
Department of Economics and Finance, University of Alabama in Huntsville, Huntsville, AL 35899

1. Introduction

The rent-seeking paradigm, which was introduced by Tullock (1967), has proven useful for exploring a variety of economic decisions that lie outside the traditional profit maximizing framework. Early applications of Tullock's insight (Becker, 1968; Krueger, 1974; Posner, 1975; Demsetz, 1976; Foster, 1981 and others) usually assumed the entire value of the rent would be dissipated by competition following the fashion of economic profits in competitive markets. In 1980 Tullock structured a simple game reflecting the decisions made in rent-seeking. The results generated by his model suggest residual rents may accrue to rent-seekers and, under certain conditions, resist dissipation. A number of studies followed Tullock's 1980 paper (Corcoran, 1984; Corcoran and Karels, 1985; Higgins, Shugart and Tollison, 1985; Tullock, 1984, 1985, and 1987) which explore the dissipation of excess rents under various assumptions.

The present paper pursues a different aspect of rent-seeking games. The impact of different cost structures on the optimal decision paths of rent-seekers is explored, and specific applications for the various constructs are offered. Amending the manner in which costs enter the game results in optimal strategies differing from those obtained in Tullock's original game. Consequently, the applicability of the rent-seeking paradigm is broadened and several social activities, such as elections, revolution, and war, which have resisted formal modeling can be constructed in a coherent manner.

2. The games

2.1. Tullock's original game

Tullock (1980a) describes his rent-seeking game as a lottery for a prize, the rent, for which the players are competing. Players buy lottery tickets to affect their probability of winning and these expenditures are retained by the lottery, i.e., ticket expenditures are not added to the prize. It is useful to restate Tullock's original game,

$$E(a) = \frac{a}{a+b} R - a. \tag{1}$$

Where a and b represent the expenditures by players A and B, respectively. The ratio of an individual's expenditure relative to the total expenditures determines the probability of the individual winning the prize or rent value, R. The expected value of the game for player A, E(a), is given by the probability of winning times the value of the rent, R, less the wager, a. The game can be generalized to any number of players. Assuming each player maximizes his or her expected value and reacts to the other player's wager, Tullock derives a Cournot-Nash type equilibrium where each player invests, $[(n-1)/n^2]R$.

Tullock (1980a) extended his game in two ways. One incorporates non-linear probabilities as a function of the bet. The second, called bias, allowed players' bets to have differing impacts on their probabilities of winning. While similar modifications can be made to the games presented below, these complications are not necessary to demonstrate the changes resulting from different cost structures. To preserve this study's focus on the characteristics of different types of rent-seeking games, a simple two person, unbiased game will be constructed for each situation. The unrestricted versions of each game, which may be designed for specific rent-seeking applications, are left for future research.

Before proceeding to the analysis of different game structures, it is useful to rewrite Tullock's game in its full expected value form,

$$E(a) = \frac{a}{a+b} (R-a) + \frac{b}{a+b} (-a), \tag{1.1}$$

which reduces to equation (1).

The first term in equation 1.1 is the probability of winning times the net rent. The net rent is the magnitude of the rent minus the cost of playing. The second term is the cost of playing, $-a$, times the probability of losing. Maximizing this expected value yields an optimal strategy for A, equation (2), which depends on the magnitudes of the rent, R, and the competitor's bet, b.

$$a = -b + \sqrt{bR}. \tag{2}$$

Player B's optimal strategy is symmetric with A's. If both players behave in accordance with their strategy of maximizing the expected value a simply Cournot-Nash equilibrium emerges, with each player betting R/4.

2.2. Elections

The structure of elections as a rent-seeking game differs from Tullock's model in that the cost of playing, campaigning for election, is not borne by the player *ex ante* of playing the game. Rather, the cost of playing is either taken out of rents by the winning participant or is contributed by third parties for the loser. The prize in an election is presumably the pay, power and prestige of the office. Some campaign activity is captured by Tullock's original game in that effort expended by the candidate is lost. However, in modern elections the largest proportion of campaign expenditures are not of this type. The bulk of campaign contributions come from third parties. Candidates run on a platform proclaiming what they will do if elected and based on their campaign promises and proclamations, third-party rent-seekers contribute to the candidate's campaign. The key difference in this game is that campaign promises are valid only if the candidate wins. Thus, the costs of campaigning falls unevenly on the candidates.[1]

Campaign promises can be viewed as conditional promises to pay, IOUs, which are issued to voters and contributors. For example, a candidate may receive a contribution from a dairy PAC in return for a promise to support subsidies for dairy producers. The contribution is spent by the candidate in his election bid. If the candidate wins, a portion of the rent accruing to his office will be expended in supporting subsidies to dairy producers. As a result, the cost of the election to the candidate is a reduction in the proportion of the rent retained. As the losing candidate is not accountable for campaign promises, the IOUs are voided, and the cost of the campaign is borne by the supporters who provided financing and/or votes. Of course, the resources expended on the campaign still represent social costs, but these costs are imposed on the candidate's supporters. As a result, a player of this game will behave differently than under Tullock's regime.

Expressing the election game in its full expected value form results in,

$$E(a) = \frac{a}{a+b}(R-a) + \frac{b}{a+b}(0); \tag{3}$$

or more simply,

$$E(a) = \frac{a}{a+b}(R-a). \tag{3.1}$$

Maximizing the expected value of this tradeoff, A's optimal expenditure is given by,

$$a = -b + \sqrt{b^2 + bR}. \tag{4}$$

As in Tullock's game, A's optimal expenditure is dependent on the magnitude of total rent, R, and the level of his opponent's activity, b. Noting that A's and

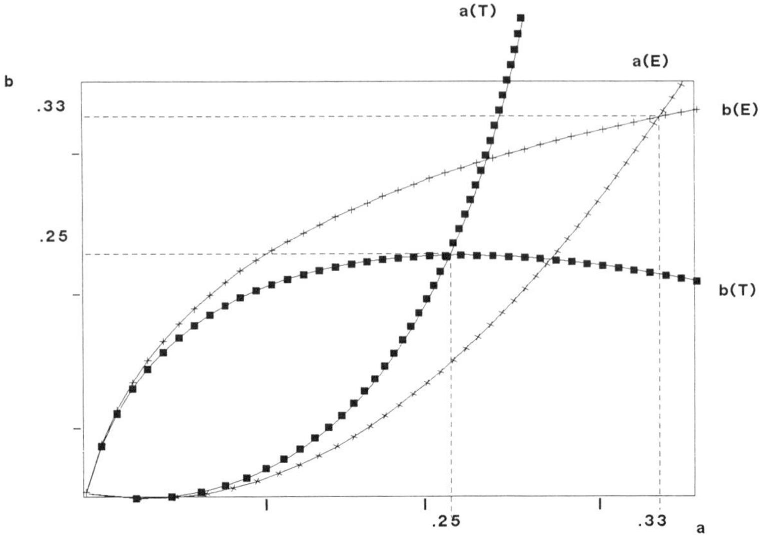

Figure 1. Lines a(T) and b(T) are the reaction functions for players A and B competing in Tullock's original game. The election game reaction functions are labeled a(E) and b(E)

B's optimal reaction functions are identical and bidding converges to a stable pair of bets, a Cournot-Nash equilibrium results where each player's optimal level of activity is equal to R/3.

Comparing this outcome with Tullock's game reveals some interesting points. First, if rent-seekers are able to shift the costs of competing to third parties in the case of a loss while extracting the cost from the value of the rent upon winning, their exposure to loss is reduced. Consequently, the optimal level of rent-seeking expenditures is increased. Still, rents are not completely dissipated. Rent-seeking expenditures sum to two-thirds of the rent value. One-third of the total rent value is extracted from the rent by the winner, and a third is borne by the losing candidate's supporters. Figure 1 shows the reaction curves of both players for the election game and Tullock's original game. The total rent value is set equal to one so the bets can be interpreted as representing the proportion of rent wagered.

In a more complete formulation, elections represent a combination of Tullock's original game and the election game. The candidate's supporters are faced with a game like the one originally presented by Tullock. Candidates, the recipients of campaign contributions, promise to support specific issues upon election. The intersection of these two components of campaign costs should prove fruitful in future modeling and empirical testing of political behavior (see Wilhite and Paul, 1988 for a further development of the election game).

2.3. War

In a war two players, countries, possess resources which they are willing to expend in an attempt to capture the rent, economic resources, held by the other. The key distinction of this game is that both players initially control some rent and may use it to play the game. This is very similar to the description of war offered by Tullock (1974). These rent values are denoted by R_a and R_b for players A and B, respectively. The formulation of this game is given by,

$$E(a) = \frac{a}{a+b}(R_a - a + R_b - b) + \frac{b}{a+b}(-R_a). \qquad (5.1)$$

The expected values for player B takes a similar form,

$$E(b) = \frac{b}{a+b}(R_a - a + R_b - b) + \frac{a}{a+b}(-R_b). \qquad (5.2)$$

As before, the first term in the equation represents A's gain from winning. In this case winning results in A retaining his rent value minus his expenditure on the competition plus B's rent minus the portion B used in the contest. The second term gives the result of losing, which is the total value of A's rent captured by the opponent. To the victor goes the spoils, the residual rent of both countries, and the loser receives noting.

Maximizing equation 5.1 yields,

$$a = -b + \sqrt{R_b b + 2R_a b}. \qquad (6.1)$$

A similar solution results for player B,

$$b = -a + \sqrt{R_a a + 2R_b a}. \qquad (6.2)$$

As in the games discussed above the optimal level of expenditure for either player is dependent on the oppnonent's effort, bet, and the value of the rents. Because there are two rent magnitudes at risk in war their relative size affects the outcome (Tullock, 1974). This complication increases the difficulty of tracking and interpreting the equilibrium. However, the problem can be simplified by reformulating equation 5.1 and 5.2 using relative rent magnitudes. Define R as being equal to $R_a + R_b$; the ratio $R_a/R = p$ and the ratio $R_b/R = 1-p$. Substituting these values into equation 5.1 and 5.2 yields the optimal reaction function, or strategy for each player, A and B.

$$a = -b + \sqrt{(p+1)bR}, \qquad (7.1)$$

and

$$b = -a + \sqrt{(2-p)aR}. \tag{7.2}$$

Recall that each player's optimal strategy is affected by the magnitude of the total rent, R, the proportional distribution of the rent, p, and the strategy adopted by the other player. Solving for the equilibrium condition yields,

$$a = \frac{2+3p-p^3}{9} R, \tag{8.1}$$

and

$$b = \frac{2+3(1-p) - (1-p)^3}{9} R. \tag{8.2}$$

If $R_a = R_b$, that is $p = ½$, the optimal bet for A is 0.375R or $0.75R_a$, with an identical solution for player B. In sum, the competitors expend 0.75 of R; which is greater than in the previously discussed games.[2]

While this equilibrium is stable, the probability of such an outcome seems remote because the expected value of the game is negative for both players. As in the negative expected value games introduced by Tulock (1980a), the players may converge to this optimum in a self-defense strategy once the game is started. This is because sunk costs are lost. However, both players would be better off by avoiding the game altogether. The introduction of player bias to reflect the military or technological advantages of one country can yield war games with positive expected values. But, for countries of relatively similar size and might the solution has a negative expected value. A result suggesting war has a negative expected value has some intuitive appeal (Tullock, 1974).

The optimal strategy in the war game depends on the relative magnitudes of the two rents at risk. Taking the derivative of the equilibrium solutions for this game, equations 8.1 and 8.2, with respect to p shows the impact of relative size on the bet. The sign of this derivative is positive for player A and negative for player B. As the rent at stake grows for one player relative to the other, the player with more at stake increases his or her investment in the game. Conversely, the smaller country reduces its level of activity in the game. This result is consistent with the observation of larger expenditures for defense by high-income countries. Additionally, it supports Tullock's (1974: 92) conclusion that ". . . it is always rational to start a war if your enemy is both rich and weak enough." Figure 2 shows the impact of a changing p level on the equilibrium of this game.

An additional application of this rent-seeking game is a *coup d'état*. Each

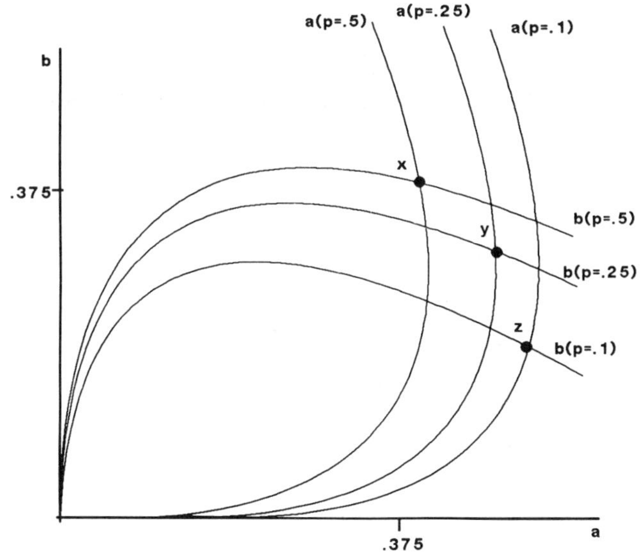

Figure 2. As the size of country A's rent grows relative to country B, the equilibrium pair of bids shifts from point X to point Y to point Z. Player A increases his bet while player B lowers his bet

player, whether the current ruling party or the revolutionary group, has access to rent and can use those resources to protect their position or attempt to capture the other's rent. Tullock (1974) observes that probably three-fourths of the violent overthrows in history have resulted from a segment of the government overthrowing the in-power group.

2.4. *The populist revolution*

The case of revolutionary activity presents another asymmetric game. In fact, this game is a special case of the previous model in which p has been set equal to 1 for the in-power group, but due to its unique attributes it is presented separately. In a revolutionary setting the in-power group or individual, termed the dictator, controls the powers of the state which allows him to extract rents from the economy and employ them to maintain his position. The revolutionary group, or outsiders, must finance rent-seeking activities from their own resource base, i.e. they cannot employ any portion of the rent for which they are competing. If the revolution is successful they receive the residual rent which consists of the original rent minus resources expended by the dictator in defending his or her position.

This game may be modeled as an "insider-outsider" contest where rent values vary for the contestants. The insider, or dictator, denoted as player A, faces a game structure,

$$E(a) = \frac{a}{a+b}(R-a) + \frac{b}{a+b}(-R) \tag{9.1}$$

If the dictator wins the game he is left with the residual rent value, while losing the game results in a loss of all rent.

The structure of the game faced by player B, the revolutionary, is given by,

$$E(b) = \frac{b}{a+b}(R-a-b) + \frac{a}{a+b}(-b). \tag{9.2}$$

If the revolutionary is successful in overthrowing the dictator he captures the rent, R, minus the costs of both players. If the revolutionary loses, the value of resources employed in his attempt to capture the rent is lost. Assuming each player maximizes the expected value of playing, the optimal strategies for players A and B are,

$$a = -b + \sqrt{b^2 + 2bR}, \tag{10.1}$$

and

$$b = -a + \sqrt{aR - a^2}. \tag{10.2}$$

note: if $a > R/2$; $b < 0$

The revolution game possesses two unique characteristics. First, while there is an equilibrium pair of bids which maximizes the expected value for both players, there is no systematic path to this equilibrium. Due to this game's unique structure, the derivation of the equilibrium value is somewhat tedious.[3] Keeping R constant at unity the optimal response path for each player can be graphed as in Figure 3. Accepting a rounding error at the fifth decimal place results in an equilibrium where $a = .37289$ and $b = .11068$. Note, in Figure 3 the adjustment process represented by the arrow does not generally converge to the equilibrium.

The game's second unique characteristic is that B's response function crosses the axis at .5R. This reflects the requirement that A's expenditure must be less than R/2 for B's expenditure amount to be positive. The reaction function suggests the dictator can reduce revolutionary activity to zero by using half the rent to defend his/her current position. While this is not a maximizing choice assuming risk neutrality, it could be chosen by a risk-averse individual. The addition of bias and other extensions reinforce this result. For example, if the dictator has technically superior weapons the proportion of the rent expended to completely suppress revolt would be reduced. Tullock (1980b) generated a pair of reaction functions resembling Figure 3 with the use of bias parameters.[4]

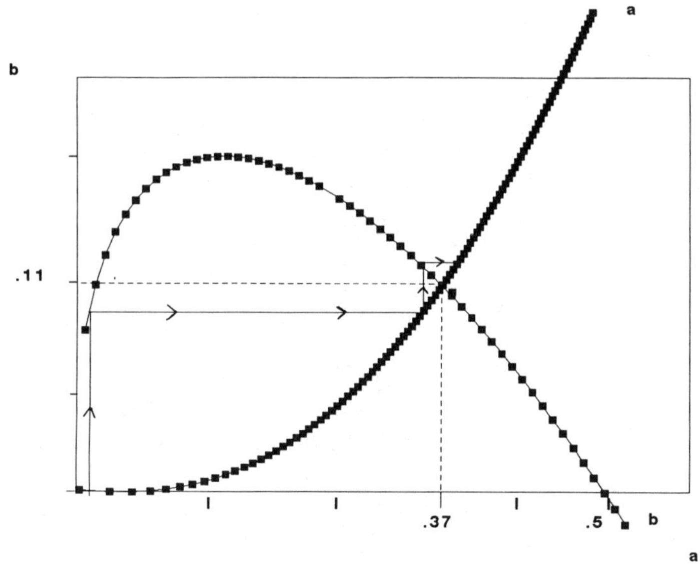

Figure 3. Because players are unable to withdraw committed resources, the bidding in the revolution game does not generally converge to an equilibrium

2.5. The lottery

In the final variation of this family of games the rent-seeking expenditures of the players are added to the rent in the way a bet in a poker game is added to the pot.[5] More precisely, as players in this game buy lottery tickets, the entire price of their tickets is added to the prize.

Here player A maximizes,

$$E(a) = \frac{a}{a+b}(R + a + b) + \frac{b}{a+b}(-a). \tag{11}$$

Taking the first derivative and setting it equal to zero, we find there is no maximum for this game. The expected value for an individual player depends on the size of R and the action of the other player, but there is no dominant level of effort defined by these parameters. There is, however, strategy. If player B holds his effort constant, the expected value of the game increases for player A as his effort increases, but if player B matches A's effort, the expected value is constant regardless of A's expenditures. Specifically,

$$\text{if } b = \bar{b},\ \lim_{a \to \infty} E(a) = R + \bar{b}, \tag{12.1}$$

and

if b = a, E(a) = ½R. (12.2)

The results of 12.1 and 12.2 are not surprising. If a player's bet is added to the prize then repeated entries are costless if he wins. The optimal strategy is to flood the lottery with tickets bearing your name. A player who is unwilling to make an infinite commitment finds the best strategy is to stay out all together.

3. Summary and conclusions

Exploring the variation in the structure of rent-seeking games widens the field of positive institutional theory. By altering the structure of Tullock's (1980) efficient rent-seeking game, some additional insight into the various possible forms of rent-seeking behavior is derived. Furthermore, the games presented demonstrate that Tullock's theory of rent-seeking has a wide variety of potential applications outside the standard profit seeking paradigm of neoclassical theory.

The rent-seeking games introduced in this paper are not an exhaustive listing of game types, but rather a demonstration of the diversity of Tullock's game and the rich variety of solutions which result. The specific structure a game takes is a function of the economic, political, and social context from which it arises. Furthermore, the resulting level of residual rent will be determined by the game's structure. As Tullock (1980) points out, this result may be the more interesting. People play games to increase their wealth by the capture of residual rents, and the magnitude of this rent is determined by the rules under which the games are played. Thus, there are incentives for players to structure their rent-seeking game to obtain a desired result.

An obvious extension of this study is the inclusion of bias, a larger number of players, and nonlinear probabilities. When a specific topic is under exploration, the bias and level of entry of additional players many generate some of the most interesting results. For example, suppose the rent-seeking model was being adopted for a study of revolution. The existence of several political parties and their allies, increasing the number of players, and the technological level of the various interest groups would be of central importance. The approach taken to resolving these issues should be applicable to a wide variety of circumstances, and this realization should substantially enrich the discourse on rent-seeking behavior and its implications.

Notes

1. A candidate could lie during the campaign, but such a strategy is inherently short-lived. Still, there are two ways to reduce the cost of campaign promises. First, candidates can address issues

they support personally, i.e., a candidate who believes in milk subsidies does not lose any latitude by promising support to MILKPAC. Second, vague campaign promises, e.g. being pro-family or anti-communist, lower the cost of campaign IOU's because there is no expectation to deliver resources on these issues.

2. This oversimplifies the war outcomes because a country can spend more than their rent value. This changes the solution because the cost of a loss is no longer fixed. For example, if $a \geq pR$, the expected value for A becomes,

$$E(a) = \frac{a}{a+b}(R-a-b) + \frac{b}{a+b}(-a)$$

and the resulting reaction function for A is; $a = -b + \sqrt{b^2 + bR}$.

3. The equilibrium value for a is,

$$a = \frac{16}{15}R + \frac{\frac{16}{75}R^2}{\sqrt[3]{6\sqrt{21}\frac{R^3}{5^{3/2}} - \frac{314}{125}R^3}} + \sqrt[3]{6\sqrt{21}\frac{R^3}{5^{3/2}} - \frac{314}{125}R^3}$$

4. Tullock's game refers to resources invested in a law suit. If the *a priori* evidence favors B, B has a favorable bias, the reaction functions resemble those presented in Figure 3.
5. While the poker game analogy is instructive, it is incomplete because a bet in poker does not affect the probability of winning when the number of players is fixed.

Investments in rent-seeking

R. KENNETH GODWIN
Department of Political Science, University of Arizona, Tucson, AZ 85721

Since the publication of a number of articles concerning efficient rent-seeking both political scientists and economists have been interested in discovering how firms make rent-seeking investments and in developing a model of that process. In addition, several writers have been interested in the question of why politicians and bureaucrats in the United States do not capture more of the benefits or rents that they provide through their policy decisions (see Tullock, 1989). In this article I attempt to move toward explaining lobbying or rent-seeking investments by examining the questions, "How do firms decide how much to spend on campaign contributions?" and "Do these decisions reflect any underlying models of decision making?"

One of the difficulties that we face in modeling a decision process is that when there are multiple objectives and individual actors weight those objectives differently, a single empirically testable decision model is difficult to construct (Hardin, 1982). We may be able to conceptualize the decision process in terms of utility maximization with relative ease, but the empirical test of this model is not straightforward. Normally we cannot test directly such a model and can only determine whether our data are consistent with what we would expect.

To examine lobbying or rent-seeking activities by firms I will limit my discussion largely to the behavior of corporate political action committees (PACs). PAC contributions represent one of many expenditures by firms to influence the political process. The advantages of concentrating on PACs are that the data are readily available and therefore the propositions developed here can be readily tested by others. The limitations of this choice are that these data omit direct lobbying, a much more extensive set of activities and expenditures. Also omitted are the numerous legal, illegal, and semi-legal activities such as providing high-paying jobs to relatives of congressmen, tips as to when to buy and sell a particular stock, and direct bribes. It must also be noted that political action committees pursue goals other than policy rewards. They are institutions that have maintenance needs and to meet these needs they give contributions not only to influence policy but also to satisfy contributors. (See Eismeier and Pollock, 1984, 1986; and Wright, 1985.)

Contributions from corporate political action committees became legal with the Campaign Finance Act of 1971 and its 1974 amendments.[1] This act and amendments made corporate PACs legal and allowed them to contribute $5,000 per election to an individual candidate. Thus, if a candidate has a primary and a general election opponent the maximum gift to him would be $10,000. Corporations have used this legislation to provide substantial contributions to federal elections. In 1978 corporate PACs provided $9.8 million to candidates for Congress and this figure had risen to $49.4 million for the 1986 elections (Sorauf, 1988). In 1975 there were 139 corporate PACs, in 1986 there were 1744. The average contribution from a corporate PAC to congressional candidate was $751 in 1984 and this figure has remained approximately constant (with adjustments for inflation) over the entire period from 1976 to 1986.

To many observers of PACs this low figure for the average contribution signifies that PACs, particularly corporate PACs, do not have a significant impact on political outcomes. The argument is that if an average campaign costs more than $250,000 and the average contribution is well under $1,000, then it is highly unlikely that corporate PAC contributions can have an effect. (See Sorauf, 1988 for this argument.) Other writers argue that PAC contributions can make a difference. If all contributions from a given industry are lumped together then the amount of money given is highly significant. For example, the 120 corporations with PACs in the chemical industry contributed $4.4 million to candidates for Congress in the 1980 elections (Schlozman and Tierney, 1986).

The empirical data concerning the impact of PAC contributions on congressmen's voting behavior is mixed. In the 1970s there appeared to be little correlation between congressional voting patterns and PAC contributions once the effects of ideology and political party were controlled. In the 1980s, however, there has been a significant increase in the impact of PAC contributions on voting outcomes and this effect is heightened if only one side of the issue is organized (Godwin, 1988).

A critical question, however, is whether congresspersons' votes are the correct variable of interest. A firm lobbies for many things other than congressional votes. For example, a defense contractor rarely lobbies for a vote for a defense appropriations bill on the floor of the House. The contractor is far more interested in how the appropriations bill is drawn up in committee. A missile contractor knows that a defense appropriations bill is going to pass, what the contractor is interested in is the price for the missile or coffee maker that the contractor supplies. This price is often negotiated with the Armed Services Committee and is written into the legislation. A rationally acting firm would provide funds to members of the Armed Services Committee if they agree to a sufficiently high price for the product being provided. The firm would not contribute to all 435 members of the House or even to those members who voted for the final appropriations bill.

There has been substantial empirical work in political science concerning what goals PACs pursue and the criteria they use to determine which candidates they will support and how much support will be given. One of the better studies of this process is that of David Gopoian (1984). Gopoian examines the giving strategies of oil, defense, and auto corporations and of labor unions. He found that oil PACs gave on the basis of ideology and key votes such as the Alaskan Lands bill; defense contractors gave on the basis of committee assignments and home district, auto PACs gave on the basis of home district and key votes, and labor unions determined contributions on the basis of key votes and political party.

When one looks at the objectives of the different organizations and firms these patterns make sense. (Of course it is relatively easy to make sense of data once you know what they look like.) Oil companies follow similar patterns to one another and the issues in which they are interested affect the entire industry. Windfall profits, drilling in wilderness areas, off-shore drilling, and decontrol are issues that affect all major oil companies. In addition, most of the issues involving big oil fall along a single ideological dimension. Conservatives tend to favor decontrol, off-shore drilling, and opening the wilderness areas; they tend to oppose windfall profits taxes. Therefore supporting conservative candidates, particularly challengers of liberals or conservatives who are challenged by liberals, makes sense in terms of policy objectives.

Labor PACs are in a similar situation to oil PACs. Key votes and ideological questions dominate their policy desires. And, the Democratic party has always been the party that favored organized labor. Their giving reflects these factors. When we get to defense PACs, for reasons discussed above, committee assignments are most important because the policy desires of defense contractors are satisfied or denied in subcommittee decisions, not on floor votes. Ideology is rarely important in these decisions and benefits are divisible among firms rather than indivisible as is the case in labor or oil policy.

Auto PACs and defense PACs give to incumbents representing their districts. For example, congressmen from Michigan are likely to get a disproportionate share of auto PAC money and congressmen from districts where defense contractors have factories get a larger than expected share of defense PAC dollars. For reasons discussed below this giving pattern fits the particularistic benefits that auto and defense PACs seek. Firms in a district expect their congressman to represent their interests in the logrolling and bargaining that typifies legislation in Congress. Auto PACs expect congressmen who have automobile plants in their district to press for benefits that will assist the industry or, better yet, the individual firm. Particularistic benefits sought include government contracts while inclusive benefits would include quotas on Japanese automobiles and domestic content legislation.

Can we develop a model that makes sense of these diverse objectives and contribution patterns? We probably cannot develop a single model that will work for all firms, but we can suggest two underlying public choice models that explain a significant portion of PAC contribution stategies. The first of these deals with the traditional collective goods and free rider problem while the second considers the diseconomies of scale that appear to occur early in PAC giving for particularistic policy rewards.

Before showing how the two models apply to rent-seeking decisions we must first distinguish between rent-seeking for non-divisible policy rewards and divisible rewards. A non-divisible reward or policy would be something like a diary price support that affects all dairy producers similarly. A divisible reward would be one such as a defense contract for a weapons system that is given to one or a few firms. We would expect that in the first case there is a free rider problem with its associated underinvestment in collective goods.[2] In the second case there is no free rider problem and firms would be expected to invest closer to the optimum amount.

Another reason that policy producers may be unable to capture a greater portion of the rents they produce is provided by Gordon Tullock (1980). In his article, "Efficient Rent-seeking," Tullock argues that it is quite possible for diseconomies of scale to occur relatively early in the lobbying process. He suggests that the traditional U-shaped production curve will not occur in rent-seeking and there will not be a point where average and marginal costs will be equal. Tullock argues that in lobbying it is not possible to assume that, in the long run, supply curves are flat or that the owners of a resource can sell that resource at its marginal cost. This is the case because lobbying investments are too specialized, and, in many cases, they are "matters of very particular and detailed good will to a specific organization" (Tullock, 1980: 98).

In addition to the problem of not being able to transfer lobbying assets investment in the lobbying process also presents interesting problems concerning the early introduction of diseconomies of scale. Take as an example of lobbying a betting game where n numer of lobbyists are pursuing m number of policies where $n > m$.[3] If we assume that each policy is worth $100 dollars and the probability of achieving a policy is a linear function of the amount the lobbying firm spends on lobbying activities, the question the lobbying firm faces is how much to spend.

In his original article, Tullock showed that in a two-firm game, assuming perfect play and complete knowledge by both firms, the amount the firms should invest is only $25, not the intuitive answer that each should purchase $50 worth of tickets. If there were 10 firms, the optimal bet would be only $9. Thus, in a linear game, the greater the number of players the smaller the investment per firm. And, in all games there is an "underinvestment" in lobbying or rent-seeking; there is an uninvested "bet" that the policy maker cannot capture.

The above lobbying lottery is too simple in that in a real lobbying situation there is likely to be a bias in favor of some betters. That is to say that some firms are likely to have a higher probable payoff for their contributions than are other firms. A firm may be advantaged or disadvantaged by factors such as the number of workers in their firm that can vote for the congressman in the next election, the support or opposition of the congressman's constituency to the proposed policy, and the proximity of the congressman's own preferences to the policy desired. When John Tower (R-Texas) was chairman of the Senate Armed Services Committee, Texas Instruments, the largest private employer in Texas, was presumably in a better position to receive a higher price for its missiles than were other firms which also built missiles but were not located in Texas. If the firms are acting rationally this bias in the expected value of an investment in rent-seeking will certainly affect their investment in the lobbying lottery.

The presence of bias for or against contributors helps us make sense of firms' decisions to give disproportionately to congressmen representing the firm's congressional district. If I am the head of a firm's political action committee and I must decide to whom the firm will contribute, I would be extremely foolish not to consider the bias involved in the weighting of contributions. In addition, Fenno (1978) showed that legislators supply numerous particularistic or divisible goods to their constituents. My contribution helps to ensure that my firm receives its share of these benefits.

Bias in the lobbying process also reduces the amount invested in rent-seeking. If we return to our earlier game of two lobbyists betting for a $100 policy reward but instead of each ticket carrying equal weight, firm A's tickets are each worth $2 while firm B's are worth only $1, the highest expected payoff for both firms comes when each bets $22 rather than the $25 when there was no bias. In this situation, assuming there are no inefficiencies resulting from the bias itself, the bias in favor of one firm over the other reduces the total amount of rent-seeking investment and society is better off.[4]

The above reasoning and examples suggest that rent-seeking is not quite as wasteful as it might be if it were not biased in favor of the contributions from firms that encourage policies popular in a representative's districts. This bias discourages bets from firms that do not have interests that are relatively congruent with the electoral interests of the politician. Thus the existing bias probably promotes effective representation and reduces wasteful rent-seeking activities.[5]

The point of the above arguments is that although the winning of the lottery (policy outcome) may be worth many thousands (or millions) of dollars, the optimal investment may still be quite small, especially if the number of lobbyists is quite large and there is bias in the system. This small investment partially explains why the number of corporate lobbies has grown quite rapidly while the average contribution to a congressman has not increased substantially.

In summary, the seemingly irrational behavior of giving relatively small contributions and concentrating them among individuals who already appear ready to vote for the bills that a corporation desires makes sense not only from the organizational maintenance perspective that political scientists have suggested, it also appears to maximize the likelihood that the firm's policy goals will be achieved. In addition, the free rider problem for non-divisible policy goals, diseconomies of scale at a very early level, and the existence of bias among legislators all lead to lower than expected investments in rent-seeking.

Notes

1. Obviously this is not the beginning of contributions by corporations to political campaigns. Corporations and their senior officers have given money in significant amounts to congresspersons since the beginning of the republic.
2. Firms may attempt to overcome the free rider problem by instructing their trade associations to make the contributions on behalf of the entire industry.
3. This is, I believe, a quite reasonable example. If one were to study the 1986 tax ''reform'' legislation it is quite obvious that there was a bidding war among competing lobbyists for the retention of tax loopholes. For a journalistic account of this bidding game see Birnbaum and Murray (1987).
4. This statement accepts Tullock's (1989) definition of rent-seeking is a behavior with a negative social impact.
5. This conclusion is similar to that reaches by Denzau and Munger (1986) who argued that a legislator who is maximizing his reelection chances will be more likely to receive contributions from interest groups whose interests are congruent with those of the legislator's constituency.

Rent-seeking for pure public goods*

ELIAKIM KATZ
Department of Economics, York University, Toronto, Ontario, Canada M3J 1P3

SHMUEL NITZAN
JACOB ROSENBERG
Department of Economics, Bar Ilan University, Ramat Gan, Israel

Abstract. In this paper we present a formal analysis of rent-seeking for public goods by two or more groups with different numbers of individuals. We begin by considering equally wealthy groups under risk neutrality, a case which constitutes our basic model. Several surprising and interesting results emerge from the analysis of this basic case. The problem is then extended to deal with (a) groups with different wealth levels, and (b) risk aversion. This last extension brings about a further crop of interesting and useful results.

1. Introduction

In the last several years the theory of rent-seeking has taken off in leaps and bounds. The early papers by Tullock (1967), Krueger (1974) and Posner (1975) have all been extended in various directions to encompass a variety of alternative scenarios and improvements upon the original theory. Thus, for example, rent-seeking has been examined in the contexts of uncertainty,[1] free entry into the rent-seeking market[2] rent avoidance as compared to rent-seeking,[3] trade,[4] the effect of rent-seeking on depletable resource policies,[5] and so on.

And yet, despite this abundance of contributions, there appears to be a major gap in the literature in that issues relating to rent-seeking for *public goods* has not, to the best of our knowledge, been directly dealt with.[6] This omission is especially surprising in view of the large number of cases when a rent sought is likely to be a public good: For example, struggles for government support between different industries clearly involve the provision of a type of public good since the rent won or lost will, in general, affect several firms (the industry) rather than an individual unit. Such struggles are very common in economic life and may involve requests for subsidies, attempts to persuade the government to impose taxes on competing industries, lobbying for relaxed regulation, etc. Another common example of a rent being a public good occurs when different locations are considered by the government for employment –

* We should like to thank Eliezer Prisman of Bar Ilan University and Barry Smith of York University for their very helpful comments and suggestions on an earlier draft of this paper.

providing government institutions and government owned corporations, or when a city council has to decide on the location of a public good such as a park. In such cases the rent to be won (the government corporation or the park being located in a given area) affects many people and has at least some attributes of public goods.

Hence, it is clear that a large percentage of rents involve public good considerations. In this paper we provide an analysis of this important issue by considering rent-seeking for a *pure* public good such as a pollution clean-up.

2. The basic model

Consider a situation in which a local authority has sufficient funds to remove pollution from one of two distinct locations under its jurisdiction.[7] The individuals living in each of these two locations would obviously like this removal of pollution done in their own area. It is assumed that whilst the clean-up costs the local authority R dollars, each individual in each neighborhood values the removal of pollution at αR dollars where $0 < \alpha < 1$.

Of course, the pollution clean-up constitutes a pure (local) public good since it has both attributes of a public good within the winning locations: First, in the location that wins, there is non-rivalness in consumption, i.e., the enjoyment (consumption) of the pollution-free atmosphere by additional individuals does not increase the cost of the clean-up or impose costs upon other individuals; second, there is non-excludability in consumption, i.e., all individuals living in the winning location can enjoy (consume) the pollution-free atmosphere and no-one in that neighborhood can be excluded.

To get down to a specific model of the problem, let the two locations be denoted by 1 and 2 respectively and assume that the numbers of individuals in locations 1 and 2 are n and m respectively. Expenditure on rent-seeking activity by individual i in location 1 will be denoted by X_i and rent-seeking activity by individual j in location 2 will be denoted by Y_j.

Now, how should rent-seeking by different individuals in different locations be mapped into the probabilities of different locations winning the pollution clean-up? To answer this we have to define the way in which the rent-seeking done by individuals, and in turn, by the whole group to which they belong, affects these probabilities. The most natural definition is an adaptation of Tullock's (1980) formulation for individual rent-seeking, which has gained wide acceptance in the literature. Thus, it is assumed that the probability that location 1 wins the pollution clean-up is given by the ratio of the total amount of money spent on rent-seeking by individuals in location 1 to the total amount of money spent on rent-seeking by all individuals in both 1 and 2.[8] Denoting the probability that location 1 will win the clean-up by Π_1, we have

$$\Pi_1 = (\sum_{i=1}^{n} X_i) / (\sum_{i=1}^{n} X_i + \sum_{j=1}^{m} Y_j) \tag{1}$$

and the probability that location 2 wins is therefore given by

$$\Pi_2 = 1 - \Pi_1 = (\sum_{j=1}^{m} Y_j) / (\sum_{i=1}^{n} X_i + \sum_{j=1}^{m} Y_j) \tag{2}$$

Hence, the expected value of the benefit to individual i (in location 1) from his rent-seeking is given by V_i, where

$$V_i = \Pi_1(\alpha R - X_i) + \Pi_2(-X_i) \tag{3}$$

Assuming risk neutrality, the problem each individual in location 1 faces is

$$\underset{X_i}{\text{Max}}\ V_i = \Pi_1\ \alpha R - X_i \tag{4}$$

Let the solution be characterized by a Cournot-Nash equilibrium. Hence, assuming a regular, interior solution, the first order condition for an optimum is

$$\frac{\partial V_i}{\partial X_i} = \frac{\partial \Pi_1}{\partial X_i}\alpha R - 1 = 0 \tag{5}$$

which yields

$$(\sum_{j=1}^{m} Y_j) / (\sum_{i=1}^{n} X_i + \sum_{j=1}^{m} Y_j)^2 = 1/(\alpha R) \tag{6}$$

Now, since α is the same for all X's and Y's, $X_i = X_j = X$ and $Y_i = Y_j = Y$ for all i and j. Condition (6) can be thus rewritten as

$$(mY) / (nX + mY)^2 = 1/(\alpha R) \tag{7}$$

Furthermore, since the problem of individuals in location 2 is symmetric with that of individuals in location 1, we have that the maximization of his rent-seeking benefit by each individual in location 2, yields, in aggregate, that

$$(nX) / (mY + nX)^2 = 1/(\alpha R) \tag{8}$$

Equations (7) and (8), therefore, characterize the Cournot-Nash equilibrium rent-seeking. Adding (7) and (8) yields

$$(nX + mY) / (nX + mY)^2 = 2/\alpha R \tag{9}$$

so that the sum total rent-seeking done by location 1 and location 2 is

$$nX + mY = \alpha R/2 \tag{10}$$

Thus the total rent-seeking done for the pure public good of is equal to only *one half of the benefit to one individual.*

In addition to this result indicating the relative smallness of the amount of rent-seeking done, several other results follow from (10). First, neither the sum total of individuals in both locations, (m + n), nor the distribution of individuals amongst these locations, affect the total amount of rent-seeking done. This appears somewhat surprising, since intuition would suggest that larger groups would suffer more from a free rider problem, a factor which would reduce their rent-seeking activity. Thus, we would have expected that rent-seeking would be a declining function of n and m. In addition, it would have seemed likely that the size of n relative to m would also affect total rent-seeking. Given equation (10), however, neither of these *a priori* suppositions seems to be borne out.

The second aspect of the result given in (10) is that it is very reminiscent of Tullock's result for two *individuals* struggling for a single, *private* good: In his paper (Tullock, 1980) the result is obtained that given a single, private good prize L, and two individuals rent-seeking for this prize, the total rent-seeking done is L/2. Our result states that if a *public* good fought over by two groups generates an *individual* benefit equal to L (in our case denoted by αR), then the sum total of rent-seeking done by (all individuals in) both groups will also equal L/2. It is as though each group, despite the free rider problem within it, acts as one individual competing with other individuals for the (single) prize.

The economic explanation for both these results seems to be that the free rider problem within each group just counterbalances the size of the total prize for the group. The reason for this is that whilst the free rider problem increases with group size, the aggregate prize also increases with group size. In other words, whilst each new individual reduces the rent-seeking done by others, the rent-seeking done by that individual is equal to the aggregate reduction of rent-seeking done by the others.

The fact that the problem reduces into one which is equivalent to rent-seeking by individuals, also explains why neither the total number of individuals in all groups nor their distribution between groups affect total rent-seeking. After all, if the n individuals in location 1 can be represented as one individual and the m individuals in location 2 can similarly be represented as one individual, neither the value n/m nor the value of m + n will matter.

Now, given the equivalence of each group (no matter its size) to one individual, one would expect, following Tullock's results, that the number of *groups* would affect the amount of rent-seeking done. This is because when t individuals compete with each other for a single prize L, Tullock's results imply that the rent-seeking done will be $(t - 1)L/t$. Thus, in the case discussed here, one would expect total rent-seeking with t groups to be $\alpha R(t - 1)/t$. It can be shown that this is, in fact, the case.

Let us now look at some further aspects of the problem. Specifically, consider the individual rent-seeking done in *each location*, the *total* rent-seeking done by each location, and the implications of this for the relative probabilities of winning the rent for location 1 and 2. Dividing (7) by (8) we obtain

$$mY = nX \tag{11}$$

so that the total rent-seeking done by each location is the same, yielding an equilibrium probability of ½ for a win by either location. This, of course, is essentially an affirmation of the logic discussed above, in which each group is seen to act as one of two identical individuals so that in equilibrium they are each equally likely to win. (Of course, it is easy to show that when there are t rent-seeking groups, the equilibrium probability of a win for any one group is 1/t.) Hence, any *a priori* intuition that the location with the larger number of individuals is less likely to win the rent as a result of its greater vulnerability to the free rider problem, is found to be incorrect in the case of a pure public good such as pollution clean-up.

However, at the individual level, it is clear that unless $n = m$, nX being equal to mY implies that $X \neq Y$. To find the amount of rent-seeking done by an individual residing in location 1 and 2, respectively, substitute nX for mY in (7). This yields

$$(nX) / (4n^2X^2) = (1/\alpha R) \tag{12a}$$

so that

$$X = \alpha R/4n \text{ and, by symmetry, } Y = \alpha R/4m \tag{12b}$$

Thus, individual members of each location *do* spend different amounts on rent-seeking, depending on the population of their location. Members of the less populous location spend *more* per capita than members of the larger group. Hence, at the individual level, the free rider effect is seen clearly, since as n or m increase, X or Y decrease respectively. Of course, since the effective aggregate prize for each location (namely $n\alpha R$ and $m\alpha R$ respectively) increases at the same rate as the free rider effect, the increased prize effect and the free rider effect will, as explained above, tend to cancel each other out in the aggregate.

3. Locations with different amount of wealth

In the last section it was assumed that α is equal for both location 1 and 2. And yet, even if the two locations are equally polluted (which is not implausible seeing that it costs R dollars to clean either one of them) one location may be wealthier than another. Given that a pollution clean-up is likely to be a normal good, the value of α for the richer neighborhood will exceed the value for α for the poorer neighborhood. Given this setting, what is the nature of the rent-seeking equilibrium?

Let 1 be the richer location, 2 be the poorer location, and α_1, α_2 be the values of α for locations 1 and 2 respectively where $\alpha_1 > \alpha_2$. Using (7) this yields that the first order condition for a maximum for individuals living in location 1 is

$$(mY) / (nX + mY)^2 = (1/\alpha_1 R) \tag{13}$$

and, by symmetry, the first order condition for a maximum for individuals living in location 2 is

$$(nX) / (nX + mY)^2 = (1/\alpha_2 R) \tag{14}$$

Adding (13) and (14) we have that

$$(nX + mY)^{-1} = (1/R)\,(1/\alpha_1 + 1/\alpha_2) \tag{15}$$

so that

$$(nX + mY) = R\tilde{\alpha}/2 \tag{15a}$$

where $\tilde{\alpha}$ is the harmonic mean of α_1 and α_2. Similarly, it is easy to show that if there are t locations involved in this rent-seeking activity, the total rent-seeking done is $\tilde{\alpha}R(t - 1)/t$, where $\tilde{\alpha}$ is, similarly, the harmonic mean of the α's.

Introducing areas with different wealth levels does not, therefore, make a major impact on the results in that once again aggregate rent-seeking is independent of the total number of individuals in all locations and of their distribution between locations. This is not all that surprising given the results of the previous section; each group acts as one individual, so that total rent-seeking is the same as total individual rent-seeking by two (or t) individuals where each individual has a different amount of wealth.

Consider, however, the effect of α_1 being different from α_2 on the aggregate rent-seeking done by *each* location. Intuition tells us that the richer area will spend more on lobbying, and thus be more likely to win the pollution clean-up. Dividing (13) and (14) yields that in equilibrium,

$$\alpha_1 \, mY = \alpha_2 \, nX \tag{16}$$

so that, since $\alpha_2 < \alpha_1$,

$$mY = (\alpha_2/\alpha_1)nX < nX \tag{17}$$

which confirms our intuition. Thus, regardless of the size of the population living in either location, the likely winner of the clean-up is the wealthier location. This would seem to confirm a general casual impression that wealthier areas within a municipality get more in the way of pure public goods (such as a pollution clean-up) than poorer neighborhoods.

Finally, note that from (16) it follows that the ratio of rent-seeking by different locations is a constant, regardless of the number of individuals living in each location. This is a generalization of the results in Section 2.

4. Risk aversion

An issue which is likely to be of some importance is the effect of risk aversion both on the amount of rent-seeking done in total and on the amount of rent-seeking done by each location. Risk aversion may, of course, play a major role in this problem, since when rent-seeking for a pure public good such as a pollution clean-up each individual is taking the risk that the other location will win.

Let us begin this case by assuming that each individual in each of the two locations, has the same initial wealth I. Furthermore, let us assume that each individual attempts to maximize the expected value of a von Neumann-Morgenstern utility function U (·) defined upon final wealth, W, where $U' > 0$, $U'' < 0$ (i.e., where the utility function displays risk aversion). U (·) is assumed to be identical for all individuals in all locations. Each individual in group 1 will thus choose X_i to

$$\max_{X_i} Z_i = \Pi_1 \, U(I + \alpha R - X_i) + (1 - \Pi_1) \, U(I - X_i) \tag{18}$$

and an analogous problem will be solved to determine Y_j by each individual in location 2.

In order to analyse the equilibrium rent in this case and relate it to the extent of individual risk aversion, we shall initially assume that the utility function of all individuals in each location is characterized by the same, *fixed*, coefficient of absolute risk aversion. Hence, each individual's utility, U, is given by

$$U = -\exp(-AW)) \tag{19}$$

where exp(•) is the exponential function, W is the individual's wealth and A is the individual's (constant) coefficient of absolute risk aversion.

Therefore, Z_i can be rewritten as

$$Z_i = -\Pi_1 \left[\exp(-A(I - \alpha R - X_i))\right] - (1 - \Pi_1)\left[\exp(-A(I - X_i))\right] \tag{20}$$

Hence, Z_i can be expressed as

$$\begin{aligned} Z_i &= kH_i \text{ where } k = \exp(-AI) > 0 \text{ and} \\ H_i &= -\exp(AX_i)\,[\Pi_1 \exp(-A\alpha R) + (1 - \Pi_1)] \end{aligned} \tag{21}$$

Hence, the value of X_i which maximizes H_i will maximize Z_i. Assuming a regular interior solution, the first order condition for a maximum is

$$\begin{aligned} \frac{\partial H_i}{\partial X_i} &= -A\exp(AX_i)[\Pi_1 \exp(A\alpha R) + (1 - \Pi_1)] - \exp(AX_i) \times \\ &\times \left[\frac{\partial \Pi_1}{\partial X_i}((\exp(A\alpha R) - 1)\right] = 0 \end{aligned} \tag{22}$$

divide (22) by $-\exp(AX_i)(\exp(-A\alpha R) - 1)$ and note that a similar condition is derived for the equilibrium of individuals in the second location. Sum the two optimizing conditions and use Tullock's probability function (1), to obtain

$$\left(\frac{\partial \Pi^1}{\partial X_i} + \frac{\partial \Pi^2}{\partial Y_j}\right) = (nX + mY)^{-1} = \frac{A(\exp(\alpha RA) + 1)}{\exp(\alpha RA) - 1} \tag{23}$$

The first result to emerge from (23) confirms the earlier result (equations (10) and (11)) that as the coefficient of absolute risk aversion tends to zero $nX = mY = \alpha R/4$. To see this, note that as A tends to zero the expression on the right hand side of (23) tends to zero over zero. This permits the use of L'Hôpital's Rule, yielding that as A tends to zero $(nX + mY)$ tends to $\alpha R/2$, so that $nX = mY = \alpha R/4$.

Intuition suggests that as the coefficient of absolute risk aversion decreases, rent-seeking will decline. This can be confirmed by considering the gradient of total rent-seeking, $T = nX + mY$, as a function of A. If this is negative for all $A > 0$, the above intuition is correct and rent-seeking is indeed a declining function of A in this region.

Differentiating T with respect to A and using (23) yields that:

$$\text{sign}(\partial T/\partial A) = \text{sign}(1 + 2A\alpha R\exp(A\alpha R) - \exp(2A\alpha R)) \tag{24}$$

It can be shown that for all $A > 0$ the right hand side of (24) is negative. Hence, concommitant with a large(er) coefficient of absolute risk aversion is a small(er) amount of rent-seeking. Furthermore, since by symmetry $nX = mY$, the rent-seeking done by each location and by each individual is similarly affected.

Next, consider the relative amounts rent-seeking done by each location when the coefficients of absolute risk aversion differ between the two locations. Let A_1 and A_2 be the coefficients of absolute risk aversion in location 1 and 2 respectively, such that $A_1 > A_2$. To analyze this case, the optimizing condition for individual i in location 1 requires replacing A by A_1 in (22). The optimizing condition for individual j in location 2 requires replacing A by A_2, X_i by Y_j and Π_1 by Π_2. Denote nX by T_1 and mY by T_2.

To determine which location does more rent-seeking in this case, the sign of the difference between nX and mY is determined: subtract the optimizing condition of j (in location 2) from the optimizing condition of i (in location 1). Since both conditions have the same, positive, denominator (T^2), only the numerator of their difference need be considered. This is

$$(T_1^2 - T_2^2) + A_1T_1 - A_2T_2 = G(A_1) - G(A_2) \tag{25}$$

where $G(A) = A(\exp(-A\alpha R) - 1)^{-1}$.

The sign of $(\partial G/\partial A)$ equals the sign of $-A\alpha R\exp(A\alpha R)$, which is negative. Therefore, if $A_1 > A_2$, the right hand side of (25) must be negative. For $A_1 > A_2$ this can only occur if $T_1 < T_2$.

Finally, consider the case of a variable coefficient of absolute risk aversion. The economics literature frequently postulates that absolute risk aversion declines with wealth. This may have profound effects on the results of this paper: It transpires that when the coefficient of absolute risk aversion is a decreasing function of wealth, $nX > mY$ if $n > m$.

This may be proved by contradiction: Let $n > m$ and assume that this implies $nX \leq mY$. Then $X < (n/m)X \leq Y$. But, given decreasing absolute risk aversion, $X < Y$ implies that A_1 will be smaller than A_2. However, from above, $nX > mY$ if $A_1 < A_2$. Hence, $n > m$ is *incompatible* with $nX \leq mY$.

Decreasing absolute risk aversion thus implies that if $n > m$, then nX will exceed mY.

Therefore, the *larger group will spend more on rent-seeking than the smaller group*, thereby increasing its probability of winning the rent. This conclusion should be contrasted with the generally accepted notion that larger groups, being diffuse, will spend less on public goods.

In some cases, therefore, the free rider effect of a large group may be modified or even reversed by the attitudes of individuals towards risk. This consideration may well have far reaching implications for other areas in the theory of public choice.

5. Conclusion

In this paper we use an adaptation of Tullock's formulation of rent-seeking and the probability of winning a rent to provide an analysis of rent-seeking for a pure public good by two or more groups consisting of different numbers of individuals. Several new and interesting results emerge. First, when individuals in all groups are identical, all groups spend the same amount on rent-seeking for the public good regardless of the number of individuals in each group. Second, the amount of rent-seeking done by two groups is equal to only one half of the benefit of the public good to a single individual. This result is extended to t groups and the total rent-seeking in that case is found to be equal to $(t - 1)/t$ times the benefit of the public good to a single individual. Third, a wealthier group will tend to spend more on rent-seeking for a public good and thus raise its chances of obtaining this good. Fourth, risk aversion reduces both aggregate and individual rent-seeking. Fifth, decreasing absolute risk aversion implies (when all individuals are identical) that a large group spends more on rent-seeking for a pure public good than a small group.

Other than these formal results, the message of this paper is that rent-seeking for a public good within a Cournot-Nash framework will tend to be very small in relation to both the aggregate value of the public good and to its cost. If an authority wishes to encourage rent-seeking for a pure public good, it may have to bring about matching behavior or develop a framework for forced contributions.

Notes

1. See Hillman and Katz (1984).
2. See Corcoran and Karels (1985), Appelbaum and Katz (1986).

3. See Appelbaum and Katz (1987).
4. See, for example, Bhagwati and Srinivasan (1982).
5. See Katz and Smith (1987).
6. See, however, Long and Vousden (1987), who do touch upon this issue, albeit in a totally different way.
7. In order to be able to focus on the rent-seeking activity for the pollution clean-up, we ignore here the source of the funds with which the clean-up will be financed. In doing this, we ignore the rent-avoiding activity done by those from whom the funds were collected in the first place. This can be justified either (1) by assuming that the money is already available and sunk rent-seeking does not matter now, or, (2) by assuming that the funds are collected all over the economy/municipality such that the many diffuse individuals which might oppose it, find the sum too small to bother with it. (On the effect of including rent avoidance in measuring waste see Appelbaum and Katz, 1986.)
8. Notice that the issue of the voting power of the two locations does not have any effect in this model. This is not because we think that the interaction of voting and rent-seeking is unimportant. Indeed, it is a topic of major importance which might alter many rent-seeking results. The reason for its omission here is that we feel that in an exploratory paper on a relatively new topic (rent-seeking and public goods) the basic issue of rent-seeking ought to be focused on. On a formal level, the fact that voting is not incorporated into the model may be justified by assuming that the two populations of the locations affected by the potential pollution clean-up are small relation to the population of the municipality as a whole. Hence, the voting power of the populations contesting the pollution clean-up can be effectively ignored. Alternatively, even if $n + m$ is large, then providing n and m are close, the maximum loss in votes from these two locations will be a small $n - m$ even if voters in the two locations vote solely on the basis of the pollution clean-up decision. Finally, given our finding of the smallness of the amount of rent-seeking done by the public for a public good, does suggest that voting rather than rent-seeking may be a more likely motivation for governments (central and local) to offer public goods.

Rent-seeking, rent-defending, and rent dissipation*

CHRIS PAUL
AL WILHITE
Department of Economics, University of Alabama in Huntsville, Huntsville, AL 35899

1. Introduction

A substantial portion of the research on rent-seeking addresses the issue of rent dissipation. This line of inquiry is drawn directly from Tullock's (1967) stated intent to identify the total social costs of monopoly. Early studies, which were concerned with the measurement of Tullock costs, simply assumed dissipation would be complete (see Becker, 1968; Kruger, 1974; Posner, 1975; and others). However, Posner (1975) and Fisher (1985) observed the question of dissipation can be answered only for overtly specified game structures.

Tullock (1980) and Rogerson (1982) introduced a rent-seeking game which yielded incomplete dissipation under a wide variety of cost conditions. In spite of Tullock's suggestion that the incomplete-dissipation result might be the more interesting, several authors responded by introducing variations of the game in attempts to obtain a general complete dissipation result (see Corcoran, 1984; Corcoran and Karels, 1985; Higgins, Shugart and Tollison, 1985; and Tullock's responses, 1984, 1985 and 1987).

Along similar lines, several authors have considered necessary conditions for excess dissipation. Lott (1987) argues that non-transferable licenses yield this result. However, Gahvavi (1989) has questioned his conclusion. Additionally, Tollison (1989) has posited the occurrence of excess dissipation when the rent seeker can generate extra-game revenue as a result of insider information generated by participation in the rent-seeking game.

Wenders (1987) addressed the social costs of rent-seeking to obtain a monopoly and concludes, "recurring or sunk, even the largest specification of the Harberger and Tullock costs of regulation may fall *far* short of the actual welfare costs. This is because the analysis concentrates on the rent-*seeking* Tullock costs and largely ignores the parallel rent-*defending* Tullock costs" (Wenders, 1987: 456, emphasis in original). Wenders is concerned with situations in which

* The authors wish to thank Randall Holcomb, Philip Porter, William Shugart and Gordon Tullock for helpful comments on an earlier version. Naturally remaining errors are the responsibility of the authors.

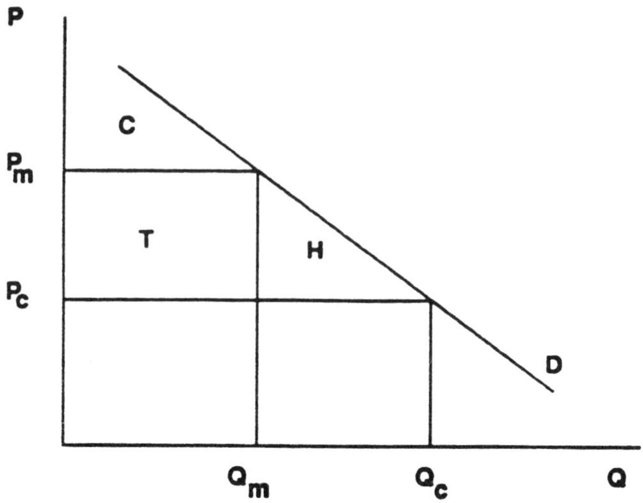

Figure 1. Competitive prices and outputs are subscripted c, and m is used for monopolies

welfare losses are larger than the sum of the Tullock rectangle (T) and Harberger triangle (H), shown in Figure 1. While he raises some interesting issues, his analysis is often incomplete and his conclusions misleading. This paper more fully develops some of these topics and presents conclusions that have not appeared in the literature.

2. Rent-seeking and rent-defending

Wenders initially consider instances of binary regulation in which the regulated price is set at either the monopoly, P_m, or the competitive, P_c, level. Adopting Posner's (1975) assumption that competition for monopoly power will transform all expected rents into welfare losses, Wenders (1987: 457) observes, " there are parallel activities and resource expenditures by those who stand to lose from restrictive regulations as they seek to defend against rent-seeking activities." Then, invoking a prisoners' dilemma mechanism, Wenders concludes dissipation is up to twice the level suggested by the traditional Tullock and Harberger costs. He writes (Wenders, 1987: 458), "why would the sum of rent-seeking and rent-defending expenditures exceed T + H? The answer lies in an analysis similar to the prisoner's dilemma theory (Magee, 1984: 47–48). Like the prisoners who both confess, neither buyers nor sellers may refrain from spending the maximum amount they each have at stake." However, Wenders fails to demonstrate how the analysis of domestic regulation presented in his paper is "similar" to the model constructed by Magee. A review of the Magee-

Young model shows it applies to a substantially different situation than the case forwarded by Wenders.[1]

The Magee-Young (1984) model is specifically formulated to represent possible outcomes of trade policy with resulting assumptions that are inappropriately applied to the incorporation of rent-defending expenditures in the regulation of a domestic industry. In the Magee-Young model all participants are owners of labor or capital and while they can choose to stay out of rent-seeking activities, they cannot escape the ramifications of its outcome; short of migrating to another country. However, in the regulation of a single domestic industry, which is Wenders' example, both resource suppliers and consumers are able to exit the rent-seeking competition and its consequences. Producers can transfer capital to competing uses and consumers can find substitutes or move to a distinct regulatory environment. Thus, seekers' ability to enter and exit the rent-seeking game nullifies the prisoner's dilemma argument posited by Wenders (see Higgins, Shughart and Tollison, 1985; and Corcoran and Karels, 1985).

Furthermore, the results cited by Wenders are interpretively different than those cited by Magee. In a single market, behavior which results in both consumers and producers being worse off requires excess dissipation of available rents or consumer surplus. However, the Magee-Young model is one of factor payments. Factor owners attempt to increase the payment per unit of resource by imposing either a subsidy on an exported good or a tariff on an imported good. Under this two factor construct both groups can be worse off, but this does not imply excess dissipation. Under the Magee-Young model, dissipation is limited to 100 percent of available rents.

2.1. The Posner model

While Wenders inappropriately applies the Magee and Young prisoners' dilemma mechanism, rent defending has some interesting welfare implications, but specific implications depend on the type of rent-seeking model employed. Wenders adopts Posner's (1975: 76) construct by assuming rent seekers bid the expected value of the transfer. In Posner's example, if ten risk-neutral firms have an equal chance of capturing a monopoly with a present value of \$1,000,000, each will spend \$100,000. The rent is completely dissipated. Assuming consumers are organized and capable of raising and spending an amount equal to producers,[2] the probability of monopoly pricing falls from 1 to .5, and the expected value of the Posner game for any one of ten producers becomes 0.1 (.5(\$1,000,000)) = \$50,000. The total expenditure of the organized consumer group is 0.5(\$1,000,000) = \$500,000. Expenditures by rent-seeking producers and rent-defending expenditures by consumers sum to the rent value of \$1,000,000. Dissipation is still complete but not excessive.[3]

To assess rent-seeking costs, the rent at stake must be identified and the model formalizing these activities selected. In the monopoly pricing case, rent-defending consumers behave similarly to rent-seeking producers because the stake for which they are competing is the same: the property right to set prices. If the right is won by producers, prices increase to the monopoly level. If consumers win, prices remain at the competitive level. Consumers may well be interested in defending the competitive price, but the return to their rent-defending expenditures is affected by their probability of winning. Wenders reached an excess-dissipation conclusion by failing to explicitly formulate the impact of consumer participation on the expected value of the contested rents.[4]

2.2. *The Tullock-Rogerson model*

As previously noted, a strategic game model of rent-seeking behavior has been posited by Tullock (1980) and Rogerson (1982). They envision seekers who influence the probability of winning by investing increasing sums in the game. With two identical risk-neutral players, A and B, the expected value of rent-seeking for player A is,

$$E(a) = \frac{a}{a + b}(T) - a, \tag{1}$$

where "a" represents A's rent-seeking expenditures, "b" is B's expenditures and T is the rent at stake. Player A maximizes the expected value, and the optimal bid, a*, depends on B's effort and the rent at stake.

$$a^* = -b + \sqrt{bT} \tag{2}$$

B faces an identical choice and generates a similar reaction function. As each player responds in turn, a Cournot-Nash-type equilibrium is attained where each player bids 1/4 of the rent value. With n players the equilibrium investment by A is $a_{eq} = [(n-1)/n^2]\ T$.[5]

Now, suppose consumers, or any party currently holding the property right to this pricing power, engage in rent-defending activities. This formulation merely changes equation (1) for the rent defender by transforming the rent to a negative value. Specifically, the defender is now competing to maintain the rent. Make player A the rent seeker and player B the rent defender. While A's expected value calculation remains unchanged B's expected value becomes,

$$E(b) = \frac{a}{a + b}(-T) - b. \tag{3}$$

B's expected value is negative. If B's rent defense is unsuccessful, all previously controlled rent is lost, while a successful defense reduces the defender's wealth by the amount of the expenditure. Solving for B's optimal response function, b*, yields,

$$b^* = -a + \sqrt{aT}\,; \tag{4}$$

a* is given by equation (2).

If both players maximize their expected value the equilibrium solutions is unchanged from the simple two-player game with $a_{eq} = (1/4)T$ and $b_{eq} = (1/4)T$. The total rent-seeking investment remains (1/2)T.[6] The equilibrium level of rent dissipation is unchanged.[7]

3. Nested games

Wenders speculatively offers another reason for excess dissipation based on successive rounds of rent-seeking. His example involves consumer groups united against a utility rate increase. Once a new rate is established invididuals compete among themselves to deflect the increase to others. As he eloquently states (1987: 457), "Lions and wolves cooperate in the hunt but scrap over the kill."

3.1. The Posner model

The issue of multi-stage or nested games is an interesting one, but again specific results depend on the model applied. Consider a two-stage Posner expected value game in which ten rent seekers pursuing a \$1,000,000 prize are divided into two groups consisting of five cooperative consumers and five united producers. The first stage of the game determines which group controls the property right; the second stage assigns the rent value to a member of the winning coalition. Players are allowed to rebid at the beginning of each stage.[8] Stage one is worth 1/2[(1/5) \$1,000,000] = \$100,000 for each of ten players, and stage two is valued at 1/5(\$1,000,000) = \$200,000 for the remaining five players. It appears twice the rent value is spend in the game. But, how useful is this result?

The total expected value for each player is a negative \$100,000.[9] Thus, a rational wealth-maximizing player would not voluntarily participate in this game. Furthermore, if one player decides to withdraw from the coalition and compete alone, the single player's potential winnings is (1/3)(\$1,000,000). The value to the competing teams is adjusted accordingly. The independent player is now breaking even, with an expected value equal to zero, while players in the coalitions continue to incur losses.[10] More importantly, all players benefit by leaving their collusive arrangements and competing independently.

This result arises because of the nature of the Posner model. The chance of an individual acquiring a monopoly right is determined by the number of bids. The award is randomly assigned. Rent-seeking expenditures are then assumed to be equal to the wager making a risk-neutral person indifferent between playing and not playing. The distinctive characteristic of the Posner model is *the level of expenditures a person commits does not affect their probability of attaining the rent.*[11] Hence, joining a coalition is not a maximizing decision, because collusive rent-seeking is costly but has no impact on the individual's probability of winning.

3.2. The Tullock-Rogerson model

The Tullock-Rogerson model allows additional expenditures to affect the probability of winning, hence collusive agreements can be wealth enhancing.[12] For example, suppose there are four identical risk-neutral seekers, A, B, C, and D. Playing independently, each will invest $[(n-1)/n_2]T = (3/16)T$ leading to aggregate dissipation of 3/4(T). Consider the formation of two coalitions, consisting of players A and B versus players C and D, who collude for the first game and compete if the first round is successful. Coalitions face two crucial decisions: (i) how to distribute first-round rent-seeking costs among members?; and (ii) how to divide profits of a win?. If these distribution questions can be settled by a pregame agreement, coalition rent-seeking is no different than games with individual players, excepting contracting and enforcement costs.

There are many instances in which this is not the case. Suppose the benefits of a successful first round of rent-seeking benefits a particular individual regardless of participation in the game. This non-excludability problem will make it difficult for the coalition to garner sufficient resources for the first round. Many, perhaps all, the beneficiaries will prefer to be free riders. Many consumer issues are of this type, and the free-rider problem may severly restrict coalition formation.

If, however, the profits of the first round of rent-seeking can be restricted to the coalition members, the question of allocating costs can be solved. Each member's willingness to pay is determined by their proportional benefit, and costs can be allocated through some traditional bargaining mechanism. However, profit distribution is still an issue. This problem of distributing first-round profits initiates a second round of rent-seeking.

Suppose two coalitions, α consisting of players A and B and β consisting of players C and D, are placed in this situation. As discussed above, the value of the second game is (1/4)T and so the expected value of this game for coalition α is:

$$E(\alpha) = \frac{\alpha}{\alpha + \beta}(.25T) - \alpha, \tag{5}$$

where $\alpha = a + b$ and $\beta = c + d$. That is, α and β represent the combined investment of coalitions consisting of players A and B and players C and D, respectively. The optimal strategy for a coalition is identical to the reaction function of the two-person game given in equation (2), but the rent at stake in the first round is only (1/4)T. The cost of competing in the first round is p(1/4) (1/4 T) = p(1/16)T for player A, and (1 – p) (1/4) (1/4)T = (1 – p) (1/16)T for B, where p and (1 – p) represent A and B's share of the first round expenditures. With the β coalition facing the same decision aggregate rent-seeking costs of the initial round equals (1/8)T. Second-round expenditures remain (1/2)T. With coalitions aggregate rent-seeking costs have *declined* to (1/8)T + (1/2)T = (5/8)T from the sum of (3/4)T in the single-stage rent-seeking game. However, this reduction does not account for coalition formation and enforcement costs.

Aggregate rent-seeking expenditures are lower in the coalition rent-seeking structure, but this result is interesting only if these collusive agreements pay. In other words, each player must be better off, or at least indifferent to the formation of coalitions. This is verified by calculating the expected value of each game for a single player. With four identical players participating in a single-stage game each player has a 1/4 chance to win T – (3/16)T and 3/4 chance to win – (3/16)T. The expected value for player A in the first game is, $E(a)_1$ = (1/4) (T – (3/16)T) + (3/4) (O – (3/16)T) = (1/16)T. In a two-stage game, returns differ depending on the result of the first game, A's expected value becomes, $E(a)_2$ = (1/4) (T – (9/32)T) + (1/4) (O – (9/32)T) + (1/2) (O – (1/32)T) = (3/32)T. The nested game yields a (1/32)T gain over the single-stage game for each of these identical players.

If rent can be restricted to identifiable participants with players facing identical choices, there is an incentive for coalitions to form and nested, two-stage, games to arise. More importantly, the creation of nested games can *reduce* aggregate welfare losses attributable to rent seeking. However, the reduction in rent-seeking expenditures will to some extent be negated by the costs associated with coalition formation and enforcement. While potential coalitions may be stifled by free-rider problems and organizational costs, rent-seeking coalitions do exist; Wenders gives examples. And, it is intuitively pleasing to find a model suggesting their existence is wealth maximizing.

4. Summary and conclusions

In the preceding analyses of rent-defending, the Posner model yielded welfare losses in excess of the combined areas of the Tullock rectangle and the Harberger triangle in only one instance. Furthermore, this particular circumstance necessitated voluntary participation in a game with a negative expected value.[13] For the Tullock-Rogerson model, the explicit addition of rent-defenders had no impact on aggregate dissipation.

In addition, this paper introduced two implications of nested games on rent-seeking theory. First, in cases where the Posner expected value bid applies, coalitions will not form. Second, coalitions arise as a result of wealth-maximizing behavior in the Tullock-Rogerson strategic game, but contrary to previous authors this model suggests, rent-seeking expenditures fall. However, the organizational and enforcement costs of coalitions reduces the welfare gain and under some circumstances may negate the gains to coalition formation.

There seem to be two common pitfalls in the analysis of welfare costs of rent-seeking activities. First, the rent at stake is often incorrectly identified. Second, the method used to allocate rents, or the structure of the game, is not explicitly formulated. Viewing rent as claims to property rights should help alleviate the problems arising from the former, and continuing research into alternative rent-seeking models represents a movement toward the latter.[14]

Notes

1. The Magee paper cited by Wenders is a secondary source which contains neither a model nor description of the prisoners' dilemma application. However, a citation within that paper, Magee and Young (1982), contains their model and analysis. The version supplied to us by Magee and cited herein is a later version dated 1984.
2. There are several problems with this assumption including the public good characteristic of non-exclusion (see Ursprung, 1989), and the differing organizational costs of consumers and producers.
3. An alternative approach would be to include a consumer coalition as an additional competitor to the ten firms. Under this formulation the expected value for all competitors is (1/11) T and the perfect dissipation result is unchanged. Curiously, if Wenders logic is accepted, i.e., all players bid the rent at stake, total dissipation would equal $11,000,000, but even Wenders does not suggest this magnitude of shortsightedness. Why are consumers less able to adjust for competition than producers? Why do producers adjust their bid to one type of competitor but not another?
4. Using a general equilibrium model, DeLorme and Snow (forthcoming) reach a similar conclusion. Specifically, they show rent-avoidance typically reduces social waste and dissipation is less than the Harberger-Tullock trapazoid as long as rent-seeking and/or rent-defending is not subsidized by the government.
5. More recently Tullock (1987) argues social losses will be higher than the efficient rent-seeking model suggests, but those issues lie outside this discussion.

6. In cases where the rent-defender is a coalition of consumers defending the competitive price, they have an additional stake equal to the value of the Harberger triangle. Their expected value is similar to equation (3) with $T' = T + H$ substituted for T.
7. The foregoing analysis implicitly assumes producers' and consumers' expenditures are equally efficient in changing the probability of capturing the monopoly rent. However, if there is a bias, say in favor of existing property rights, the magnitude of dissipation would be reduced further.
8. Some interesting arrangements are omitted. For example, coalitions could negotiate contracts defining the proportion of expenditures provided by each member of the team and rules governing the distribution of the rent if their coalition wins. Or, the rules of the game could limit all bids to the beginning (no bids in stage two). In these cases Posner's original conclusion holds.
9. Wenders claims his essay points to excess dissipation for costs that are either recurring or sunk. Not only do bidders play negative sum games, but they do so repeatedly.
10. Total dissipation also differs. If the independent player wins the first round, there is full dissipation as no expenditure occurs in round two. Double dissipation occurs only when the first round is won by a coalition.
11. Naturally, a person could play twice, but each bid is an independent decision.
12. There are several interesting ways to formulate two-stage games and many yield unique results. Unfortunately, a comprehensive review would lead us far astray. The case explored here was selected because it seemed to be in line with Wenders' thinking.
13. Tollison's (1989) ''superdissipation'' appears to be a viable theory for excess dissipation.
14. For example, Hillman and Riley (1989) and Paul and Wilhite (1990) present several rent-seeking structures applicable to a variety of situations.

COLLECTIVE RENT DISSIPATION*

Shmuel Nitzan

The theory of rent seeking was initiated by Tullock (1967, 1980), followed by Krueger (1974) and Posner (1975) and, more recently, extended in various directions by Allard (1988); Appelbaum and Katz (1986*a*, *b*, *c*); Gradstein and Nitzan (1989); Hillman and Katz (1984, 1987), Hillman and Samet (1987); Hillman and Riley (1989); Katz *et al.* (1990); Long and Vousden (1987); Ursprung (1990) and Varian (1989). The purpose of this paper is to extend this theory by introducing the possibility of collective-group rent seeking with voluntary individual decisions regarding their extent of participation in the collective rent-seeking efforts.

The type of rent seeking I consider has the following characteristics: (i) a number of groups of individuals compete for a single rent, (ii) the rent is indivisibly allocated in the sense that a single group wins the entire rent, (iii) the rent exhibits private good characteristics and therefore it can be divided among the members of the winning group and (iv) group members decide voluntarily on the extent of their rent-seeking efforts. Common examples of this type of rent seeking are the struggles for the budgets at the discretion of politicians by various interest groups (parties, localities, industries, etc.).

In imperfectly discriminating[1] *collective* rent-seeking contests substantial dissipation of the contested rents is usually not the case. The reduced dissipation rate is obtained in small or large-number contests, with risk neutral or risk averse potential rent seekers and with homogeneous or heterogeneous agents. Reduced dissipation in our extended group rent-seeking model is basically due to two factors: the free-riding incentives within the groups competing on the rent and the deterrent group-size effects – since rents are subtractable, an increase in group size reduces the individual members' shares in the rent. Both of these factors depend on the rules applied by the groups to distribute rents among their members. In this study I focus on mixed rules that distribute part of the rent on an egalitarian basis and the rest on the basis of the principle 'to each according to his relative effort'. The main results provide the relationship between the proportion of the rent dissipated in equilibrium and the following parameters: the number of competing groups, the size of the groups, the distribution rule applied by the groups and the characteristics of the individual players: their endowed wealth and attitudes towards risk. It is shown that, in general, the extent of rent dissipation is positively related to the

* I am very much indebted to John Hey, Arye L. Hillman, Nava Kahana and two anonymous referees for their useful comments and suggestions. I also wish to express my appreciation to Moshe Glazman for his help in data processing.

[1] In an imperfectly discriminating contest an ultimate winner is not designated, but rather, each contending group is assigned a probability of winning the rent. For an analysis of perfectly discriminating individual rent-seeking contests see Hillman and Samet (1987) and Hillman and Riley (1989).

number of contesting groups, and is inversely related to the degree of 'egalitarianism' in distributing the rents and to the degree of individual risk aversion. The effect of the total number of potential rent seekers is ambiguous. Thus, in contrast to earlier studies that deal with individual rent seeking, in our setting an increase in population may reduce the extent of rent dissipation. Finally, wealth variability may also set a bound on the possible outlays on the rent seeking activities.

The basic elements of the extended model of collective rent seeking are introduced in Section I. In Section II, I study the special case where all groups distribute rents according to relative effort. The diametrically opposed case where all groups distribute rents equally among their members is analysed in Section III. In Section IV I consider the general case of groups applying the same mixed distribution rule. Individuals are initially assumed to be risk neutral and identical in their endowed wealth. The only asymmetry allowed in the basic extended model is the variability in group-size. The analysis of the extended collective rent-seeking model with heterogeneous players (agents are endowed with different wealth levels and are characterised by different attitudes towards risk) is presented in Section V. The empirical applicability of the extended approach is discussed and illustrated in Section VI. Section VII contains a brief summary of the main conclusions.

I. VOLUNTARY PARTICIPATION IN COLLECTIVE RENT SEEKING

Consider n interest groups confronting the opportunity of winning a prespecified prize S. This prize is referred to as a contestable rent. We focus on Tullock's (1980) special case of an imperfectly discriminating contest where the political process cannot discriminate among the competing groups to designate a winner with certainty, but rather the outcome of the contest is the assignment to each group of a probability that it wins the contest. Specifically, group i's probability of success in the contest, π_i, is given by the value of its outlay X_i, $X_i = \sum_{k=1}^{n(i)} X_{ki}$, relative to the total outlays X, $X = \sum_{j=1}^{n} X_j$, made by all groups engaged in the rent seeking activities. That is,

$$\pi_i(X_1, \dots, X_n) = \frac{X_i}{\sum_{j=1}^{n} X_j} = \frac{X_i}{X}. \qquad (1)$$

Let us denote by $n(i)$ the number of individuals in group i. The size of the groups is given exogenously and is held constant, i.e. inter-group mobility is not allowed in our model. Initially individuals are assumed to be identical risk neutrals endowed with wealth y. The expected payoff of a representative individual in group i, individual ki, from being engaged in the rent seeking activity is assumed to be given by:

$$V_{ki} = \pi_i\{y + Sf_{ki}[X_{1i}, \dots, X_{ki}, \dots, X_{n(i)i}] - X_{ki}\} + (1 - \pi_i)(y - X_{ki}), \qquad (2)$$

where $f_{ki}[X_{1i}, \dots, X_{ki}, \dots, X_{n(i)i}]$ is the rule applied by group i for distributing the prize S.[2] Usually the proportion of the rent S obtained by individual ki depends on the outlays by him and by the other members of his group who try to help his group win the rent. Here I focus on the following family of distribution rules:

$$f^a_{ki}\,[X_{1i},\ldots,X_{n(i)i}] = \frac{(1-a)\,X_{ki}}{X_i} + \frac{a}{n(i)}. \tag{3}$$

That is, a proportion a of the rent is distributed on egalitarian grounds and the rest is distributed according to relative effort. When $a = 1$, each member in group i receives $1/n(i)$ of the rent regardless of his personal effort. When $a = 0$ the member ki receives X_{ki}/X_i of the rent. Substituting (1) and (3) into (2) we get:

$$V_{ki} = \frac{X_i}{X}\left\{y + S\left[(1-a)\frac{X_{ki}}{X_i} + \frac{a}{n(i)}\right] - X_{ki}\right\} + \frac{(X-X_i)}{X}(y-K_{ki}). \tag{4}$$

In the current extended N-person rent-seeking game, $N = \sum_{i=1}^{n} n(i)$, the payoff function of player ki, $k = 1,\ldots,n(i)$, $i+1,\ldots,n$, is given by (4) and his strategy set is the interval $[0, y]$. In the pure strategy Nash equilibrium of this game, holding the other players' outlays fixed, each individual ki solves the problem:

$$\underset{X_{ki}}{\text{Max}}\; V_{ki} = S(1-a)\frac{X_{ki}}{X} + \frac{SaX_i}{n(i)X} + y - X_{ki} \tag{5}$$

s.t. $0 \leqslant X_{ki} \leqslant y$,

where $\quad X_i = \sum_{k=1}^{n(i)} X_{ki} \quad \text{and} \quad X = \sum_{i=1}^{n} X_i.$

The first order condition for a global interior maximum of expected utility for individual ki is:[3]

$$\frac{\partial V_{ki}}{\partial X_{ki}} = S(1-a)\left(\frac{X-X_{ki}}{X^2}\right) + \frac{Sa}{n(i)}\left(\frac{X-X_i}{X^2}\right) - 1 = 0. \tag{6}$$

In a symmetric Nash equilibrium, identical players who are members of the same group receive the same payoff, that is, $X_{ki} = x_i$ for every i, $i = 1,\ldots,n$ and

[2] In my model the divisible rent S is wholly distributed among the members of the winning group that applies the sharing rule f^a_{ki}. Recently, Long and Vousden (1987) studied a different setting assuming that the individual contestants compete for a share of a divisible rent rather than the whole of an indivisible rent. In their variant of the individual rent-seeking game the rent being contested is fixed or variable, but each player's share is uncertain.

[3] V_{ki} is concave in X_{ki} since

$$\frac{\partial^2 V_{ki}}{\partial X^2_{ki}} = S(1-a)\frac{-2(X-X_{ki})}{X^3} + Sa\frac{-(X-X_i)}{X^3} < 0.$$

$k, k = 1, \ldots, n(i)$. Hence, by (6), an interior equilibrium is characterised by the following set of conditions: for $i = 1, \ldots, n$,

$$\frac{S(1-a)(X-x_i)}{X^2} + \frac{Sa(X-X_i)}{n(i)\,X^2} = 1, \tag{7}$$

and

$$0 \leqslant x_i \leqslant y.^4 \tag{8}$$

II. EQUILIBRIUM UNDER DISTRIBUTION OF RENTS ACCORDING TO RELATIVE EFFORT

For $a = 0$, (7) reduces to:

$$S(X-x_i) = X^2. \tag{9}$$

Consequently, in equilibrium under rent distribution according to relative effort, for every i and j, $x_i = x_j = x$. This implies that (9) can be rewritten as

$$S[(N-1)x] = XNx, \tag{10}$$

so total rent seeking outlays by all groups are given by:

$$X = S(N-1)/N. \tag{11}$$

This amount is equal to the total outlays obtained in Tullock's original game with N players individually competing on the rent S. In addition to the equivalence between the rent-seeking outlays in the two different games, several interesting observations can be made. First, the distribution of individuals among the groups and the number of groups do not affect the total amount of rent seeking done. However, the total rent-seeking outlay of a group is proportional to its size. This means that, regardless of group size, the distribution rule generates positive incentives to participate in the collective group that just counterbalance the negative size effect due to free riding and to the inverse relationship between the individual share in the rent and the size of the group. A larger group is therefore more likely to win the rent. A larger group size is advantageous for the group since in equilibrium its chances of winning are equal to $n(i)/N$. However, the expected net benefit of every individual, regardless of his group affiliation, is equal to $S/N-[S(N-1)]/N^2 = S/N^2$.[5]

Note that an implicit assumption of the model is that relative effort can be costlessly observed and rewarded. If this simplifying assumption is modified

[4] Henceforth the analysis focuses on interior equilibria. Equilibria with a corner solution for the members of some groups are possible. By the Kuhn-Tucker conditions, if $x_i = y$ for individuals in group i, then $x_j = y$ for individuals in any group j such that $n(j) \leqslant n(i)$. If $x_i = 0$ for individuals in groups i, then $x_j = 0$ for individuals in group j such that $n(j) \geqslant n(i)$. Note, however, that $X_{ki} = 0$ for every k and i cannot be a Nash equilibrium since in such a situation every individual is induced to spend some positive yet very small amount on rent seeking which will guarantee that his group wins the rent and that his payoff is increased.

[5] Note that the individual budget constraints (8) imply that equilibrium exists provided that total rent seeking done is smaller than total available resources, i.e. $S[(N-1)/N] \leqslant Ny$. If $S > N^2y/(N-1)$, in equilibrium each individual's expenditure on rent seeking is equal to y. In such a case entry of agents (an increase in N) may secure the existence of an interior equilibrium. However, a decrease in N cannot generate equilibrium in the reduced game. Note that for $a = 0$ there exist no equilibria with $x_i = 0$ for any group i.

and such costs are explicitly introduced into the model, total rent-seeking outlays would tend to decline and, of course, be more complexly related to the parameters of the rent-seeking environment.

III. EQUILIBRIUM UNDER EQUAL DISTRIBUTION OF RENTS

For $a = 1$, (7) reduces to:

$$\frac{X-X_i}{X^2} = \frac{n(i)}{S}. \qquad (12)$$

By summing over $i = 1, \ldots, n$, we get:

$$\frac{X(n-1)}{X^2} = \frac{N}{S}, \qquad (13)$$

or,

$$X+\frac{(n-1)}{N}S. \qquad (14)$$

Total rent seeking done is increasing with the number of competing interest groups and is decreasing with the total population. Under the egalitarian distribution rule the proportion of the rent dissipated will be considerably smaller than 1 when n is sufficiently small and N is sufficiently large. In marked contrast to the previous case, such reduced dissipation rate is due to the predominant free-riding incentives within the groups. By (12), for every i,j,

$$\frac{X-X_i}{X-X_j} = \frac{n(i)}{n(j)}. \qquad (15)$$

When $n(i) > n(j)$, (15) implies that the larger group i spends less on the rent-seeking activities relative to the smaller group j. The most likely winner of the rent is the group with the smallest number of members. In other words, under equal distribution of rents among group members, the negative free-riding effect dominates the positive group-size effect and, therefore, $n(i) > n(j) \Rightarrow X_i < X_j$. When $n = 2$, by (15), we obtain that:

$$\frac{X_1}{X_2} = \frac{n(2)}{n(1)}. \qquad (16)$$

That is, the relative expenditure on rent seeking done by the two groups is fixed and equal to the inverse of their relative size. This yields an equilibrium probability of $n(2)/[n(1)+n(2)]$ for a win by group 1 and a probability of $n(1)/[n(1)+n(2)]$ for a win by group 2. Total rent seeking done in group 1 is equal to $Sn(2)/N^2$ and rent seeking in group 2 is equal to $Sn(1)/N^2$. The expected benefit to an individual member in group 1 is equal to

$$\frac{Sn(2)}{Nn(1)}\left(\frac{N-1}{N}\right).$$

When $n(1) > n(2)$ his benefit is smaller than

$$\frac{Sn(1)}{Nn(2)}\left(\frac{N-1}{N}\right)$$

the expected benefit of a member in group 2. For the individual member, an increase in the size of his group is disadvantageous. As already noted, the extent of rent dissipation in equilibrium is invariant to the distribution of agents over the groups.[6]

IV. EQUILIBRIUM UNDER MIXED DISTRIBUTION RULES

For mixed distribution rules, $0 < a < 1$. In this general case, by summing (7) over $i = 1, \ldots, n$, and rearranging terms we get:

$$\frac{(1-a)\,N+na-1}{X} = \frac{N}{S}, \tag{17}$$

which implies that,

$$X = SD \quad \text{where} \quad D = \frac{(1-a)\,N+na-1}{N}. \tag{18}$$

Total outlays on rent seeking in society depend on the number of competing groups n, on the total population N, and on the degree of egalitarianism in distributing rents, a. For any N and a, the degree of rent dissipation D is positively related to the number of competing groups n, i.e. $\partial D/\partial n = a/N > 0$. If society is partitioned into more groups total rent seeking is increased. For any given N and n, the degree of rent dissipation D is inversely related to a, i.e. $\partial D/\partial a = n/N - 1 < 0$. An increase in the proportion of the rent distributed equally among group members reduces the total outlays on rent seeking. D ranges between $(n-1)/N$ and $(N-1)/N$, the two extreme values obtained respectively for $a = 1$ and $a = 0$. A society applying a more egalitarian rule for distributing rents within groups is less wasteful. One can think of a number of policies inducing groups to shift to such a waste-reducing intra-group allocation rule. A clear example is the imposition of certain constraints on the possible uses of the prespecified prize by the winning group. In particular, earmarking the prize for the provision of a non-excludable yet divisible public good implies that the intra-group sharing rule is, in fact, egalitarian. Finally, the effect of total population on the degree of rent dissipation is ambiguous. Specifically:

$$\frac{\partial D}{\partial N} \gtreqless 0 \quad \text{if} \quad a \lesseqgtr \frac{1}{n}. \tag{19}$$

The total population effect on rent dissipation is neutralised when $a = 1/n$. When $a > 1/n$ ($a < 1/n$) an increase in total population reduces (increases) the proportion of rent dissipation.

In a mixed society different groups may use different distribution rules. In such societies interior equilibria need not exist. For example, in the two-groups case where $n(1) > 1$ and $n(2) > 1$, if the two groups apply the two polar sharing

[6] The collective rent-seeking game with the egalitarian distribution rule possesses an interior equilibrium provided that $S(n-1)/N \leqslant Ny$, or $S \leqslant N^2y/(n-1)$. Existence of an interior equilibrium under the egalitarian distribution rule is consistent with a wider range of prespecified rents relative to the previous case of distribution according to relative effort (see footnote 5).

rules equilibrium never exists. If the two groups apply mixed distribution rules, the problem of non-existence of equilibrium arises when the variability between the two sharing rules is sufficiently large or when the two groups are equally populous and sufficiently large (see Nitzan (1990) for a detailed analysis of the problem of nonexistence of equilibrium in two-group rent-seeking contests).

V. HETEROGENEOUS AGENTS

A. *Different Endowments of Wealth*

Suppose that the risk neutral individuals are endowed with wealth levels that differ across groups. That is, $y_{ki} = y_i$ for each individual in group i, and with no loss of generality, $y_1 \leqslant y_2 \leqslant \ldots \leqslant y_n$. If all groups use the same rule to distribute rents among their members, any change in the egalitarian wealth distribution considered so far leaves the aggregate equilibrium outlays on rent seeking SD unchanged (see (18)), provided that an interior Nash equilibrium still exists. By (8), the equilibrium outlays on rent seeking of an individual member in group i cannot exceed y_i. A necessary condition for the existence of equilibrium is that the total resources expended are lower than total wealth or, $S \leqslant N\bar{y}/D$, where $\bar{y}$ is the average wealth. Since, in general, some of the individual budget constraints are not satisfied even when the above total budget constraint is satisfied, more stringent necessary conditions can be derived. For example, when $a = 0$, I have shown that $x_i = x_j = x = S(N-1)/N^2$. The individual budget constraint requires that for each i, $S \leqslant N^2 y_i/(N-1)$, which implies that the less stringent condition, $S \leqslant N^2\bar{y}/(N-1)$ is satisfied.[7]

B. *Different Attitudes Towards Risk*

In general, individuals differ both in terms of endowed wealth and in terms of their attitudes towards risk. Suppose that individuals differ only across groups and denote by U_i the continuous, differentiable, strictly increasing and concave utility of a representative individual in group i. An interior Nash equilibrium is now characterised by the following conditions: For $i = 1, \ldots, n$,

$$\frac{(X-X_i)}{X^2} U_i\left\{y + S\left[(1-a)\frac{X_{ki}}{X_i} + \frac{a}{n(i)}\right] - X_{ki}\right\}$$
$$+\frac{X_i}{X} U_i'\left\{y + S\left[(1-a)\frac{X_i X_{ki}}{X_i^2} + \frac{a}{n(i)}\right] - X_{ki}\right\}$$
$$-\frac{(X-X_i)}{X} U_i(y - X_{ki}) - \frac{X-X_i}{X} U_i'(y - X_{ki}) = 0, \qquad (20)$$

and

$$0 \leqslant x_i \leqslant y. \qquad (21)$$

Since U_i is continuous, strictly increasing and concave, it can be shown that there exist $S_1, S_2, \ldots, S_n, S_i < S$, such that the equilibrium of the extended rent-seeking game with risk neutral individuals, each facing his respective S_i is

[7] If an interior equilibrium does not exist, an increase in N may secure it. With heterogeneous players, a decrease in n and in N, may also give rise to the existence of an interior equilibrium.

precisely the same as the equilibrium of the game when players are risk averse and the rent is equal to S. Put differently, $S_1, \ldots, S_n$ are the risk neutrality equivalent rents which make each individual choose the same outlay on rent seeking in equilibrium under risk neutrality as in equilibrium under risk aversion. S_i depends, in particular, on U_i, y_i and $n(i)$.[8]

By summing (7) over $i = 1, \ldots, n$ and rearranging terms, we obtain that in this general case of heterogeneous resources and possibly different attitudes towards risk, total rent seeking outlays are given by:

$$X = S^h D, \tag{22}$$

where S^h is the harmonic mean of the players asymmetric valuations – the risk neutrality equivalents. Risk aversion thus reduces the extent of rent dissipation since $S^h < S$.[9]

Tullock (1980) studied the symmetric case where $N = n$ and individuals are risk neutral and, hence, $S_i = S$ for every i. In that case (22) reduces to:

$$X = S(N-1)/N. \tag{23}$$

Hillman and Riley (1989) analysed the case of asymmetric valuations where $N = n$. In that case (22) reduces to:

$$X = S^h(N-1)/N. \tag{24}$$

Katz *et al.* (1990) examined the case where $n = 2$, the rent is a pure public good and individuals in the two groups are risk neutral who have asymmetric valuations of the rent which are given by $\alpha_1 S$ and $\alpha_2 S$. If we set $\alpha_1 = 1/n(1)$ and $\alpha_2 = 1/n(2)$ we can interpret $\alpha_i S$ as the share of our (private good) rent obtained by the members of group i when they apply the polar egalitarian distribution rule. In such a case, by (22), the total rent seeking done is given by:

$$X = \frac{S}{1/\alpha_1 + 1/\alpha_2} = \frac{S}{n(1)+n(2)} = \frac{S}{N}.^{10} \tag{25}$$

Our analysis of the extended game of collective rent seeking leads to the conclusion that, in general, rent dissipation is likely to be much smaller than the contested rent since the number of competing groups n is usually considerably smaller than N, groups distribute rents among their members at least partly on egalitarian grounds, $a > 0$, and even an increase in the

[8] Note that even if all risk averse individuals share the same utility, the individual risk neutrality equivalent rents would in general differ across groups. Such heterogeneity in the risk neutrality equivalent rents is due to the heterogeneity in the size of the competing groups – the equilibrium strategy of player i is affected by his group size $n(i)$ (see (20)).

[9] When $N = n$ the individual risk neutrality equivalent rents are identical, $S_i = S^r$ for all $i, i = 1, \ldots, N$. Hence $X = S^r D = \delta DS$, where $\delta < 1$. If N is sufficiently large and S is sufficiently small, $\delta = (y - SR)/y$ where R is the coefficient of relative risk aversion. For a proof see the Appendix in Hillman and Katz (1984).

[10] The general case of multi-group rent seeking for a pure public good with asymmetric valuations is equivalent to the case of collective private rent seeking with equal sharing of the rent, provided that the asymmetric valuations in the former case are equal to the equal shares obtained by individuals in the latter case. The expenditure on rent seeking in such a case is given by (22) which reduces to (14), i.e. $X = [(n-1)/N]\,S$. Note that under multi-group rent seeking for a pure public good with symmetric valuations, Katz *et al.* (1990) obtain that $X = [(n-1)/n]\,S$, where S represents the common valuation of the public good. This result is therefore distinct from any of the results obtained in the current study.

population N may result in reduced rent-seeking efforts. In short, $D = [(1-a)N + na - 1]/N$ can be considerably smaller than 1. Risk aversion would only reduce this tendency to dissipate even further since for risk averse individuals S^h is smaller than S.

VI. RENT-SEEKING FOR BUDGETARY ALLOCATION: REVISED ESTIMATES

Recently, Katz and Rosenberg (1989) offered preliminary estimates for the proportion of government spending and the proportion of GNP wasted in rent seeking for the government's budgetary allocation in twenty countries. Their attempted estimation of rent seeking induced by the government budget is based on the following two assumptions:

(a) The annual value of the contestable rents is equal to the total change in the government's budget (S).

(b) The aggregate value of the resources wasted by the competitors attempting to win the rents is equal to S.

Assumption (b) is consistent with Tullock's (1980) model provided that the rents exhibit private good characteristics, the potential rent beneficiaries are individuals rather than groups of individuals, and the number of competitors is sufficiently large. Relying on the same data base used by Katz and Rosenberg (1989), I have revised their rent-seeking estimates by substituting assumption (b) with the following assumption:

(b′) Of the total change in the government's budget, one-third is private good transfers to individuals, one-third is private good transfers to groups and one-third finances the provision of public good rents. The extent of rent dissipation associated with the transfers to individuals is one. The rent-seeking outlays generated by transfers to interest groups are given by (18). The extent of rent dissipation in the public-good-rent-seeking games is given by $(n-1)/n$ (see footnote 10).

Since the number of competing groups, n, and the number of individual rent seekers, N, differ across countries, the extent of rent dissipation in different countries is no longer the same. I have used the number of political parties represented in the legislative bodies and the total number of legislators as rough proxies for n and N. The average rent seeking as a proportion of the budget, R_c, and as a proportion of GNP, W_c, for the sample of twenty countries is given in Table 1. These estimates are calculated assuming that the same intra-group sharing rule is used in all countries. The table contains the estimates corresponding to the two polar cases, $a = 1$ and $a = 0$. The average rent seeking as a percentage of the budget ranges from 0·9% to 7·13% when $a = 0$ and from 0·47% to 3·76% when $a = 1$. Rent-seeking outlays as a percentage of GNP range from 0·13% to 3·79% when $a = 0$ and from 0·07% to 2·08% when $a = 1$. The last two columns of Table 1 contain the rent-seeking estimates obtained by Katz and Rosenberg (1989). Comparison of these earlier estimates with the revised estimates clearly reveals that in my extended setting, which is based on assumptions (a) and (b′), the measures used as a first approximation

Table 1

Rent Seeking as a Proportion of Budget (R_c) and GNP (W_c)

Country	$R_c(a = 1)$	$R_c(a = 0)$	$W_c(a = 1)$	$W_c(a = 0)$	R_c^*	W_c†
France	0·0047	0·0090	0·0019	0·0036	0·0128	0·0051
FR Germany	0·0051	0·0097	0·0007	0·0014	0·0138	0·0020
Switzerland	0·0080	0·0147	0·0007	0·0013	0·0210	0·0019
Belgium	0·0080	0·0149	0·0028	0·0051	0·0213	0·0073
UK	0·0094	0·0178	0·0033	0·0062	0·0255	0·0089
Sweden	0·0096	0·0181	0·0034	0·0064	0·0259	0·0092
Canada	0·0096	0·0182	0·0022	0·0041	0·0261	0·0059
USA	0·0103	0·0196	0·0023	0·0043	0·0280	0·0062
Australia	0·0107	0·0200	0·0030	0·0057	0·0287	0·0081
Spain	0·0108	0·0204	0·0024	0·0046	0·0292	0·0066
Kenya	0·0146	0·0277	0·0036	0·0069	0·0397	0·0099
Greece	0·0199	0·0369	0·0047	0·0087	0·0528	0·0125
Chile†						
Korea	0·0225	0·0425	0·0037	0·0069	0·0608	0·0099
Italy	0·0270	0·0511	0·0098	0·0185	0·0731	0·0265
Israel	0·0292	0·0528	0·0208	0·0379	0·0758	0·0543
Turkey	0·0284	0·0538	0·0066	0·0124	0·0770	0·0178
Indonesia	0·0288	0·0549	0·0066	0·0126	0·0785	0·0180
Mexico	0·0384	0·0710	0·0066	0·0122	0·1016	0·0175
Egypt	0·0376	0·0713	0·0912	0·0363	0·1019	0·0519

* See Table 1 in Katz and Rosenberg (1989).
† See Table 2 in Katz and Rosenberg (1989).
† Given that in Chile political power is concentrated in the hands of a military dictator, I did not feel that the competitive rent-seeking models are applicable. This is the reason for the absence of estimates of R_c and W_c for this country.

for the waste generated by rent-seeking activities for government spending are considerably smaller than those based on assumptions (a) and (b). When $a = 1$, the estimates are reduced by an average factor of about 2·7, given the revised assumption (b′). When $a = 0$, the estimates are reduced by a factor of 1·4. Finally, note that the rankings of the countries by W_c or R_c according to my revised estimates are different from the rankings obtained by Katz and Rosenberg (1989). The differences in these rankings would be more clear cut had I allowed differential intra-country sharing rules.

VII. CONCLUSIONS

A. *The Extent of Rent Dissipation*

The evident empirical significance of earlier results on complete rent dissipation is that the social cost associated with a contestable rent can be inferred by observing the value of the rent itself.[11] The detailed and hard-to-come-by information on individual outlays made in the course of the rent-seeking process thus becomes unnecessary. In our collective rent-seeking setting the evaluation of the social cost associated with rent seeking requires not only observation of the value of the rent, but also of the number and size distribution

[11] See Hillman (1989), chapter 6 for the conditions under which the complete dissipation assumption is appropriate.

of the contesting groups and of the rule adopted by groups for allocating the rent among their members. This increases the complexities that arise in seeking to infer from the value of an observed rent the value of the resources used in quest of the rent.

In the general collective rent seeking game analysed in the preceding section, the total rent seeking done in equilibrium is equal to $S^h D$. This implies that the extent of rent dissipation is positively related to the number of groups participating in the contest with the exception of the polar case where rent is distributed wholly according to relative effort. Rent dissipation is inversely related to the proportion of the rent distributed equally among the group members. The total population effect, however, is ambiguous. In contrast to earlier studies dealing with a rent which is a private good, Tullock (1967, 1980); Higgins *et al.* (1985); Hillman and Riley (1989); or with a rent which is a public good, Katz *et al.* (1990); I obtain that an increase in the number of potential rent seekers N may reduce the extent of rent dissipation. This occurs when the proportion of the rent distributed according to the egalitarian principle is sufficiently close to one, in particular, when a is larger than $1/n$.

For given individual utilities and a given sharing rule, there exists a constant trade off (which can be positive or negative, depending on whether (na) is larger or smaller than unity) between the number of competing groups and the total number of potential rent seekers which keeps the extent of rent dissipation unaltered. This rate of substitution between N and n is equal to $dN/dn = -a(1-a-c)$, where c is the constant proportion of rent dissipation.

B. *Neutrality*

My analysis yields the following three neutrality results:[12]

(1) A change in the distribution of individuals across the n groups always leaves the extent of rent dissipation unchanged.

(2) In the polar case of distribution according to relative effort, a change in the number of competing groups n leaves the extent of rent dissipation unchanged.

(3) A change in the number of agents N leaves the extent of rent dissipation unchanged when $a = 1/n$.

C. *Does Group Size Matter?*

Are groups with a larger number of members more likely to win the contest? Is the expected payoff of an individual who is a member in a larger group higher than expected payoff of a member in a smaller group? Do members of the more populous groups spend more per capita than members of the less populous groups? For risk neutral players and the two polar distribution rules I obtain the following answers:

(1) In the polar case of rent sharing according to relative effort, the individual outlays on rent seeking and their expected payoffs are independent

[12] These results depend on the constant returns to scale assumption embodied in the probability function defined in (1) – each lobby's probability of winning a contest is equal to the value of its rent-seeking outlays relative to total outlays. Under decreasing (increasing) returns to scale the equilibrium rent-seeking outlays are smaller (larger) relative to the case of constant returns to scale for any given intra-group sharing rule.

of group size. More populous groups thus spend more on rent seeking and, accordingly, their chances of winning the rent are higher. This result is of interest because it casts doubt on the conventional wisdom that large groups almost always have a comparative disadvantage in mobilising political influence. In the standard view large groups are predicted to be successful only when rent seeking is produced as a byproduct of activities which are intended to perform some function in addition to rent seeking. On the 'by-product' theory of large pressure groups see Olson (1965).

(2) In the polar case of rent distribution according to the egalitarian principle, the more populous group spends less on rent seeking activities and, consequently, it is less likely to win the contest relative to smaller groups. The comparative advantage of a smaller group in mobilising political influence is due to its lesser vulnerability to the free-rider effects. The expected benefit of its individual members are higher than those of individuals who are members of more populous groups. For the individual member of a larger group size is disadvantageous.

D. *The Long Run Effects on Group Size and on the Intra-Group Sharing Rule*

(1) In the long run inter-group mobility might be possible. In such a case the number of groups and their size should also be endogenously determined in the rent-seeking game. For risk neutral players who control their entry/exit decisions to/from lobby groups, under the egalitarian sharing rule smaller groups offer their members higher expected benefits. This implies that in the long-run equilibrium the economy consists of single-individual groups. In contrast, in a proportional rewards economy the expected benefit to an individual is independent of group size. This implies that in the long run the short-run equilibria of Section II are consistent with any size distribution of the competing groups.

(2) In the long run, the intra-group sharing rule may be determined endogenously either by a central planner or by the individual rent seekers. In the former case, a central planner (a politician) who maximises the rent-seeking expenditures (see (18)) will adopt the polar rule distributing rents according to relative effort. A central planner who minimises the rent-seeking expenditures (see (18)) or one who maximises the aggregate utility of the players in my extended rent-seeking game ($\Sigma_i \Sigma_k V_{ki}$) will adopt the polar egalitarian sharing rule. If the individual players choose the sharing rule as well as their rent-seeking outlays (see (5)), and the intra-group sharing rules are determined by applying a special majority rule, it can be shown that the long-run intra-group equilibrium sharing rule is indeterminate: any pair (a, X) with $0 \leqslant a \leqslant 1$ and X as given by (18) is an equilibrium outcome of the long-run rent-seeking game.

Bar-Ilan University

Date of receipt of final typescript: April 1991.

A general analysis of rent-seeking games*

J. David Pérez-Castrillo
Thierry Verdier
DELTA Joint Research Unit (CNRS EHESS ENS), 48 Bd Jourdan, F-75014 Paris

Abstract. In this paper we reconsider the basic model of "efficient rent seeking." We stress the importance of the shape of the players' reaction curve in order to understand the impact of the technology of rent-seeking on the structure of the outcome of the game. We give a complete characterization of the pure strategy equilibria. Moreover, the possibility of preemption by a Stakelberg leader is discussed according to the nature of the technology of rent-seeking available to the agents.

1. Introduction

The literature on efficient rent-seeking has expanded quite rapidly since the seminal work of Tullock (1980) and there has been quite a lot of debate and controversies around the subject. Typically, the basic discussion raised two interrelated points of interest. First was the question of the structure of the equilibria that should emerge in the rent-seeking process and notably whether the equilibria should be symmetric or not. Secondly was the point that complete dissipation of rents in rent-seeking processes does not necessarily occur even when there was competition and free entry among the participants.

A certain number of works have tried to investigate both points. Corcoran (1984) and Corcoran-Karels (1985) extended Tullock's model to a long-run setting and tried to endogenize the number of participants in the rent-seeking process through free entry. It was then found that under some circumstances there was total dissipation of rents. Tullock (1984) and (1985) pointed out the difficulties with the long-run solution depending on whether the technology of rent-seeking was with decreasing or increasing returns of scale; and secondly they commented that in a-priori symmetric rent-seeking models, there was a strong presumption of the possibility of asymmetric behavior of the participants.

Hillman-Samet (1987a) have touched the problem through the use of mixed-

* We would like to thank an anonymous referee for his useful comments

strategies. In their model, rent-seeking is a contest in which the rent prize is allocated to the greatest outlay. They found that if no initial bet was imposed in order to participate in rent-seeking, then on average one would observe total dissipation of rents. Here again Tullock (1987) questioned the reasonability of mixed-strategies in the context of rent-seeking. As Hillman-Samet (1987b) rightly replied, the critic of Tullock was in fact more fundamental by raising the difficult question of the use and interpretation of mixed-strategies in game theory in general.

As it comes out from the preceding discussion, it seems that we are still "in the swamp" inspite of the many efforts undertaken. However, a potential way to "drier lands" is perhaps to go back to "the roots", reconsider more systematically the basic model of rent-seeking and analyse explicit its properties. In this respect, one point has not probably received the attention that it deserves. It is the rigorous determination of the optimal behavior of a participant given its strategic environment, namely the exact derivation of the "reaction" curve is important because one can reasonably think that much of what can be said about the rent-seeking game is certainly connected with the shape of this reaction curve.

The main purpose of this paper is to try to fill this gap by investigating systematically the properties of the reaction function of a particular participant to a rent-seeking game. As we will show, this will provide us with some insights why the case with decreasing returns of scale in the technology of rent-seeking is very different from the case with increasing returns. Moreover, with the explicit specification of this reaction curve in mind, we will analyse rigorously the nature of the equilibria of the rent-seeking game in the short run as well as in the long run. We will discuss the problem of symmetry or asymmetry of the equilibria and reconsider the basic problem of rent-seeking dissipation in this kind of game.

Our analysis also enables us to consider the importance of the technology of the shape of rent-seeking's shape in rent-seeking games where there is an asymmetry between the agents: one agent being in a dominant position over the others and acting as a Stackelberg leader. Here again, according to the type of technology used by the players, the properties of the reaction curve help us identify the conditions where the Stackelberg leader effectively preempts the other agents from entering actively in the race for political favors.

The plan of the paper is the following. In Section 2 we describe the basic model and derive explicitly the reaction curve of a particular agent given his strategic environment. Section 3 derives necessary conditions for an equilibrium to exist. Section 3 derives necessary conditions for an equilibrium to exist. Section 4 analyses the structure of the Nash equilibria of the rent-seeking game when the number of the potential participants is exogenously fixed. In Sectoin 5 we consider the case of the long-run competition with an endogenous number of agents. Section 6 considers the problem of preemption in a leader-follower framework. Finally Section 7 concludes.

2. The model

We consider a rent-seeking process involving N participants. For example, one may think of N firms in a particular industry and bidding for the attribution of some monopoly right. A particular agent is noted by the indice i ($i \in \{1,..,N\}$). The rents which are the object of the competition may be represented by a prize X. Each agent i makes a bet a_i in the rent-seeking process and following Tullock (1980) and Corcoran (1984), we suppose that his probability of winning this prize X is given:

$$\Pr(a_i, a_{-1}) = \frac{a_i^r}{a_i^r + \sum_{\substack{j=1 \\ j \neq i}}^{n}} \tag{1}$$

where $r \geq 0$ caracterizes the returns of scale of the technology of rent-seeking. When $r \leq 1$ the technology of rent-seeking may be considered with decreasing returns of scale while when $r > 1$ the technology is with increasing returns. For simplicity, as we will consider initially only the decision problem of a single agent i, we will omit the indice i and note $B = \sum_{\substack{j=1 \\ j \equiv i}}^{N} a_j^r$. Now the expected profit of our agent may be written as:

$$E\Pi(a) = \frac{a^r}{a^r + B} X - a \tag{2}$$

and his decision program is simply to maximize his expected profit $E\Pi(a)$, taking as given his "strategic environment B" and under the constraint the $a \geq 0$. The first order condition of this program yields for an interior solution:

$$a^{1-r}(a^r + B) = r\, B\, X \tag{3}$$

Let note $a = a(B)$ the "reaction curve" of our agent given an "outside" competition B from the other agents, that is the best response to B. We pose also the useful notation $A(B) = (a(B))^r$. Then we have the following proposition characterizing this best response function:

Proposition 1

1) If $r \leq 1$; then the best response $a(B)$ is strictly positive for all $B > 0$ and is determined by the first order condition (3).
2) If $r > 1$; two cases are possible:
   For $B \leq M(r,X)$, then $a(B)$ is strictly positive for $B > 0$ and determined by the first order condition (3), and $a(0) = 0$.
   For $B > M(r,X)$, then $a(B) = 0$.
   where $M(r,X) = \dfrac{(r-1)^{r1-} X^r}{r^r}$

Proof: See the Appendix 1.

The preceding proposition strikingly separates the case where the technology of rent-seeking is with decreasing or constant returns of scale ($r \leq 1$) from the case where the technology has some increasing returns of scale ($r > 1$). In the case of $r \leq 1$, the agent will always find in its interest to invest strictly positively in the rent-seeking process. On the contrary, in the case $r > 1$, he does invest in rent-seeking only if the "outside" competition (represented by the term B) is not too important. In fact, the outside competition has to be lower than a certain level $M(r,X)$ which is increasing in the amount of the rent. For levels of B higher than that amount, the agent simply does not participate actively in rent-seeking.

The next step is to analyse how does the agent react to changes of his strategic environment B. The following proposition characterizes the shape of the best response function $a(B)$.

Proposition 2

1) $a'(B) \leq 0$ (equivalently $A'(B) \geq 0$) if and only if: $A(B) \geq B$.
2) $\forall$ B, $A'(B) > -1$.

Proof:

1) Simple differentiation of equation (3) yields the result.
2) See Appendix 2

Propositions 1) and 2) define three possibilities for the shape of the function $A(B)$. They are represented in Figures 1 to 3. Typically, when we are in the case $r \leq 1$, the function is increasing at first when the outside competition is weak and decreases continuously as B increases. On the other hand, for the case $r > 1$, the function $A(B)$ jumps discontinuously from a positive level to zero as B passes through $M(r,X)$. This discontinuity is essentially due to the nonconvexity of the profit function of the agent in the case $r > 1$. When $r > 2$ the reaction curve in its positive part is always increasing while in the case $1 < r < 2$ it is first increasing and then decreasing in Figure 3).

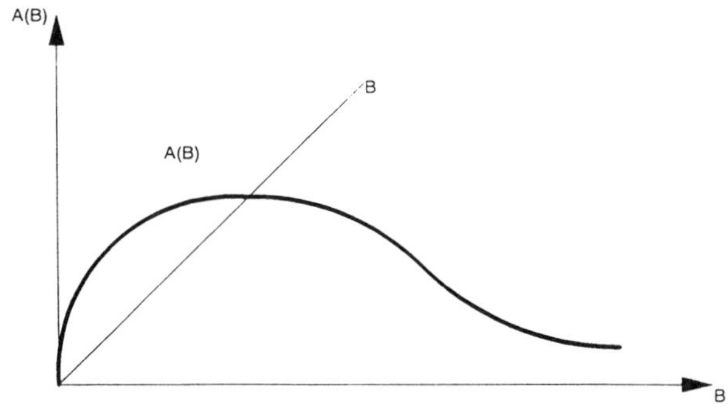

Figure 1. Reaction curve in the case r ≤ 1.

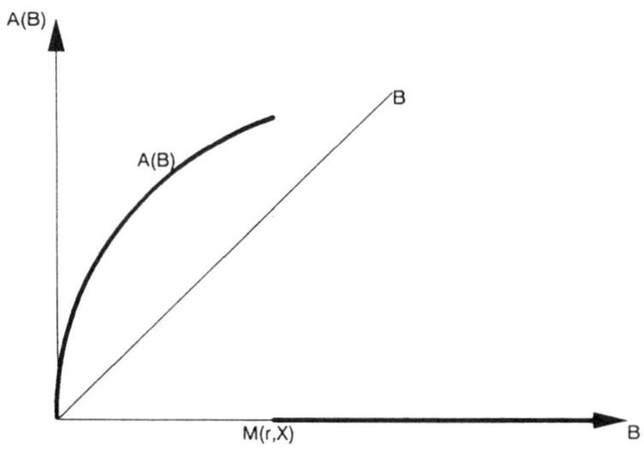

Figure 2. Reaction curve in the case r ≤ 2.

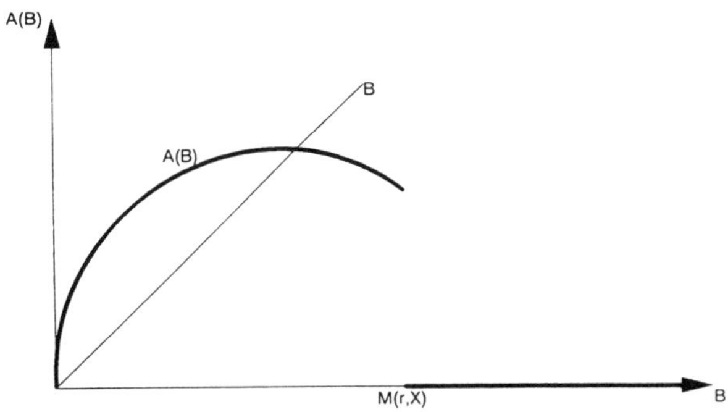

Figure 3. Reaction curve in the case 1 < r < 2.

Having completely examined the behavior of our single agent, we are now in a position to consider the characterization of the equilibrium of the rent-seeking process. In a first step we give some results about the equilibrium in outlays for a given number of active agents. This will be useful to analyse subsequently the structure of equilibria when the number N of agents involved is fixed and then to discuss the problem of entry and endogenization of N.

3. Non-cooperative rent-seeking equilibria

In this section we show that in a Nash equilibrium with a given number of *active* agents, those active agents necessarily make the same bet. While this is always taken for granted in the literature, it is not however as obvious as it seems. There are numbers of symmetric models in economic theory which in fact admit asymmetric equilibria. We give then a characterization of this symmetric equilibrium in outlays.

We first have the following lemma:

Lemma 1: In a rent-seeking Nash equilibrium with K active agents, necessarily those agents invest all the same amount of resources.

Proof: Let us consider a rent-seeking Nash equilibrium with K active agents and suppose that two active agents i and j devote respectively in this equilibrium the amounts a_i^* and a_j^* with $a_i^* \neq a_j^*$. Let us note $H^* = \sum_{k \neq i,j} a_k^{*r}$ in which a_k^* is the investment made by another agent active in this rent-seeking equilibrium. Then from proposition 2) we have:

$$a_i^{*r} - a_j^{*r} = A(a_j^{*r} + H^*) - A(a_i^{*r} + H^*) < (a_i^{*r} + H^*) - (a_j^{*r} + H^*) = a_i^{*r} - a_j^{*r}.$$

which is absurd. Hence the lemma results. Q.E.D.

We may now characterize a Nash equilibrium with K *active* agents ($K \leq N$) by the following proposition which gives the usual symmetric characterization of the rent-seeking equilibrium in bets.

Proposition 3:
A Nash equilibrium with K active agents is such that all agents invest the same amoung a* (K) of money in rent-seeking with

$$a^*(K) = \frac{K-1}{K^2} r X.$$

A necessary condition for the existence of such an equilibrium in the case of $r > 1$ is $K < \frac{r}{r-1}$. The equilibrium expected profit fo each agent actively involved in rent-seeking is then:

$$E\Pi^*(K) = \frac{(1-r)K + r}{K^2} X. \tag{4}$$

Proof: From lemma 1) we derive that there can only be symmetric equibria with K active agents. To characterize the symmetric equilibria we substitute B in equation (3) by $(K-1)a^r$. This gives the equilibrium level a* (K). Finally, substituting this level in (2) gives the equilibrium expected profit. This equilibrium can exist only if the equilibrium profit is positive. As

$$E\Pi^* (K) = \frac{(1-r)K + r}{K^2} X = \frac{r-1}{K^2} \left[\frac{r}{r-1} - K \right] X > 0$$

This is equivalent to the condition that $r \leq 1$ or

$$r > 1 \text{ and } K < \frac{r}{r-1}. \qquad \text{O.E.D.}$$

4. Rent-seeking with a fixed number N of agents

Our point now is an attempt to clarify somehow the discussion raised by Tullock (1980) on the nature of the equilibria of this game of rent-seeking. A certain number of studies have dealt with this problem from a different point of view (see notably Corcoran, 1984; Corcoran and Karels, 1985; Hillman and Samet, 1987a). For this purpose, we will use the preceding propositions in order to classify the conditions of existence and stability of the Cournot-Nash equilibria of this static game.

In this section we discuss the case where the total number of agents potentially interested in rent-seeking is fixed to some number N (≥ 2). While a useful step of analysis for the general situation of endogenous N, this case is in itself already interesting. For example, if the rents to be distributed ared monopoly rents specific to a particular industry, we may reasonably suppose that in the short run the firms already in the market have some informational advantage over the potential entrants about those rents and the best way to lobby for them. Therefore the rent-seeking game will be played with a fixed number of firms.

We have the following proposition characterizing completely the Nash equilibria of rent-seeking for a fixed number of agents $N \geq 2$. ($N = 1$ is trivial case)

Proposition 4:

a) If $r \leq 1$, then there is a unique Nash equilibrium in which all the N agents are active players and each of them invests $a^* = \frac{N-1}{N^2} r X$. Moreover, the equilibrium expected profit for each agent is equal to:

$$E\Pi^* = \frac{(1-r)N + r}{N^2} X > 0$$

b) If $r > 1$ and $N \leq \frac{r}{r-1}$, then a symmetric equilibrium with N active players exists with the same characteristics as in case a). ($E\Pi^* = 0$ only if $N = \frac{r}{r-1}$)

c) If $r > 1$ and $N > \frac{r}{r-1}$, let N^* the highest number such that $N^* \leq \frac{r}{r-1}$. Then if $N^* > 1$, the Nash equilibria in pure strategies are asymmetric. Moreover, there exists an equilibrium with N^* be active agents and $N-N^*$ non-active agents in which each of the active players devotes $a^* = \frac{N^*-1}{N^{*2}} r X$ of resources to rent-seeking and receives a profit $E\Pi^*$ = resources to rent-seeking and receives a profit $E\Pi^* = \frac{(1-r)N^* + r}{N^{*2}} X$ positive. Each of the non-active players invests 0 and has a null profit.

Proof: See Appendix 3.

As it was already mentioned in the literature, we observe a strong difference between the case $r \leq 1$ and the case $r > 1$. In the case where the technology of rent-seeking is with constant or decreasing returns of scale, there is for a fixed number of agents a unique Nash equilibrium which is symmetric. In the case of increasing returns of scale, if the number of possible participants is not too high, here again there is a unique symmetric equilibrium with all agents participating actively in the rent-seeking activity. However, when the number of agents potentially interested in rent-seeking is higher than a certain level, we find a multiplicity of equilibria which are asymmetric and in which there are N^* devoting the same amount of resources to rent-seeking and $N-N^*$ staying inactive. The active agents derive a perhaps small but strictly positive profit while the inactive agents receive nothing. The reason for the mujltiplicity of equilibria comes two reasons. The first one is the obvious indeterminacy of who will be the active agents or the inactive agents.

The second one is more intricate and comes from the fact that there may be an asymmetric Nash equilibrium with N^* active agents and an asymmetric Nash equilibrium with $N^* - 1$ active participants. (It is not difficult to show that an equilibrium with $N^* - 2$ active agents cannot exist.) As a matter of fact, this happens when we are in the following configuration for N^*:

$$(N^*-1)\, a^*(N^*-1) > M(r) > (N^*-1)\, a^*(N^*). \tag{5}$$

Reconsidering proposition 1), those inequalities simply say that if a potential participant anticipates that $N^* - 1$ agents play $a^*(N^* - 1)$ then he does not bet anything and thus we observe effectively a Nash equilibrium with $N^* - 1$ active agents. But, similarly, if the agent anticipates that the $N^* - 1$ play $a^*(N^*)$ then he has some incentive to make a positive bet which in this case will be his best response $a^*(N^*)$ and consequently we may also observe a Nash equilibrium with N^* active agents.

It is interesting to see that the number N^* does not depend on the number of potential players N. This will have some importance in the following section when we consider a rent-seeking process with free entry. Note finally that we have characterized all the equilibria in pure strategies of this game of rent-seeking.

5. Rent-seeking with free entry

In this section we discuss the case where the number of players in the gaem is not a-priori fixed. The results of proposition 4) show us that in the case $r \leq 1$, for any number of agents N, there is always a unique equilibrium in which the expected payoffs are strictly positive. There is therefore always some incentive for a potential entrant to decide to participate in rent-seeking. Here, in the ideal theoretical case, as was pointed out rightly by Corcoran and Karels (1985), the equilibrium entails a very large number of agents, each of them undertaking an infinitesimal bet and competing for some expected profit which tends from above to zero (Tullock 1984). Note however that in this kind of setting we do observe a convergence of the total amount of outlays to the rent prize when the number of participants N tends to infinity only when $r = 1$

$$\lim_{N \to \infty} \frac{N\, a^*(N)}{X} = r \tag{6}$$

In this sense, the rents prize cannot be necessarily a good proxy for the amount of resources spent in rent-seeking.

One can easily solve the indeterminacy of the number of participants by introducing some little fixed fee to pay at the beginning of the rent-seeking process or equivalently some small range of increasing returns of scale in the technology. In that case profits need not be zero but would remain relatively small.

If $r > 1$, then as long as $N < N^*$, any potential entrant has some incentive to enter in the game. As we observed in the previous section, when $N > N^*$, an agent contemplating entry will not engage in the process of rent-seeking because by doing this he will receive a negative expected payoff. Therefore the only possible solution with free entry is N^* agents undertaking rent-seeking and obtaining a strictly positive but generally small expected profit. Rents are not completely dissipated.

6. Stackelberg leader behavior

Until now we have supposed that all the agents were identical and therefore a natural way to model their behavior was to view them all as Nash players. However, in many cases we find situations where firms or agents are not placed symmetrically in the rent-seeking game. Some of them may possess superior knowledge about the rent-seeking environment and may have better connections with the politicians before the beginning of the race to political favors. This kind of situation calls for a different type of modelization of the game and a leader-follower framework seems to be appropriate in this case. In order to analyse the consequences of such an asymmetry, let us consider the case where one of the agents plays as a Stackelberg leader compared to the other agents. In such a case he may use strategically his capacity of commitment of playing the first "shot" in order to obtain a better outcome in the rent-seeking game.

A particular interesting point to analyse in this context is how the shape of the technology of rent-seeking is related to the capacity of preemption of the lader of the game. As a matter of fact, we will see below that a technology of rent-seeking with increasing returns to scale ($r > 1$) allows the agent playing as a Stackelberg leader to preempt successfully the other players and forbid them the possibility of active entry in the rent-seeking game.

This is most simply seen by considering the case of a K-person natural rent-seeking game with free entry. In that case we know from proposition 4) that only K agents can be active players in a Nash equilibrium of the rent-seeking game.

Now suppose that player 1 plays as a Stackelberg leader compared to the other players. It is easy to see that by playing M(r,X) as a bet, he is able to preempt the other players by preventing them from any possible active entry in the rent-seeking game. Is it in his interest to do that? In order to give an answer to this question we need some few more notations. Let us note the profit function of agent 1 as:

$$E\Pi(a,B) = \frac{a^r}{a^r + B} X - a$$

Let assume that player 1, as a Stackelberg leader, bets first $a \geq 0$. The other agents play then between themselves as Nash players and there is an resulting Nash equilibrium with free entry between them. Let denote E as the set of the active agents in this equilibrium and let $b_i^*(a)$ be the bet of agent i, $i \in E$, and

$E\Pi_i^*(a)$ the profit he receives (which both depend of course on the amount a previously chosen by the Stackelberg leader). Thus we should have the following inequality:

$$a + \sum_{i \in E} b_i^*(a) \geq M(r,X)$$

This inequality ensures that any agent $j \notin E$ is not interested in participating in rent-seeking. But then we have:

$$E\Pi(M(r,X),0) \leq E\Pi\,(a + \sum_{i \in E} b_i^*(a),0) \tag{7}$$

where $E\Pi(.,0)$ is the profit function of player 1 when he is the only one to play actively in the rent-seeking process. Moreover, as the technology of rent-seeking is with increasing returns of scale ($r > 1$), it is easy to see that: $\forall\, a \geq 0$ such that $b_i^*(a) > 0$

$$E\Pi(a+(a+\sum_{i \in E} b_i^*(a),0) > E\Pi(a,(a+\sum_{i \in E} b_i^*(a))+(a+\sum_{i \in E} b_i^* E\Pi_i^*(a) \geq$$
$$\geq E\Pi(a,\, (a + \sum_{i \in E} b_i^*(a)) \tag{8}$$

From equations (7) and (8) we see that agent 1 has an interest, as a leader of Stackelberg, to bet $M(r,X)$ and preempt all the other potential players. The interesing point to note here is the fact that his possibility of total preemption of the Stackelberg leader is only feasible because of the non-convexity associated with the technology of rent-seeking. In the case of $r < 1$, it is easy to see that a leader of Stackelberg cannot preempt the other players from entering actively in the game. In that case the Stackelberg leader will still have an advantage over the other players but his power will be obviously more limited than in the case with increasing returns of scale.

7. Conclusion

In this paper, we have tried to investigate more closely the implications of the rent-seeking technology on the shape of the typical reaction curve of an agent wishing to participate in rent-seeking. We saw that in the case of decreasing return of scale, this reaction curve is continuous in the bets of the other agents. On the contrary the case with increasing returns of scale shows a sharp discontinuity in the reaction curve. This systematic analysis of the reaction curve allowed us to discuss, in a consistent framework, the problem of "efficient rent-seeking'' and the natural structure of competition that is supposed to appear in such games. In this respect, according to the type of the technology of rent-seeking, we characterize completely the type of pure strategies Nash equilibria that may result in the game.

Moreover, we have been able to investigate also the consequences of forms of strategic behavior that depart from the traditional Nash behavior. We considered the case where one of the agents has some kind of superior position compared to the other agents, namely he acts as a Stackelberg leader with respect to the other participants of the rent-seeking. We show that a technology with increasing returns of scale enables the leader to preempt the other players from entering actively into the race for rents.

Evidently several extensions have not been explored in this paper. An interesting one may be to consider different alternative assumptions on the conjectures that one agent forms about the others' reaction to his behavior and to study the implications of those assumptions on the nature of the resulting equilibria of the rent-seeking game. Another interesting question would also be to consider rent-seeking processes where participants acquire explicitly some form of experience in the way to efficiently rent-seek bureaucrats. In that way we would have a fully dynamic rent-seeking process where memory effects take place (see Cairns,, 1989, for a first analysis of dynamic rent-seeking games). While all those extensions are obviously beyond the scope of this paper, we believe that the basic results that we get there are nevertheless a useful step in our understanding of rent-seeking processes.

Appendix 1

Let $\phi(a) = a^{1-r}(a^r + B)^2$. The first order condition equation states:

$$\phi(a) = r\,B\,X \tag{3}$$

Then in a point a that satisfies (3) we have:

$$E\Pi(a) \geq 0 \Leftrightarrow \frac{a^r X}{a^r + B} - a \geq 0 \Leftrightarrow \frac{a(a^r + B)}{r\,B} - a \geq 0$$

$$\Leftrightarrow a \geq ((r-1)B)^{\frac{1}{r}} \tag{A1.1}$$

In the case $r \leq 1$, condition (A1.1) is always satisfied. Let us consider the case $r > 1$. In that case the function $\phi(a)$ verifies:

$$\phi'(a) \geq \Leftrightarrow -(r-1)a^{-1} + 2ra^{r-1}(a^r + B)^{-1} \geq 0$$

$$\Leftrightarrow a^r \geq \frac{r-1}{r+1}B$$

and thus ϕ is decreasing for $a \leq \left[\frac{r-1}{r+1}B\right]^{\frac{1}{r}}$ and increasing thereafter. Condition (4.A) is then verified if and only if:

$$\phi\left[(r-1)^{\frac{1}{r}}\; B^{\frac{1}{r}}\right] \leq r\,B\,X \Leftrightarrow \frac{((r-1)B)^{\frac{1}{r}}}{(r-1)B}(rB)^2 \leq r\,B\,X$$

$$\Leftrightarrow B \leq \frac{(r-1)^{r-1}}{r^r}X^r$$

and we pose in the text $M(r,X) = \frac{(r-1)^{r-1}}{r^r}X^r$. OED.

Appendix 2

a(B) is defined by:

$$a^{1-r}(a^r + B)^2 - r\,B\,X = 0 \Leftrightarrow$$

$$\Leftrightarrow A^{\frac{1}{r}}(A + B)^2 - r\,A\,B\,X = 0 \tag{A2.1}$$

Differentiating (A2.1) we obtain that:

$$\frac{dA}{dB} = \frac{-2\,A^{\frac{1}{r}}\,(A+B) + r\,A\,X}{\frac{1}{r}\,A^{\frac{1}{r}-1}\,(A+B)^2 + 2\,A^{\frac{1}{r}}\,(A+B) - r\,B\,X} \tag{A2.2}$$

* Let us show that the denominator of the right member of equation (A2.2) is positive in all point A(B) verifying (A2.1).

$$\frac{1}{r}\,A^{\frac{1}{r}-1}\,(A+B)^2 + 2\,A^{\frac{1}{r}}\,(A+B) - r\,B\,X > 0$$

$$\Leftrightarrow \frac{1}{r}\,A^{\frac{1}{r}-1}\,(A+B)^2 + 2\,A^{\frac{1}{r}}\,(A+B) - A^{\frac{1}{r}-1}\,(A+B)^2 > 0$$

$$\Leftrightarrow \left[\frac{1}{r} - 1\right] A^{-1}\,(A+B) + 2 > 0$$

$$\Leftrightarrow (A+B)\,(1-r) + 2\,r\,A > 0 \tag{A2.3}$$

thus the denominator of the right hand side of equation (A2.2) is positive if and only if we have inequality (A2.3). When $r \leq 1$ this inequality is automatically satisfied. If $r > 1$, on the decreasing part of A(B) we have that $A + B > 2\,A$, hence

$$(A+B)\,(1-r) + 2r\,A > A > 2\,A\,(1-r+r) > 0$$

and thus the sign of the denominator of (A2.2).

** Let us show now that $\frac{dA}{dB} > -1$. This is equivalent to showing that

$$r\,A\,X > -\frac{1}{r}\,A^{\frac{1}{r}-1}\,(A+B)^2 + r\,B\,X$$

$$\Leftrightarrow r\,A\,X > -B\,X + r\,B\,X$$

$$\Leftrightarrow A > \frac{r-1}{r}\,B$$

Let B^* the point where the curve A(B) intersect the line $A = \frac{r-1}{r}\,B$

Then the property $\frac{dA}{dB} > -1$ is verified for all point B if and only if $B^* > M(r)$. We may calculate B^* easily.

$$\left[\frac{r-1}{r}\right]^{\frac{1}{r}} B^{*\frac{1}{r}} \left[\frac{r-1}{r}\,B^* + B^*\right]^2 - r\,\frac{r-1}{r}\,B^{*2}\,X = 0$$

which gives:

$$B^* = \frac{(r-1)^{r-1}\,r^{2r+1}}{(2r-1)^{2r}}\,X^r$$

hence $B^* > M(r) \Leftrightarrow \frac{(r-1)^{r-1}\,r^{2r+1}}{(2r-1)^{2r}}\,X^r > \frac{(r-1)^{r-1}}{r^r}\,X^r$

$$\Leftrightarrow r^{3r+1} > (2r-1)^{2r}$$

inequality which is always verified for $r \in [1, \frac{3}{2}]$. (When $r > \frac{3}{2}$ the reaction curve is always increas- and thu trivially the property is verified).

OED.

Appendix 3

a) For the case $r \leq 1$. From proposition 3) we know that for any $K \leq N$ there is a unique rent-seeking equilibrium with K active agents. In each equilibrium the active agents derive a strictly positive profit. Suppose now that $K < N$ and let us consider the stability of the equilibrium associated with this K. In order to do this we have to examine the behavior of one of the non-active agents. Has he got any incentive to stay inactive? By becoming active and anticipating that his expected profit will be the one of an active agent in a the new resulting equilibrium with $K+1$ agents, he obtains a strictly positive expected payoff which is higher than staying inactive and contemplating an equilibrium with K active agents in which he receives 0. Hence in any equilibrium with K active agents the non-active agents always have an incentive to enter actively in the game. Moreover, it is not difficult to show that if agent $K+1$ takes as completely given the bets of the other K agents, he has also an incentive to participate actively in the rent-seeking process. Therefore the unique Nash equilibrium and the only stable solution is the equilibrium with all the N agents active in rent-seeking. The conclusions on the equilibrium amount of resources and profits then follow immediately from proposition 3).

b) In the case where $r > 1$ and $N \leq \frac{r}{r-1}$, from proposition 3) there exists an equilibrium with N active agents. For the same reasons as in a) it constitutes the only stable equilibrium.

c) In the case $r > 1$ and $N > \frac{r}{r-1}$, we consider N^* the number such that $N^* \leq$ r $< N^* + 1$. Hence:

$$\frac{1}{r-1} < N^* < \frac{r}{r-1} \qquad \text{(A3.1)}$$

Moreover, in the case of $N^* \geq 3$, those inequalities imply that $r \leq \frac{3}{2}$. Now it is easy to see from proposition 3) that $E\Pi^*(N^*) \geq 0$. For the same reasons as previously, all equilibria with K active agents for $K < N^*$ are not stable. Moreover, again from proposition 3), no equilibria with K active agents exist for $K > N^*$. We want to show now that any equilibrium with N^* is stable. In order to do this, we have to show that $E\Pi^*(N^*+1) < 0$. In that case, no inactive agent will have any incentive to move from the position of no investment. Showing that $E\Pi^*(N^*+1) < 0$ is equivalent, after some manipulation to show that:

$$N^*\left[\frac{N^*-1}{N^{*2}}\, r\, X\right]^r > \frac{(r-1)^{r-1} X^r}{r^r}$$

which is equivalent to

$$N^{*1-2r}(N^*-1)^r > (r-1)^{r-1}\, r^{-2r} \qquad \text{(A3.2)}$$

But then it is easy to see that for all $N \leq \frac{r}{r-1}$, the function $N \rightarrow N^{1-2r}(N-1)^r$ is increasing in

N and therefore recalling equation (A2.1) we find that:

$$N^{*1-2r}\,(N^*-1)^r > \left[\frac{1}{r-1}\right]^{1-2r}\left[\frac{1}{r-1}-1\right]^r = (r-1)^{r-1}\,(2-r)^r > (r-1)^{r-1}\,r^{2-r}.$$

The last inequality follows from $(2-r)^r > r^{-2r}$ which is always true for $r \in [1,\frac{3}{2}]$. This demonstrates inequality (A2.2) and finally proves that any equilibrium with N* is stable. OED

More efficient rent-seeking – A Münchhausen solution*

WOLFGANG LEININGER
Fachbereich Wirtschafts- und Sozialwissenschaften, Postfach 500500, DW-Dortmund 50, Deutschland

1. Introduction

In the by now standard Tullock model of rent-seeking (Tullock, 1980) fulfillment of the rent-dissipation hypothesis advanced by Tullock (1967) and Posner (1975) is rather the exception than the rule. Using a game-theoretic model, Tullock showed that in non-cooperative Cournot-Nash equilibrium the extent of rent-dissipation crucially depends on the (scale) returns to individual rent-seeking expenditures. His seminal work, in particular the 'intellectual mire' (Tullock, 1980) presented by increasing returns to such expenditure (which may lead to non-existence of Cournot-Nash equilibrium) has subsequently attracted considerable attention (see, e.g., Hillman and Katz, 1984; Higgins, Shughart and Tollison, 1985; Corcoran and Karels, 1985; Michaels, 1988; and Allard, 1988). While all of these contributions have shed new light on the issue, they did not satisfactorily solve the basic modeling problem, which obstinately kept its status as an 'intellectual swamp' (Tullock, 1985). The present contribution is an attempt to point to a way out of this swamp by questioning the appropriateness of the Cournot-Nash solution concept for Tullock's original problem. Equivalently, we question the modeling device of having rent seekers move *simultaneously*.

Simultaneity of moves in the efficient rent-seeking model is imposed on the presumption that all players have an interest to be a first-mover and hence competition for the first move would yield this simultaneity (Tullock, 1980: 107–108; 1985: 260). As a consequence, an exogenous imposition of sequentiality would be (and has been) considered artificial. The present paper challenges this view by showing that the basic presumption that rent-seekers will always compete for the first move in the Tullock model is unfounded. We

* Freiherr Karl Friedrich Hyronymus von Münchhausen (1720–91), renowned German braggart ('The Baron of Lies'), once told the story that during fighting in Russia he went astray with his horse into a swamp. In acute danger he rescued himself from sinking into mud by grabbing his tuft and pulling himself out. (Raspe, 1785; Bürger, 1786).

specify a simple two-player version of the model in which the basic question whether rent seekers move simultaneously or whether they move sequentially, with one playing the role of a leader and the other acting as a follower, is decided *endogenously* (through rent seekers preferences). Our surprising answer is that the seekers – if left with the *choice* of moving simultaneously or sequentially – agree (!) to move in a particular sequential order. Since most of the widely discussed problems connected with the Tullock model have their origin in the simultaneity issue or – equivalently – in the use of the static Cournot-Nash solution concept, this basic insight might pave a way out of these difficulties. At least it shows, that "the behavior in a dynamic lottery" (Corcoran and Karels, 1985, on Tullock's 1980-model) should be properly examined with the help of an explicitly dynamic model.

The present paper sets out a 'nucleus model' for such an analysis by reconsidering Tullock's model also from a dynamic point of view. It consists of several stages (determining the order of moving and the actual moves) and – equally important – is analyzed with the help of dynamic solution concepts from non-cooperative game theory. In particular, we do not use (Cournot-) Nash equilibrium, but its dynamic extension of (subgame) perfect equilibrium (Selten, 1965; 1975). In its limited framework the paper provides a complete theoretical resolution of the potentially paradoxical implications of the Tullock model, that have dominated the subsequent literature (e.g. Corcoran, 1984; Corcoran and Karels, 1985; Tullock, 1985; and Michaels, 1988), while – at the same time – predicting lower costs of rent-seeking to society. Its main 'applied' message therefore is that the design of rent-seeking competitions in an institutional framework should take into account and nurture the dynamic nature of rent-seeking competitions in order to realize efficiency gains. A similar point has been made by Leininger (1991) with respect to rent-dissipation in patent races.

The structure of the model specified below is overly simplistic. It has been chosen deliberately for several reasons: firstly, the simplifications are imposed for pedagogical reasons to make the logic behind the drastically different results as transparent as possible; secondly, and closely related to the first point, they allow the technicalities of the analysis imposed by the more stringent solution concept to be kept at a 'digestible' level for non-game theorists. Yet they do point out the sequential modeling principles and the impact of the dynamic solution concept. Thirdly, and important from a theoretical modeling point of view, this simple two-player model can be used as a 'building stone' of more general many-players many-stages models since it will form a basic subgame of such extensions. For example in a 'truly' dynamic game, in which players move several times in a sequential order (and not just once as in the present model) the solution of the present model is of strategic importance since it provides a 'common threat point'. (This issue is taken up in a more general and deeper game-theoretic analysis of rent-seeking by Leininger and Yang, 1990).

The paper is organized as follows: Section 2 sets out an extension of Tullock's game, in which players also have to decide on the timing of their bids. Section 3 contains a detailed analysis of this game and its subgames. Section 4 uses this analysis to determine the unique equilibrium of the extended game, which always yields sequential play of the rent-seeking game. Section 5 relates this result to the previous literature while Section 6 offers some concluding remarks.

2. An extension of the Tullock model

The purpose of this section is to formalize the question whether rent seekers should really be expected to move simultaneously. For this we draw on the very recent literature on the endogeneous timing of moves in oligopoly games (see, e.g., Anderson and Engers, 1989; and Hamilton and Slutsky, 1990). Since the issue of the endogeneous determination of the order of moving in a game is a complex one, we first try to outline the guiding principles in an non-technical way.

Recall that Tullock (1980) proposed a model, in which n rent seekers compete for a prize (rent) of size (value) V. If a player i makes an expenditure of x_i in order to capture the rent his probability of success is assumed to be given by

$$p_i = \frac{x_i^r}{x_i^r + \sum_{j \neq i} x_j^r}$$

where x_j denotes the simultaneous expenditure by his rival j, and r reflects the marginal cost incurred by influencing the size of p_i. Consequently, a bid for V of x_i yields expected profits for player i of

$$\pi_i = p_i \cdot V - x_i = \frac{x_i^r}{x_i^r + \sum_{j \neq i} x_j^r} \cdot V - x_i,$$

which he tries to maximize by a suitable choice of x_i taking into account the optimizing behavior of this rivals. In a (Cournot-)Nash equilibrium all players make expenditures of

$$X_i^* = \frac{(n-1)}{n^2} \cdot r \cdot V.$$

Hence, depending on n and r, competition for the rent may dissipate in the aggregate less or more expenditure than V. The socalled 'rent-dissipation hypothesis' does not hold. In fact, if x_i exceeds V/n (i.e., $\frac{(n-1)}{n} \cdot r > 1$) then π_i^* becomes negative and it would be individually rational not to bid at all. Alas, everyone else behaving in this individually rational way makes it profitable to bid! Players are likely to be drawn into a wasteful competition, which escalates bids up to the level of x_i^* as no proper equilibrium exists.[1]

Now suppose that a player not only has to decide on the size of his bid x_i but also when to make this bid. Let us consider the simple case of two rent seekers who can either bid 'Early' (= E) or 'Late' (= L). If their timing decisions are the same, simultaneous play results, if they are different, a sequential game arises. Note that the choice of timing is *not* 'Earlier' or 'Later'; i.e., players *cannot* choose whether they want to be leaders or followers as this always depends on the other player's decision. The decision of an individual bidder with respect to the timing is made in ignorance of the rival's decision and is assumed to be binding. It is then revealed to the rival. That is, the extended game has the following two-stage-structure:

Stage I: Players simultaneously decide whether they move 'Early' (E) or 'Late' (L).

Stage II: The result of Stage I is revealed and the rent-seeking game is played with simultaneous moves, if this result is (E, E) or (L, L), and sequential moves, if this result is (E, L) or (L, E). (In the latter case player 1 is the leader after (E, L) and player 2 is the leader after (L, E)).

Analysis of this two-stage game requires an analysis of the sequential versions of the rent-seeking game in addition to the solution of the simultaneous game: a player's decision at Stage I will depend on the expected (equilibrium) pay-offs of the games acailavailable at Stage II. This is seen most clearly, if one considers a stylized game tree of the extended game:

Players 1 and 2 simultaneously choose between 'E' and 'L': this is modeled here as player 1 choosing first (hence not knowing player 2's choice) and then player 2 making his choice not knowing of the result of player 1's earlier decision; i.e., the decision modes g_1 and g_2 can not be distinguished by player 2 and form a single information set (labeled 2). After these decisions both players can see which of the information sets $g_3 - g_6$ has been reached and each player then makes his bid knowing the timing of his rival's bid. Alternatively, one can interpret Stage I as an 'announcement stage' (Hamilton and Slutsky, 1990), in which players simply announce their intents with respect to their timing.

Our aim is to determine the subgame perfect equilibrium of this extended stage-game, in which a player's strategy consists of two components: a decision

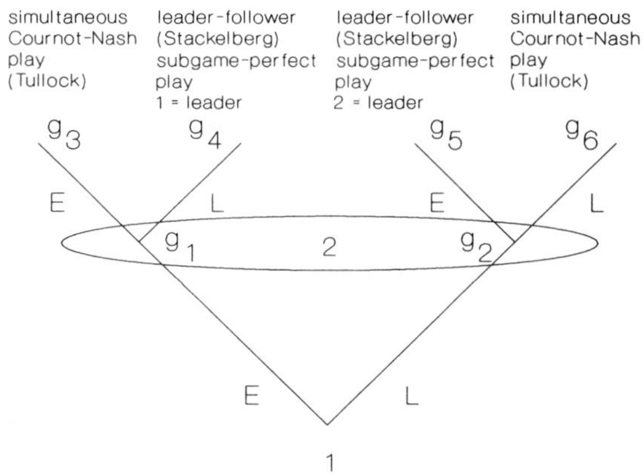

Figure 1. The extensive form of the two-stage game.

when to move and a bid x. More formally, a player has to specify a tupel (T, x) subject to $T \in \{E, L\}$ and $x : \{E, L\} \chi \{E, L\} \rightarrow [0, \infty)$. The game is analyzed in a backwards inductive fashion. We first determine the solution of the four possible subgames of the game arising after play at Stage I; i.e., the solution of the rent-seeking games after (E, E), (E, L), (L, E) or (L, L) has been chosen. We then substitute the obtained equilibrium pay-offs for the subgames of the game depicted in Figure 1 and solve the reduced game to determine the equilibrium timing decisions. We claim, that players always choose different times for their move and hence play the rent-seeking game *sequentially* at Stage II.

3. Timing and rent-seeking

We now apply the extended two-player model of the previous section to the rent-seeking problem.

We choose the following specification of Tullock's model: there are two players, X and Y, who compete for a rent they value at V_x (player X) resp. V_y (player Y). For the introduction of this kind of asymmetry we refer to Hillman and Riley (1989). (Allard, 1988, considers another asymmetric situation in which players have different abilities to influence the probability of winning in their favour). We denote a bid (expenditure) by player X (resp. Y) by x (resp. y).

The probability of winning for player X when bids x and y are submitted is then given by

$$p_x(x, y) = \frac{a \cdot x}{a \cdot x + y}$$

implying that the probability of winning for player Y is given by

$$p_y(x, y) = 1 - p_x(x, y) = \frac{y}{a \cdot x + y}.$$

Thus we consider Tullock's original model (with $r = 1$) with the possibilities of bias (if $a \neq 1$), reflecting differential advantages, and non-identical assessments of the value of the rent opportunity among players (if $V_x \neq V_y$). Determination of the equilibrium of the extended rent-seeking game will depend on a comparison among the pay-offs for individual players resulting from simultaneous play and the two possible versions of sequential play. That is, each player has to compute and compare his pay-off as a leader resp. follower to the simultaneous play outcome of familiar Cournot-Nash equilibrium.

3.1. Simultaneous play

If the two players move simultaneously the unique Cournot-Nash equilibrium is given by

$$x^* = \frac{a \cdot v}{(a+v)^2} \cdot V_x \text{ and } y^* = \frac{a \cdot v}{(a+v)^2} \cdot V_y$$

where $v = V_y/V_x$. Hence the sum of rent-seeking expenditures is given by

$$x^* + y^* = \frac{a \cdot v}{(a+v)^2}(V_x + V_y).$$

Note that with different valuations the players will submit *different* bids. In contrast, with identical valuations – irrespective of the bias – they will submit identical bids (Tullock, 1980).

These bids determine the probabilities of winning and expected pay-offs as

$$p_x(x^*, y^*) = \frac{a}{a + v} \text{ and } p_y(x^*, y^*) = \frac{v}{a + v},$$

$$\pi_x^* = \frac{a}{a+v} \cdot V_x - \frac{a \cdot v}{(a+v)^2} \cdot V_x = \frac{a^2}{(a+v)^2} \cdot V_x \text{ and}$$

$$\pi_y^* = \frac{v}{a+v} \cdot V_y - \frac{a \cdot v}{(a+v)^2} \cdot V_y = \frac{v^2}{(a+v)^2} \cdot V_y.$$

Obviously, bias in his favor or a higher valuation increase a player's expected pay-off in equilibrium. With no bias ($a=1$) and identical valuations V ($v=1$) the familiar solution of $x^* = y^* = 0.25$ V results and both win with probability 0.5. With different valuations the player with the higher valuation bids more. With no bias ($a=1$) this results in a higher probability of winning (and thus higher expected profits) for him:

$$p_x \gtreqless p_y \Leftrightarrow V_x \gtreqless V_y \text{ and}$$

$$\pi_x^* \gtreqless \pi_y^* \Leftrightarrow V_x \gtreqless V_y.$$

If one also considers bias then the formulas show in a precise way how these two influences combine to an overall effect. In particular, they neutralize each other if $a = v$, resp. $aV_x = V_y$.

In summary, the pay-offs for players X and Y in the two-stage game are

$$(\pi_x^*, \pi_y^*) = \left(\frac{a^2}{(a+v)^2} \cdot V_x, \frac{v^2}{(a+v)^2} \cdot V_y\right)$$

if (E,E) or (L,L) have been chosen at Stage I.

3.2. *Sequential play*

We now examine the two possibilities of sequential play, in which each player once assumes the role of the leader and the role of follower.

i) Player X moves first (has chosen E at Stage I) and player Y moves second (has chosen L at Stage I).

In this case player Y has to decide on his bid y *given* the bid x of player X who moved before him. Hence player Y maximizes the expected payoff

$$\pi_y(x,y) = \frac{y}{a \cdot x + y} \cdot V_y - y.$$

The first-order condition is given by

$$\frac{a \cdot x}{(a \cdot x + y)^2} \cdot V_y = 1$$

and hence $y = (a \cdot x \cdot V_y)^{1/2} - a \cdot x$.

This solution only makes sense if $y \geq 0$ since a player cannot make a negative bid. In case of a negative value of the above mathematical expression for y player Y bids 0; i.e., does not bid at all. This happens for sufficiently high opening bids of player X. That is, the follower's optimal bid as a function of the leader's opening bid is given by

$$y(x) = \begin{cases} (a \cdot x \cdot V_y)^{1/2} - a \cdot x & \text{if } x \leq \frac{1}{a} \cdot V_y \\ 0 & \text{if } x \geq \frac{1}{a} \cdot V_y \end{cases}$$

The follower only responds with a positive bid y if the leader's bid is less than $1/a\ V_y$.

Player X, the leader, takes into account this optimal follower behavior when deciding on his opening bid; i.e., he *anticipates* that an opening bid of x will draw a response of y(x).

He thus maximizes his expected pay-off by maximizing the expression

$$\pi_x\,(x,y) = \frac{a \cdot x}{a \cdot x + y(x)} \cdot V_x - x$$

or – if we substitute the expression for y(x) –

$$\pi_x\,(x,y) = \begin{cases} \left(\frac{a\ x}{V_y}\right)^{1/2} \cdot V_x - x & \text{if } x \leq \frac{1}{a} \cdot V_y \\ V_x - x & \text{if } x \geq \frac{1}{a} \cdot V_y \end{cases}$$

The first-order condition of this problem for $x \leq 1/a \cdot V_y$ is given by

$$\frac{1}{2}\left(\frac{a \cdot x}{V_y}\right)^{1/2} \cdot \frac{a}{V_y} \cdot V_x = 1$$

which yields

$$x^* = \frac{a \cdot V_x^2}{4 \cdot V_y} = \frac{a}{4v} \cdot V_x.$$

The leader's optimal bid x* draws a response

$$y(x^*) = (a \cdot x \cdot V_y) - a \cdot x^* = \frac{a \cdot V_x}{2}\left[1 - \frac{a}{2v}\right].$$

For $x \geq 1/a \cdot V_y$ $\pi_x(x,y)$ is trivially seen to become maximal at $x = 1/a \cdot V_y$.

Since $x^* \leq 1/a \cdot V_y$ if and only if $V_x \leq 2/a\ V_y$, we can specify the equilibrium bids as functions of the parameters V_x and V_y as follows

$$x_L^* = \begin{cases} \dfrac{a}{4v} \cdot V_x & \text{if } 0 \leq V_x \leq \dfrac{2}{a} V_y \\ \dfrac{1}{a} V_y & \text{if } \dfrac{2}{a} V_y \leq V_x \end{cases}$$

and

$$y_F^* = \begin{cases} 0 & \text{if } 0 \leq V_y \leq \dfrac{a}{2} V_x \\ \dfrac{a \cdot V_x}{2}\left[1 - \dfrac{a}{2v}\right] & \text{if } \dfrac{a}{2} V_x \leq V_y \end{cases}$$

The leader bids according to the x*-solution for valuations $V_x \leq 2/a\ V_y$. If $V_x = 2/a\ V_y$ he bids $1/a\ V_y$ which draws a zero bid from the follower. Hence there is no need for the leader to bid more, even if he has higher valuation than $2/a\ V_y$, as the follower only submits a positive bid if his valuation is less than $2/a\ V_y$.

Figures 2 and 3 depict the optimal bids as functions of the bidders' valuations. (The follower's bid approaches $a/2\ V_x$ asymptotically.)

Comparison of the formulas for x* and y* yields:

Both players submit a positive bid if and only if $V_y > aV_x/2$. Otherwise only the leader bids (and wins with probability 1).

Figure 4 visualizes this optimal bidding behavior in $V_x - V_y$ space.

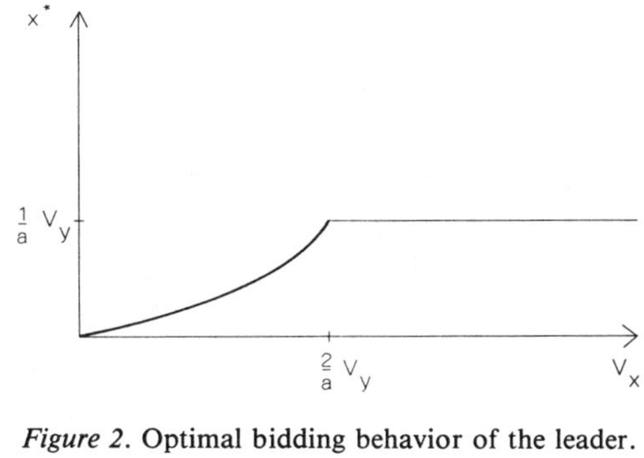

Figure 2. Optimal bidding behavior of the leader.

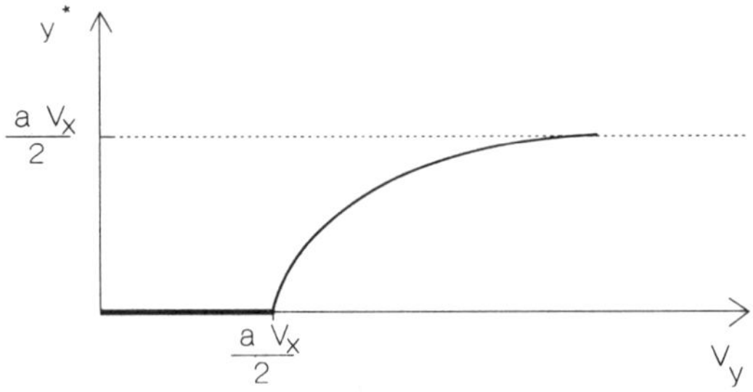

Figure 3. Optimal bidding behavior of the follower.

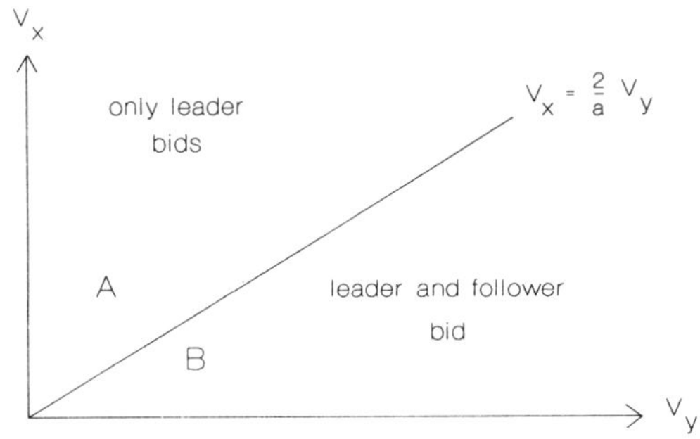

Figure 4. Bidding in equilibrium with leader X.

In region A the pay-off for the leader is given by

$$\pi_x^* = V_x - 1/a\, V_y > 0$$

while the follower's pay-off is $\pi_y^* = 0$.

In region B, in which both players bid, we get

$$p_x(x^*,y^*) = \frac{a \cdot x^*}{a \cdot x^* + y^*} = \frac{a}{2v}$$

and consequently

$$\pi_x^* = \frac{a}{4v} \cdot V_x > 0 \qquad \text{and}$$

$$\pi_y^* = \left[1 - \frac{a}{2v}\right]^2 \cdot V_y > 0.$$

In summary, the pay-offs in the two-stage game for players X and Y are (L = leader, F = follower)

$$(\pi_x^L, \pi_y^F) = \begin{cases} \left(V_x - \frac{1}{a} V_y, 0\right) & \text{if } V_x \geq \frac{2}{a} V_y \\ \left(\frac{a}{4v} \cdot V_x, \left[1 - \frac{a}{2v}\right]^2 \cdot V_y\right) & \text{if } V_x \leq \frac{2}{a} V_y \end{cases}$$

if (E,L) has been chosen at Stage I. Note that bids and pay-offs vary continuously in V_x resp. V_y.

ii) Player Y moves first (has chosen E at Stage I) and player X moves second (has chosen L at Stage I)

In this case a completely analogous derivation yields:

The leader Y bids according to

$$y_L^* = \begin{cases} \frac{v}{4a} \cdot V_y & \text{if } 0 \leq V_y \leq 2a\, V_x \\ a \cdot V_x & \text{if } 2a \cdot V_x \leq V_y \end{cases}$$

and the follower X bids

$$x_F^* = \begin{cases} 0 & \text{if } 0 \leq V_x \leq \frac{V_y}{2a} \\ \frac{V_y}{2a}\left[1 - \frac{v}{2a}\right] & \text{if } \frac{V_y}{2a} \leq V_x \end{cases}$$

Both players submit a positive bid if and only if $V_x > V_y/2a$. Otherwise only the leader Y bids and wins with certainty.

The pay-offs in the two-stage game for players X and Y are now

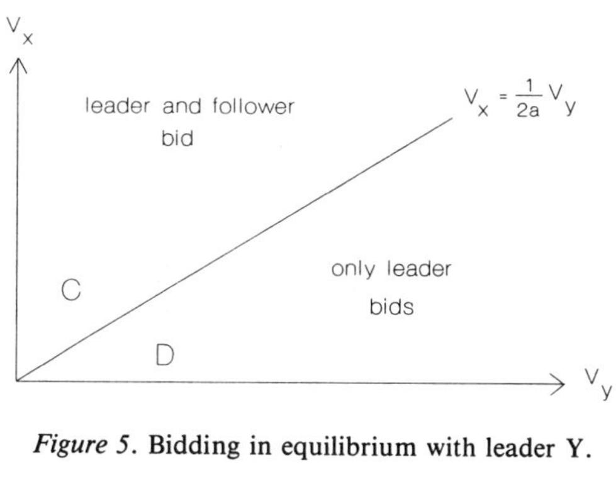

Figure 5. Bidding in equilibrium with leader Y.

$$(\pi_x^F,\pi_y^L) = \begin{cases} (0, V_y - a\cdot V_x) & \text{if } V_x \le \dfrac{1}{2a} V_y \\ \left(\left[1-\dfrac{v}{2a}\right]^2 \cdot V_x, \dfrac{v}{4a} V_y\right) & \text{if } V_x \ge \dfrac{1}{2a} V_y \end{cases}$$

if (L,E) has been chosen at Stage I.

This completes the analysis of the subgames at Stage II.

4. Equilibrium

The previous analysis reduces our problem to the analysis of the following reduced game in normal form in which players only have to decide on their timing.

X \ Y	E	L
E	Π_x^*, Π_y^*	Π_x^L, Π_y^F
L	Π_x^F, Π_y^L	Π_x^*, Π_y^*

Figure 6. Pay-offs in the normal form of the extended game.

This normal form is equivalent to the extensive form (game tree) after the subgames have been replaced by their (unique) solutions (Figure 7).

Equilibrium analysis of this simple game yields our first main result. Let us call player X 'stronger' than player Y if and only if $a \cdot V_x > V_y$. We then get:

Theorem 1

i) With players of different strength ($aV_x \neq V_y$) there is a unique subgame perfect equilibrium of the extended game, in which the weaker player moves first and the stronger player moves second.

ii) With players of equal strength ($aV_x = V_y$) players are indifferent among moving first, second or simultaneously. Hence there are multiple equilibria which all yield the same equilibrium pay-offs (resulting from the same equilibrium bids).

Proof: See Appendix.

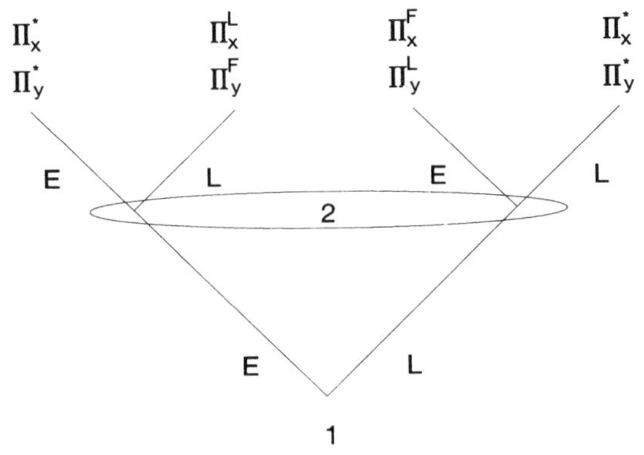

Figure 7. Pay-offs in the extensive form of the extended game.

Hence the case with players of equal strength is somewhat degenerate, here both sequential play equilibria are equilibria of the extended game. The simultaneous Cournot-Nash equilibrium, too, is an equilibrium of the extended game. The proof of this theorem clearly shows that while it is true that both players prefer leading to simultaneous play it is *not* true that this implies competition for the first move. The latter would only arise if for both following is worse than simultaneous play. This is not the case in our model: the sequential solution referred to in the theorem *pareto-dominates* simultaneous play (i.e., is also preferred by the follower!).

Theorem 1 has a very desirable consequence.

Theorem 2

i) If $aV_x \neq V_y$ then total expenditures in the unique equilibrium of the extended game are always less than total expenditure in simultaneous play.

ii) If $aV_x = V_y$ total expenditures in sequential play and simultaneous play are the same.

Theorem 2 follows immediately from the fact that *the preferred* sequential play Pareto-dominates simultaneous play. In quantitative terms it is tedious (but straightforward) to check that

$$x^*_L + y^*_F < x^* + y^* \qquad \text{if } aV_x < V_y \qquad \textit{and}$$
$$x^*_F + y^*_L < x^* + y^* \qquad \text{if } aV_x > V_y.$$

Hence our solution, which determines the order of play endogeneously, is *more efficient* than the Cournot-Nash solution considered in the previous literature. This reinforces a point made by Hillman and Riley (1989) in a simultaneous move game, namely, that asymmetric valuations tend to decrease rent-seeking expenditures.

Intuitively the two players behave as follows: They 'meet' and observe their individual strength (in particular, how player X's strength aV_x compares to player Y's strength V_y). After showing off their muscles to each other it is 'common knowledge' which of them is the stronger one. The stronger one then exploits (with the consent of the weaker one) the situation as follows: both players know that if he goes first he rationally would make a sizeable bid reflecting his true strength, to which the (weaker) follower for his part would choose his optimal response. This way the greater strength of the stronger player is brought to bear by the factual opening bid. However, the stronger player realizes that he need not exert his powers as much. The weaker player, realizing that any bold opening move would run into a heavy counter bid by the stronger player, would act well-behaved as a first-mover and make a moderate opening bid reflecting his 'inferiority'. The (stronger) follower's *optimal* reaction is then also more moderate while still giving him the better end. This way the greater strength of the stronger player is brought to bear via the (rational) *expectations* of the weaker player. It thus needs no materialization by an actual (expensive) bid and *both* players prefer this situation.

5. Comments on the literature

We have analyzed a simple model in some detail. We now want to discuss some general lessons which can be drawn from it. Our analysis yielded *sequential* realization of the rent competition as an endogeneous result of players interaction. This is probably the strongest justification for sequential play possible. Yet even in less ideal circumstances should the design of sequential mechanisms for the conduct of rent competitions be considered. This is for the simple, but important reason that in a *sequential* competition a player would never bid more than his expected value, if he behaves (sequentially) rational. Thus, in properly designed sequential rent competitions the strange phenomena of individually or socially 'irrational' high bids (caused by non-existence of static Cournot-Nash equilibrium) cannot occur. For example, if players of the general rent-seeking game of Section 2 (n players, $r = 1$) would move sequentially one after the other, a subgame perfect equilibrium would still exist and none of them – whatever the value of r – would bid more than his expected value in it. In making his decision, each player would take into account the amount of expenditures made by previously moving players *and the optimal reactions of later players*. In contrast, players are *assumed* to behave myopically in pseudo-dynamic adjustment to the Cournot-Nash solution as described in Tullock (1980: 106): The simultaneous two-player solution of the rent-seeking game with $V_x = V_y = 100$ has each player bid 75 (for an expected pay-off of 50!). Tullock (1980: 106), explains this outcome by the following argument:

Suppose, for example, that we start with both parties at 50. Smith raises to 51. With the exponent of r = 3, the increase in the probability that he will win is worth more than 1 – in fact, considerably more. If Jones counters, he also gains more than 1 by his investment. By a series of small steps of this sort, each one of which is a profitable investment, the two parties will eventually reach 75, at which point there is no motive for either one to raise or lower his bid by any small amount.

Smith's behavior is very short-sighted and only profitable on the presumption that there is *no* reaction by Jones. At the same time, Smith can clearly see that Jones has a strong incentive to react (which would trigger off further rounds of escalating bids). Taking this into account Smith should not bid, neither should Jones. In fact, in a truly dynamic game, in which the two players could perform such a sequence of bids alternatingly, the initial position of both having sunk 50 would never arise in the first place (see Leininger and Yang, 1990), if players are assumed to behave rationally.

Tullock (1980) notes that there is a precommitment strategy: if one player would put in 75 *first* and present the other with a *fait accompli*, the other player would not bid (and the first mover would make a certain profit of 25). Yet he maintains that *both* would try to be first and dismisses the suggestion of a more sensible sequential behavior by a referee, who argued a first bid of about 55 would be high enough in order to prevent the then follower from bidding. The referee's idea was taken up by Corcoran and Karels (1985) in a slightly different context. They were interested in long-run rent-seeking behavior and considered so-called 'pre-emptory' (or – as they called in new industrial organization-preemptive) bids which are just high enough to prevent the potential entry of *later* moving players. Our analysis shows that such preemptive bids do rarely constitute *optimal* sequential behavior. Only if the preempting player is strong enough in relation to the other player, is actual preemption optimal. In all other cases it is overly expensive. Bidding less than the preemptive value and let the other enter with a (small) positive bid is more profitable. Hence one can expect that analyses of long-run behavior, in which players behave sequentially optimal (i.e., in accordance with subgame perfect equilibrium), will lead to results different from those presented by Corcoran and Karels (1985). That the preemptive behavior of incumbents described in Corcoran and Karels's model does not constitute a non-cooperative equilibrium is the underlying reason for Tullock's critique of it (Tullock, 1985: 260). His fear that competition for the (first!) preemptive bid might unduly complicate the matter, is weakened by the present analysis. Pre-emption is neither optimal nor necessarily desirable if it is available as an optimal option in some circumstances. For example, in our two-player model with $a = 2$, $V_x = 15$ and $V_y = 10$ (i.e. $v = 2/3$) player X as the by far stronger player ($aV_x = 30 > 10 = V_y$) could preempt Y with a bid of

$1/a\ V_y = 5$. This would be optimal, if he moved first, and lead to an expected pay-off of $15-5 = 10$ (see the formulas for x_L^* and y_F^*). If, on the other hand, he would not preempt and move second, he would reply with a bid of

$$\frac{V_y}{2a}\left(1-\frac{v}{2a}\right) = \frac{10}{4}\left(1-\frac{1}{6}\right) = \frac{25}{12} \text{ to the first bid of y of size}$$

$$\frac{v}{4a} \cdot V_y = \frac{1}{12} \cdot 10 = \frac{5}{6} \text{ (see the formulas for } y_L^* \text{ and } x_F^*\text{).}$$

His pay-off now is $\pi_x^F = \left[1-\frac{v}{2a}\right]^2 \cdot V_x = \frac{125}{12} > 10.$

Hence he prefers to wait and does not preempt.

6. Concluding remarks

The preceding analysis shows that strategic interaction in rent-seeking competitions does not lead to competition for the first move. This conclusion is derived from a model which contains Tullock's original model as a subgame; players could opt to play the original game but avoid to do so in equilibrium. Instead, they agree to play a sequential version of Tullock's game. This, in our view, is a strong indictment of the practice to specify a simultaneous move game for the analysis of rent-seeking behavior. We have admittedly examined an extension of a simple version of the Tullock game, notably one in which Cournot-Nash equilibrium exists and does not present a particular 'irrationality' problem. Indeed, our extended game could not have a subgame perfect equilibrium, if one of its subgames (namely, the original Tullock game) did not have an equilibrium. Nevertheless, if a solution is rejected when it exists (see our analysis), why should we then be overly bothered when it does not exist? We showed that imposition of simultaneous play on rent seekers does hurt rent seekers. However, the (correct) sequential play does not hurt rent seekers. Moreover, it always exists. There are strategic (competitive) forces at work which accomodate best to sequential play of the competition. There is also an efficiency gain from not moving simultaneously. Players use the additionally offered variable (time) *strategically* to soften competition in the original variable (expenditure). While this strategic behavior is wasteful to society in many contexts of industrial organization (e.g., product differentiation is used to soften price competition) it is beneficial in the present context since competing for rents itself is wasteful.

This suggests that rent-seeking behavior should be analyzed with the help of dynamic (and not static) non-cooperative games. Our specification of the subgames in which players move sequentially is only a very moderate beginning in this respect. A more sophisticated effort is contained in Leininger and Yang (1990). It emerges from these investigations that if rent seekers can act sequentially they will wisely avoid the swamp lurking in the Tullock game, and should they ever get in by accident would immediately resort to the Münchhausen method to get out (by not engaging in further bidding). Clearly, there are many issues awaiting future research.

Note

1. There does exist a mixed strategy equilibrium for the special limiting case that the highest bid wins with certainty (see Hillman and Samet, 1987, for symmetric valuations and Hillman and Riley, 1989, for an extension including the case of asymmetric valuations).

Appendix

In order to prove Theorem 1 we first state

Lemma 1: $\pi_x^L > \pi_x^F$ if and only if $\pi_y^L < \pi_y^F$.

That is, if X prefers to be a leader, Y prefers to be a follower and vice versa. I.e., if players *had* to play sequentially, they would always agree on the order of play (which depends on a, V_x and V_y).

Proof: In view of Figures 4 and 5 we have to consider three cases:

i) $0 < V_x < \frac{1}{2a} V_y$ (equivalently: $v > 2a$)
In this case we have $\pi_x^F = 0$ and hence $\pi_x^L > \pi_x^F$. On the other hand, we have

$$\pi_y^L = V_y - a \cdot V_x \text{ and } \pi_y^F = \left(1 - \frac{a}{2v}\right)^2 V_y$$
$$= V_y - \frac{a}{v} \cdot V_y + \frac{a^2}{4v^2} V_y = V_y - a \cdot V_x + \frac{a^2}{4v^2} \cdot V_y.$$

Consequently, $\pi_y^L < \pi_y^F$.
X wants to lead and Y wants to follow.

ii) $\frac{1}{2a} V_y \le V_x \le \frac{2}{a} V_y$ (equivalently: $v \in [a/2, 2a]$)
Now we have that

$$\pi_x^L > \pi_x^F \Leftrightarrow \frac{a}{4v} > \left(1 - \frac{v}{2a}\right)^2$$
$$\Leftrightarrow \frac{a}{4v} - 1 > \frac{v^2}{4a^2} - \frac{v}{a} = \frac{v}{a}\left(\frac{v}{4a} - 1\right)$$

At the same time, we have

$$\pi_y^L > \pi_y^F \Leftrightarrow \frac{v}{4a} > \left(1 - \frac{a}{2v}\right)^2$$
$$\Leftrightarrow \frac{v}{4a} - 1 > \frac{a^2}{4v^2} - \frac{a}{v} = \frac{a}{v}\left(\frac{a}{4v} - 1\right)$$
$$\Leftrightarrow \left(\frac{a}{4v} - 1\right) < \frac{v}{a}\left(\frac{v}{4a} - 1\right)$$

i.e., X and Y never prefer the same position.

iii) $\frac{2}{a}\ V_y < V_x$ (equivalently: $v < a/2$)

In this case $\pi_y^F = 0$ and hence $\pi_y^L > \pi_y^F$.

But $\pi_x^L = V_x - \frac{1}{a}\ V_y$ and $\pi_x^F = \left(1-\frac{v}{2a}\right)^2 \cdot V_x$

$= V_x - \frac{1}{a} \cdot V_y + \frac{v^2}{4a^2} \cdot V_x$ and thus $\pi_y^L > \pi_y^F$.

X wants to follow and Y wants to lead.

This completes the proof of Lemma 1.

Lemma 2: It is always the weaker player, who wants to lead, and the stronger player, who wants to follow.

Proof: Let us refer to the three cases considered in the proof of Lemma 1.

The claim obviously holds in cases i) and iii): in case i) we have $aV_x < 1/2\ V_y$ and thus Y being far stronger than X, while in case iii) $aV_x > 2V_y$ holds and thus X being far stronger than Y.

In the intermediate case ii) it is not clear a priori whom of the players is the stronger one. We thus have to consider two subcases compatible with $1/2a\ V_y \leq V_x \leq 2/a\ V_y$ (resp. $v \in [a/2, 2a]$):

a) $a \cdot V_x < V_y$ (equivently: $a<v$): X is weaker. We have $v \in (a,2a]$ and hence

$$\pi_x^L = \frac{a}{v4} \cdot V_x,\ \pi_x^F = \left(1-\frac{v}{2a}\right)^2 \cdot V_x$$

Because of Lemma 1 it suffices to show that X wants to lead; i.e., that $\pi_x^L > \pi_x^F$. For this we have to show.

$$\frac{a}{4v} > \left(1-\frac{v}{2a}\right)^2 \text{ for } v \in (a, 2a].$$

Viewed as functions of v the two expressions have the following interpretation: $a/4v$ is a hyperbola with value 1/4 at $v = a$, while $(1-v/2a)^2$ is a parabola with value 1/4 at $v = a$ and value 0 at $v = 2a$, which is its vertex. I.e., the two functions cross at $v = a$ and are both monotonically decreasing and convex on [a,2a]. Since the value of $a/4v$ at $v = 2a$ exceeds 0 the above inequality must hold.

b) $a \cdot V_x > V_y$ (equivalently: $a>v$): X is stronger.

Now it suffices to show that X wants to follow. For this to hold we have to show that

$$\frac{a}{4v} < \left(1-\frac{v}{2a}\right)^2 \text{ for } v \in \left(\frac{a}{2}, a\right).$$

This now follows – by the same arguments as above – from the fact that the value of $a/4v$ at $v = a/2$ is 1/2 which is less than 9/16, the value of $(1-v/2a)^2$ at $v = a/2$.

This completes the proof of Lemma 2.

Note that if $aV_x = V_y$ or $a = v$ then players are equally strong. Now they are indifferent between going first or second ($\pi_x^L = \pi_x^F$ and $\pi_y^L = \pi_y^F$).

Lemma 3: The commonly preferred sequential solution also is commonly preferred to the simultaneous solution.

Proof: We have to consider two cases:

a) $a \cdot V_x > V_y$ resp. $a > v$

We know: In simultaneous play the pay-offs are (π_x^*, π_y^*), wheras in sequential play the pay-offs are (π_x^F, π_y^L) since Y wants to lead and X to follow.

Clearly, we must have $\pi_y^L > \pi_y^*$. This follows from the fact that equilibrium of simultaneous play is determined by the intersection of the two reaction curves, while equilibrium in sequential play is determined by the leader's most preferred point on the follower's reaction curve.

For the follower X we have:

$$\pi_x^F > \pi_x^* \Leftrightarrow \left(1 - \frac{v}{2a}\right)^2 \cdot V_x > \frac{a^2}{(a+v)^2} \cdot V_x$$

$$\Leftrightarrow \frac{2a - v}{2a} > \frac{a}{a+v} \Leftrightarrow a > v$$

and the claim follows.

b) $a \cdot V_x < V_y$ resp. $a < v$: completely analogous.

Lemmas 1–3 imply that the commonly preferred sequential solution is a subgame perfect equilibrium of our game.

Lemma 4: The commonly preferred sequential solution is the *unique* subgame perfect equilibrium of our extended game.

Proof: To establish this assertion we have to show that the other sequential solution is *not* commonly preferred to simultaneous play. We only consider the case $aV_x < V_y$ resp. $a < v$: We have to show that (π_x^*, π_y^*) is *not* Pareto-dominated by (π_x^L, π_y^F).

Surely, $\pi_x^L > \pi_x^*$. But now we have $\pi_y^F > \pi_y^* \Leftrightarrow \left(1 - \frac{a}{2v}\right)^2 V_y > \frac{v^2}{(a+v)^2} \cdot V_y$

$$\Leftrightarrow \frac{2v - a}{2v} > \frac{v}{a+v} \Leftrightarrow a < v$$

and thus $\pi_y^F < \pi_y^*$.

This completes the proofs of Lemma 4 and Theorem 1.

Still somewhat muddy: A comment

GORDON TULLOCK
Department of Economics, University of Arizona, Tucson, AZ 85721

Perez-Castrillo and Verdier[1] seem to have solved the bulk of the first level mathematical puzzles in my "Efficient Rent-Seeking". There still remains the second order of puzzle mentioned in my first article, the question of which "agent" (to use their terminology) will be the one or more who buys tickets in this lottery. This, I am happy to say, is somewhat easier than the original problem, but until it is solved we can't claim to understand the issue in general.

Let me begin with a case where r is less than 1. In these declining marginal efficiency cases Perez-Castrillo and Verdier follow the conventional approach and point out that there usually is some minimum cost, postage for example. Hence there is a restriction on the minimum bid.

This is of course true, but it raises another problem. Suppose that in the lottery for $100, r is 1/3. Further suppose that it costs $3 in actual resource expenditures to get your lottery ticket. According to Table 6.2 in "Efficient Rent Seeking,"[2] we see that 10 people are the right number for this amount. Each of these 10 would be investing $3 to get a 1 in 10 chance of $100 and this is obviously not equilibrium.

The procedure investigated in "Efficient Rent-Seeking" when r is less than 1 is that as more people invest, the average amount invested by each person goes down and there is no true equilibrium. With a minimum effective bid of $3.00, however, we would anticipate that not 10 but 33 people would invest their $3 which is the minimum resource cost of a ticket. This is an equilibrium, but a peculiar one.[3]

This particular set of circumstances, i.e. when r is less than 1, is one in which preclusive bidding is not possible. Indeed, the person proposing to get in with a large sum should break his investment up into a lot of small pieces, as small as possible, and make a lot of small bids. The reader will recall that not very long ago an Australian syndicate bought 5 million $1 tickets in the Virginia State Lottery and collected $27 million dollars.[4] Of course, in this case there is no evidence it was equilibrium.

Since the Virginia State Lottery Commission has changed the rules to make this harder in the future, the lottery may never reach an equilibrium of this sort.

In essence, they raised the private cost of buying a lottery ticket and perhaps the normal private purchase of 2 or 3 million tickets is in equilibrium under those circumstances. Strictly speaking, of course, where there is an effective minimum bid r is 1 at that bid.

If r is greater than 1, then we have two distinct areas. When r is between 1 and 2, N* can be quite a large number. In cases where r is 2 or above, N* is always 1. Incidentally, they talk to some extent about the symmetry or asymmetry of the investments here and it's a little hard to see what that terminology means if r is above 2.

From the standpoint of the agents wondering whether to buy tickets in the lottery, there are three different types of game. In the first they can buy a certain number of tickets and then either increase their holdings or cash them in and take back their money right up to the time the drum is spun and the number is withdrawn. In the second, you can buy any number of tickets you wish and increase the number at any time, again up to the time the drum is spun, but you can't cash them in and withdraw. In the third, you must make a single purchase and that's it.

The first of these would correspond to many speculative market where you can get in and out very easily.[5] The second is what I think most people thinking of rent-seeking regard as normal. Once you give a congressman an expensive evening's entertainment, there is no way you can get the money back. The third would be the case of the sealed bid. It's apparently little used in rent-seeking, and, hence, I shall give it relatively little attention.

Let us begin with the case in which you can withdraw your investment at any time and assume that this is costless. Further, I'd like to use a particular game which is easy to think about, specifically one where there are only two agents and r is equal to 3.

Let me assume as a starting point that both of them have already bought $50 worth of tickets for a $100 prize. Agent A now goes up to $75. In doing so, he increases his probability of winning so that his expected value goes up by $27 so, per se, that is a sensible investment. Agent B now has a choice. He can match agent A's bid by going up to $75 which will increase the value of his expectancy from the £23, which it is after agent A went up to $75, to $50 which looked at by itself once again is a sensible investment, or he can get out.

Assume that he goes up to $75 and then both of the players begin making strong statements about how they are going to stick regardless. In fact, there is no reason to try to cash in their chips and get out until the very last minute, since there is always some chance that the other party will do so first.

The question there is whether it is sensible to cash in at the last minute. Note both of the parties face this problem and neither one can wait until after the last minute to cash in his own lottery tickets and get out. The last minute is, after all, the last minute.

If agent A thinks that agent B will withdraw with exactly 50% probability and agent B thinks that agent A will withdraw with exactly 50% probability, they each own a right with a present discounted value of $75, but if they both stick they have an expectancy of − $25. If either one thinks that the chance that the other will check out is greater than 50% he should stay in, and if he thinks it is less than 50% he should get out.[6]

We have here an example of the paradox of the liar. The situation in which, if there is a correct strategy, and it can be computed by A, then B can compute what A's correct strategy is. He can then use whatever his best strategy in return and in general that will mean that A's strategy is not really the best, i.e. there is no optimal strategy. This is the problem that led Pascal to give up on games of strategy. They lead to an infinite regress.

Now in this particular case there is, as it happens, a mixed strategy.[7] The problem is that if I think my opponent in this game in which we both put in $75 is going to actually have an exactly 50% chance of staying in or leaving (let us say I saw him flip a coin) I am now free to do anything, depending on extrinsic matters. I may for example be risk averse. Or I may dislike him and want to make sure that he doesn't win. The strategies provided by those two different preferences are both costless in expectancy terms and hence the sensible thing is to ignore the expectancy and make up my mind. Unfortunately, once again, this is true for both agents and there is no true solution to the game.

What about the situation in which you can buy a certain number of tickets and then can buy more but cannot take money out of the game? The first thing to be said is that if r is much above 1, whoever gets in first can lay a preclusive bid. For example, $99 by A would keep B from making any purchase at all and hence is pretty much a guarantee of $1 profit.

Of course, $99 is not the most profitable way of precluding your opponent. You would want the lowest possible amount. Unfortunately, this is a difficult problem. It is particularly difficult in the area of r between 1 and 2 because in this case there are apt to be a considerable number of people investing unless you preclude all of them. If they do invest there is no guarantee of any profit for anyone.

Let us return to our simple case where there are only two agents and r is 3. Assume temporarily that A is thinking of a preclusive bid and is attempting to calculate the appropriate one. Unfortunately this is not an easy problem if he wants to make the minimum preclusive bid.

Depending on what he thinks the other party will do and what he thinks he will do in response to the other party and what he thinks the other party will think he will do in response, etc. it can be any number from about 30 to about 60. If A goes too low B can dash in with, let us say, 75 and preclude A from raising his bid. If he bids too high he is investing money innecessarily. Unfortunately, if he stops to carefully work out this problem he will probably be beaten by B who dashes in with some large number, perhaps 75, without thinking about the matter.

Of course it's not essential that any party make a preclusive bid. If, however, an individual party does not make a preclusive bid then almost anything can happen. It's easy to develop scenarios in which a preclusive bid is made by nobody and in which almost any outcome that you want to specify occurs. Unfortunately, for reasons we will discuss later, making a preclusive bid is a very risky strategy also.

In the real world, this is not the only calculating problem. A high Hollywood executive explaining [anonymously] to the New York Times how Sony lost $45 million on a single film said: "This business is so competitive, so cynical, so absolutely cutthroat that before you have a chance to digest information you start moving."[8] Putting it differently, a preclusive bid is necessarily highly risky. You can't afford to stop and think the matter over because if you do somebody will get in ahead of you.

Of course you can put in a small amount of money and then go up. Indeed, rent-seeking works just that way. You invite the congressman out to dinner and make up your mind at that point whether you will have more dinners or more resources invested in that particular issue. You take into account what other people are doing. Unfortunately, if r is above 1 and you get into this kind of a game, costs are generally sunk and the odds are that the total amount invested by all of the rent-seekers will be greater than the prize. The only really good motive for small initial investments would be as a strategic investment in finding out what your rivals are going to do.

There is a possible solution, but before we deal with it let us turn to our third category, the case in which you are permitted to make only one bid. As far as I know this is not common in rent-seeking activities, but for completeness we should at least mention it and point out that it raises the same problem. Once again, what you want to do is get your bid in first and have a preclusive one. Of course if some kind of sealed bid technique is used you can't even do that.

Consider the situation if there are a number of problems of either our second or third type coming up. The case of Hollywood firms deciding what movies to produce is of course a clearcut example, but so is the situation in Washington in which the highly paid lobbyists of the various industries and labor unions must decide how much they will put into lobbying different congressmen.

There is in biology a solution to this kind of problem which is called the hawk-dove equilibrium.[9] What we would expect is that there would be a large number of agents who would decide to stay out of business completely and another large number of agents who would make a profession of attempting preclusive bids for various opportunities. Note I say attempt because it is clear that they would miscalculate, they don't have time to calculate accurately. The miscalculation would frequently mean that more than one agent put his money down and only one won the lottery.

The hawk-dove equilibrium in this case would be that there would be enough people who are engaging in the strategy of making quick investments in the rent-seeking lottery so that the return that they had over time would be roughly the same as that of those who made no such investments. In other words, any potential profit would be competed away, but competed away not in the individual lottery but over the universe of all lotteries and all agents.

Note that this leaves us with no solution for any individual lottery. All we know about it is that there is a preclusive bid which somebody can make first, but he will not know exactly how big it is and further, he won't actually know the value of the lottery because the agents have to make their bids without careful calculation. If they spend time carefully calculating, somebody else will get in ahead of them.

The business would appear to be a nerve-wracking one and as far as we can tell that is indeed true. Back in the days when stomach ulcers were a major disease we would have predicted many of them among Hollywood producers and lobbyists in Washington. Those people, of course, with the specialized talents which make it possible to make these calculations quickly and with a somewhat lower error rate than other people have would be very highly rewarded.

Once again, note that here there is no social gain from this activity. We would anticipate that enough bids would be made so that any potential profits would be more or less eroded away. It would not be true that for any particular agent making bid for any particular lottery that the expectancy would be a normal profit. Sometimes they would make a lot of money and sometimes they would lose a lot of money, i.e. Sony's $45 million.

In both the case where r is below 1 and r is above 1, we have situations where although we can predict the outcome, mainly as a result of the work of Perez-Castrillo and Verdier, the outcome is inefficient. Resources are wasted in investments which simply transfer rents from one group of potential rent-seekers to another. There is an equilibrium, but it's not a nice equilibrium.

Notes

1. "A general analysis of rent-seeking games" in *Public Choice* 73.3 (April 1992): 335–350.
2. Buchanan, Tollison and Tullock (Eds.) (1980), *Toward a Theory of the Rent-Seeking Society* (College Station: Texas A&M University Press), pp. 97–112.
3. They mention in passing the possibility that r would turn up somewhere. This seems to me to be a dubious solution to the problem, but they don't analyze it and I will follow their example.
4. "Despite violation, Virginia to pay a lottery jackpot of $27 million" in *The New York Times* 11 March 1992; A13.
5. Usually with a small cost.
6. There is an alternative to getting out which is to go down to a low number. For example, A might go down to 1 on the theory that if B goes down to 0 you get the money at a low price and if he doesn't he will lose only a little bit. The problem with this is, again, it's symmetrical – the same strategy is open to both.

7. For my general criticism of mixed strategies, briefly summarized in the following few sentences of the text, see ''Games and preference'' in *Rationality and Society* 4.1 (January 1992): 24–32.
8. ''Tracking the tailspin of 'Radio Flyer''' in *The New York Times* (9 March 1992): B1.
9. For an explanation and an application to other economic problems, see my ''Hawks, doves and free riders'' in *Kyklos*, 45 (1992): Fasc. 1, 25–36. German translated excerpts were published in *Wirtschafts Woche* (8 November 1991): 132–134.

Cooperation by Credible Threats: On the Social Costs of Transfer Contests Under Uncertainty

by

CHUN-LEI YANG *

A transfer-seeking contest for the well-known Dollar-Auction as a limit case is modeled in an infinite horizon noncooperative setting. Some kind of mild but credible threat to retaliate is shown to constitute a Markov-stationary subgame perfect equilibrium. Introducing an entry barrier to, and uncertainty about, the transfer issue at stake, this contest is shown to perform efficiently in the sense that both contenders bid δ, the entry fee, in equilibrium. This is in stark contrast to the common scenario of fully-dissipating rent-seeking frequently presented in economic theories of politics, and can be interpreted as a resolution of the well-known Tullock paradox. (JEL: D 72, C 73, D 74, L 51)

1. Introduction

The social cost of monopoly is the sum of the traditional dead weight loss plus the monopoly rent: this is POSNER's message [1975]. Free entry to competition for a rent must cause, relying upon common sense economic wisdom, the dissipation of the whole rent competed for. This hypothesis has been so popular that many economists began using it to econometrically estimate the social loss of monopoly to a national economy.[1]

However, it is the nature of most politically contestable rents that free entry, and therefore perfect competition, does not exist. In particular, if the issue is to make some transfer between two interest groups as it happens through reform of taxation, protection, and regulation policies etc., there may be only two parties involved: for instance, subsidy beneficiaries vs. tax payers of some specific tax issue, or domestic consumers vs. domestic industries in search of protection against foreign competitors. In such situations, one proper way of assessing the social cost of rent-seeking is to deal with a micro-model where the

* This paper is based on Essay 4 of my PhD thesis submitted at the Economics Department of University Dortmund. I am indebted to Wolfgang Leininger and Rabah Amir for invaluable conversations and detailed comments. I am also grateful to three anonymous referees for helpful comments.

[1] See TOLLISON [1982] for further literature.

direct interactions, together with their consequences for the parties involved, are clearly defined.

A very influential formal model in this direction was framed by TULLOCK [1980]: in his model, a finite number of rent-seekers undertake efforts to influence political decision-making concerning some *artificially contrived* rents. As the emphasis is on the determination of the total amount of expenditure outlaid during the contest, the very complicated structure of political decision processes has been abstractly modeled as a stochastic device which chooses the winner of the contest. Put differently, from the viewpoint of each contender (and outside observers as well), the policy decision is made randomly and what he can do is to influence the performance of that random variable in his favor by exerting efforts. It is then reasonable to assume that the probability of winning the contest for a participant depends positively on his own investment and negatively on that of his opponents.

In the cases where simultaneous-move Nash equilibrium in pure strategies can be proven to exist, it is to be observed that the full-dissipation hypothesis is valid only in one specific case, while in other cases a large part of the rent is indeed dissipated in terms of expenditures. However, there is a serious problem associated with this approach, which TULLOCK [1985] himself has described as an "*intellectual swamp*": namely, for a range of values of the parameter r which can be interpreted as a measure of the *intensity* of competition [2], there exists no Nash equilibrium in pure strategies.[3] For the limit case ($r = \infty$), which is also known as the Dollar-Auction game in the literature,[4] HILLMAN and SAMET [1987] have shown the existence of a simultaneous-move Nash equilibrium in mixed strategies leading to a confirmation of the full-dissipation hypothesis.

One source of the problems of the approach mentioned above is the assumed simultaneity of the once-and-for-all investment acts, as important features – such as reacting to each other's offensives – are thereby abstracted away. LEININGER [1993] develops a model in which both the simultaneous and the sequential (Stackelberg) modes are possible outcomes in a two-stage game, but where only the latter endogenously prevails in subgame perfect equilibrium. He shows that the total expenditure to rent-seeking is in general smaller than in the original Tullock case. An approach using an infinite horizon game is followed in LEININGER and YANG [1993] where contenders invest into rent-seeking alternatingly in a sequential way and both of them have the same valuation of the rent.

The main message emerging is that there always exists some subgame perfect equilibrium, the strategic behavior involved being reminiscent of the famous

---

[2] For $r > 2$, to be precise. The meaning of r is also implicitly defined in the formulae (1) in the next section.

[3] A formal proof of its existence in mixed strategies is recently available from the author on request.

[4] Cf. SHUBIK [1971] or LEININGER [1989].

Tit-for-Tat pattern, such that only half of the value of the prize under consideration is expended as outlays, no matter how *intensive* the competition is. In fact, every contender always has the opportunity to modify his bid in case his opponent has increased his previous bid one stage ago. The quite mild, but credible, threat to simply adopt the opponent's bid is strong enough to prevent the contest situation from escalating. The equilibrium is characterized by a *preemptive* bid of exactly half the value of the rent by the first mover.

YANG [1992] extends this analysis to the general case of arbitrary valuations of the rent by the contenders. He shows that preemption can only prevail in equilibrium with sufficiently similar valuations, while with large differences in valuation preemption turns out to be too expensive for the players. Equilibrium can now be characterized by 'almost efficient' outcomes: facing similar Tit-for-Tat-like threats, everyone only makes a very low bid indeed.

In the present paper, this almost-efficiency property will be further extended to the common-valuation case of LEININGER and YANG [1993]. For this purpose we introduce a kind of entry fee, which is interpretable as the significance level of effort that is necessary to activate the responsible political instances.[5] Think of the case in which some interest-lobby intends to initiate a value transfer from other citizens to its own clientele – e.g. a specific protection policy for the domestic electronic industry. It is then appropriate to assume that the lobby first needs to articulate its desire to the public to some minimum extent, thus incurring some minimum expenditure, before the issue can ever be seriously considered by the government or other responsible authorities.

However, it is not appropriate in this example to assume that the lobby can perfectly anticipate the value of such a protection policy, as this depends on the exact stipulations of that (sought-for) policy in its final approved form. It is more realistic to envision a continual revelation of uncertainties about the value of this rent-seeking issue during the whole process preceding the final decision of the government. Such uncertainty will be introduced in section 4 in various stylized simple forms. It can then be shown that the outcome in which both contenders bid just the entry fee is to be expected in a (Markov-stationary) subgame perfect equilibrium: almost-efficiency results whenever that entry fee can be considered small. This is in stark contrast to the outcome in the simultaneous-move game with entry fee (HILLMAN and SAMET [1987]) and to the preemption outcome of games without an entry fee.[6]

A theoretical resolution of Tullock's paradox – that in reality much less outlay is observable than predicted by the rent-dissipation hypothesis[7] – is thereby offered. Beyond the observation that some genuine noncooperatively sustained *cooperative* outcome results, it is emphasized that this *cooperative*

---

[5] This device was introduced into the literature on rent-seeking by HILLMAN and SAMET [1987].

[6] Notice, however, that the introduction of uncertainty is necessary for our results.

[7] TULLOCK [1988, 470 f]: "... the puzzle of why the total expenditures ... is still rather small compared to the value of the favors."

outcome does not depend on the identity of the initial bidder, which may give the present model a more realistic appeal. This is hoped to mitigate doubts expressed by sceptics who object to sequential modeling on the grounds of the ad hoc determination of the initial mover. In the last section, the paper concludes with some further interpretations and ideas concerning the present model as well as the problem of rent-seeking in general.

2. The Model

Let us think of the transfer-seeking contest as an auction game in which two players X and Y are involved. It would be helpful in this context to view a lobbyist as trying to cause some income transfer from some victim group to his clientele.

At the very beginning, i.e. before the activation of the transfer issue, the value parameter V is a random variable, the distribution of which is known. The auction is opened by a bid $a_1 \in \mathbb{R}_+$, say, by player X (our lobbyist). If this bid exceeds some minimum outlay δ, then *nature* is assumed to move to resolve the uncertainty about V. Knowing the exact realization of V, player Y (an agent of our victim group) is to make his bid $a_2 \in \mathbb{R}_+$.[8]

For our lobbyist, all this may mean that he has first to send off his lawyers and other staff members to contact some friendly-minded parliamentarians, and to advertise through the press etc. Responding to these actions, those parliamentarians will then work out the bill which delineates the exact terms (aggregated in our V) of the intended income transfer, since this must take account of political feasibility constraints if it is to ever come before the Parliament. And this is assumed to happen before any organized resistance on behalf of the victim group gets started. (However ad hoc this assumption may admittedly appear, discussions in section 4 will show that it is *not* crucial for the prevalence of cooperative outcomes.)

Formally, the auction goes on with X and Y alternately making some *admissible* bids $a_{t+2} \geqq a_t$ for $t \in \mathbb{N}$, which are interpretable as the contenders' aggregated (sunk) efforts. It is ended if one of X and Y is no longer willing to bid any further, which is expressed by a simple repetition of one's own last bid. Furthermore, the auction is closed at some time $t = 2, 3, \ldots$ when $a_t = a_{t-2}$.[9] We assume

[8] An alternative model is to require the activation of the transfer issue as soon as at least one player has shown sufficient interest, i.e. min $\{a_1, a_2\} \geqq \delta$. For the reasons given in footnote 19, the cooperative outcome would still remain sustainable.

[9] From the viewpoint of modeling device, this is equivalent to saying that there is some random deadline of time beyond which any further effort will remain ineffective – for instance the voting is over. This can be seen from the fact that both models share the feature that there exists no predetermined last mover with some distinguished power of threat. Regarding the rule of closing, one can also assume that the bids are then repeated forever – which may make a more perfect analogy to thinking that the contenders will remain inactive from then on till the (random) deadline takes effect.

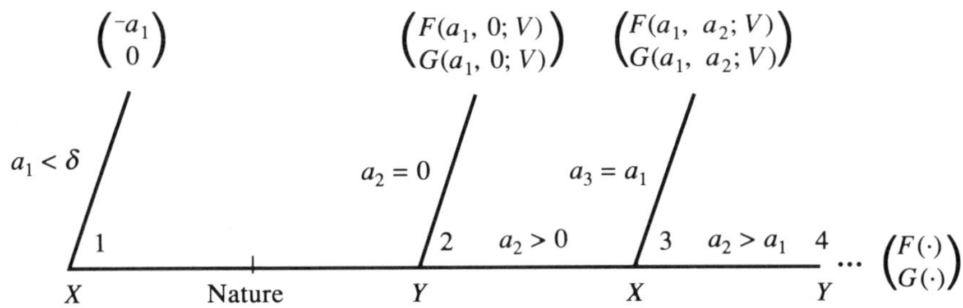

Figure 1

Game Tree

$a_0 = 0$. If, however, player X's first bid a_1 lies below the required minimum δ, the auction is closed immediately without any award of the (uncertain) rent sought – it is quite obvious that nothing would happen if, for example, our lobbyist's lawyers contacted only one parliamentarian who did not think he was able to convince enough colleagues to support any such bill. This would mean the end of the story unless more efforts follow. The extensive structure of this auction game is illustrated in the game tree in figure 1. If the auction is closed in some period t, then the payoffs to X resp. Y are assumed to be:

(1)
$$F(x, y) = \frac{Vx^r}{x^r + y^r} - x,$$
$$G(x, y) = \frac{Vy^r}{x^r + y^r} - y,$$

where $(x, y) = (a_{t-1}, a_t)$ for t even and $(x, y) = (a_t, a_{t-1})$ for t odd denotes the final bids by X and Y in the auction; V is the value of the transfer in consideration; and $r \geqq 2$ is supposed to be some natural number, to keep the analysis transparent.[10] However, if $a_1 < \delta$, the players get the payoffs $-a_1$ and zero respectively.

For possibly infinite play, i.e. $a_{2t+1} > a_{2t-1}$ and $a_{2(t+1)} > a_{2t}$ for all t, we formally define the payoffs to any admissible sequence $\{a_t\}_{t \in \mathbb{N}}$ as

(2)
$$F(\{a_t\}_{t \in \mathbb{N}}) = \lim_{t \to \infty} \left(\frac{a^r_{2t+1}}{a^r_{2t+1} + a^r_{2t}} V - a_{2t+1} \right)$$
$$G(\{a_t\}_{t \in \mathbb{N}}) = \lim_{t \to \infty} \left(\frac{a^r_{2t}}{a^r_{2t+1} + a_2^{a\,t}} V - a_{2t} \right).$$

[10] In fact, the case in which $r < 2$ can be interpreted to provide some milder climate of competition, such that 'almost efficient' outcomes can be sustained even without the uncertainty and the entry fee modeled here (see Essay 3 of Yang [1992]).

Owing to the admissibility constraints, the limits always exist in the extended reals.[11]

Observe that, as shown in HILLMAN and RILEY [1989], a transfer contest as discussed here can be more precisely described than we have done, by using an additional variable that characterizes the fact that the loser of such a contest has to (partially) bear the cost of the rent. However, as the analysis remains essentially the same, we have abstained from that formulation for the sake of simplicity. Interested readers are referred to an early version of the present paper (YANG [1991]) where that more precise formulation was adopted.

Also, it should be mentioned that HILLMAN and SAMET [1987] first modeled the entry fee in the simultaneous Dollar-Auction rent-seeking game which they called "minimum outlays for participation." In contrast to their model where the entry fees have no real influence on the total amount of expenditure, it can be shown, for a class of uncertainty specifications in the present paper, that the equilibrium bid for both players is only the entry fee. This can indeed be interpreted as a (forced) victory of rationality in overcoming some Prisoner-Dilemma-like situation.

3. Equilibrium Analysis in the Deterministic Case

Throughout this section it is assumed that V is deterministic. In this form, the game described in the last section is identical to the infinite horizon model of LEININGER and YANG [1993] up to the additional feature of an entry fee δ and the fact that there is no move of nature here to determine the first bidder. So, I may refer to that paper for a formal game theoretic description of information sets, histories, strategies etc. relevant for a general analysis.

In this paper, the analysis is restricted to so-called Markov-stationary strategies and Markov-stationary subgame perfect equilibrium as the solution concept. In contrast to a "normal" strategy of a player in an extensive form game, which assigns an action to every conceivable history at every stage t, a player's Markov-stationary strategy depends only on the current state of the play – usually identified with the payoff relevant terms for one's current decisions – independently of the stage and of the pre-history that has led to the current state.

In our game, the state at time t is identified with the last two bids $\{a_{t-2}, a_{t-1}\}$, the only factor which determines the final payoff if the game happens to stop at t. From the game rules it can be seen immediately that the space of accessible states for player X resp. Y is $\Omega_X = \{(x, y) \in \mathbb{R}^2_+ : x \geqq \delta\} \cap \{(0, 0)\}$ resp.

[11] If both $\{a_{2t}\}_{t\in\mathbb{N}}$ and $\{a_{2t-1}\}_{t\in\mathbb{N}}$ are bounded, then the limits exist due to monotonicity of these sequences. If e.g. $\{a_{2t}\}_{t\in\mathbb{N}}$ is bounded whereas $\{a_{2t-1}\}_{t\in\mathbb{N}}$ not, then $F(\cdot) = -\infty$, $G(\cdot) = -\lim_{t\to\infty} a_{2t}$. If both are unbounded then both get the payoff $-\infty$.

$\Omega_Y = \{(x, y) \in \mathbb{R}^2_+ : x \geqq \delta\}$. Any *Markov-stationary strategy* for X resp. Y can be identified with some mapping $\sigma_X : \Omega_X \subset \mathbb{R}^2_+ \to \mathbb{R}_+$ such that $\sigma_X(x, y) \geqq x$ resp. $\sigma_Y : \Omega_Y \subset \mathbb{R}^2_+ \to \mathbb{R}_+$ such that $\sigma_Y(x, y) \geqq y$.[12]

Since SELTEN'S [1965], [1975] seminal work the solution concept of *subgame perfect equilibrium* (*SPE*) has become standard in analyzing extensive form games, replacing traditional Nash equilibrium. Simply speaking, SPE requires some stronger self-enforcing property of the equilibrium strategy combination, in the sense that a Nash equilibrium has to be induced in any conceivable subgame. In other words, decisions must be optimal even with information sets which are not expected to be reached by carrying out the designated equilibrium strategies: a strategy satisfying this criterion does not make any *empty* threats.

A *Markov-stationary SPE* (*MSPE*) is simply a SPE using only Markov-stationary strategies. To be precise, let $s_{(x, y)_i}(\sigma_X, \sigma_Y)$ denote the final state induced by the Markov-stationary strategies σ_X and σ_Y in the subgame that starts at the state (x, y) with player i at move. Then, a pair (σ_X, σ_Y) constitutes a MSPE iff $\forall (x, y) \in \mathbb{R}^2_+$:

$$\sigma_X \in \arg\max_{\sigma'_X} F(s_{(x, y)_X}(\sigma'_X, \sigma_Y))$$

if it is X's turn to make a bid (at (x, y)) and

$$\sigma_Y \in \arg\max_{\sigma'_Y} G(s_{(x, y)_Y}(\sigma_X, \sigma'_Y))$$

if it is Y's turn to make a bid.[13] It means that (σ_X, σ_Y) induces a Nash equilibrium at any stage (x, y).[14]

Notice that MSPEs have the nice property that only little information is needed for the players to make their decisions; hence, a rational player need not have an unlimited memory and calculation capacity to be able to find the optimal actions. For the analysis, it is only relevant for a player to know what

---

[12] To avoid misunderstanding, notice that (x, y) represents X's and Y's actual bids; depending on the odd- or evenness of t, it maybe $(x, y) = (a_{t-1}, a_t)$ or $(x, y) = (a_t, a_{t-1})$.

[13] Note further that only the part $\sigma'_i|_{[x, \infty) \times [y, \infty)}$ in the formulas above is of any relevance for the issue of subgame perfection.

[14] From the definition above one easily can see how the solution concept of Nash equilibrium may allow for absurd threats. E.g. strategies

$$\sigma_X(x, y) = \begin{cases} \max\{\epsilon, x\}, & \text{if } y = 0 \\ 4V + x, & \text{otherwise} \end{cases} \qquad \sigma_Y(x, y) = \begin{cases} V + y, & \text{if } x < \epsilon \\ y, & \text{otherwise} \end{cases}$$

form a Nash equilibrium with the final state $(\epsilon, 0)$. Yet, if Y bids ϵ at the state $(\epsilon, 0)$, receiving a negative payoff by bidding $4V + x$ is not in X's own interest – since he could get $\frac{V}{2} - \epsilon > 0$ if he stops bidding right away.

(payoff) to expect when moving at any specific state reached. In fact, the structure of our game fortunately enables us to conclude that every player's optimal action in remote states (far from the origin) turns out to be uniquely determined, independently. The consequence is that the SPE behavior can be derived uniquely (backwards with regard to accessible sets of states), except for a relatively small-sized area adjacent to the origin. To show this, the following lemma is needed where the locally best response curves are characterized. Recall, however, that those curves are only of restricted relevance for the players' actual action because the game is terminated only when one player has repeated his own previous bid.

Lemma 1. X's resp. Y's local best response curve can be represented parametrically by

$$R_X(t) = \begin{cases} x_F(t) = rVt^r(1+t^r)^{-2} \\ y_F(t) = t\,x_F(t) \end{cases} \tag{3}$$

respectively

$$R_Y(t) = \begin{cases} x_G(t) = t\,y_G(t) \\ y_G(t) = rVt^r(1+t^r)^{-2} \end{cases} \tag{4}$$

for $t \in \left(0, \left(\frac{r+1}{r-1}\right)^{\frac{1}{r}}\right)$.

Proof: The first order condition for X is

$$F_x = \frac{rVx^{r-1}y^r}{(x^r+y^r)^2} - 1 \stackrel{!}{=} 0\,. \tag{5}$$

Inserting $y = tx$ into (5) yields (3). Checking the second order condition then yields that (3) represents some local maximum iff $t \in \left(0, \left(\frac{r+1}{r-1}\right)^{\frac{1}{r}}\right)$. Q.E.D.

Let us now consider figure 2. The horizontally resp. vertically hatched area (with the lower bound $\tilde{R}_X$ resp. $\tilde{R}_Y$) represents states for which R_X resp. R_Y also depicts the (globally) maximal choices among the admissible ones there, for player X resp. Y. (Compare also the partial curvature shown in figure 4 to check that the graphs are drawn properly.) The basic rationality assumption about individual behavior requires X (resp. Y) to stop the game immediately at any state outside the horizontally (resp. vertically) hatched area, by repeating his previous bid – since any continuation of the game therefrom would make him strictly worse off. Anticipating these considerations which are also commonly known, X's (resp. Y's) best action at some state (x, y) with $y \geqq \frac{rV}{4}$ (resp.

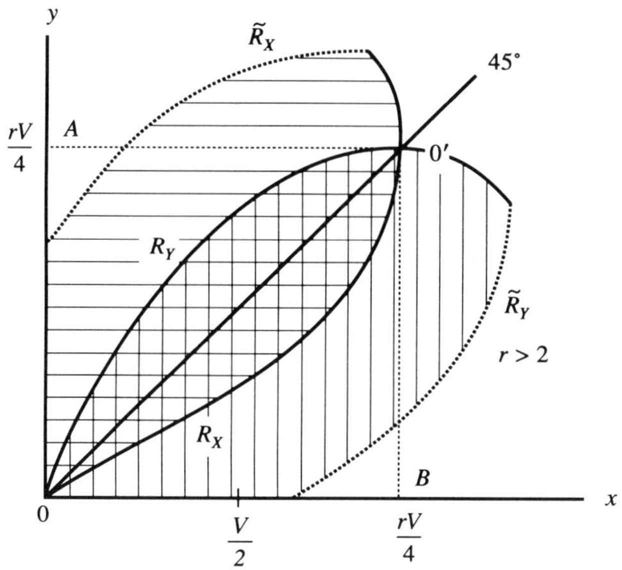

Figure 2
Locally Best Responses

$x \geqq \frac{rV}{4}$), in particular, is to switch to R_X (resp. R_Y) or to give up, whichever is better.

To obtain a MSPE, it remains to consider the states within the hatched areas in the square $OBO'A$. For this purpose, let us consider the *Tit-for-Tat* (TFT) behavior which roughly speaking means that every player threatens to counter with his opponent's current bid. This threat is understood as a mild one since the players signal their contention with an equal division of the rent. To provide a proper definition for the analysis, however, let us first delineate the area in which TFT may pay at all.

Lemma 2. Let

(6) $$T_X(t) := (x_{T,X}(t), y_{T,X}(t)) := \left(\frac{V}{2}\ \frac{t^r - 1}{2(t-1)(t^r+1)},\ \frac{V}{2}\ \frac{(t^r-1)t}{2(t-1)(t^r+1)}\right)$$

(7) $$T_Y(t) := (x_{T,Y}\ t), y_{T,Y}\ t)) := \left(\frac{V}{2}\frac{t(t^r-1)}{2(t-1)(t^r+1)},\ \frac{V}{2}\frac{t^r-1}{2(t-1)(t^r+1)}\right)$$

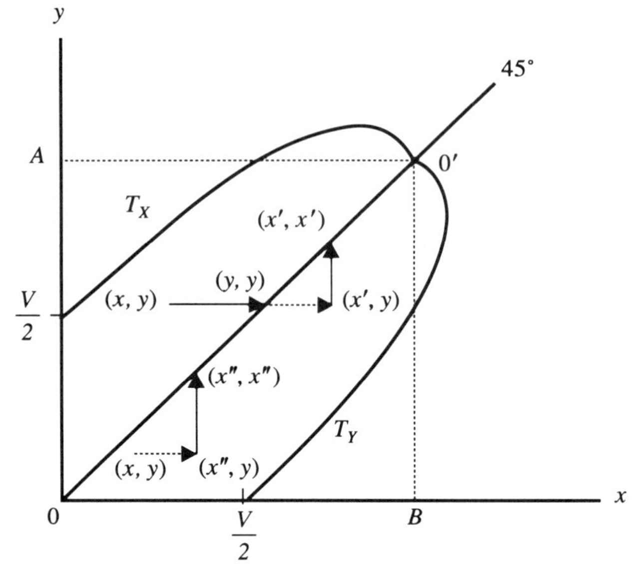

Figure 3

TFT Regions and MSPE

Bold-faced arrows represent SPE moves according to σ defined by (8) and (9), while dotted arrows represent some off-equilibrium behavior and $r > 2$.

where $t > 1$. Then, $\forall (x, y) \in \mathbb{R}_+^2$:

$$F(y, y) \geqq F(x, y) \text{ if } \exists t > 1 : x \in [x_{T,X}(t), y],\ y = y_{T,X}(t);$$
$$G(x, y) \geqq G(x, y) \text{ if } \exists t > 1 : x = x_{T,Y}(t),\ y \in [y_{T,Y}(t), x].$$

Proof: Straightforward: insert $y = tx$ into the equation $F(x, y) = F(y, y)$ for X; and analogously for Y. *Q.E.D.*

The curves just defined in this lemma are shown in figure 3. We are now able to define formally what we will refer to as TFT-strategies in this paper.[15]

$$(8) \qquad \sigma_X(x, y) = \begin{cases} x_F(y) & \text{if } y \geqq \dfrac{rV}{4} \text{ and } F(x_F(y), y) \geqq F(x, y) \\ y & \text{if } x_{T,X}(y) < x \leqq y \text{ and } y \leqq \dfrac{rV}{4} \\ \dfrac{V}{2} & \text{if } (x, y) = (0, 0) \\ x & \text{otherwise} \end{cases}$$

[15] A TFT behavior can not always be supported as some credible threat, for instance outside the square $OAO'B$ as discussed before.

$$(9)\qquad \sigma_Y(x, y) = \begin{cases} x_G(x) & \text{if } x \geqq \frac{rV}{4} \text{ and } G(x, y_G(x)) \geqq G(x, y) \\ x & \text{if } y_{T,Y}(x) < y \leqq x \text{ and } x \leqq \frac{rV}{4} \\ y & \text{otherwise.} \end{cases}$$

Here, $x_F(y)$ resp. $x_{T,X}(y)$ denote the x-value corresponding to y on the curve R_X resp. T_X; and $y_G(x)$ and $y_{T,Y}(x)$ are defined accordingly. By X's playing of σ_X and Y's playing of σ_Y, every player indeed adheres to the TFT-behavior in the square $OAO'B$ of figure 3 up to (including) the curves T_X and T_Y, as illustrated by the boldfaced arrows. (Recall that X's resp. Y's action at any state (x, y) can be graphically represented by a horizontal resp. vertical line section connecting (x, y) with the resulting state.) Let us call this area *retaliation area.* Outside that area – between T_X (resp. T_Y) and the 45°-line within the square $OAO'B$, player X (resp. Y) is recommended, by σ_X (resp. σ_Y), to stop the game immediately by repeating his own last bid.

The TFT-strategy combination (σ_X, σ_Y) indeed constitutes a MSPE. Consider for instance X's decision, given that Y is expected to use his TFT-strategy σ_Y. Let the actual state be (x, y). At first, because of the TFT property of σ_Y, for every final state $s_{(x,y)_X}(\tilde{\sigma}_X, \sigma_Y)$ that is accessible by X's deviating to some $\tilde{\sigma}_X$ in the state (x, y), there exists some bid $x' \geqq x$ such that the expected final state $(x', \sigma_Y(x', y))$ yields X no less a payoff than does $s_{(x,y)_X}(\tilde{\sigma}_X, \sigma_Y)$. It means that the analysis can be restricted to considering X's one-step decision at $(x, y)_X$ only. Among the one-step accessible states at (x, y), those of (x, y), (y, y) and $(x_{T,Y}(y), y)$ resp. $(x_{\tilde{R}_Y}(y), y)$ can be shown to constitute a payoff dominant subset for player X, where $(x_{\tilde{R}_Y}(y), y) \neq (x_{\tilde{R}_Y}(y), y_G(x_{\tilde{R}_Y}(y)))$ denotes some point satisfying $G(x_{\tilde{R}_Y}(y), y) = G(x_{\tilde{R}_Y}(y), y_G(x_{\tilde{R}_Y}(y)))$, i.e. the lower bound $\tilde{R}_Y$ as illustrated in figure 2.[16]

For more details, let us examine more closely figure 3. If $x < y$, X must expect, because of σ_Y, that any bid $x' \in (y, x_{T,Y}(y))$ (i.e. diving into Y's retaliation region, as shown by the dotted arrow) leads to the final state (x', x') on the 45°-line that makes him strictly worse off than the state (y, y) which results if σ_X is followed. If $x \geqq y$, X obviously prefers stopping the game right away yielding the final state (x, y) to any bid $x'' \in (x, x_{T,Y}(y))$ which gives Y the chance to retaliate causing the final state (x'', x''). Since making a bid so large that Y has no further incentive at all to continue (i.e. $x' > x_{T,Y}(y)$) is never a better decision than stopping at the 45°-line, which is illustrated in figure 4 and briefly proved in the Appendix. The decision $\sigma_X(x, y)$ is in fact a best one. If y is high enough so that X must bid $x_{\tilde{R}_Y}(y)$ in order to "drive away" the opponent, then X even has a strict incentive to go to (y, y) because $x_{\tilde{R}_Y}(y) \geqq x_{T,Y}(y)$ in an area where X's partial payoff is continuously decreasing. Anywhere, the recommendations of σ have proved to be the (*subgame perfectly*) optimal ones. This then

[16] Recall that one's payoff is monotone decreasing in the rival's (final) bid.

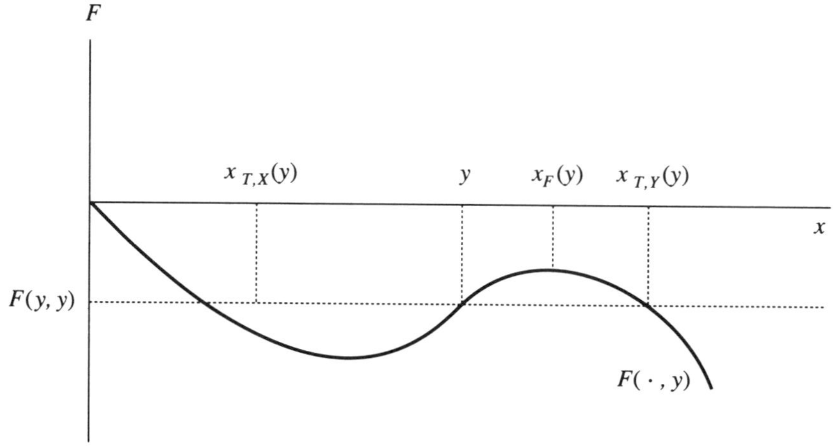

Figure 4
Bimodality of Partial Payoffs.

completes the heuristic proof of the following basic statement for our further analysis:[17]

Proposition 1. For $\delta \in [0, \frac{1}{2}V]$, (σ_X, σ_Y) constitutes a *MSPE* in which X opens with a bid $\frac{1}{2}V$ and Y makes a closing bid of zero. The equilibrium payoffs are $\frac{1}{2}V$ for X and 0 for Y.

It can be observed from the proposition that, on the equilibrium path, the first bidder X moves to the border of Y's retaliation region immediately. The reason for this "aggressive" action of preemption is the discontinuity of the payoffs at the origin: no transfer or rent awarding would take place if no investment into the contest could be recognized "publicly." By insertions into (8) and (9), it can be easily checked that any bid $a_1 \in [\delta, \frac{1}{2}V)$ by X will cause Y's retaliation in line with the TFT-strategy σ_Y which will yield X the payoff $\frac{1}{2}V - a_1$ that is smaller than his equilibrium one. This means the introduction of $\delta > 0$ has no influence on our equilibrium analysis as long as V is assumed to be deterministic, which is similar to a result in Hillman and Samet [1987].

4. *Uncertainty Cases*

From the last section we have seen that the first bidder behaves preemptively in our infinite horizon game if the term V is known at $t = 1$. If, however, one

[17] A complete formal proof and further characterizations can be found in Leininger and Yang [1993], which is a special case of Yang [1992].

agrees that the exact size of V may not be determined unless some necessary political process has been activated after recognition of some significant effort level coming from the contenders, it seems appropriate to assume that the first bidder treats the term V as a random variable at the very beginning. As discussed in section 2, this uncertainty is assumed to be resolved as soon as the rent-seeking issue has attracted some significant bid $a_1 \geqq \delta$ by X.

Assumption 1. V is a random variable uniformly distributed on the support $[V_1, V_2] \subset \mathbb{R}_+$. The resolution of uncertainty w.r.t V takes place at $t = 2$ if $a_1 \geqq \delta$.

Proposition 2. Under assumption 1,

$$\text{if } 0 < \delta \leqq \frac{V_2 - V_1}{4} = \min\left\{\tfrac{1}{2}EV, \tfrac{1}{2}(V_2 - EV)\right\},$$

where $EV = \frac{1}{2}(V_1 + V_2)$ denotes the expected value for V, then (δ, δ) is a *MSPE* outcome.

Proof: Let σ_X^* be a modification of σ_X, with the only difference that $\sigma_X^*(0, 0) = \delta$. Since the uncertainty is resolved at $t = 2$ if $a_1 \geqq \delta$, the property of a MSPE in the certainty case implies that (σ_X^*, σ_Y) makes up a MSPE no matter which state $(a_1, 0)$ be reached, due to the previous proposition 1.[18]

Anticipating these equilibrium continuations, the first bidder X has to assess the situation at the origin (0, 0) as follows: if he makes a high bid $a \geqq \frac{1}{2}V_2$, Y will certainly be preempted from making any positive bid; too low a bid $a < \delta$ means no activation of the rent-seeking issue, hence merely sunk cost on his part; a bid $a \in [\delta, \frac{1}{2}V_1]$ that is high enough to activate the issue implies that Y will certainly answer with the bid $a_2 = a$, such that the winning probability is $\frac{1}{2}$ for both; any bid $a \in [\frac{1}{2}V_1, \frac{1}{2}V_2]$ will turn out to be preemptive, if and only if the realization of the random variable V is such that Y has no profitable positive bid while facing the opponent's TFT behavior in equilibrium continuation. Hence, X's expected payoff by bidding $a_1 = a$ is

$$F^E(a) = \begin{cases} -a, & a < \delta \\ \displaystyle\int_{V_1}^{V_2} \left(\frac{1}{2}V - a\right) \frac{dV}{V_2 - V_1}, & a \in [\delta, \tfrac{1}{2}V_1] \\ \displaystyle\int_{V_1}^{2a} (V - a) \frac{dV}{V_2 - V_1} + \int_{2a}^{V_2} \left(\frac{1}{2}V - a\right) \frac{dV}{V_2 - V_1}, & a \in [\tfrac{1}{2}V_1, \tfrac{1}{2}V_2] \\ \displaystyle\int_{V_1}^{V_2} (V - a) \frac{dV}{V_2 - V_1}, & a \geqq \tfrac{1}{2}V_2 \end{cases} \tag{10}$$

[18] In fact, an equivalent definition of SPE is to require that at any subgame a SPE starting therefrom is to be induced.

For $a \in [\frac{1}{2}V_1, \frac{1}{2}V_2]$ we have

$$F^E(a) = EV - a - \frac{1}{2(V_2 - V_1)} \int_{2a}^{V_2} V dV$$
$$= EV - a - \frac{1}{2(V_2 - V_1)} \frac{1}{2}(V_2^2 - (2a)^2).$$

Therefore

$$\frac{d}{da}F^E(a) = -1 + \frac{2a}{V_2 - V_1}$$
$$\frac{d^2}{da^2}F^E(a) = \frac{2}{V_2 - V_1} > 0$$

which means F^E is strictly convex and must reach its maximum at one of the corners of the interval $[\frac{1}{2}V_1, \frac{1}{2}V_2]$. We then conclude that

$$\max_{a \in [\frac{1}{2}V_1, \frac{1}{2}V_2]} F^E(a) \in \left\{ \int_{V_1}^{V_2} \left(V - \frac{1}{2}V\right) \frac{dV}{V_2 - V_1}, \int_{V_1}^{V_2} \frac{1}{2}(V - V_1) \frac{dV}{V_2 - V_1} \right\}$$
$$= \left\{ EV - \frac{1}{2}V_2, \frac{1}{2}(EV - V_1) \right\}.$$

On the other hand, the global maxima for the intervals $a \in [\delta, \frac{1}{2}V_1]$ resp. $[\frac{1}{2}V_2, \infty)$ are obviously:

$$\tfrac{1}{2}EV - \delta \quad \text{resp.} \quad EV - \tfrac{1}{2}V_2 .$$

It is then obvious that:

$$\max_{a \in \mathbb{R}_+} F^E(a) \in \left\{ 0,\ EV - \frac{1}{2}V_2, \frac{1}{2}EV - \delta \right\}.$$

What is then implied is that $a = \delta > 0$ is the only optimal decision for the first bidder X if: $\delta < \frac{1}{2}EV$ and $\delta < \frac{1}{2}(V_2 - EV)$.[19] However, if $a_1 = \delta$ is chosen at

[19] At this stage, it can be seen that a modification of the game rule such that both players are given the power to activate the transfer issue as mentioned in footnote 9 will not rule out the cooperative outcome. The only difference is that if $a_1 < \delta$ then Y is given the role player X had in this proof. Recall that the uncertainty is resolved as soon as the transfer issue is activated, Y will carry out exactly the same calculation up to the case of $a_1 \in [0, \delta]$. (A higher a_1 will have the effect that Y is more likely to choose the cooperative bid $a_2 = \delta$, since Y would have to invest more to force X giving up bidding further, due to the sunk cost effect of $a_1 > 0$.) No matter what Y does, however, any $a_1 < \delta$ by X is dominated by $a_1 = \delta$ since giving the active role away to the rival never pays in this model. Thus, the same conclusion as in this proposition can be stated for the modified case.

$t = 1$, the equilibrium continuation yields $a_2 = \delta$, $a_3 = \delta$ which leads to the final state of (δ, δ) and the equilibrium payoffs $(\frac{1}{2}\tilde{V} - \delta, \frac{1}{2}\tilde{V} - \delta)$ where $\tilde{V} \in [V_1, V_2]$ is some realization of the random variable $\tilde{V}$. This completes the proof. *Q.E.D.*

Roughly speaking, the smaller δ and the larger the term $\frac{1}{2}(V_2 - EV)$, the more likely is the cooperative behavior, in contrast to the preemptive one, to be expected in such an infinite horizon game. This is not surprising. With a bid $a_1 = \delta$, X can get the payoff $\frac{1}{2}V - \delta$ with certainty, which is only by δ less than his highest payoff $\frac{1}{2}V$ in the MSPE of the certainty case. If δ is low while the consequences of the uncertainty are quite severe, he will prefer bidding δ to get some certain payoff.

The strong impact of Tit-for-Tat type behavior – to induce people to restrain themselves in a conflict situation, thus yielding an efficient outcome – is revealed once more in an infinite horizon noncooperative setting.[20] In our particular model this cooperative outcome is even robust against the roughness of competition in terms of varying V, as can be read directly from the propositions.

A further interesting aspect of this cooperative outcome is its robustness against modifications of the model setting. That the cooperative outcome remains the solution in a modified mode of the *activation* rule has already been discussed in footnote 19. In the following, some intuition is given to illustrate the robustness of this outcome if the timing of the resolution of uncertainty is changed. The modification of the model is expressed in the following assumption.

Assumption 2. The random variables V are realized with probability p at $t = 2$ and $(1 - p)$ at $t = 3$.

The associated game tree is illustrated in figure 5.

Quite obvious is the observation now that, for p very close to 1, the expression $F^E(a)$ in (10) may change only slightly and therefore proposition 2 is valid for a slightly smaller upper bound of those entry fees δ that induce cooperation.

Consider the opposite extreme case of $p = 0$, i.e. the resolution of the uncertainty evolves only after Y's bidding a_2. Anticipating the MSPE continuation with the strategy pair (σ_X, σ_Y) in any certainty case, player Y is expected to bid $a_2 = a_1$ as a reaction to player X's ('cooperative' or 'preemptive') bid a_1 if $\delta \leqq a_1 < E\frac{1}{2}V$, because his expected payoff is $EG(a_1, a_1) = E\frac{1}{2}V - a_1$. If $a_1 \geqq E\frac{1}{2}V$, Y rather prefers bidding zero. If, however, $a_1 < \delta$, Y may be cooperative by bidding $a_2 = \delta$ or preemptive, as X does in the $p = 1$ case. Anticipating this behavior of player Y, player X at $t = 1$ has his optimal action among $a_1 = \delta$ and $a_1 = E\frac{1}{2}V$ only. While $a_1 = E\frac{1}{2}V$ leads to the expected payoff $E\frac{1}{2}V$, $a_1 = \delta$ yields him only $a_1 = E\frac{1}{2}V - \delta$. This implies that for the extreme case of $p = 0$

[20] In contrast to the models of repeated games, however, there are no stage payoffs here. A further important feature is also the finiteness of the equilibrium play.

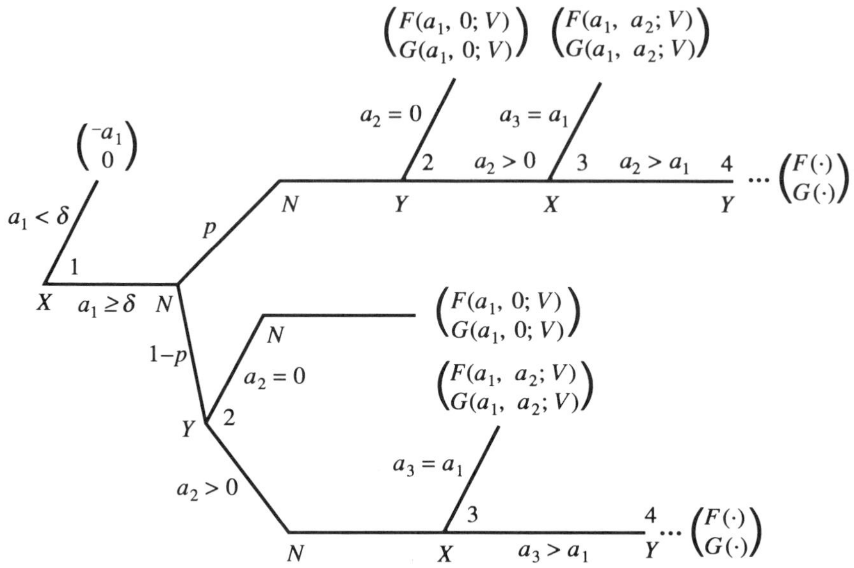

Figure 5

Modified Game Tree

the cooperative outcome (δ, δ) is not sustainable by (σ_X, σ_Y). However, the above consideration leads to the insight that $p = 0$ is the only case where (δ, δ) is not sustainable. Thus, we can conclude:

Proposition 3. Under assumption 2, if $p \neq 0$ then there exists some $\bar{\delta}(p) > 0$ such that (δ, δ) is a MSPE outcome if $\delta < \bar{\delta}(p)$. Furthermore, $\bar{\delta}(p) \to 0$ if $p \to 0$.[21]

But this is not yet the complete story. From the analysis just completed, one inevitably comes to the insight that risk-averse players are more likely to cooperate than risk-loving ones. In fact, if player X is risk-averse, even for the extreme case of $p = 0$ the cooperative outcome is sustainable. Furthermore, the upper limit $\bar{\delta}(p)$ of sustainable entry fees can then be extended for all p. Also, the specific form of the (independent) distributions is not necessary for the results as a careful re-reading of the proofs may reveal.

The analysis of this section can now be interpreted to offer a resolution of Tullock's paradox in the following form: if the contenders for a rent have the almost unrestricted opportunity to retaliate and if there are some (not too high) institutional barriers to entry and uncertainty about the cake at stake, then the observed low levels of outlays in the real world can be explained as the result

[21] For the sake of completeness, it should be mentioned that if $\delta > \bar{\delta}(p)$, then the preemption result of proposition 1 is valid.

of some kind of forced rationality through credible threats. Possible aggressive actions may be the expression of the limits of (institutional) frameworks favorable for cooperation; such limits include for instance high entry costs, misspecification of the uncertainties involved, and the presence of risk-loving contenders.

5. Concluding Remarks

"Institutions," to cite North [1991], "are the humanly devised constraints that structure political, economic and social interactions." They have been established mainly to capture the gains from trade; otherwise, they typically fail to survive over time. In an ideal framework, Buchanan and Tullock [1962] have shown that an institution, the constitution to be precise, serving this goal can be established upon the unanimous agreement among rational ('selfish') individuals. However, how an efficient institution in the real world works, whether in form of laws, habits, common sense or something else, is difficult to identify, even though we may often be able to notice the efficiency of the outcomes. And even if an efficient institution can be figured out in detail, it still remains almost insurmountable an obstacle to exactly explore the evolutionary process leading to it.

The main message of the present paper is to show that there exists some institutions of rent-seeking which yields an almost efficient outcome. The framework set by this institution can be identified with the infinite horizon structure of the auction game analyzed, supplemented by features such as minimum outlays and uncertainties within political processes. The Tit-for-Tat conduct can be understood *both* as some outcome inherent to this rent-seeking institution *and* as an established institution itself within the rent-seeking – one that may have resulted from *some* evolutionary process of its internalization (among potential rent-seekers across possible rent-seeking issues). As an indication that such internalization may already have taken place in the society, the observation that credible Tit-for-Tat-like threats are commonly conceded among the economic as well as political citizens can be instanced. This kind of *rationalizing* of cooperative behavior in a noncooperative setting is, in fact, a starting motivation for this paper.

The model presented does have a great deal of realistic appeal. The modeling of the entry cost is adapted to reflect the fact that only qualified agents of interest groups involved are permitted to take part and the cost of their establishments cannot be without influence on the final outcome of the issue at stake. It takes time before it is absolutely clear how the rent in consideration is exactly to be valued via the responsible authorities: this has led to the assumption of uncertainty. In regard to the sequential structure, it is not assumed that the real world rent-seeking is infinite; this infinite horizon modeling device, to cite Rubinstein [1991], "is supposed to assist us with analysing situations in which players are examining a long-term situation without assigning in their reasoning a special status for the end of the world,"

which is just what people do in sequentially interactive, real world conflict situations. The independence of our cooperative outcome from the identitiy of the arbitrarily fixed first bidder, as shown, may also make it less severe of an ad hoc assumption. No doubt, however, the analysis presented here is only one of partial equilibrium. It remains to be investigated whether a model can be found which endogenizes the variable δ among others.

Yet, if the government is in charge of designing a rent-seeking auction and is supposed to be interested in some efficient outcome, then there already exist models satisfying this requirement. For instance, a stage of simultaneous participation decisions by paying fee δ can be designed to preceed our infinite alternate bids auction, where the MSPE outcome (δ, δ) would take place regardless of whether the terms c and V are random.

Finally, the symmetry property assumed, while making life easier, is not necessary for the major intention of this paper. In YANG [1992], some kind of quasi Tit-for-Tat can be sustained as MSPE.

Zusammenfassung

Der Wettbewerb um institutionell bedingte Renten oder Transfers ist modelliert als ein Auktionsspiel von unendlicher Zeitdimension. Das bekannte Tit-for-Tat Verhalten kann als glaubwürdige Drohung im Markov-Stationären teilspielperfekten Gleichgewicht gestützt werden. Die Einführung einer minimalen Investition zur Aktivierung des Transfer-Seeking-Aktes sowie die Einführung von Unsicherheit bewirkt, daß im Gleichgewicht beide Konkurrenten nur diese minimale Investition bieten. Dieses "effiziente" Ergebnis steht im krassen Gegensatz zur gängigen These der "Full-Dissipation" aus den Theorien der Politischen Ökonomie und kann zudem als eine Auflösung des sogenannten "Tullock-Paradox" interpretiert werden.

Appendix

To prove proposition 1, some further insights into the features of the underlying payoff functions are needed which are briefly sketched in this appendix.

The bimodal property of the partial payoff function $F(\cdot, y)$ illustrated in figure 4 results from lemma 1 and the fact that the first order condition (5), when reformulated, can be expressed as a polynomial in the variable x with two changes of its signs of coefficients which leads to the conclusion that the first order condition either has two positive roots or non at all, according to the

Sign-rule by Descarte (BRONSTEIN and SEMENDJAJEW [1981]). Incorporating this into the second order condition it is then straightforward to conclude

Lemma 3. If $y > \frac{r^2-1}{4r}\left(\frac{r+1}{r-1}\right)^{\frac{1}{r}} V$, then (5) has no positive solution. If $y \leqq \frac{r^2-1}{4r}\left(\frac{r+1}{r-1}\right)^{\frac{1}{r}} V$, then (5) has exactly two positive solutions $\underline{x}(y) \leqq \bar{x}(y)$, where $\bar{x}(y)$ denotes the local maximum and $\underline{x}(y)$ denotes the local minimum. Furthermore, if $y \leqq \frac{rV}{4}$, then $\underline{x}(y) \leqq y \leqq \bar{x}(y)$.

Another crucial result used for proposition 1 is that the TFT behavior $\sigma_X(x, y) = y$ never makes X worse off compared to the aggressive, sweeping-aside action of $\sigma_X(x, y) = x_{T,Y}(y)$. He is in fact indifferent between these two points as illustrated in figure 4.

Lemma 4. $\forall y \in (0, \frac{rV}{4}]: F(y, y) = F(x_{T,Y}(y), y)$.

Proof: Let $y = \frac{V}{2}\frac{t^r-1}{2(t-1)(t^r+1)}$ for some $t > 1$, then

$$F(x_{T,Y}(y), y) - F(y, y)$$

$$= V(1+t^{-r})^{-1} - \frac{V}{2}\frac{t(t^r-1)}{2(t-1)(t^r+1)} - \left(\frac{V}{2} - \frac{V}{2}\frac{t^r-1}{(t-1)(t^r+1)}\right)$$

$$= \frac{V[2(t-1)t^r - t(t^r-1) - (t-1)(t^r+1) + (t^r-1)]}{2(t-1)(t^r+1)} = 0.$$

Q.E.D.

Effort Levels in Contests: The Public-Good Prize Case

KYUNG HWAN BAIK
Department of Economics, Appalachian State University, Boone, NC 28608, USA

Abstract

We examine the equilibrium individual players', groups', and total effort levels expended in a contest where groups compete with one another to win a group-specific public-good prize and the players choose their effort levels simultaneously and independently.

1. Introduction

A contest is a situation in which individual agents or groups compete with one another by expending effort to win a prize. Examples include R&D competition, rent-seeking and rent-defending contests, competition for promotion, election campaigns, litigation, and sports events. Contests have been studied by many economists [see, e.g., Loury (1979), Tullock (1980), Rosen (1986, 1988), Dixit (1987), Hillman and Riley (1989), Reinganum (1989), and Ellingsen (1991)].

Despite the vast literature, however, contests in which groups compete to win group-specific public-good prizes have not been explicitly studied. The purpose of this paper is to examine the individual players', groups', and total effort levels expended in such contests. To do so, we consider a contest in which groups compete with one another to win a group-specific public-good prize, the players choose their effort levels simultaneously and independently, and the players value the prize differently.

Contests involving group-specific public-good prizes are easily observed. For example, consider a contest in which people in different locations compete to win the designation of location of a government institution, a government-owned corporation, or a new highway. All people living in the winning location benefit from the prize won. Competition between consumers and firms over a monopoly position provides another example. If consumers win the contest, all consumers enjoy the rent defended.

2. The model

Consider a contest in which n groups compete with one another by expending effort to win a prize. The number of the groups is greater than unity: $n > 1$. Group i consists of m_i risk-neutral players. Let x_{ik} be the irreversible effort level expended by player k in group i and let X_i represent the effort level expended by all the players in group i: $X_i = \sum_{j=1}^{m_i} x_{ij}$. Effort levels are nonnegative and are measured in units commensurate with the prize. Let $p_i(X_1, \ldots, X_n)$ be the probability that group i wins when the effort levels of the groups are $(X_1, \ldots, X_n)$. Then the probability-of-winning function for group i can be written as

$$p_i = p_i(X_1, \ldots, X_n),$$

where $\sum_{j=1}^{n} p_j = 1$.

Assumption 1. We assume that $\partial p_i/\partial X_i \geq 0$, $\partial^2 p_i/\partial X_i^2 \leq 0$, $\partial p_i/\partial X_j \leq 0$, and $\partial^2 p_i/\partial X_j^2 \geq 0$ for $j \neq i$. We further assume that $\partial p_i/\partial X_i > 0$ and $\partial^2 p_i/\partial X_i^2 < 0$ when at least one $X_j > 0$, and $\partial p_i/\partial X_j < 0$ and $\partial^2 p_i/\partial X_j^2 > 0$ when $X_i > 0$.

In Assumption 1, we assume that each group's probability of winning is increasing in its own effort level and is decreasing in opponent's effort level. The marginal effect of each group's effort level on its own probability of winning decreases as its effort level increases. Finally, the marginal effect of opponent's effort level on each group's probability of winning decreases as opponent's effort level increases.

The prize is a public good within each group. Valuations of the prize may differ across players in the contest. Let v_{ik} represent the valuation of the prize of player k in group i.

Assumption 2. Without loss of generality, we assume that $v_{ih-1} \geq v_{ih} > 0$ for $h = 2, \ldots, m_i$.

Although players in each group have the same goal of winning the group-specific public-good prize, they choose their effort levels independently. We assume that all of the above is common knowledge.

The expected payoff of player k in group i is

$$\pi_{ik} = v_{ik} p_i(X_1, \ldots, X_n) - x_{ik}.$$

Given effort levels of all the other players in the contest, let $\widetilde{x}_{ik}$ denote the best response of player k in group i. Then $\widetilde{x}_{ik}$ is obtained by

$$\widetilde{x}_{ik} = \arg\max_{x_{ik}} \; v_{ik}p_i(X_1, \dots, X_n) - x_{ik}$$
$$\text{such that } x_{ik} \geq 0.$$

The first-order condition for this problem is

$$v_{ik}(\partial p_i/\partial X_i) - 1 = 0 \qquad \text{for } \widetilde{x}_{ik} > 0 \tag{1}$$

or

$$v_{ik}(\partial p_i/\partial X_i) - 1 \leq 0 \qquad \text{for } \widetilde{x}_{ik} = 0. \tag{2}$$

If player k in group i expends a positive effort level, his marginal gross payoff, $v_{ik}(\partial p_i/\partial X_i)$, must be equal to his marginal cost, 1, at that effort level. If he chooses zero effort, his marginal gross payoff must not exceed his marginal cost at that zero effort. His marginal gross payoff, $v_{ik}(\partial p_i/\partial X_i)$, decreases in his effort level, x_{ik}, due to Assumption 1. This implies that the second-order condition for this maximization problem is satisfied and $\widetilde{x}_{ik}$ is unique.

We assume that the players in the contest choose their effort levels simultaneously and we employ a Nash equilibrium as the solution concept. A Nash equilibrium occurs when each player's effort level is the best response to the effort levels of the other players.

Let x^*_{ik} and X^*_i denote the equilibrium effort level of player k in group i and the equilibrium effort level of group i, respectively. Let $(X^*)_{-i} \equiv (X^*_1, \dots, X^*_{i-1}, X^*_{i+1}, \dots, X^*_n)$.

Definition 1. Given the other groups' equilibrium effort levels, $(X^*)_{-i}$, group i's player-k-best response, $\widetilde{X}_i(k)$, is defined as

$$\widetilde{X}_i(k) = \arg\max_{X_i} \; v_{ik}p_i(X_i, (X^*)_{-i}) - X_i$$
$$\text{such that } X_i \geq 0.$$

Group i's player-k-best response, $\widetilde{X}_i(k)$, represents the best response of group i as a whole to the other groups' equilibrium effort levels when player k's valuation of the prize is taken into account. The first-order condition for this maximization problem is

$$v_{ik}(\partial p_i/\partial X_i) - 1 = 0 \qquad \text{if } \widetilde{X}_i(k) > 0 \tag{3}$$

or

$$v_{ik}(\partial p_i/\partial X_i) \; - \; 1 \; \leq \; 0 \qquad \text{if } \widetilde{X}_i(k) \; = \; 0. \tag{4}$$

The term, $v_{ik}(\partial p_i/\partial X_i)$, decreases in X_i due to Assumption 1. Therefore, the second-order condition is satisfied and group i's player-k-best response, $\widetilde{X}_i(k)$, is unique.

Lemma 1. $\widetilde{X}_i(h{-}1) \; \geq \; \widetilde{X}_i(h)$ for $h \; = \; 2, \ldots, m_i$.

Proof. Since the term, $v_{ik}(\partial p_i/\partial X_i)$ in first-order conditions (3) and (4) decreases in X_i, we obtain that for any h and k, $\widetilde{X}_i(h) > \widetilde{X}_i(k)$ holds if $v_{ih} > v_{ik}$ and $\widetilde{X}_i(h) = \widetilde{X}_i(k)$ holds if $v_{ih} = v_{ik}$. This and Assumption 2 yield Lemma 1. □

Lemma 2. Given the other groups' equilibrium effort levels, $(X^*)_{-i}$, *group i's equilibrium effort level is neither greater nor less than group i's player-1-best response,* $\widetilde{X}_i(1)$.

Proof. Let X_i be the effort level of group i. First, suppose that $X_i > \widetilde{X}_i(1)$ holds. Then by Lemma 1, $X_i > \widetilde{X}_i(1) \geq \widetilde{X}_i(k)$ holds for any k, where $1 \leq k \leq m_i$. This and Assumption 1 imply that $v_{ik}(\partial p_i/\partial X_i) - 1 < 0$ for any k (see first-order condition (3)). Looking at first-order condition (1), then, we know that for any player expending a positive effort level, his effort level is not the best response to the effort levels of all the other players in the contest since his marginal gross payoff is less than his marginal cost. Therefore, group i's effort level X_i is not an equilibrium one.

Next, suppose that $X_i < \widetilde{X}_i(1)$ holds. Then looking at first-order condition (3) and using Assumption 1, we know that $v_{i1}(\partial p_i/\partial X_i) - 1 > 0$ holds at group i's effort level X_i. This implies that first-order condition (1) or (2) for player 1 does not hold. His marginal gross payoff is greater than his marginal cost at his effort level. Thus, his effort level is not the best response to the effort levels of all the other players in the contest. Therefore, group i's effort level X_i is not an equilibrium one. □

Lemma 2 implies that given the other groups' equilibrium effort levels, group i's equilibrium effort level equals group i's player-1-best response: $X_i^* = \widetilde{X}_i(1)$. Using this, we construct equilibrium effort levels of the players in group i in Lemma 3.

Lemma 3. Given the other groups' equilibrium effort levels, $(X^*)_{-i}$, (a) *if* $v_{i1} > v_{i2}$, *then* $x_{i1}^* = \widetilde{X}_i(1)$ *and* $x_{ih}^* = 0$ *for* $h = 2, \ldots, m_i$, *and* (b) *if*

$v_{i1} = v_{it} > v_{it+1}$ for some t, then $\sum_{j=1}^{t} x_{ij}^* = \widetilde{X}_i(1)$ and $x_{ih}^* = 0$ for $h = t+1, \ldots, m_i$, where $2 \leq t \leq m_i$.

Proof. (a) Consider first the case where $\widetilde{X}_i(1) = 0$. By Lemma 1, $\widetilde{X}_i(k) = 0$ holds for any k, where $1 \leq k \leq m_i$. Then it follows from first-order condition (4) that if group i's effort level is zero, then $v_{ik}(\partial p_i/\partial X_i) - 1 \leq 0$ holds for any k. This implies that if all players in group i expend zero effort, first-order condition (2) is satisfied for each player in group i. Therefore, given the other groups' equilibrium effort levels, $(X^*)_{-i}$, and zero effort of the other players in group i, zero effort is the best response of each player in group i.

Next, consider the case where $\widetilde{X}_i(1) > 0$. Using first-order condition (3) and Assumption 1, we obtain: If group i's effort level equals $\widetilde{X}_i(1)$, then $v_{i1}(\partial p_i/\partial X_i) - 1 = 0$ and $v_{ih}(\partial p_i/\partial X_i) - 1 < 0$ for $h = 2, \ldots, m_i$ hold since $v_{i1} > v_{i2}$. Hence, if player 1 expends $\widetilde{X}_i(1)$ and the rest of the players in group i choose zero effort, first-order condition (1) is satisfied for player 1 and first-order condition (2) is satisfied for each of the rest. Therefore, the proposed effort level of each player in group i is his best response to the other groups' equilibrium effort levels, $(X^*)_{-i}$, and the proposed effort levels of the other players in group i.

Finally, we show that there are no other equilibrium effort levels of the players in group i. Suppose on the contrary that $(x_{i1}, \ldots, x_{im_i})$ are the equilibrium effort levels of the players in group i such that $X_i = \sum_{j=1}^{m_i} x_{ij} = \widetilde{X}_i(1)$ and $x_{it} \neq 0$ for some t, where $2 \leq t \leq m_i$. Then since first-order condition (1) must be satisfied for player t, at these effort levels $v_{it}(\partial p_i/\partial X_i) - 1 = 0$ must hold. Since $v_{i1} > v_{it}$, it follows from first-order condition (3) and Assumption 1 that at these effort levels $v_{it}(\partial p_i/\partial X_i) - 1 < 0$ must also hold. This leads to a contradiction.

(b) The proof of part (b) is similar to that of part (a) and therefore omitted. □

If one and only one player in a group has the highest valuation, the equilibrium effort levels of the players in the group are unique. Only the hungriest player expends positive effort. If more than one player in a group has the highest valuation, the equilibrium effort levels of the players in the group are not unique. It is possible, in this case, that some hungriest players expend zero effort. Note, however, that in both cases, group's equilibrium effort level is equal to its player-1-best response to the other groups' equilibrium effort levels.

We describe the equilibrium individual players', groups', and total effort levels in Proposition 1 which follows immediately from Lemmas 2 and 3.

Proposition 1. If a player in a group expends positive effort at a Nash equilibrium, his valuation of the prize must be the highest one in his group. The equilibrium groups' and total effort levels equal those resulting when only one of the hungriest players in each group competes for the prize.

The first part of Proposition 1 implies that a player whose valuation of the prize is less than somebody else's in his group expends zero effort and thus is a free rider. The second part implies that the number of players and the distribution of valuations in each group do not affect groups' and total effort levels as far as the highest valuation of the group does not change. To obtain the equilibrium groups' or total effort levels, one only needs to consider a reduced contest with n hungriest players, one for each group.

3. Conclusion

We have examined the equilibrium individual players', groups', and total effort levels expended in a contest where groups compete with one another to win a group-specific public-good prize, the players choose their effort levels simultaneously and independently, and the players value the prize differently. We have demonstrated the following. If player's equilibrium effort level is positive, he must be one of the hungriest players in his group. The equilibrium effort level of a player whose valuation of the prize is less than somebody else's in his group is zero. The equilibrium groups' and total effort levels depend neither on the number of players in each group nor the distribution of valuations in each group. They depend on the valuation of the hungriest player in each group and the number of groups in the contest.

More on more efficient rent seeking and strategic behavior in contests: Comment

SHMUEL NITZAN
Department of Economics, Bar-Ilan University, 52900 Ramat-Gan, Israel

In Leininger (1993) it is shown that the basic presumption that rent seekers will always compete for the first move is unfounded. More specifically, in a two-player two-stage, Tullock's (1980) type rent-seeking contest the rent seekers agree to move in a particular order. Specifically, assuming that the players decide both on the size of their bids and also on when to make them (early or late), they agree that the weaker player (the one with the lower valuation of the rent and/or with the lower ability to influence the probability of winning in his favor) moves first, i.e., the weaker player becomes the Stackelberg leader in the sequential rent-seeking contest. In other words, in the unique subgame perfect equilibrium of this contest, the weaker player moves first and the stronger player moves second. Furthermore, the equilibrium rent-seeking outlays are lower than the total rent-seeking expenditures in the Nash equilibrium of the simultaneous (non sequential) rent-seeking contest (see Theorem 1 and Theorem 2 in Leininger, 1993).

Leininger's elaborate and insightful analysis is carried out assuming, first, that the two players, say player 1 and player 2, compete for a rent K they value respectively at V_1 and V_2 and, second, that their respective winning probabilities are

$$p(x_1, x_2) = \frac{ax_1}{ax_1 + x_2} \quad \text{and } 1 - p(x_1, x_2),$$

where x_1 and x_2 are the submitted bids. With no loss of generality one can assume that $K = V_2$.

Resorting to Dixit's (1987) more general two-player contest on a fixed rent K where $p(x_1, x_2)$ is assumed to take the logit form, $p(x_1, x_2) = \dfrac{f_1(x_1)}{f_1(x_1) + f_2(x_2)}$ ($f_i(0) > 0$ and $f_i'(x_i) > 0$, $i = 1,2$), Baik and Shogren (1992) obtain the same results. That is, they prove (in a direct and very economical way) that strategic behavior with endogenous order of moves leads to under investment in effort compared with the equilibrium outcome in the simultaneous move contest. The underdog (the weaker player whose chance of winning the contest is lower than one half at the Nash equilibrium of the simultaneous contest) acts as the leader while the favorite (the stronger player whose chance of victory exceeds one half at the Nash equilibrium) waits, sizes up his opponent's effort, and then move (see Proposition 1 in Baik and Shogren, 1992).

To obtain Leininger's model as a special case, let $f_1(x_1) = abx_1$ and $f_2(x_2) = x_2$ where $b = \frac{V_1}{V_2}$. The multiplicative term ab represents the combined asymmetry between the players. The component a captures the differential advantage associated with the players' rent-seeking efficiency whereas b reflects the asymmetry in the players' assessment of the contested rent.

The condition $ab \gtrless 1 \Longleftrightarrow aV_1 \gtrless V_2$ determines wether player 1 is the stronger (weaker) player. To show that Leininger's results are implied by the main result of Baik and Shogren it remains to be shown that this same condition also determines whether player 1 is the favorite (the underdog). This is indeed the case since when the two players move simultaneously the equilibrium probability of player 1 winning the contest is given by (see Leininger, 1993: 48):

$$p(x_1^*, x_2^*) = \frac{a}{a+\frac{V_2}{V_1}} = \frac{a}{a+\frac{1}{b}} = \frac{1}{1+\frac{1}{ab}} .$$

Hence, $ab \gtrless 1 \Longleftrightarrow p(x_1^*, x_2^*) \gtrless \frac{1}{2}$ ..

Theorem 1 and Theorem 2 in Leininger (1993) constitute a special case of Proposition 1 in Baik and Shogren (1992). While these results were clearly developed independently, Baik and Shogren's results constitute both a simplification and generalization of Leininger's results.

Modelling rent-seeking contests

Shmuel Nitzan*

Department of Economics, Bar-Ilan University, 52900 Ramat-Gan, Israel

Abstract

This survey focuses on alternative ways of modelling rent-seeking contests. My primary concern is with the relationship between the extent of rent dissipation and the underlying contest characteristics: e.g., the number of players, their attitudes toward risk, the asymmetry among the players, the source of the rent, the nature of the rent or the nature of the rent setter. The survey concludes with a brief description of attempts to endogenize various components of the rent-seeking contest.

Key words: Rent-seeking contests; Rent dissipation

JEL classification: D72

1. Introduction

The emerging theory of rent seeking was first surveyed by Tollison (1982) and more recently by Brooks and Heijdra (1989). There was a natural need at the time to define the basic concepts (e.g., natural vs. artificial rents, rent seeking vs. profit seeking), clarify the main ideas, implications and messages of the theory and discuss its normative and positive aspects.

In the passing decade the rent-seeking literature has gathered momentum and advanced in many directions. On the one hand, the simplicity and stylized nature of the game-theoretic rent-seeking model studied by Tullock (1980) made it a natural starting point for numerous interesting extensions and modifications. On the other hand, considerable attention has been attracted by some unresolved controversies, in particular, regarding the

* Parts of this paper were written while visiting the Department of Economics at the University of Bonn and the Tinbergen Institute at the University of Amsterdam. The support of the Sonderforschungssbereich and the Tinbergen Institute is gratefully acknowledged. I am also indebted to Jan Potters and Caspar de Vries for their helpful comments on an earlier draft of the paper.

question of the social costs of rent seeking. The purpose of the current work is to survey the alternative modelling of strategic 'winner take all' rent-seeking contests and to discuss their success in shedding light on some issues related to the measurement of the social waste associated with the rent-seeking process.[1] My chief concern will be with the relationship between the rent-seeking expenditures and the nature of the contest, the characteristics of the contested rents and the relevant parameters of the political-economic environment.

The rent-seeking contests on which I focus share the following characteristics:

(i) The contest is an N-player strategic game, $N \geqslant 2$.
(ii) The contested rent is indivisible in the sense that one 'winner takes all'.
(iii) The players expend effort (resources) to increase their probability of winning the rent.

These characteristics define the scope of the survey. While allowing a very rich class of models they exclude that part of the literature on interest groups, lobbying or regulation framed in terms of a *single agent* doing the rent seeking, *non-strategic* agents or agents lobbying for a *share* of the rent. The studies of Bhagwati (1980, 1982), Becker (1983, 1985), Kruger (1974) and Posner (1975), as well as the more recent contributions of Cairns (1989), Cairns and Long (1991) and Long and Vousden (1987) remain therefore beyond our general framework. I also almost disregard the game-theoretic models of interest groups based on a vote function and campaign contributions, a composite utility function or strategic transmission of information. For a useful review of these approaches the reader is referred to Potters and van Winden (1993). Since my primary concern is with alternative modelling of rent-seeking contests, no attention is paid to the applications of the theory in specific economic contexts (e.g., Anam (1982), Hillman (1982), Rodrik (1986), Mayer and Riezman (1987) – the reader is referred to Hillman (1989) for a comprehensive survey), to the studies attempting to empirically estimate the implications of the alternative models on the social costs of rent seeking (e.g., Laband and Sophocleus, 1989; Dougan, 1991; Katz and Rosenberg, 1989) and to the experimental work (e.g., Millner and Pratt, 1989, 1991; Shogren and Baik, 1991).

The literature that will be reviewed is closely related to the literature on incentives in elimination tournaments (Rosen, 1986; Lazear and Rosen, 1981;

[1]Assuming that rent-seeking expenditures have no social value, they are conceived herein as the real resources wasted in the rent-seeking process. Of course, the other possible component of the social cost of a contestable rent is the allocative inefficiency (deadweight losses) associated with the rent.

Nalebuff and Stiglitz, 1983), R & D rivalry and patent competition (Dasgupta and Stiglitz, 1980; Dasgupta, 1986; Leininger, 1991), electoral competition (Snyder, 1989), entry and entry deterrence in oligopolistic competition (Tirole, 1988) and, more generally, contest theory (Dixit, 1987) and auction theory (Riley and Samuelson, 1981; Milgrom and Weber, 1982). Undoubtedly, these literatures inspired some of the ideas and models in the rent-seeking literature. The fruitfulness of applied game theory in the past twenty years, especially in different industrial organization contexts, has certainly been a major factor accounting for the ongoing 'second wave' of contributions to the theory of rent seeking which started in the eighties and on which the current survey focuses.

In the following section I introduce the basic rent-seeking contest and discuss the effect of asymmetry in rent seekers' characteristics, risk aversion and uncertainty of rents on the extent of rent dissipation. Section 3 presents six extensions of the basic contest. In the first extension the source of the rent is taken into account and incorporated into the contest. In the second extended contest the competitors are no longer individuals, but groups of individuals. In the third extension the contested rent is allowed to possess public good attributes. The possibility of a rent awarded by a committee is considered in the fourth extension. The fifth line of extension is concerned with dynamic contests. Finally, I consider two examples of multiple-rent contests. The survey concludes with a brief description of attempts to endogenize various components of the (basic and extended) rent-seeking contests.

2. The basic rent-seeking contest

Consider N agents confronting the opportunity of winning a prespecified fixed prize, the contestable rent, R. The outcome of this static, non-stratified, 'winner takes all' contest on a private-good rent is the assignment to each player, rent seeker i, of a probability that he wins the contest. If player i's effort level in units commensurate with the rent is x_i, then the probability that he wins the rent is $\pi_i(x_1, \ldots, x_N)$ where $\sum_{i=1}^{N} \pi_i(x)=1$ and π_i is nondecreasing in x_i and nonincreasing in x_j, $j \neq i$. Assuming that agent i's payoff is given by his expected utility, V_i, the static rent-seeking game may possess Nash equilibria in pure or in mixed strategies. The rent-seeking literature is concerned with the existence and characterization of Nash equilibria and, in particular, with the relationship between total rent-seeking outlays in equilibrium and the value of the contested rent. The ratio D between these two values is called the extent of rent dissipation. This ratio is important for empirical applications since it can serve as a direct measure for inferring the value of the resources spent on the contested rent from its value.

When $x^* = (x_1^*, \ldots, x_N^*)$ is a Nash equilibrium in pure strategies, $D = \sum_{i=1}^{N} x_i^*/R$. When the outcome of the rent-seeking contest is a mixed strategy equilibrium, $D = \mathrm{E}(\sum_{i=1}^{N} x_i)/R$, where $\mathrm{E}(\sum_{i=1}^{N} x_i)$ is the expected total rent-seeking outlays given the players' equilibrium mixed strategies.

The analysis of the basic rent-seeking game depends on the assumptions made regarding the contest outcome functions, $\pi_i(x)$,[2] and the number and characteristics of the players, viz., their endowments, lobbying capabilities and preferences (attitudes towards risk, valuations of the rent and, in general, their utilities) which determine their strategy sets and their payoffs, V_i. Let us turn to some special cases starting with Tullock's (1980) rent-seeking contest.

2.1. *Symmetry and risk neutrality*

When the probabilistic contest outcome functions are symmetric and of the logit form, then

$$\pi_i(x) = \frac{f(x_i)}{\sum_{i=1}^{N} f(x_i)},$$

where f is an increasing function. This logit form is used for contest analysis by Baik and Shogren (1992), Dixit (1987), Gradstein (1991), Rosen (1986) and Snyder (1989). In his seminal contribution to the rent-seeking literature, Tullock (1980) made the special assumptions that $f(x_i) = x_i^r$, $r > 0$ and that the identical rent seekers are risk neutral. In this case the payoff function of player i, V_i, is equal to his expected profit, that is,

$$V_i = \pi_i(x)R - x_i = \frac{x_i^r}{\sum_{j=1}^{N} x_j^r} R - x_i.$$

In this contest, if an interior Nash equilibrium in pure strategies exists, then the extent of rent dissipation is at most one as $D = r(N-1)/N$.[3] For recent comprehensive studies of Tullock's rent-seeking game see Cleeton (1989) and Perez-Castrillo and Verdier (1992). The extent of rent dissipation is increasing in the number of rent seekers and in the parameter r, the marginal return to lobbying outlays. This conclusion is generalizable to any symmetric

---

[2] These functions are also called the success probability, winning probability, contest success, or influence functions (see Potters and van Winden (1993)).

[3] Such equilibria exist if and only if $r \leqslant N/(N-1)$. Mixed-strategy Nash equilibria exist when $r > (N-1)/N$, but the possibility of over dissipation of rents – which was conjectured in the earlier literature – does not arise in equilibrium (see Baye et al. (1993b)).

contest[4] where π_i is of the logit form. Namely, the extent of rent dissipation is a decreasing function of the degree of concavity of $f(x_i)$ and an increasing function of the number of players (see Gradstein, 1991). The rent-seeking outlays are maximal when f is linear. In Tullock's game, when the returns from outlays made are constant, $r=1$, $D=(N-1)/N$. In this widely used model, apparently because of its greater analytical tractability, the rent is totally dissipated when the number of rent seekers is sufficiently large. However, in small-number contests the rent is not fully dissipated. In particular, in the minimal, two-player game, only half of the rent is dissipated.

In perfectly discriminating contests with symmetric valuations the rent is fully dissipated, even when the number of rent seekers is small (Hillman and Samet, 1987; Hirshleifer and Riley, 1978; Moulin, 1986). In such contests identical players are risk neutral and

$$\pi_i(x)=\begin{cases}1/m & x_i \text{ is one of the } m \text{ maximal elements in } x_1,\ldots,x_N,\\ 0 & \text{otherwise.}\end{cases}$$

That is, the contender making the highest outlay wins the prize with certainty. If several contenders make the highest outlay, they win the prize in equal probability. In perfectly discriminating rent-seeking contests which are, in fact, first-price all-pay auctions (Baye et al., 1993a), mixed strategy equilibria exist and in equilibrium the expected value of the rent-seeking outlays equals the common valuation of the rent R, i.e., $D=1$.

In perfectly and imperfectly discriminating basic contests complete rent dissipation is not to be expected due to three main reasons: the rent seekers are usually risk averse, the rent seekers are usually heterogeneous and contests are often characterized by additional uncertainty which goes beyond the uncertainty regarding the ultimate winner of the contested rent.

2.2. Risk aversion

When the identical rent seekers are risk averse, there exists $R^e<R$, such that the equilibrium of the rent-seeking game with risk-neutral players competing for the prize R^e is the same as the equilibrium of the contest with the risk-averse players competing for the prize R. Put differently, R^e is the risk-neutrality equivalent rent which makes each player choose the same equilibrium rent-seeking outlay under risk neutrality as in equilibrium under risk aversion. As expected, rent dissipation in the presence of risk aversion is

[4] In a symmetric contest the rent seekers are identical. In particular, rent valuations by all players are equal and $f_i(x_i)=f(x_i)$ for any i.

reduced relative to the case where the rent seekers are neutral. Risk aversion implies incomplete dissipation of the rent (Hillman and Katz, 1984; Hillman and Samet, 1987).

2.3. *Asymmetry*

Under complete information and heterogeneous valuations of the contested rent by risk neutral players, the extent of rent dissipation is reduced, Hillman and Riley (1989). In perfectly discriminating contests asymmetric valuation acts as a barrier to entry and only the two agents with the highest valuations contest the prize. Moreover, the player with the lower valuation is inhibited in his outlays by the awareness to the higher valuation of his rival. Asymmetric equilibria may imply higher dissipation of the rent relative to the symmetric equilibrium (Baye et al., 1990).

In Tullock's game with $r=1$, the value of the rent-seeking outlays made in equilibrium is $((N-1)/N)R^h$, where R^h is the harmonic mean of the players' valuations of the rent R. When the rent seekers have different endowments of wealth and/or different attitudes towards risk, there exist risk-neutrality equivalent rents, $R_1^e, R_2^e, \ldots, R_N^e < R$, such that rent dissipation is incomplete. Specifically, $D = R^{eh}(N-1)/RN$, where R^{eh} is the harmonic mean of the risk-neutrally equivalent rents (Nitzan, 1991a).

Asymmetry in individual lobbying capabilities yields similar results. The case of asymmetric cost structures in a two-player contest is analyzed in Paul and Wilhite (1990). Allard (1988) and Leininger (1993) study Tullock's game when players have different abilities to influence the probability of winning in their favor. Gradstein (1991) analyzes a contest with risk-neutral players assuming that

$$\pi_i(x) = \frac{a_i f(x_i)}{\sum_{j=1}^{N} a_j f(x_j)}$$

($a_j > 0$, $\sum_{j=1}^{N} a_j = 1$ and f is increasing, weakly concave and $f(0)=0$). Here a_i can be interpreted as player i's prior likelihood to win the contest. Gradstein shows that in a two-player contest the extent of rent dissipation is decreasing in the asymmetry between the players' lobbying strength. For $f(x_i) = x_i$, this result is generalized to n-player contests. Specifically, an equalizing spread in the distribution of the players' lobbying capabilities increases the equilibrium rent-seeking outlays.

2.4. *Uncertain rents*

In the various modelling of the rent-seeking contest mentioned so far, it has been assumed that one of the rent seekers wins the rent R with certainty. But often this assumption is not satisfied because under certain circumstances the rent is uncertain in the sense that in some positive probability nobody wins it. If this type of uncertainty is allowed, the expected value of an awarded prize is less than R and, consequently, rent dissipation is clearly reduced. Kahana and Nitzan (1993) study a contest where such rent uncertainty is due to imperfect government credibility. Uncertainty about the ability to maintain the rent (a monopoly position) is considered in Jadlow (1985).[5] Other types of rent uncertainty are discussed in the sequel when I refer to extended contests that take into account the source of the rent and the possibility of rent-avoidance activities by third parties (e.g., consumer organizations) and the possibility of rent sharing (Ellingsen, 1991; Rama, 1993; Schmidt, 1992). See also Gradstein, Nitzan and Slutsky (1992) for a general discussion of the effect of uncertainty on interactive behavior.

In the basic rent-seeking contest the amount of the expended resources is increasing in the individual risk-neutrality equivalents of the rent and in the intensity of competition on the rent as measured by the number of competitions or by the degree of homogeneity in their characteristics. The extent of rent dissipation is therefore usually incomplete due to risk aversion and uncertainty about the award of the rent, or due to the existence of a small number of rent seekers or the asymmetry in the competitors' rent valuations, endowments, attitudes toward risk or lobbying effectiveness.

In extended contests there are other reasons for the incomplete dissipation of the rent. In the next section I discuss several such reasons that have to do with issues that so far have been disregarded. Specifically, these reasons relate to the source of the rent (whether it is internal or external to the contest); the nature of the competitors (whether the rent is contested by individuals or by groups of individuals); the nature of the rent (whether it is a private-good or a public-good rent); the nature of the agent setting the rent (whether the rent is set by an individual or by a committee) and the nature of the contest (whether it is static or dynamic and whether it is a single or a multiple-rent contest).

3. Extended contests

3.1. The source of the rent

In the basic rent-seeking contest the source of the fixed pre-existing rent is disregarded. When the source of the rent is internal, viz., some of the players

[5] Uncertainty concerning other contenders' valuations of the rent has been analyzed by Hillman and Riley (1989). They show that such uncertainty increases the dissipation of rents because it erodes the barrier to entry or inhibition on active participation in the contest.

losing the contest pay the rent, the contest is slightly altered becoming a basic transfer contest. A player facing the risk of paying part of the rent might be expected to expend resources not only in an attempt to win the transfer, but also in an attempt to avoid the loss. In general, we would expect transfer contests to be more wasteful. Somewhat surprisingly, in Tullock's symmetric version of the transfer contest with $r=1$, if the transfer is equally paid by the $N-1$ losers, then the value of the expenditures made in the attempt to win the contest equal the value of the transfer received by the winner (Appelbaum and Katz, 1986a). In the symmetric perfectly discriminating version of this transfer contest the resources expended by the players exceed the transfer (Hillman and Riley, 1989).

When the source of the rent is external, that is, the rent involves deadweight losses or transfer of resources by agents who do not participate in the basic contest, a plausible modelling of the situation requires an extension of the basic contest that takes into account the possible response of the affected parties. In Appelbaum and Katz (1986a) and Wenders (1987) rent-avoidance activities lead to an increase of the resources expended in the contest. In contrast, in the more general setting studied by Ellingsen (1991) and Schmidt (1992), rent defending activities by consumers may lead to underdissipation of the rent. In these extended rent-seeking contests, consumers' participation implies that the rent associated with the monopoly status cannot be taken for granted. This reduces the expected profit of the rent-seeking firms and, in turn, their expenditures. Furthermore, it turns out that total rent-seeking expenditures of both firms and consumers may also be reduced since, in equilibrium, consumers' lobbying efforts can be more than matched by the reduction in firms' lobbying efforts. For similar reasons Bhagwati (1982) characterizes lobbying activities as directly wasteful but as potentially 'indirectly' productive. Rama (1993) proposes a further extension of the rent-seeking contest by adding to the competing firms and consumers the workers (or trade unions) who attempt to win a share of the rent created by restrictive regulation.

3.2. The nature of the competitors

In the basic rent-seeking contest the rent is contested by individuals. But often the rent is sought by groups of individuals and in such a case the competition in the corresponding extended contest becomes a stratified competition: the competing groups consist of competing individuals, Farrell and Lander (1989). Modelling group rent seeking requires therefore the introduction of explicit assumptions regarding intra-group competition that supplement the assumptions on inter-group competition.

Consider the following natural extended stratified n-group rent-seeking contest, Nitzan (1991a). The assumptions of the basic contest are adapted to the inter-group competition. Let $N(i)$ be the number of members in groups i, $i=1, \ldots, n$. The total number of players in the extended game is $N=\sum_{i=1}^{n} N(i)$. Each of these players decides voluntarily on the extent of his rent-seeking efforts, x_{ki}, $i=1, \ldots, n$, $k=1, \ldots, N(i)$. The effort made by group i is x_i, $x_i=\sum_{k=1}^{N(i)} x_{ki}$. The probability that group i wins the rent is $\pi_i(x_1, \ldots, x_n)$.[6] Finally, suppose that in every group a mixed rule is applied to distribute the rent among its members; a proportion a of the rent is distributed on an egalitarian basis and the rest is distributed on the basis of the principle 'to each according to his relative effort'.[7,8]

In the above group rent-seeking contest rent dissipation is usually reduced relative to the basic contest. This is due to two basic reasons. First, within the groups there are free-riding incentives. Second, the intensity of competition in an extended contest is, in general, lower than the intensity of competition in the basic contest because the number of competitors in the former case is smaller. For example, under Tullock's assumptions regarding π_i and with $r=1$ and identical risk-neutral players, the extent of rent dissipation is equal to

$$D=\frac{(1-a)N+na-1}{N}.$$

If the group applies the egalitarian distribution rule ($a=1$), $D=(n-1)/N<(N-1)/N$. When the rent is wholly distributed according to relative effort ($a=0$), $D=(N-1)/N$, as in Tullock's basic rent-seeking contest. Note that an implicit assumption of this extended model is that effort can be costlessly observed and rewarded. If this simplifying assumption is modified and such costs are explicitly introduced into the model, total rent-seeking outlays would tend to decline. In any event, the extent of rent dissipation is positively related to n, the number of contesting groups as long as $a>0$ and it is inversely related to a, the degree of egalitarianism in distributing the rent. However, the effect of the total number of rent seekers, N, is ambiguous.[9] As in the basic contest setting, asymmetry among rent seekers, risk aversion and rent uncertainty still tend to reduce the extent of rent dissipation.

---

[6] Notice that if $n(i)=1$ for every i, $N=n$ and the extended game reduces to a basic contest.

[7] Two special cases of this extended group rent-seeking contest are analyzed in Lee (1993a) and Baik (1993). The former study focuses on a two-group contest assuming that $a=1$. The contest analyzed in the latter study is equivalent to a $[(N-m)+1]$-group contest with $(N-m)$ single-member groups and one m-member group. See also Paul and Wilhite (1991).

[8] When different groups apply different sharing rules, the extended game need not have an equilibrium, see Nitzan (1991b).

[9] $\partial D/\partial N \geqslant 0 \Leftrightarrow a \leqslant 1/n$.

3.3. *The nature of the rent*

In group contests over a perfectly divisible private-good rent, free-riding incentives and the fact that the number of competing groups, n, is usually smaller than the number of individual rent seekers, N, tend to reduce the individual players' rent-seeking efforts. These considerations are also relevant when the group contest is over a public-good rent (e.g., a publicly funded park, pollution removal by a local authority from one of the locations under its jurisdiction, etc.) which costs R dollars (Katz et al., 1990; Ursprung, 1990).[10] When the contested rent has public good attributes there are other considerations that may explain underdissipation of the rent. In particular, when the group contest is over a pure public-good rent, i.e., there is a perfect non-excludability and perfect non-rivalness in the consumption of the rent within the group winning the contest, the free-riding incentives are maximal since, by definition, the public good is wholly and equally consumed by all members of the winning group. On the other hand, the pure publicness of the rent implies that the rent is not shared as in the group contest over the private-good rent. This induces the individual players to increase their rent-seeking efforts. It turns out that under Tullock's assumptions with $r=1$, the negative free-riding incentives within the groups just counterbalance the positive 'rent size' effect. Assuming that all players value the public good rent at αR dollars, $0<\alpha<1$, in such a case total rent-seeking outlays are equal to $(n-1)\alpha R/n$. That is, the value of the resources expended in the contest is smaller than the value of the public good to a single individual. Clearly, rent-seeking efforts tend to be very small relative to the aggregate value of the contested public-good rent (see Katz et al., 1990) and Ursprung (1990) for a discussion of a number of other issues that arise in a contest over a public-good rent).

3.4. *The nature of the rent setter*

In the basic rent-seeking contest it has been implicitly assumed that the award of the rent is to be made by a single agent who is typically an administrator or a politician. However, the decision of awarding the rent is often made by a committee and not by an individual rent setter. In such a case the rent seekers would try to affect the deliberations of the committee by expending resources that are distributed among the committee members. Modelling an extended rent-seeking contest with committee decisions on the award of the rent requires explicit assumptions regarding the characteristics

[10] Rent seeking for public goods is also studied in Magee et al. (1989) using a model with competing interest groups that do not interact strategically. See also Varian (1989).

of the committee and, in particular, the number of the committee members and the decision rule that they use. Congleton (1984) studies a stylized two-person, committee-directed, rent-seeking contest assuming that the committee consists of three homogeneous members who apply a simple majority rule. He examines the effect of committee versus one-man administration in a perfectly discriminating contest and in Tullock's rent-seeking contest. His main argument is that in both cases relatively smaller efforts tend to be invested to influence the deliberations of committees than those of single administrators. Two reasons account for this tendency. First, since more people have to be influenced under committee administration, the participation threshold is greater and thus more prohibitive. Second, the absence of stable majority coalitions in the committee allows the rent seekers to economize on efforts devoted to influencing the committee deliberations by targeting alternative majority coalitions. This interesting claim needs, however, to be formally demonstrated in both contexts explored by Congleton (1984). The analysis of more general extended committee-directed rent-seeking contests certainly deserves further careful attention.

3.5. The nature of the contest

The rent-seeking contests considered so far have been modelled as static non-cooperative games in normal form in which the rent seekers move simultaneously. The analysis of these contests resorted exclusively to the Nash equilibrium solution concept. But in the political-economic reality rent seeking often has a dynamic nature. The challenge of extending the static rent-seeking contest to a dynamic one was undertaken by Baik and Shogren (1992), Leininger (1993), Leininger and Yang (1992) and Yang (1991).[11] These studies demonstrate that in a dynamic setting the extent of rent dissipation is reduced relative to the outcome in the corresponding static rent-seeking contest.

Leininger and Yang (1992) analyze a two-player dynamic rent-seeking contest with finite or infinite alternating bids. The contest outcome functions are assumed to be of Tullock's type. In the infinite-move game, which is considered as the more appropriate model, threats and counter-threats in a tit-for-tat subgame perfect equilibrium make implicit collusion possible. This implies a reduction in the extent of wasteful rent-seeking efforts relative to the static contest.

Baik and Shogren (1992) and Leininger (1993) study a two-player, two-stage contest in which a player's strategy consists of two components: the timing of his move (making his rent-seeking outlay early or late) and his

[11] See also Cairns (1989), Stephan (1993) and Wirl (1991).

rent-seeking effort. In the first stage of the game the players simultaneously decide whether to move early or late.[12] If both players make the same timing decision, the rent-seeking contest is played with simultaneous moves. If the players make different timing decisions, the game is played sequentially. When the contest outcome functions are of the logit form, there is a unique subgame perfect equilibrium in which the weaker player (the player with the lower valuation of the rent and/or the lower lobbying effectiveness) moves first. Total rent-seeking expenditures are smaller than those of the Nash equilibrium of the static (simultaneous move) contest.[13,14]

3.6. Multiple-rent contests

The rent-seeking literature is typically concerned with contests (basic or extended) over a single prespecified rent. The study of multiple-rent contests has hardly begun. I conclude this section by pointing to two preliminary attempts of modelling multi-rent contests. In the first case the same players are assumed to simultaneously confront several fixed rents. In the second case the assignment of a single rent is assumed to give rise to a multi-tiered rent-seeking contest.

Gradstein and Nitzan (1989) analyze a stylized game of competitive allocation of fixed resources by N identical players on m prespecified relatively high (advantageous) indivisible rents. In this so called advantageous multiple rent seeking game the contest outcome functions are assumed to be perfectly discriminating. The game can be interpreted therefore as a generalized first-prize all-pay auction. It turns out that in this multi-rent contest rent seekers concentrate their resources on single objects. This occurs regardless of whether the prizes are equally or differently valued by the players. The equilibrium ratio between the number of players concentrating on any two prizes approximates the ratio between their respective values.

Hillman and Katz (1987) explore the possibility of a single rent that, in a

---

[12] The first stage can be interpreted as an announcement stage, Hamilton and Slutsky (1990).

[13] Tullock (1980, 1985) argues that the assumption of simultaneous moves is justified since the players have an incentive to be first movers. Leininger (1993) challenges this argument by pointing to his finding that, in the endogenously determined order of moves, the players do not compete for the first move, that is, they agree on a particular sequential order which makes the weaker player the leader in the game.

[14] Wirl (1991) studies a two-player infinite-horizon game of lobbying. His lobbying game, which is not a contest as defined herein, is modelled as a differential game and its subgame perfect equilibrium in linear feedback strategies is shown to yield rent-seeking efforts which are considerably smaller than the expenditures associated with an open-loop equilibrium. A finite-horizon contest over a prize awarded at the final stage of the game in which only open-loop strategies are allowed is studied in Waldow (1989).

first stage, may give rise to two contests, one for the rent itself, and another to designate the bureaucrat who is to become the beneficiary of part of the resources expended in the course of the contest over the initial rent. A further contest is formed if part of the resources expended in the second contest also become a prize to be contested. And so the process continues. This finite sequence of contests is analyzed assuming that in each contest the probabilistic outcome function is of Tullock's type with $r=1$. The analysis focuses on the relationship between the value of the rent, the transfers (bribes) made in the course of this multi-rent contest and the value of real resources expended in rent seeking.

4. Endogenous contests

Given my space constraint, the description of the efforts to endogenize the components of the rent-seeking contest will be brief. This part of my review is organized in accordance with the sequence of contests as introduced in the preceding sections. The implications of endogenous contests on the extent of rent dissipation will be only very briefly highlighted.

The early analysis of the basic rent-seeking contest led researchers to try to endogenize the number of participants in the contest. This task was initially undertaken by allowing free entry into the contest (long-term competition). In Tullock's version of the basic rent-seeking contest with identical risk-neutral players and $r=1$, the introduction of free entry results in complete dissipation of the rent (Corcoran, 1984; Corcoran and Karels, 1985; Perez-Castrillo and Verdier, 1992; Tullock, 1984).[15] Exploring an alternative two-player contest, Higgins et al. (1985) established a similar result. In their setting there exists a symmetric mixed strategy equilibrium in which the rent is expectationally dissipated. Hillman and Riley (1989) derive the rule limiting entry to Tullock's type contest with $r=1$ and asymmetric rent valuations. They show that the number of agents actively participating in the contest is small, unless valuations of the rent are very similar. This implies that, in general, rent dissipation will be incomplete. Similarly, in a perfectly discriminating contest with asymmetric valuations of the rent, free entry into the contest does not imply a large number of contenders. Again, asymmetric valuations act as a barrier to entry and, in turn, reduce the extent of rent dissipation. A different approach is proposed by Michaels (1988) who studies a version of Tullock's basic contest with entrance fees. His focus is on the number of rent seekers which is optimal from the rent setter's (the politician's) point of view. Other attempts to endogenize the number of rent

[15] The effect of changes in the value of the rent and in the entry fee on the number of rent seekers is studied in Appelbaum and Katz (1986b).

seekers in extended contests in which the source of the rent is taken into account and in extended two-stage contests with strategic entry deterrence can be found in Appelbaum and Katz (1986c), Gradstein (1991) and Baye, Kovenock and de Vries (1993a). In the two-stage contest analyzed in the latter study, given a set of potentially active rent seekers, the politician determines in the first stage of the game the subset of rent seekers actually participating in the contest. In the second stage of the game, a first-price all-pay auction determines the outcome of the contest. It turns out that the politician has an incentive to preclude from participation in the contest the potential rent seekers most valuing the rent. This interesting finding means that in this context rent dissipation is, again, incomplete.

Endogenization of other parameters of the basic rent-seeking contest is in its infancy stage. See, however, Glazer (1993), Michaels (1988) and Kahana and Nitzan (1993) that contain preliminary attempts to endogenize, respectively, the contest outcome function, the parameter r of Tullock's logit contest outcome function and the duration of the contest. The common feature of the above studies is that they all view the relevant parameter as a control variable determined by a politician who maximizes his wealth and, therefore, the total rent-seeking expenditures.[16]

More efforts have been directed to the endogenization of the contested rent. Appelbaum and Katz (1986c) study a three-player game where the rent setter (a regulator offering a rent to firms) is himself a rent seeker (seeking the support of consumers–voters). In their extended contest the value of the rent is determined endogenously.

Gradstein (1993a) studies two alternative extended contests with endogenously determined rents. In the static version, the basic contest is supplemented with an exogenous function relating (positively) the value of the rent to the rent seekers' efforts. In the second sequential version of the extended contest, the rent setter (the government) becomes a player who sets the value of the contested rent in the first stage of the game. In the context of two different extended two-group contests over a public-good rent, Ursprung (1990) and Riaz et al. (1991) endogenize the contested rent, or more precisely, the rent seekers' valuations of the rent.[17] Notice that when the rent is variable, the extent of rent dissipation is only a partial and, in general, unsatisfactory measure of the efficiency implications of rent seeking, even when no deadweight losses are associated with the rent.

Recently, several attempts have been made to endogenize group formation and group sharing rules in extended group rent-seeking contests over a

[16] See also Guttman, Nitzan and Spiegel (1992) for a study of the possibility of endogenizing the rent seekers' altruistic utilities.

[17] Ursprung's (1990) contest is more general as he endogenizes the rent seekers' valuations by embedding the extended rent-seeking contest into a spatial model of candidate competition.

private-good rent. The endogenization of group formation is based on the introduction of long-run inter-group mobility (Lee, 1992; Nitzan, 1991a). Alternative modes of endogenous determination of sharing rules are discussed in Nitzan (1991a), Lee (1993) and Baik (1993). The long-run intra-group sharing rule can be extremely egalitarian, based only on individual efforts or indeterminate, depending on whether it is set by a central planner or by the rent seekers. Of course, in the former case the nature of the sharing rule depends on the objective function of the planner and in the second case it depends on the assumptions made on the mechanism applied by the individuals to determine the sharing rule.

The endogenous determination of the order of moves in a two-player two-stage rent-seeking contest was already discussed in the preceding section. Baik and Shogren (1992) and Leininger (1993) are, so far, the only studies concerned with endogenizing elements of dynamic rent-seeking contests.

Let me finally turn to the challenge of endogenizing multiple-rent contests. Politically contestable rents may take the form of individual private-good transfers, group private-good transfers or group public-good transfers. The determination of governmental transfer patterns is a complex process and the question is can the theory of (endogenous) rent seeking shed some light on it. One possible approach is to view the transfer pattern as a variable which is under the control of an optimizing politician. Adopting this approach, Nitzan (1993) explores the possibility of specialization in the 'provision of transfers' and derives the relationship between the parameters of the extended multiple-rent contest and the preferred kind of transfer. The parameters of the model are the distribution of potential rent seekers across groups, the sharing rule used within groups to distribute the private-good transfers and the relative value of a dollar spent on the provision of a (local) public good.

5. Concluding remarks

I have confined my attention in the current work to alternative modelling of rent-seeking contests. My primary concern has been with the question how do different contests affect the extent of rent dissipation.[18] The difference between contests can be in terms of the value of the parameters of the same type of contest or in terms of the underlying contest characteristics.

---

[18] The broader efficiency implications of rent seeking, especially in a general equilibrium political-economic setting, and their implications in terms of evaluating alternative forms of government intervention are beyond the scope of the current review. For an interesting evaluation of governmental provision of public goods in the presence of rent seeking (see Gradstein (1993b)).

The last part of the paper is devoted to the important and intriguing question how are rent-seeking contests determined. Namely, how are they affected by the interaction among potential rent seekers and rent setters as well as any other affected agents who all operate in some given political-economic environment. Whereas the study of questions about the nature of contest equilibria seems to have reached an advanced stage, the analysis of equilibrium or endogenous contests has reached only a very preliminary and inadequate stage of development. Future progress in this direction will constitute a significant contribution to the theory of rent seeking, public choice and, more generally, to political economy.

Cooperative rent-seeking*

BRUCE G. LINSTER
Department of Economics and Geography, United States Air Force Academy, Colorado Springs, CO 80840-5701

Abstract. This paper presents an analysis of cooperation in the context of a repeated rent-seeking game which can be thought of as modeling bilateral situations such as military/political conflict, labor/business lobbying, gang/illegal activities, or criminal/civil law suits. The potential for mutually advantageous agreements is explored using the repeated nature of the game as the mechanism which sustains the cooperation. The Nash bargaining solution is applied to symmetric as well as asymmetric rent-seeking situations. The asymmetries can derive from the players valuing the rent differently or choosing sequentially.

1. Introduction

Gordon Tullock's (1980) game theoretic model of rent-seeking activities provides a framework for analyzing competition for politically contestable rents and the equilibrium level of rent dissipation. His approach awards the prize to the winner of a lottery-like contest with a probability depending on the size of her contribution relative to the total contributions.[1] The degree of rent dissipation in this model depends on the number of players and parameter values for the contest success function. This paper examines a simplified version of Tullock's (1980) rent-seeking game allowing the players to cooperate for their mutual advantage. Specifically, the players can make agreements in a bargaining stage followed by an infinitely repeated version of the rent-seeking game.

Many authors have extended Tullock's (1980) model in various ways. Corcoran (1984), for example, considers the model in a long run setting and finds rents will be completely dissipated if free entry is allowed. Corcoran and Karels (1985) take the analysis further allowing different types of long-run competitive response. More recently, Hillman and Riley (1991) allow players to value the prize differently, while Katz, Nitzan, and Rosenberg (1990) examine the game with a public good as the prize. Linster (1993a, 1993b) analyzes this type

* The author gratefully acknowledges helpful comments by Bill Beck, Tom Homewood, and an anonymous referee.

of contest when played sequentially and when players care who wins if it is someone else. Additionally, Tullock (1974) offers a similar model of arms reduction negotiation, but the present model has many other applications.

This model of cooperative rent-seeking is similar in spirit to the standard models of collusion from industrial organization theory. Just as collusion between duopolists is not a reasonable result in a one-shot duopoly game, cooperation between the players cannot be supported as an equilibrium outcome if the rent-seeking game is played only once. However, if the rent-seekers play this game repeatedly, a cooperative outcome can be supported as a perfect equilibrium[2] under some conditions. The situations lending themselves to the type of analysis presented here include bilateral political/military conflict, gang or organized crime activities, labor/business lobbying activities, criminal/civil law suits, and other environments where only two competitors naturally emerge.

The exposition begins by showing how repeated interaction can lead to sustaining cooperative equilibrium outcomes. To put this in the context of rent-seeking models, a simplified version of Tullock's (1980) game is then briefly discussed. Next, cooperative agreements in symmetric and asymmetric situations[3] are considered separately. Finally, the results are summarized.

2. Cooperation in repeated rent-seeking games

Since the agreements will generally be illegal or the players may not be subject to external policing, the enforcement mechanism for cooperative rent-seeking must be the participants' self-interest. Such agreements in the one-shot game described by Tullock (1980) would be very difficult to sustain because both players have incentive to cheat on any agreement worth negotiating. However, rent-seekers often face repeated interaction with each other in the real world, and this repetition can allow for cooperative equilibrium behavior. As long as the future is important enough (or the probability of another rent-seeking encounter is high enough) cooperation can be sustained as a perfect equilibrium outcome of the infinitely repeated game.

To see how cooperation can be sustained in the repeated rent-seeking game, suppose an agreement yields a payoff vector (R_1, R_2) per period. Since we are now considering a repeated game, strategies must describe how a player will respond if his opponent cheats, and the simplest one terminates the deal and plays the one-shot Nash equilibrium strategy forever. It is important now to show the players have no incentive to deviate from the agreement.

Suppose the Nash equilibrium payoff vector of the one-shot game is (P_1, P_2), and player i gets T_i if she cheats, with $T_i > R_i > P_i$. Consider player i's possible payoffs in the repeated game if her discount factor is $\delta \in (0,1)$ – indicating either true discounting or that the game continues after each stage with probability δ. If both players cooperate, player i gets a payoff $A_i = R_i + R_i\delta + R_i\delta^2 + \ldots$, but if she decides to defect at time N, she secures $B_i = R_i + R_i\delta + R_i\delta^2 + \ldots R_i\delta^{N-1} + T_i\delta^N + P_i\delta^{N+1} + P_i\delta^{N+2} + \ldots$. Player i should comply with the agreement if $A_i \geq B_i$, which will be true if $\delta \geq (T_i - R_i)/(T_i - P_i)$. In other words, if the future is important enough, the players have incentive to comply with the agreement, and the strategies described above form a perfect equilibrium. This argument also rationalizes cooperation in the infinitely repeated Prisoners' Dilemma and collusion in duopoly theory.

Since a plethora of payoff vectors satisfying the above conditions exists, the Nash bargaining solution (NBS) will be used to select a unique payoff vector for cooperative situations. The NBS selects the payoff vector satisfying four axioms. In the context of this model, the NBS requires that the agreed outcome is Pareto efficient and treats the players symmetrically in the sense that the outcome is unchanged if they are labeled differently.

To formalize this idea somewhat, consider a bargaining situation (X, d) where X, the bargaining set, is the cooperative payoff region (or set of possible payoff vectors) in the repeated rent-seeking game with free disposal, and d is the disagreement point (the unique Nash equilibrium/subgame perfect equilibrium of the one-shot game). The NBS, then, is a function which maps a bargaining situation, (X, d), into an ordered pair (U_1, U_2) representing the agreed payoffs to the players. In the situations under consideration, the NBS is $F(X, d) = (1/2)t + (1/2)s$ where t and s are the Pareto efficient points in the bargaining set where one player gets his disagreement payoff and the other gets the entire surplus.[4] This is depicted in Figure 3.

Interestingly, other axiomatic bargaining solutions lead to the same unique outcome in this cooperative rent-seeking game. It can easily be shown that the NBS yields the same split as the Kalai-Smorodinski and Maschler-Perles bargaining solutions in this model,[5] indicating the outcomes presented here are robust to changes in the axioms regarding how irrelevant alternatives, or possible outcomes away from the bargaining solution, are treated.

3. The model

Consider a simple version of the one-shot rent-seeking game Tullock (1980) and Hillman and Riley (1987) analyzed. Two players – player I and player II – compete for something of value, and the probability the prize goes to player i is the ratio of his payment to the sum of both players' expenditures. The players are risk neutral, so the payoff functions can be described as

$$U_i(x_1, x_2) = \begin{cases} x_i v_i/(x_1+x_2) - x_i, & \text{if } x_1 \text{ or } x_2 > 0; \\ v_i/2, & \text{otherwise.} \end{cases} \tag{1}$$

where v_i, the value player i assigns winning the prize, is strictly positive and common knowledge among the players. The players' contributions are measured as x_1 and x_2.

Tullock (1980) actually considered the case where player i wins with probability $x_i^r/(x_1^r + x_2^r)$, and the players value the prize equally. The formulation under consideration here is a special case of his model with $r = 1$. However, like Hillman and Riley (1987) the valuations assigned the rent may vary between the players. This type of contest is similar to a lottery – making contributions is akin to purchasing lottery tickets.

The unique Nash equilibrium contributions are represented by the intersection of the players' best reply functions. Solving player i's first-order utility maximization condition for x_i yields (for $i \neq j$)

$$BR_i(x_j) = \begin{cases} (v_i x_j)^{1/2} - x_j, & \text{if } x_j \in (0, v_i]; \\ 0, & \text{if } x_j > v_i \end{cases} \tag{2}$$

Both best reply functions are simultaneously satisfied at the Nash equilibrium contribution vector $(x_1^*, x_2^*) = (v_1^2 v_2/(v_1+v_2)^2, v_1 v_2^2/(v_1+v_2)^2)$, making the equilibrium payoff vector $(U_1^*, U_2^*) = (v_1^3/(v_1+v_2)^2, v_2^3/(v_1+v_2)^2)$.[6]

The Nash equilibrium of the one-shot rent-seeking game is illustrated in Figure 1, where the players' best reply functions along with the indifference curves representing the equilibrium utility levels are depicted. The interior of the shaded region represents deals where both players achieve more than the Nash equilibrium payoffs. This stage game's structure makes cooperation unlikely in the one-shot version but sustainable if the game is infinitely repeated. Suppose the players choose the strategy which responds to defection by perpetually choosing the one-shot Nash equilibrium contribution. If the players agree to contributions (x_1^C, x_2^C) in the shaded region of Figure 1, player i's payoff from complying with the agreement is $R_i = U_i(x_1^C, x_2^C)$. If one of the players, say player II, decides to cheat on the agreed level of contributions, she will choose $x_2^{BR} = BR_2(x_1^C)$ and obtain $T_2 = U_2(x_1^C, x_2^{BR}) > R_2$ for the round in which she defects and $P_2 = U_2(x_1^*, x_2^*) < R_2$ in all subsequent plays of the stage game. Thus, the argument presented in Section 2 indicates cooperation can be sustained if the future is important enough.

If the rent-seeking stage game is played as a Stackelberg game, the equilibrium outcome differs if and only if the players value the prize differently. Assuming player I moves first, the unique subgame perfect equilibrium can be

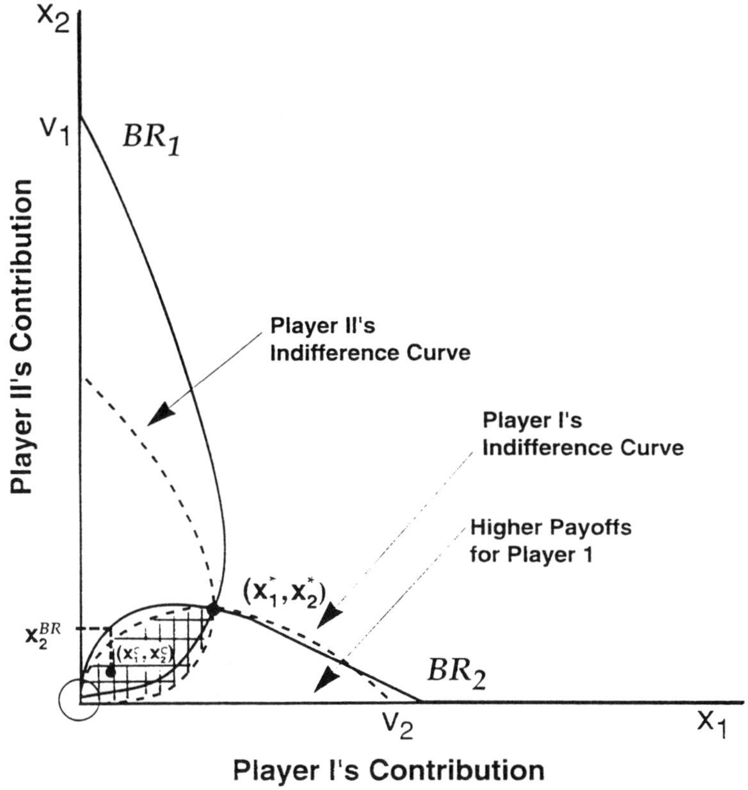

Figure 1. Nash equilibrium in the simultaneous-move rent-seeking game.

found by substituting player II's best reply function into player I's payoff function and solving the first order maximization condition for x_1. Then player II's equilibrium contribution can be determined by evaluating her best reply function at player I's equilibrium contribution. The unique subgame perfect equilibrium contributions for the Stackelberg game are

$$(x_1^*, x_2^*) = (\min\{v_1^2/4v_2, v_2\}, \max\{(v_1/2) - v_1^2/4v_2, 0\}), \tag{3}$$

and the equilibrium payoff vector is

$$(U_1^*, U_2^*) = (\max\{v_1^2/4v_2, v_1 - v_2\}, \max\{v_2 - v_1 + (v_1^2/4v_2), 0\}). \tag{4}$$

The contributions and payoffs in (3) and (4) depend on the players' relative valuations for the prize. When the first player values the prize at least twice as much as the second player, the first player's equilibrium contribution will be the value the second player assigns to the prize, and the second player will con-

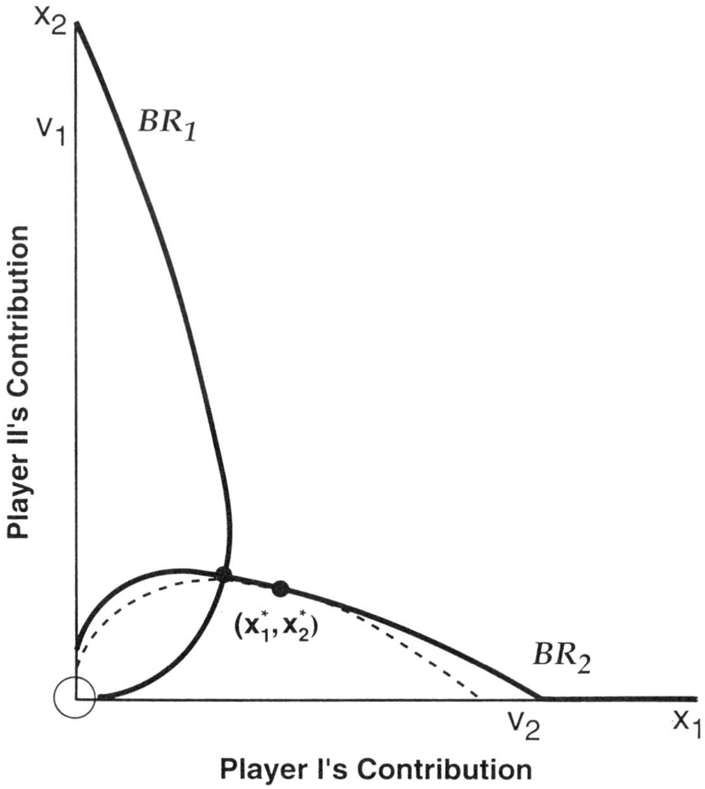

Figure 2. Stackelberg equilibrium in the rent-seeking game.

tribute nothing. The outcome of a Stackelberg game with an interior solution is depicted in Figure 2.[7]

4. Symmetric cooperative rent-seeking

Consider first the completely symmetric situation where the players move simultaneously and $v_1 = v_2 = v$. Without loss of generality, the value of the prize is normalized to unity ($v = 1$), and the contributions are proportions of the contestable rent. Additionally, this analysis begins assuming "transferable utility," which should not cause much alarm since risk neutral players will be indifferent between getting the rent with a probability q and getting the proportion q of the rent with certainty.

The bargaining set for the repeated rent-seeking game, X, must be determined along with the disagreement point, d. The greatest possible joint payoff the players can split is $v = 1$, which is available when neither contributes

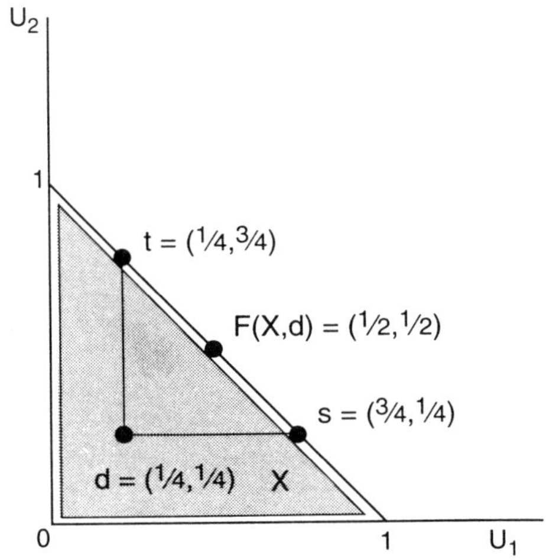

Figure 3. The Nash bargaining solution in a symmetric rent-seeking situation.

anything[8] ($x_1 = x_2 = 0$). If they fail to reach agreement they will get the Nash equilibrium payoff of d = (1/4, 1/4) in each play of the stage game. The bargaining situation, (X, d), is depicted in Figure 3, and determining the NBS is straightforward because the game is symmetric; F(X, d) = (1/2, 1/2) or the players split the maximum payoff evenly. Neither player makes a contribution, and no transfer is required.

If a player cheats on this agreement in a single play of the game, she earns a payoff arbitrarily close to one.[9] However, cooperation is sustainable if the rent-seeking situation is repeated. Since $R_i = 1/2$, $P_i = 1/4$, and T_i can be very close to one, cooperation will be incentive-compatible if the players do not discount the future too much. This means cooperation can be sustained if the players' discount factors are greater than 2/3.

5. Asymmetric cooperative rent-seeking with transferable utility

Now consider games where the players assign different values to the contestable rent, perhaps resulting from the players' varied circumstances. For example, an auto maker producing predominantly small cars may value import restrictions more highly than one making large autos. These dissimilar valuations complicate analysis of the repeated rent-seeking game somewhat. The solution concept is still the Nash bargaining solution applied to the cooperative payoff region of the rent-seeking game with the unique one-shot Nash/subgame perfect equilibrium as the disagreement point.[10] However, the cooperative payoff region is an open set in the asymmetric cooperative rent-seeking situation

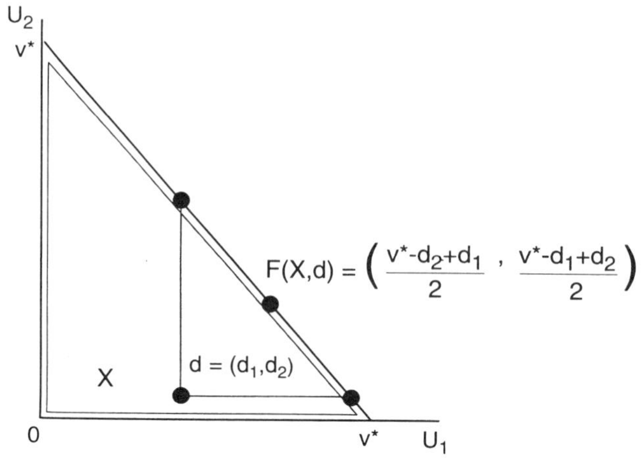

Figure 4. Asymmetric rent-seeking situation with transferable utilty.

(violating one of the requirements of the NBS) unless a minimum rent-seeking expenditure is imposed on those choosing to contribute more than zero. To simplify the analysis, initially assume the minimum contribution is $\epsilon \in (0,(v_1 - v_2)/2)$ with the players labeled so $v_1 > v_2$. The above assumptions ensure the bargaining set is closed, and permit analysis of the game with no minimum expenditure by taking the limit of the cooperative solution as the minimum contribution gets arbitrarily small ($\epsilon \rightarrow 0$).

An important difference between the asymmetric and the symmetric games is that the strategy choice where both players contribute zero no longer maximizes the joint payoffs. Instead, the sum of the players' payoffs is greatest when only the player with the larger valuation (player I) contributes ϵ; therefore, the cooperative payoff region is bounded by the line defined by $U_1 + U_2 = v_1 - \epsilon = v^*$. The joint payoff is $(v_1 + v_2)/2$ if both players contribute zero, but if player I makes the minimum contribution while player II contributes nothing, the total payoff is $v^* = v_1 - \epsilon$, which is strictly greater than $(v_1 + v_2)/2$ by assumption.

The solution to this asymmetric cooperative rent-seeking game, F(X, d), is depicted in Figure 4. The disagreement point, $d = (v_1^3/(v_1 + v_2)^2, v_2^3/(v_1 + v_2)^2)$, is the Nash equilibrium payoff vector of the one-shot rent-seeking game. The cooperative outcome in this repeated game is, then, $F(X, d) = ([(v_1 - \epsilon)/2] + (v_1^3 - v_2^3)/[2(v_1 + v_2)^2], [(v_1 - \epsilon)/2] - (v_1^3 - v_2^3)/[2(v_1 + v_2)^2])$. These payoffs are obtained when player I makes the minimum contribution, ϵ, and wins the prize with certainty. Then he makes a side payment of $[(v_1 - \epsilon)/2] - (v_1^3 - v_2^3)/[2(v_1 + v_2)^2]$ to player II.

As ϵ vanishes, $\lim_{\epsilon \rightarrow 0} F(X, d) = ((v_1/2) + (v_1^3 - v_2^3)/[2(v_1 + v_2)^2], (v_1/2) - (v_1^3 - v_2^3)/[2(v_1 + v_2)^2])$, or player I (the player valuing the prize more highly) gets half his valuation plus half the difference between the one-shot game equilibrium payoffs. Player II secures player I's payoff less the difference between their one-shot game equilibrium payoffs.

Now briefly consider the case where the minimum contribution is at least half the difference between the valuations, or $\epsilon \geq (v_1 - v_2)/2$, with the players still numbered so $v_1 > v_2$. The cooperative payoff region is bounded by the line $U_1 + U_2 = (v_1 + v_2)/2 = v^*$, and the cooperative outcome, $([(v_1+v_2)/4] + (v_1^3 - v_2^3)/[2(v_1+v_2)^2],\ [(v_1+v_2)/4] - (v_1^3 - v_2^3)/[2(v_1+v_2)^2])$, is achieved when neither player makes a contribution and player II makes a side payment equal to half the difference between their single play Nash equilibrium payoffs minus one-quarter the difference between their valuations. This situation is depicted in Figure 4.

Asymmetry may also arise if the rent-seeking competition is played as a Stackelberg game and the players value the rent differently (see Linster, 1993b). Now the players are identified by the order in which they choose – player I chooses first and player II follows.

The equilibrium payoffs in the one-shot Stackelberg rent-seeking game depend on the relative values the players assign the rent. Consider first the case where $v_1 \leq 2v_2$. (Again a small minimum contribution, ϵ, is necessary). The cooperative payoff region is bounded by the line $U_1 + U_2 = \bar{v} - \epsilon = v^*$ where $\bar{v} \equiv \max\{v_1, v_2\}$ for notational simplicity. If the Stackelberg rent-seeking game is played once, the unique subgame perfect equilibrium payoff vector is $(U_1^*, U_2^*) = (v_1^2/4v_2,\ v_2 - v_1 + (v_1^2/4v_2))$. With (U_1^*, U_2^*) as the disagreement point for the bargaining situation, the cooperative outcome is $((\bar{v} - \epsilon - v_2 + v_1)/2,\ (\bar{v} - \epsilon + v_2 - v_1)/2)$. Allowing ϵ to get arbitrarily small, the player valuing the prize more gets his valuation minus half his opponent's valuation, and the lower valuation player secures half of her own valuation. Interestingly, although the disagreement point changes with which player goes first, the cooperative outcome is independent of the order.

If the difference between v_1 and v_2 is no more than 2ϵ (or $|v_1 - v_2|/2 \equiv v^* \leq \epsilon$), the bargaining set is bounded by the line defined by $U_1 + U_2 = (v_1 + v_2)/2$. The NBS applied to this region with the one-shot Nash equilibrium payoffs for the disagreement point yields the payoff vector $((3v_1 - v_2)/4,\ (3v_2 - v_1)/4)$ – neither player makes a contribution, and the player valuing the rent less pays one-quarter the difference between the values to the other player. Again, the order in which the players choose is irrelevant.

Now consider the case where $v_1 \geq 2v_2$. In the Stackelberg rent-seeking game the equilibrium payoff vector is $(v_1 - v_2, 0)$, and using this as the disagreement point for the bargaining situation, the NBS payoff vector becomes $((v_1 - \epsilon + v_2)/2,\ (v_1 - \epsilon - v_2)/2)$. As $\epsilon \rightarrow 0$ player I gets the mean of the two valuations, and player II obtains half the difference between them.

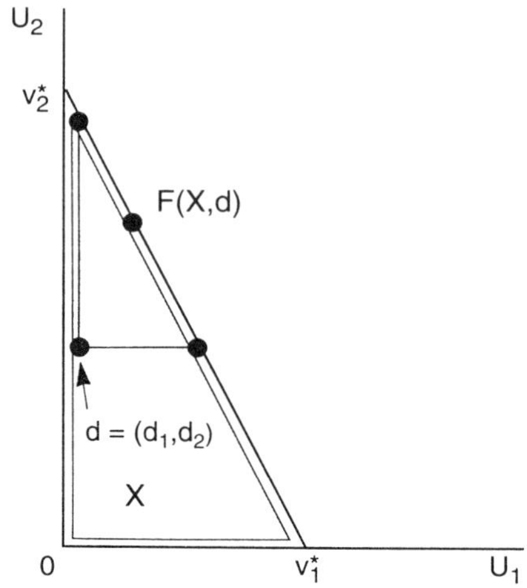

Figure 5. Asymmetric rent-seeking situation without transferable utility.

6. Cooperative rent-seeking without transferable utility

The possibility of side payments simplified the above analysis. Although utility transfers may not be achievable in some cases, gains from cooperation may still exist. This section considers the cases where side payments are not feasible.

Without transferable utility, defining a suitable cooperative payoff region is more problematic than in the earlier examples. To keep X convex and closed, the model is modified so the minimum total of the contributions for the prize is $\epsilon > 0$. This assumption removes the possibility that neither player makes a contribution and someone wins the prize. More formally, the utility function for both players evaluated at the point (0, 0) is now $U_i(0, 0) = 0, i \in \{1, 2\}$ (this assumption becomes irrelevant as $\epsilon \rightarrow 0$). The cooperative payoff region in the modified model becomes $\{(U_1, U_2) | U_2 \leq v_2^* - (v_2^* U_1/v_1^*)\}$ where $v_i^* \equiv v_i - \epsilon$, depicted in Figure 5.

Again, the NBS can be applied to the bargaining set with the Nash/subgame perfect equilibrium as the disagreement point. The calculations are straightforward, but the expression for the bargaining solution is rather messy, so only the limit of the solution as $\epsilon \rightarrow 0$ will be described. In the simultaneous move game the NBS yields the payoff vector $(v_1^2/(v_1 + v_2), v_2^2/(v_1 + v_2))$. This means that as $\epsilon \rightarrow 0$, both players get their one-shot game equilibrium payoff plus the contributions they would have made in the noncooperative game. In the Stackelberg game the cases where $v_1 \leq 2v_2$ and $v_1 \geq 2v_2$ (where v_1 is the first player's valuation) must be considered separately. The limit of the solution to the game as $\epsilon \rightarrow 0$ with $v_1 \leq 2v_2$ is the payoff vector $(\frac{v_1}{2} - \frac{v_1^2}{8v_2} + \frac{v_1^3}{8v_2^2}, \frac{v_2}{2}$

$+ \frac{v_1}{8} - \frac{v_1^2}{8v_2}$). If player I values the prize at least twice as much as player II does, the solution is $(v_1 - \frac{v_2}{2}, \frac{v_2^2}{2v_1})$.

In the above expressions, the contributions the players make have not been explicitly described. However, their payments can be completely characterized by noting that $x_1 + x_2 = \epsilon$, and the utility functions yield the payoffs indicated by the Nash bargaining solution.

7. Summary

This paper has presented an analysis of a simple version of the Tullock (1980) rent-seeking model when the players have an opportunity for cooperation. The enforcement mechanism in this game is repetition of the rent-seeking situation. If the game is repeated and the players care enough about the future, cooperation can be sustained.

When the rent-seeking situation is symmetric the cooperative outcome has neither player making expenditures in pursuit of the prize. Both players are as likely to win as in the one-shot stage game, but there are no wasteful rent-seeking expenditures. Changing the symmetric simultaneous move game into a Stackelberg game has no impact on the cooperative outcome.

In rent-seeking situations where the prize has different values to the players, the cooperative rent-seeking outcomes depend upon whether or not the game is played sequentially. Again, the Nash bargaining solution was applied to the cooperative payoff region. Here both players share the surplus available through cooperation. Situations in which utility is assumed to be nontransferable were also analyzed.

An important result of this analysis is that rent-seeking expenditures are minimal when the players are able to cooperate. In the symmetric case there is no expenditure of resources, and in the asymmetric case the rent-seeking expenditure is equal to some minimum amount introduced primarily to close the bargaining set. Tullock (1980) identified the fundamental problem to be addressed in these models as finding ways to reduce the wasteful rent-seeking expenditures. This paper lends some insight to how wasteful expenditures may be avoided in repeated rent-seeking situations. In bilateral conflict situations it is in the interest of both parties to reach an agreement since they can make a deal in which both sides are better off. The Nash bargaining solution can be used to predict an outcome in this situation. There are many settings in which rent-seeking games are repeated, and the players can cooperate to their joint advantage.

Notes

1. See Buchanan (1980) for an excellent introduction to this problem.
2. Aumann (1981) provides an excellent discussion of equilibria in repeated games.
3. Although the word "collusive" could easily be used here, these agreements will be called "cooperative" to avoid any negative connotations.
4. For more details and an excellent discussion of this, see Binmore (1992: 180–191).
5. A more detailed explanation of these bargaining solutions can be found in Shubik (1982: 194–200).
6. Linster (1993b) shows how to find the Nash equilibrium in this game.
7. For a detailed description of how these curves are derived for both the Stackelberg and simultaneous-move games, see Linster (1993b).
8. To see this, notice $U_1 + U_2 = (x_1+x_2)/(x_1+x_2) - (x_1+x_2) = 1 - (x_1+x_2) < 1$ as long as $x_1 + x_2 > 0$, and $U_1 + U_2 = 1$ if $x_1 + x_2 = 0$.
9. To see that this is true, let one of the players cheat by making a contribution of $\gamma > 0$ which is arbitrarily close to zero. Then he will have a payoff of $1-\gamma$, which is arbitrarily close to one.
10. For an excellent discussion of bargaining and the Nash Bargaining solution, see Binmore (1992).

Dynamic Rent-Seeking Games

WOLFGANG LEININGER*

LS Wirtschaftstheorie, Universität Dortmund, Postfach 500500, D-44221 Dortmund, Germany; and Department of Economics, Boston University, 270 Bay State Road, Boston, Massachusetts 02215

AND

CHUN-LEI YANG*

LS Wirtschaftstheorie, Universität Dortmund, Postfach 500500, D-44221 Dortmund, Germany

The present paper analyses rent-seeking games in which competitors for a rent can act and react finitely or infinitely often. It argues for an infinite-move model as the most appropriate specification of a model of rent-seeking. Dynamic equilibrium analysis of this game suggests that wasteful expenditures in rent-seeking competitions are lower than previously studied static (simultaneous-move) games predict. *Journal of Economic Literature* Classification Numbers: D72, C73.

1. INTRODUCTION

The existence of contrived economic rents represents a source of potentially large social welfare losses. This is the basic insight provided by the theory of rent-seeking, which focuses on the incentives to divert (otherwise productive) resources into activities which aim to win or defend such rents. This view was pioneered by Tullock (1967) who argued that the social costs of monopoly not only consist of the traditional "dead-weight"

* We are indebted to two anonymous referees and claim property rights to all remaining errors. Leininger expresses his gratitude to the Economics Department at Boston University for a pleasant stay while revising this article.

loss but also the wasteful (rent-seeking) cost of its formation. With respect to the size of the latter cost, Posner (1975) advanced the so-called rent dissipation hypothesis: since rent-seeking itself is a competitive activity, the entire monopoly rent will be competed away in the rent-seeking competition.

This relation between the value of a contestable rent and the value of resources expended in the competition for it, however, does not apply in general. A first and subsequently very influential game-theoretic model of rent-seeking competitions due to Tullock (1980) predicts underdissipation of the rent. Only for a limiting version (involving a deterministic rent-seeking process) could the rent-dissipation result be confirmed (Hillman and Samet, 1987). In addition, it was shown that risk-aversion on behalf of rent-seekers (Hillman and Katz, 1984), heterogeneous individual valuations of the contested rent (Hillman and Riley, 1989), and public-good properties of the rent-generating activity (Ursprung (1990), Katz *et al.* (1990)) contribute systematically to underdissipation of the contested rent. All these results were obtained in static (one-shot) models of the rent-seeking process. In contrast, Leininger (1993) shows that the (simultaneous) static Nash equilibrium concept may not be appropriate for the analysis of the rent-seeking problem as formulated by Tullock (1980). Retaining the feature that each player can only move once, but endogenizing the order of moves, he shows that players want to conduct the competition *sequentially* (and not *simultaneously*) which yields higher payoffs due to lower expenditures.

In the present paper, we use the original model by Tullock (1980) and reexamine it by formulating a truly *dnyamic* structure of the rent-seeking process. We do not derive this structure endogeneously, but take Leininger's (1993) argument as sufficient justification for considering, a priori, extensive forms of sequential rent seeking. What emerges from this approach is a more stable and less menacing picture of a "rent-seeking society": we show that threats and counter-threats in a dynamic version of Tullock's rent-seeking process make "implicit collusion" possible (and rational). Unlike in many other circumstances involving implicit collusion, this is a desirable result in this context: if players collude (implicitly) they soften *wasteful* competition! Hence we provide a further basic rationale for underdissipation of a rent. It stands to reason that the introduction of any of the above mentioned instances, which were shown to reduce expenditures in static rent-seeking competitions, in our dynamic framework leads to a further strengthening of the underdissipation prediction.

The paper is organized as follows: in Section 2 we briefly review Tullock's (1980) model and provide some technical results for use in later sections. Section 3 treats models of rent-seeking with finitely many stages while Section 4 advances a model with infinitely many stages. In this model we identify a prominent subgame perfect equilibrium, which makes use of tit-for-tat strategies. Section 5 offers some concluding remarks.

2. Preliminary Results

This section is devoted to some basic calculations in the original Tullock model of rent-seeking. For simplicity, we assume throughout the whole paper that there are only two players (i.e., rent-seekers), denoted by X and Y, who have the same valuation V for the rent. For reasons of brevity, only the most important technical characterizations are included here.

Tullock (1980) modeled the rent-seeking game in a simultaneous mode by using the Cournot–Nash equilibrium. Players X and Y compete for the prize (rent) of size V by making expenditures (resp., bids) x and y in order to capture the rent. This leads to overall expected profits of

$$\begin{aligned} F(x, y) &= \frac{Vx^r}{x^r + y^r} - x \quad \text{for player } X, \\ G(x, y) &= \frac{Vy^r}{x^r + y^r} - y \quad \text{for player } Y, \end{aligned} \tag{1}$$

where the probability of winning (depending on the expenditures x and y) is given by $x^r/(x^r + y^r)$ for X (resp., $y^r/(x^r + y^r)$ for Y). Note that (1) presumes that all bids represent sunk costs, i.e., are to be treated as non-retrievable investments. The parameter r determines the marginal (expected) return on such an investment.

Tullock shows that in a static (Cournot–)Nash equilibrium players make expenditures of

$$x^* = y^* = \frac{rV}{4}.$$

Hence, depending on r, competition for V may dissipate in the aggregate lower or higher expenditure than V. In fact, if $r > 2$ (i.e., $x^* = y^* > V/2$) expected profits become negative and it would be individually rational not to bid at all. Alas, everyone else behaving in this way makes it profitable to bid! There does not exist an equilibrium in pure strategies.

We now have a closer look at some of the structural properties of this simple auction game. Since the auction is symmetric w.r.t. the roles of players, all results obtained for one player apply—mutatis mutandis—for the other.

Lemma 1. (a) *For any* $r \geq 2$, $F(\cdot, y)$ *possesses exactly one local maximum* $\bar{x}(y)$ *and one local minimum* $\underline{x}(y)$ *with* $\underline{x}(y) \leq \bar{x}(y)$ *if* $y \leq [(r^2 - 1)/4r][(r+1)/(r-1)]^{1/r}V$. *If* $y \leq rV/4$, *then* $\underline{x}(y) \leq y \leq \bar{x}(y)$.

(b) *The (locally) best reaction curve* R_X *can be represented as*

$$R_X(t) = \begin{cases} x_F(t) = rVt^r(1+t^r)^{-2} \\ y_F(t) = tx_F(t) \end{cases} \tag{2}$$

for $t \in (0, ((r+1)/(r-1))^{1/r})$.

(c) *If, however,* $y \geq [(r^2-1)/4r]((r+1)/(r-1))^{1/r}V$, *then* $F(\cdot, y)$ *has no positive extremal point.*

Proof. Let $t := y/x$; the first order condition

$$F_x(x, y) = rV\left(1 + \left(\frac{y}{x}\right)^r\right)^{-2} \frac{y^r}{x^{r+1}} - 1 = 0 \tag{3}$$

then leads to the expression $R_X(t)$ immediately. Looking at the second order condition, it turns out that

$$\begin{aligned} F_{xx} &= rVt^r x^{-2}(1+t^r)^{-3}[2rt^r - (r+1)(1+t^r)] \\ &= rVt^r x^{-2}(1+t^r)^{-3}[(r-1)t^r - (r+1)] < 0 \\ \Leftrightarrow t &< ((r+1)/(r-1))^{1/r}. \end{aligned} \tag{4}$$

This proves part (b). Now, rewriting the first order condition again in terms of (x, y), we get

$$x^{2r} + 2y^r x^r - rVy^r x^{r-1} + y^{2r} = 0. \tag{5}$$

The (sign-)rule of Descartes (cf. Bronstein and Semendjajew, 1981, p. 189) tells us that if any polynom has the signs of its coefficients changed k times, then the number of its positive roots must be $k - 2h \in \{0, 1, 2, \ldots\}$ for some adequate $h \in \{0, 1, 2, \ldots\}$, where $k - 2h = 0$ means non-existence of any positive root. For (5) where $k = 2$, this implies that it either possesses two positive roots or none for any given $y \geq 0$. In the case of existence, there is a local maximum $\bar{x}(y) > ((r-1)/(r+1))^{1/r}y$, due to the proof of part (b). From $\lim_{x \to 0} F_x(x, y) = -1$, the smallest positive root of $F_x(\cdot, y)$, $\underline{x}$, can never be a local maximum. Hence, $\underline{x}(y) \in (0, \bar{x}(y))$. That $\underline{x}$ is indeed a local minimum results from the continuity of $F_x(\cdot, y)$ and the fact of $\bar{x}$ being a local maximum. The last statement of part (a) can be seen additionally by inserting $x = y$ into (3) which yields $F_x(y, y) = rV/4y - 1 \geq 0$, if $y \leq rV/4$. This proves part (a).

Part (c) is proved by verifying $(d/dt)y_F(t) \geq 0$ for all $t \in (0, ((r + 1)/(r - 1))^{1/r})$ and inserting $t = ((r + 1)/(r - 1))^{1/r}$ into $y_F(t)$. ■

For notational simplicity we also use the terms $x_F(y)$, $y_F(x)$ to denote X's reaction curve $R_X(t)$ and $x_G(y)$, $y_G(x)$ for Y's reaction curve $R_Y(t)$, which is symmetric to $R_X(t)$ with respect to the 45° line.

Without proof we state the following characterization of indifference curves under consideration.

LEMMA 2. (a) *Let* $I_{X,w} := \{(x, y) \in \mathbb{R}^2_+ : F(x, y) = w\}$ *denote X's indifference curve yielding him payoff w. Then,* $I_{X,w}$ *can be represented by*

$$I_{X,w}(t) = \begin{cases} x_I(t) = V(1 + t^r)^{-1} - w \\ y_I(t) = tx_I(t) \end{cases} \qquad t \in \left[0, \left(\frac{V - w}{w}\right)^{1/r}\right]. \tag{6}$$

(b) *If* $w > V/2$, *then* $\forall (x, y) \in I_{X,w}$: $y/x < 1$. *If* $w \leq T\ V/2$, *then* $y = x$ *on the curve* $I_{X,w}$ *iff* $x = y = V/2 - w$.

Some implications of Lemma 2 are illustrated in Fig. 1.

Now we are able to characterize a player's payoff in terms of his opponent's local reaction curve.

LEMMA 3. (a) $G(R_X(t))$ *has a local minimum at* $t = 1$ *and a local maximum at some* $t^* \in (0, 1)$.

(b) $\forall t < 1$: $G_y(x, y)|_{R_X(t)} > 0$.[1]

Proof.

$$G(t) := G(R_X(t)) = V(1 + t^{-r})^{-1} - rVt^{r+1}(1 + t^r)^{-2} \tag{7}$$

$$\begin{aligned} G'(t) &= rVt^{r-1}(1 + t^r)^{-3}[(r - 1)t^{r+1} + t^r - (r + 1)t + 1] \\ &= rVt^{r-1}(1 + t^r)^{-3}(t - 1)[(r - 1)t^r + r\sum_{k=1}^{r-1} t^k - 1]. \end{aligned} \tag{8}$$

Since $\Gamma(t) := (r - 1)t^r + r\sum_{k=1}^{r-1} t^k - 1$ is monotone increasing, $\Gamma(0) = -1$, and $\Gamma(1) = r^2 - 2 > 0$ if $r \geq 2$, we conclude that there exists some $t^* \in (0, 1)$ such that

$$G'(t) \leq 0 \Leftrightarrow t \in [t^*, 1]$$

[1] See also Fig. 4 for an illustration.

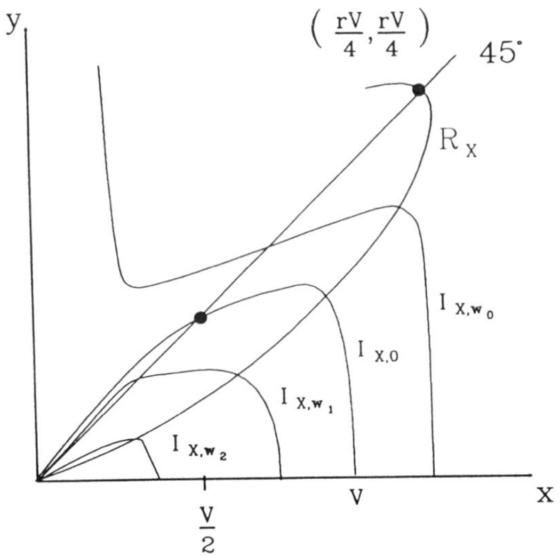

FIG. 1. Indifference curves: $w_0 \in (-\infty, 0)$, $w_1 \in (0, V/2)$, $w_2 \in (V/2, V)$.

which implies that t^* maximizes and $t = 1$ minimizes $G(t)$ locally. This proves (a). Furthermore,

$$\begin{aligned} G_y(x, y)|_{R_X(t)} &= \left(rV\left(1 + \left(\frac{x}{y}\right)^r\right)^{-2} \frac{x^r}{y^{r+1}} - 1\right)\Bigg|_{R_X(t)} \\ &= rVt^{-r}(1 + t^{-r})^{-2}(rVt^{r+1}(1 + t^r)^{-2})^{-1} - 1 \qquad (9) \\ &= t^{-1} - 1 > 0 \\ &\Leftrightarrow 0 \leq t < 1. \quad \blacksquare \end{aligned}$$

$R_X(t^*)$ is often called the interior Stackelberg solution when Y is the Stackelberg-leader and X is the Stackelberg-follower. Part (b) of Lemma 3 says that on X's reaction curve, Y always has an incentive to marginally increase his bid level as long as $y/x < 1$. Together with Lemma 1, it also implies that the partial payoff $G(x, \cdot)$ restricted onto the interval $[y_F(x), \infty)$ is unimodal with a maximum if there is any extremal point.

The following lemma is not difficult to prove.

LEMMA 4. (a) $(d/dt)F(R_X(t)) < 0$.

(b) $F(x_F(y), y) = 0 \Leftrightarrow y = [(r-1)/r](r-1)^{-1/r}V$.

This lemma tells us that a player's payoff decreases along his own reaction curve forever.

3. Finite Alternating Bids Models of Rent-Seeking

We now replace Tullock's (1980) simultaneous move model of rent-seeking by a model that allows players to bid several times alternatingly.

Let $N \in \mathbb{N}$ denote the number of bidding stages. $(a_1, \ldots, a_N)$ then denotes a sequence of bids, in which odd-numbered bids refer to the behaviour of the first moving player and even-numbered bids to that of the second moving player. This sequence has to satisfy the condition $a_t \geq a_{t-2}$ for all $t = 3, \ldots, N$, which reflects the fact that (accumulated) investments in rent seeking are sunk. The payoffs to the two players are determined by the final (accumulated) bids of a_{N-1} and a_N as

$$F(a_1, \ldots, a_N) = \frac{V \cdot a_N^r}{a_N^r + a_{N-1}^r} - a_N$$

and

$$G(a_1, \ldots, a_N) = \frac{V \cdot a_{N-1}^r}{a_{N-1}^r + a_N^r} - a_{N-1}$$

if X is the last moving player; resp., the other way round if Y is the last moving player. More technically, the game at hand is described as follows: at each stage t the set of feasible actions, S_t, of the player who is to move at this stage can be represented by $S_t = [0, \infty)$. When a player bids at t, he is perfectly informed about previous play; i.e., he knows the history of previous bids $(a_1, \ldots, a_{t-1}) \in S_1 \times \cdots \times S_{t-1}$. For notational convenience we introduce an initial state $(a_{-1}, a_0) = (0, 0)$, i.e., $S_0 = \{(0, 0)\}$, so that any history up to t, h_t, is an element of $H_t = S_0 \times S_1 \times \cdots \times S_{t-1}$. The choice of a player at t is constrained to a subset of S_t, namely $\overline{S}_t(h_t) = [a_{t-2}, \infty)$, $t = 1, \ldots, N$. A feasible strategy at t for a player is now given by a function s_t: $H_t \rightarrow S_t$ such that $s_t(h_t) \in \overline{S}_t(h_t)$. Any complete list of strategies at t, $(s_1, \ldots, s_N)$ then determines a unique path $h_{N+1}(s_1, \ldots, s_N) = (a_{-1}, a_0, a_1(s_1, \ldots, s_N), \ldots, a_N(s_1, \ldots, s_N))$ in the game. $h_{N+1}(s_1, \ldots, s_N)$ emanates from the initial state and follows the recursive relations $t = 1, \ldots, N$, $a_t(s_1, \ldots, s_N) = s_t(h_t)$, where $h_t = (0, 0, a_1(s_1, \ldots, s_N), \ldots, a_{t-1}(s_1, \ldots, s_N))$. Given the path $h_{N+1}(s_1, \ldots, s_N)$, the players receive the payoffs as specified above. Note that only the last two components, namely $a_{N-1}(s_1, \ldots, s_N)$ and $a_N(s_1, \ldots, s_N)$, matter in this respect. Note also that our description encompasses the situation in which a player "gives up" after having bid a_{t_0} at t_0, say. The strategies at t, for $t > t_0$, which he controls, would then just repeat the bid a_{t_0}, which is the smallest feasible bid at $t_0 + 2$, until the end. We are interested in strategies $(s_1, \ldots, s_N)$ for the two players (or, more precisely, their respective agents at t) which form a subgame perfect equilibrium (Selten, 1965, 1975). Such strategies must induce a Nash equilibrium in *any* subgame of our game. To be precise, $(s_1^*, \ldots, s_N^*)$ is a subgame perfect equilibrium (SPE) if, for all $t = 1, \ldots, N$ and for any history $h_t \in H_t$,

$$\text{(E)} \qquad s_t^*(h_t) \in \arg \max_{a \in \overline{S}_t(h_t)} U_t(h_t, a, s_{t+1}^*(h_t, a), \\ s_{t+2}^*(h_t, a, s_{t+1}^*(h_t, a)), \ldots, s_N^*(h, a, \ldots)),$$

where $U_t \in \{F, G\}$ depending on the identity of the player who moves at t.

Condition (E) requires that for *all* conceivable histories $h_t \in H_t$ (and not just the eventually realized one) the bid of the player, who moves at t, is a best response to the strategies employed after t.

The goal of this section is to characterize the sets of SPE payoffs if $N = 2$, resp. $N = 3$, first; and our main result is that, for any $N \in \mathbb{N}$ finite, the set of equilibrium payoffs is identical either to the $N = 2$ or to the $N = 3$ case.

Without loss of generality we assume that player Y is always the last bidder throughout this section. The first bidder in the $N = 2$ case is X, making bid a_1; after Y's concluding bid, a_2, the game ends and X obtains $F(a_1, a_2)$ and Y obtains $G(a_1, a_2)$. It is obvious that X has only two choices of relevance: either making the interior Stackelberg-leader bid $x_G(t^*)$ while expecting Y's bid to be $y_G(t^*)$ or preempting Y by making a bid so large that Y is left with no incentive to make any positive bid at all.

Formally, we state the following.

PROPOSITION 1. *For any $r \geq 2$, the only subgame perfect equilibrium with $N = 2$ consists of the strategies $a_1 = x_p := [(r-1)/r](r-1)^{-1/r}V$, $a_2 = 0$. The only SPE payoff is then $(1 - [(r-1)/r](r-1)^{-1/r})V$ for the first bidder X and zero for the last bidder Y.*

Before proving this proposition we state a technical lemma needed there.

LEMMA 5. *There exists no $t \geq 0$ solving the system*

$$\begin{cases} y = rVt^r(1+t^r)^{-2} \\ x = ty \\ 0 < t \leq \left(\dfrac{r+1}{r-1}\right)^{1/r} \\ x = V(1+t^{-r})^{-1} - pV \quad \textit{where}\; p := 1 - \dfrac{r-1}{r}(r-1)^{-1/r}. \end{cases} \tag{10}$$

That is, Y's reaction curve (the first two equations) does not intersect X's indifference curve yielding payoff pV (the last equation).

Proof. From the equations in (10) we get

$$(1 + t^{-1})^{-1} - p = rt^{r+1}(1 + t^r)^{-2}. \tag{11}$$

Let $\gamma = t^{-1}$, (11) is reformulated as

$$p\gamma^{2r} + (2p - 1)\gamma^r + r\gamma^{r-1} + p - 1 = 0. \tag{12}$$

Changing the variable once more by $z = \gamma - ((r - 1)/(r + 1))^{1/r}$, one gets

$$p\left(z + \left(\frac{r-1}{r+1}\right)^{1/r}\right)^{2r} + (2p-1)\left(z + \left(\frac{r-1}{r+1}\right)^{1/r}\right)^{r} + r\left(z + \left(\frac{r-1}{r+1}\right)^{1/r}\right)^{r-1}$$

$$+ p - 1 = p\sum_{k=r+1}^{2r}\binom{2r}{k} z^k \left(\frac{r-1}{r+1}\right)^{(2r-k)/r} + \left[p\binom{2r}{r}\left(\frac{r-1}{r+1}\right) + (2p-1)\right] z^r$$

$$+ \sum_{k=1}^{r-1} z^k \left[p\binom{2r}{k}\left(\frac{r-1}{r+1}\right)^{(2r-k)/r} + (2p-1)\binom{r}{k}\left(\frac{r-1}{r+1}\right)^{(r-k)/r}\right. \tag{13}$$

$$\left. + r\binom{r-1}{k}\left(\frac{r-1}{r+1}\right)^{(r-1-k)/r}\right]$$

$$+ p\left(\frac{r-1}{r+1}\right)^2 + (2p-1)\frac{r-1}{r+1} + r\left(\frac{r-1}{r+1}\right)^{(r-1)/r} + p - 1 = 0.$$

Now we recall that a sufficient condition for (13) possessing no positive root is that all coefficients occurring are non-negative. However, if (13) has no positive root, then (12) has no root larger than $((r - 1)/(r + 1))^{1/r}$, therefore (11) has no root in the interval $(0, ((r + 1)/(r - 1))^{1/r}]$ which means that (10) possesses no solution.

The coefficients for z^k, $k = r + 1, \ldots, 2r$, are obviously positive. For $k = 1, \ldots, r - 1$,

$$-\binom{r}{k} + r\binom{r-1}{k}\left(\frac{r-1}{r+1}\right)^{-1/r} = \binom{r}{k}\left(-1 + (r-k)\left(\frac{r-1}{r+1}\right)^{-1/r}\right) \geq 0 \tag{14}$$

implies that these coefficients are non-negative. From $p = 1 - [(r - 1)/r](r - 1)^{-1/r}$ we have, for $k = 0$ and $\forall r \geq 2$,

$$p\left(\frac{r-1}{r+1}\right)^2+(2p-1)\frac{r-1}{r+1}+r\left(\frac{r-1}{r+1}\right)^{(r-1)/r}+p-1$$

$$=\left(\frac{r-1}{r+1}+1\right)\left(p\frac{r-1}{r+1}+p-1\right)+r\left(\frac{r-1}{r+1}\right)^{(r-1)/r}$$

$$=\frac{r}{r+1}\left[2\left(p\frac{2r}{r+1}-1\right)+(r-1)\left(\frac{r-1}{r+1}\right)^{-1/r}\right]$$

$$\geq\frac{r}{r+1}[2(p-1)+r-1]>0.$$

For $k = r$, it is true that

$$p\binom{2r}{r}\frac{r-1}{r+1}+(2p-1)=p\left[\binom{2r}{r}\frac{r-1}{r+1}+2\right]-1\geq 0$$

$$\Leftrightarrow 1-\frac{r-1}{r}(r-1)^{-1/r}\geq\left[\binom{2r}{r}\frac{r-1}{r+1}+2\right]^{-1}.$$

However, since $\binom{2r}{r}[(r-1)(r+1)] = (2r/r)\cdot(2r-1)/(r-2)\cdot\ldots\cdot[(r+3)/2]\cdot[(r+2)/1] > r$ and $(r-1)^{-1/r} \leq 1$, the last inequality is valid for all $r \geq 2$. This completes the proof. ■

Proof of Proposition 1. From Lemma 4(b) interpreted symmetrically for Y, we know Y's optimal bid is $a_2 = 0$ if $a_1 > x_p$. If X makes some bid $a_1 < x_p$ then Y always has strict incentive to bid $a_2(a_1) = y_G(a_1) > 0$; in this case, X would bid $a_1 = x_G(t^*)$, the interior Stackelberg point. From Lemma 5 we know that the payoff $pV = V - x_p > 0$ for X is not obtainable at any point of R_Y. Since $\lim_{t\to\infty} F(R_Y(t)) = 0$ and therefore $(0, F(x_G(t^*), y_G(t^*))] \subset F(R_Y)$ from the continuity of $F(R_Y(t))$, it is immediate that

$$F((x_p, 0)) = pV > \max F(R_Y) = F(x_G(t^*), y_G(t^*)).$$

The last point is also made transparent in Fig. 2. ■

Y as the first and the last bidder in a three rounds game is able to commit himself to retaliate at the last round after bidding a certain amount at the first stage (see Fig. 2). Having recognized this, one can conclude that Y can ensure himself at least a payoff of $(1 - y_{pp})V$ where y_{pp}, used as a_1 by Y, is such that X at the second stage finds no bid $a_2 > 0$ which would yield him non-negative payoff while anticipating Y's best reaction at the last stage. Though our intuition strongly suggests that this kind of pre-preemption is the only candidate for SPE, we technically have not been

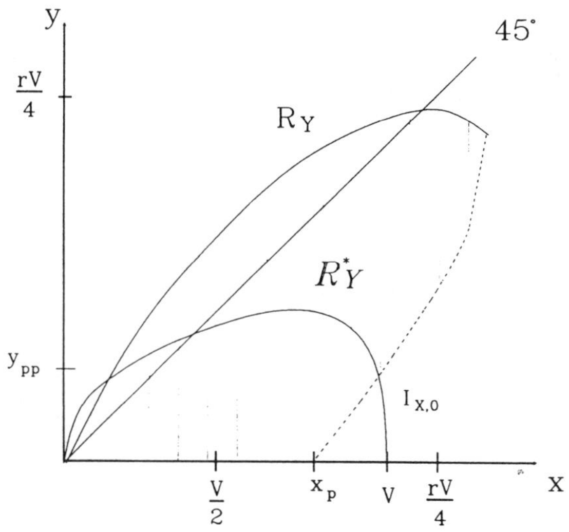

FIG. 2. Preemption and pre-preemption.

able to rule out another kind of equilibrium called *sub-Stackelberg* which says there may be some bid y_s such that X finds it best to make a bid $a_2 = x_G(y_s)$; i.e., Y gives X a chance to react with a positive bid and prefers this sub-Stackelberg solution to pre-preemption. We informally explained the following.

PROPOSITION 2. *For* $r \geq 2$, $N = 3$, *let* $y_{pp} := \min y$ *such that*

$$\begin{cases} x = V\left(1 + \left(\frac{y}{x}\right)^r\right)^{-1} \\ G(x, y) \leq G(x, y_G(x)) \\ x \geq pV, \end{cases} \tag{15}$$

where $y_s := \max \{y_{ss}, y_G(t^*)\}$ *and* $y_{ss} := \min y$

$$s.t. \begin{cases} G(x, y) \leq G(x, y_G(x)) \\ x \geq pV \\ F(x_G(y), y) \geq F(x, y). \end{cases} \tag{16}$$

Then, either $(0, G(0, y_{pp}))$ *or* $(F(x_G(y_s), y_s), G(x_G(y_s), y_s))$ *is the SPE payoff, depending on Y's preference between* $(0, y_{pp})$ *and* $(x_G(y_s), y_s)$. *And* $\#SE(3) = 2$ *iff Y is indifferent.*

We are now about to show the most striking result of this section which says that the structure of SPE payoffs for any finite rounds alternating bids model is exhaustively analysed by considering the cases $N = 2$ and $N = 3$.

PROPOSITION 3. *Let $SE(N)$ denote the set of SPE payoffs of the N-rounds game. Then $SE(2N) = SE(2)$ and $SE(2N + 1) = SE(3)$ $\forall N \in \mathbb{N}$.*

Proof. Consider the $2N$-rounds game first. X is the first bidder and Y the last one. It is clear that, by bidding $x_p + \varepsilon$ at once, X can always ensure himself the payoff $F(x_p + \varepsilon, 0)$, $\forall \varepsilon > 0$ as in the two-rounds case. Suppose there were some other SPE. Let $(\tilde{x}, \tilde{y}) = (a_{N-1}, a_N)$ be the last two bids. Since we proved that the preemption is preferred to any point of Y's reaction curve R_Y, $(\tilde{x}, \tilde{y})$ has to be outside or just on the border of Y's retaliation region $\mathcal{R}_Y^*$. This implies, however, that $(\tilde{x}, \tilde{y})$ can yield no more payoff to X than $(x_p, 0)$ does and therefore $(F(x_p, 0), 0)$ is the only SPE payoff.

In a $(2N + 1)$-rounds game, Y is both the first and the last bidder. From Proposition 2 we know that Y's payoff in $SE(3)$ is unique. It is trivial to see that Y always can ensure his $SE(3)$-payoff because he is able to threaten to retaliate credibly even though he may not have strict incentive to do so. Suppose that $SE(3)$ is single-valued and the sub-Stackelberg case occurs for $N = 3$. Since pre-preemption is dominated by $(x_G(y_s), y_s)$, the only positive SPE outcome which yields Y a higher payoff has to be $(x_G(y^*), y^*)$ for some $y^* < y_s$ which implies $a_{2N-1} \leq y^*$, $a_{2N-2} \leq x_G(y^*)$. However, due to the properties of sub-Stackelberg (Proposition 2), X either has strict incentive to go beyond Y's retaliation region, causing a large loss to Y, or to bid $a_{2N} = x_G(t^*) = x_G(y_s)$ which causes $a_{2N+1} = y_G(t^*) = x_G(y_s)$, which in turn implies that there is no other SPE payoff in the case of sub-Stackelberg. If pre-preemption is to be expected with $N = 3$, a similar argument shows that Y is not able to get more payoff in any SPE either. The cases when $SE(3)$ happens to be double-valued can be handled the same way—mutatis mutandis. This completes the proof. ■

The three-stage model is more "asymmetric" from a strategic point of view than the two-stage model. This can be seen most easily from an interesting observation regarding the limit behaviour of equilibrium bids: in the two-stage ($2N$-stage alike) model we get that the preemptive (equilibrium) bid x_p converges to V, the valuation of the rent held by the bidder, as the parameter r approaches infinity and thus we get approximately full rent dissipation. In the three-stage ($2N$ + 1-stage alike) model, however, numerical experimentation suggests that Y's opening bid converges to zero as r approaches infinity; i.e., there is no profit dissipation at all! The player moving first *and* last can exert such strong strategic powers that his rival is (rationally) forced to abstain from competing. This is illustrated in Table I.

TABLE 1

PREEMPTION AND PRE-PREEMPTION

r:	2	3	4	8	15	30	70
x_p	50	52.91	56.99	68.61	78.28	86.40	92.79
y_{pp}	50	49.68	49.73	38.85	25.67	15.17	7.66

Note. Calculated for $V = 100$. x_p is X's preemptive bid in $N = 2$. y_{pp} is Y's pre-preemptive bid in $N = 3$.

In most real rent-seeking competitions none of the competitors can be singled out to have such an outstanding strategic position, in which it is up to him to have the first and last word. In some cases, which for this reason we might term "rigged," however, this might be true. In any case, we would like to defend our analysis for two reasons: first, it sheds light on the strategic incentive structure for individual players in the competition and, second, it helps, ex post, to identify an appropriate model for the underlying conflict situation. Our analysis shows that it is of overriding importance that both players know who is to move last. This knowledge, however, is in general not shared by rent-seekers in actual competitions. This insight necessitates the search for a rent-seeking model in which there is no a priori known last bidder. Such a model is presented in the next section.

4. An Infinite Alternating Bids Model

The following infinite alternating bids model is to be understood as *modeling* device to capture the fact that players cannot be sure of who is moving last (and *not* as a description of a potentially endless struggle for a rent). Players perceive this information as highly relevant (see our previous results) and thus take account of it in their strategic reasoning. With perfect information, however, this cannot be modeled by a finite move game. Since our infinite model is thus meant to represent a *different* interactive decision problem there is a priori no reason, let alone need, for a "convergence result" in the sense that the equilibrium behaviour of our finite bids models should approach equilibrium behaviour of the infinite bids model as we expand the finite games. On the contrary, one rather would expect structurally different results since the strategic reasoning applied by the rent seekers is different.[2]

[2] In any case, given that equilibrium behaviour in the finite models always "oscillates" around $SE(2)$ and $SE(3)$, the question is settled a priori in favour of "non-convergence" mathematically.

4.1. *Rules of the Infinite Alternating Bids Game*

We extend the model of Section 3 to allow for infinite sequences of (alternating) bids by the two rent-seekers. A move of nature is also incorporated now at the very beginning. Nature will choose (with equal probability) one of the two players as the first mover. We denote the realization of nature's move by a_{-2} with $a_{-2} \in \{X, Y\}$.

So let $N = \infty$; a play of the game can now be identified with a sequence $h_\infty = (a_{-2}, a_{-1}, a_0, a_1, \ldots)$, where $a_{-2} \in \{X, Y\}$ and $(a_1, a_2, \ldots)$ denotes the history of alternating bids emanating from the initial state $(a_{-1}, a_0) = (0, 0)$. The definition of a stragegy at t, $t = 1, 2, \ldots$, remains unchanged, so that, as before, a complete list of strategies at t, $(s_1, \ldots, t_t, \ldots)$, determines a unique path of bids, $h_\infty(s_1, \ldots, s_t, \ldots)$, via the same (but now infinitely often applied) recursions. The payoffs resulting from such a path have now to be defined as

$$F(h_\infty) = \begin{cases} \lim\limits_{t\to\infty} \left(\dfrac{V \cdot a_{2t}^r}{a_{2t}^r + a_{2t-1}^r} - a_{2t} \right) & \text{if } a_{-2} = Y \\[2ex] \lim\limits_{t\to\infty} \left(\dfrac{V \cdot a_{2t-1}^r}{a_{2t-1}^r + a_{2t}^r} - a_{2t-1} \right) & \text{if } a_{-2} = X \end{cases}$$

with $G(h_\infty)$ defined analogously.

Since each player's bids have to form a monotonically increasing sequence these payoffs are well-defined (although they may reach $-\infty$). Note that this specification reduces to the previous one, if we define a play to be *finite*, if and only if there exists $N_0 \in \mathbb{N}$ such that $a_t = a_{t-2}$ for all $t \geq N_0$.

A subgame perfect equilibrium is now given by a sequence $\{(s_t^*)_{t\in\mathbb{N}}\}$ of strategies at t such that, for all t and any history $h_t \in H_t$,

$$\text{(E}'\text{)} \qquad s_t^*(h_t) \in \arg\max\nolimits_{a \in \bar{S}_t(h_t)} U_t(h_t, a, s_{t+1}^*(h_t, a), s_{t+2}^*(h_t, a), \ldots).$$

where $U_t \in \{F, G\}$, as defined above depending on the value of a_{-2} as part of the given h_∞.

Since for every player at any bidding state t the payoff relevant part of a history $h_t = (a_{-2}, a_{-1}, a_0, \ldots, a_{t-1})$ consists only of (a_{t-2}, a_{t-1}) and *not* the entire history, it is natural to restrict strategies at t to be of an adequately simple type. We call a strategy at t, s_t, *Markovian* if $s_t(h_t) = s_t(h_t')$ for all $h_t, h_t' \in H_t$ satisfying $a_{t-2} = a_{t-2}'$ and $a_{t-1} = a_{t-1}'$; i.e., s_t only conditions on the relevant *state* given by the present (accumulated) bids of the two players. Adopting the notation saving convention that the first component of the state variable always refers to player X's last bid and the second one always to Y's last bid, we denote a Markovian strategy at t by a function σ_t: $\mathbb{R}_+^2 \to \mathbb{R}_+$ such that $\sigma_t(x, y) \geq x$ if player X is to move at t, resp. $\sigma_t(x, y) \geq y$ if player Y is to move at t. A *Markovian* SPE is then just an SPE in Markovian strategies.

4.2. *Tit-for-Tat and Subgame Perfect Equilibrium*

We now show that tit-for-tat strategies (TFT) form an SPE of our game. In a TFT a player exactly copies another player's move. As a threatening device this is a moderate one in the sense that it is entirely left to the opponent to "choose" the sort of treatment he will receive from him. If credible this mechanism prevents the bidding from escalating.

We begin with some useful characterization of TFT strategies.

LEMMA 6. (a) *Let*

$$T_X(t) := (x_{T,X}(t), y_{T,X}(t)) \\ := \left(\frac{V}{2}\frac{t^r - 1}{(t-1)(t^r+1)}, \frac{V}{2}\frac{(t^r-1)t}{(t-1)(t^r+1)}\right). \tag{17}$$

Then for any $x < y$, it pays for X to play TFT; i.e., $F(y, y) \geq F(x, y)$, iff $\exists t > 0$: $x \geq x_{T,X}(t)$, $y \leq y_{T,X}(t)$.

(b) $\forall x \leq \frac{rV}{4}$: $y_G(x) \leq y_{T,X}(x)$; i.e., *R_Y lies below T_X, where $y_{T,X}(x)$* $:= y_{T,X}(x_{T,X}^{-1}(x))$.[3]

Proof. (a) For any $x < y$,

$$F(y, y) - F(x, y) = \frac{V}{2} - y - \frac{Vx^r}{x^r + y^r} + x = \frac{V}{2} - (t-1)x - \frac{V}{1 + t^r} \geq 0$$

$$\Leftrightarrow x \leq \frac{V}{2}\frac{t^r - 1}{(t-1)(t^r+1)},$$

while

$$y = tx = \frac{V}{2}\frac{(t^r-1)t}{(t-1)(t^r+1)} \qquad \text{and} \qquad t > 1.$$

(b) From Lemma 3 we induce that, for all $x \leq rV/4$, $G(x, \cdot)$ is unimodel with a maximum. The claim is then equivalent to stating that $\forall t \geq 1$ and $x \leq rV/4$,

[3] An alternative interpretation is illustrated in Fig. 4, namely, that R_Y lies in X's activity set A_X.

$$G_y(x, y)|_{T_X} = rV\left(1 + \left(\frac{x_{T,X}(t)}{y_{T,X}(t)}\right)^r\right)^{-2} x^r_{T,X}(t) - 1$$

$$= rV(1 + t^{-r})^{-2}t^{-r}\left(\frac{V}{2}\frac{t(t^r - 1)}{(t-1)(t^r+1)}\right)^{-1} - 1$$

$$= \frac{2rt^{r-1}(t-1)}{(t^r+1)(t^r-1)} - 1 \leq 0.$$

However, the last inequality is valid since $\min_{z \in \mathbb{R}} \cosh z = \cosh 0 = 2$ and therefore

$$t^{2r-1} - 1 - 2rt^{r-1}(r-1)$$

$$= (t-1)\left(\sum_{k=0}^{2r-1} t^k - 2rt^{r-1}\right)$$

$$= (t-1)t^{r-1}\left(\sum_{k=1}^{r-1} (t^k + t^{-k}) + t^{2r-1} + 1 - 2r\right)$$

$$= (t-1)t^{r-1}\left(\sum_{k=1}^{r-1} \cosh(k \ln t) + t^{2r-1} + 1 - 2r\right)$$

$$\geq 0. \quad \blacksquare$$

A crucial result for the main proposition of this section is the following lemma.

LEMMA 7. $\forall x \in (0, rV/4]$: $G(x, x) = G(x, y_{T,X}(x))$.

Proof. Let $x = (V/2)((t^r - 1)/[(t-1)(t^r+1)])$ for some $t > 1$, then it follows immediately that

$$G(x, y_{T,X}(x)) - G(x, x) = 0. \quad \blacksquare$$

Now we are about to relate TFT strategies to equilibrium. Consider the Markovian strategies

$$\sigma^T_X(x, y) = \begin{cases} x_F(y) & \text{if } y \geq \frac{rV}{4} \wedge F(x_F(y), y) \geq F(x, y) \\ y & \text{if } x \leq y \leq y_{T,X}(x) \wedge y \leq \frac{rV}{4} \\ V/2 & \text{if } (x, y) = (0, 0) \\ x & \text{otherwise,} \end{cases} \tag{18}$$

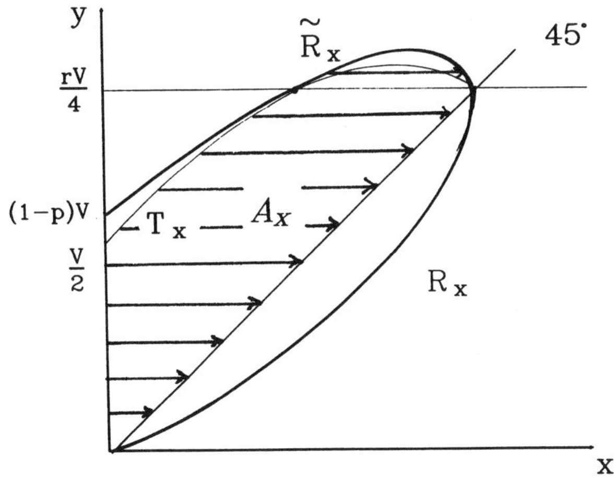

FIG. 3. TFT strategy and activity set. According to σ_X^T, X moves to the border of the hatched region A_X as shown by the arrows.

$$\sigma_Y^T(x, y) = \begin{cases} y_G(x) & \text{if } x \geq \frac{rV}{4} \wedge G(x, y_G(x)) \geq G(x, y) \\ x & \text{if } y \leq x < x_{T,Y}(y) \wedge x \leq \frac{rV}{4} \\ V/2 & \text{if } (x, y) = (0, 0) \\ y & \text{otherwise,} \end{cases} \tag{19}$$

where $x_F(\cdot)$ (resp. $y_G(\cdot)$) denotes X's (resp. Y's) best reaction curve and $x_{T,Y}(y)$ (resp. $y_{T,X}(x)$) denotes the x-coordinate (resp. y-coordinate) of the TFT-border T_Y (resp. T_X) given y (resp. given x). For any $r > 1$, σ_X^T can roughly be depicted as in Fig. 3.

PROPOSITION 4. *(σ_X^T, σ_Y^T) is a SPE in Markovian strategies with expected equilibrium payoffs $(V/4, V/4)$. Its equilibrium path has the chosen first bidder bidding $V/2$ and the other player bidding zero.*

Proof. We have to show that at any state $(x, y) \in \mathbb{R}_+^2$ the strategies $(\sigma_{X,(x,y)}^T, \sigma_{Y,(x,y)}^T)$ induced form a Nash equilibrium. Let us define some auxiliary notation first. At any state (x, y), the set of remaining accessible states for X and Y independent of σ^T is the area

$$W_X(x, y) = \{(x', y'): x' > x, y' \geq y\} \cup \{(x, y)\}$$

and (20)

$$W_Y(x, y) = \{(x', y'): x' \geq x, y' > y\} \cup \{(x, y)\}.$$

Furthermore, the strategies σ_i^T, $i = X, Y$, are essentially described by the *activity set*

$$A_X = \{(x, y): \sigma_X^T(x, y) > x\}$$
$$A_Y = \{(x, y): \sigma_Y^T(x, y) > y\}. \tag{21}$$

Therefore, if at some state (x, y) the opponent's continuation behaviour is believed to follow σ^T, then player i's choice of continuation strategy $\sigma_{i,(x,y)}^T$ will lead to some expected final state in the set

$$Z_i(x, y) = W_i(x, y) \backslash A_{-i} \tag{22}$$

for $i = X, Y$ while $-i$ denotes i's oppnent. Put differently, given σ_{-i}^T, player i never expects the game to end up in A_{-i}. What we have to show is hence that, for all (x, y), if i is to move at (x, y) then the σ^T-induced final state in the subgame $\Gamma((x, y)_i)$ is preferred to $Z_i(x, y)$ by i.

Since $(x, y) >_x W_X(x, y)$,[4] if $x \geq rV/4$, and $(x, y) >_Y W_Y(x, y)$, if $y \geq rV/4$ as implied by Lemma 1, stopping the game under those conditions is in fact optimal (as is prescribed by σ^T). We now define σ^T on the remaining states in $[0, rV/4] \times [0, rV/4]$. We first consider player X. Recall that a player's payoff monotonically decreases in his opponent's final bid, hence the σ^T-accessible set $Z_X(x, y)$ is dominated by its lower bound

$$\underline{Z}_X(x, y) = \overline{Z_X(x, y)} \backslash \overset{\circ}{\overline{Z_X(x, y)}}, \tag{23}$$

i.e., the optimal accessible state for X in (x, y) is contained in $\underline{Z}_X(x, y)$. The set of candidates for optima can further be reduced to

$$\tilde{Z}_X(x, y) := \underline{Z}_X(x, y) \cap \{(x', y'): y' \leq \max\{y'': (x, y'') \in \overline{A_Y}\}\}, \tag{24}$$

because X's local best response curve satisfies $R_X \cap (0, rV/4]^2 \subset \overline{A_Y}$ as shown in Lemma 6(b), and because, from the point $x_F(y)$ on, X's partial payoff is even decreasing in his own bid, due to Lemma 1. For the same reason, X's optimal accessible state at some subgame (x, y) with $x \geq x_F(y)$ is (x, y) itself, which is exactly what σ^T prescribes.

Let us now consider the case $x \in [y, x_F(y)]$. Then, $\tilde{Z}_X(x, y) \backslash \{(x, y)\}$ consists of the point D on the lower bound of A_Y and the curve section $\widetilde{CB}$ as displayed in Fig. 4. From the technical lemmata previously proved,

[4] "$l >_i k$" is to be read as "i (not necessarily strictly) prefers l to k" henceforth.

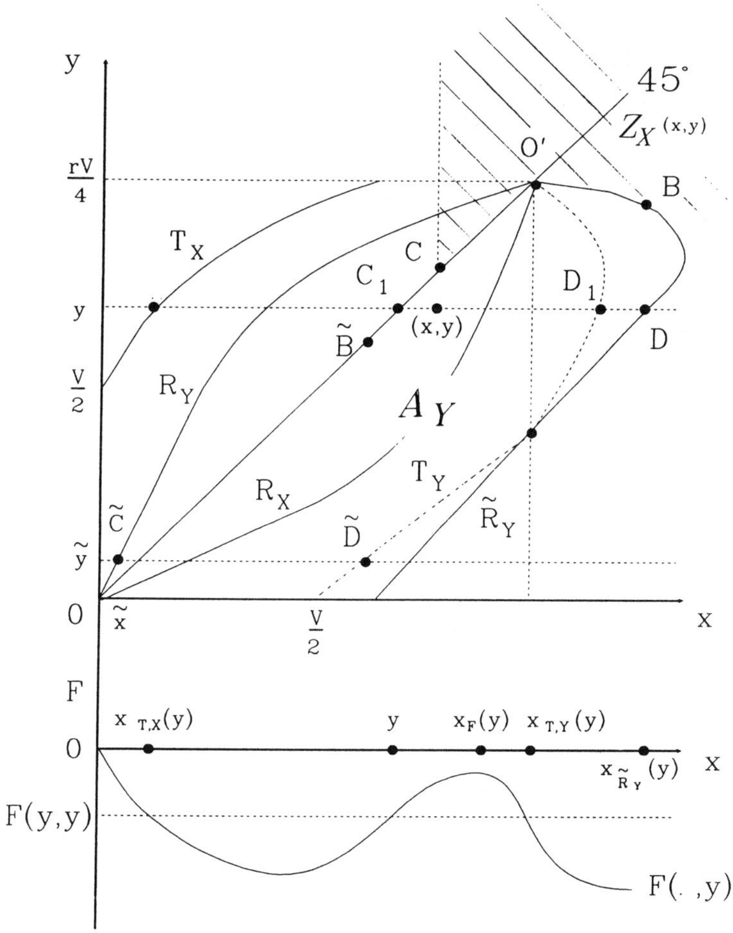

FIG. 4. Optimal accessible states and SPE.

we induce

$$C_1 >_X (\overline{CO'} \cap \widetilde{CB}), D_1 >_X D >_X D >_X B >_X \widetilde{O'B}, (x, y) >_X C_1 \sim_X D_1, \quad (25)$$

where $C_1 = (y, y)$, $C = (x, x)$, $D = (\bar{x}(y), y)$, and $B = (\bar{x}(y), \bar{y}(\bar{x}(y)))$ with

$$\bar{x}(y) = \max\{x' : (x', y) \in \overline{A_X}\} \text{ and } \bar{y}(x) = \max\{y' : (x, y') \in \overline{A_X}\} \quad (26)$$

while $D_1 = (x_{T,Y}(y), y)$. In fact, if y is such that $\bar{x}(y) \leq rV/4$, then $D = D_1$ and $\widetilde{CB} \subset \overline{CO'}$; and if y is such that $x_G(y)/y \geq ((r+1)/(r-1))^{1/r}$, then $D = B$. Yet, independent of these cases, the conclusion from (25) is that it is optimal for X to stop the game as recommended by σ^T because $(x, y) >_X \tilde{Z}_X(x, y)$. An illustration is given in Fig. 4.

The case $x < y$ in the square $(0, rV/4]^2$ remains. Here, the additional set of relevant σ^T-accessible states at (x, y), compared to the $x \geq y$ case, is the line section $[x, y] \times \{y\}$. From Lemma 1, this set is either dominated by $C_1 = (y, y)$ or by (x, y) dependent on the relation $(x, y)\ (\gtrless)\ (y, y)$ itself. Together with (25), we conclude that σ^T's recommendation at $(x, y)_X$ indeed leads to the optimal accessible state if the opponent Y is expected to stick to σ_Y^T.

Finally, if $(x, y) = (0, 0)$, then the best state for X to reach is $(V/2, 0)$ by preemptively bidding $\sigma_X^T(0, 0) = V/2$, because Y is recommended not to retaliate on the lower bound of his activity set A_Y.

For symmetry reasons the same arguments hold for player Y. Thus (σ_X^T, σ_Y^T) are best reactions to each other which determine payoffs and bids as claimed. ■

Threats and counterthreats in a TFT equilibrium rationally restrain competitors from entering into escalatory behaviour which would exhaust further their resources. This "implicit collusion"-like behaviour, probably best known from the theory of repeated games, is now obtained in a truly dynamic model of the bidding process (which made its proof somewhat involved).

A very interesting property of the TFT equilibrium is that equilibrium strategies do *not* depend on r, the parameter governing the stochastic success rate of an investment. TFT strategies thus are seen to eliminate the increasingly severe effects of r on the riskiness of investments by players as r increases. This is worth noting since it is precisely this effect which causes the instability (leading to non-existence of equilibrium) in the static game. In the limit, i.e., $r = \infty$, the probability function chosen by Tullock converges to the certainty case of the Dollar Auction Mechanism

$$\lim_{r\to\infty} \frac{x^r}{x^r + y^r} = \begin{cases} 0 & \text{if } x < y \\ 1/2 & \text{if } x = y \\ 1 & \text{if } x > y, \end{cases}$$

i.e., whoever bids more wins with certainty. This deterministic auction model has played a prominent role in the analysis of escalation phenomena (see, e.g., Shubik, 1971; O'Neill, 1986; and Leininger, 1989). It has also been used by Leininger (1991) to study patent races, which may be interpreted as a particular instance of rent-seeking (the rent accruing from the patent awarded). In a static version it was introduced to the rent-seeking literature by Hillman and Samet (1987).

5. Concluding Remarks

The early literature on rent-seeking presumed that the rent dissipation hypothesis holds. Subsequently, several rationales for the underdissipation of a contested rent have been provided (Hillman and Katz, 1984; Hillman and Riley, 1989; Ursprung, 1990; and Katz *et al.*, 1990). Our analysis points to a new fundamental reason for expecting underdissipation: the sequential (dynamic) conduct of rent-seeking competitions. If rent-seekers (inter)act more than just once, the (credible) threat of escalating the bidding leads players to be more restrained and to make lower bids. This has been shown by the use of rather simple bidding strategies. Players apply tit-for-tat reasoning, which is of considerable behavioural appeal. In doing so they make strategic use of the time variable in order to soften competition for the rent. Less competition here, however, means less waste and is hence socially beneficial.

Yang (1992, 1993) explores further consequences of this insight. For example, with a "minimum outlay for participation" in the rent competition, $\delta > 0$, say, it is possible that equilibrium bids stay at (δ, δ), resulting in aggregate expenditures of a mere 2δ. This is in stark contrast to the work by Hillman and Samet (1987), who introduced this device in a static model and showed a full rent dissipation result to hold. This indicates that the consideration of dynamic aspects in the modeling of rent-seeking processes forms an important ingredient of a solution to the so-called "rent-seeking paradox"; namely, that rents seem to get appropriated on the basis of expenditures which represent only a fraction of their value (Tullock, 1988).

The solution to the Tullock rent-seeking game when R > 2: Mixed-strategy equilibria and mean dissipation rates*

MICHAEL R. BAYE
The Pennsylvania State University, Dept. of Economics, University Park, P 16802

DAN KOVENOCK
Purdue University, Dept. of Economics, West Lafayette, IN 47907

CASPER G. DE VRIES
Erasmus Universiteit Rotterdam/Tinbergen Instituut, Oostmaaslaan 950, 3063 DM Rotterdam

Abstract. In Tullock's rent-seeking model, the probability a player wins the game depends on expenditures raised to the power R. We show that a symmetric mixed-strategy Nash equilibrium exists when R > 2, and that overdissipation of rents does not arise in any Nash equilibrium. We derive a tight lower bound on the level of rent dissipation that arises in a symmetric equilibrium when the strategy space is discrete, and show that full rent dissipation occurs when the strategy space is continuous. Our results are shown to be consistent with recent experimental evidence on the dissipation of rents.

1. Introduction

In Tullock (1980) the following interesting rent-seeking game is described. Consider two players who bid for a political favor commonly known to be worth Q dollars (Q > 0 and finite). Their bids influence the probability of

* An earlier version of this paper circulated under the title, "No, Virginia, There is No Overdissipation of Rents." We are grateful to Dave Furth and Frans van Winden for stimulating conversations, and for comments provided by workshop participants from the CORE-ULB-KUL IUAP project, Purdue University, Pennsylvania State University, Rijksuniversiteit Limburg, and Washington State University. We also thank Max van de Sande Bakhuyzen and Ben Heijdra for useful discussions, and Geert Gielens for computational assistance. An earlier version of the paper was presented at the ESEM 1992 in Brussels and the Mid-West Mathematical Economics Conference in Pittsburgh. All three authors would like to thank CentER for its hospitality during the formative stages of the paper. The second author has also benefited from the financial support of the Katholieke Universiteit Leuven and the Jay N. Ross Young Faculty Scholar Award at Purdue University. The third author benefitted from visiting IGIER where part of the paper was written. The third author also benefitted from grant IUAP 26 of the Belgian Government.

receiving the favor. Let x and y denote the bids of agents 1 and 2 respectively, and let $\pi(x,y)$ denote the probability the first agent is awarded the political favor. The payoff to agent 1 from bidding x when the other agent bids y is

$$U_1(x|y) = \pi(x,y)Q - x, \tag{1}$$

while that of player two is symmetrically defined:

$$U_2(y|x) = [1 - \pi(x,y)]Q - y$$

Because the politician awarding the prize may have other considerations, or because he can only imperfectly discriminate between the bids (if bids are not made in the money metric), the high bidder is not guaranteed the prize. This is a common assumption in (1) the principal-agent literature (Lazear and Rosen, 1981; Nalebuff and Stiglitz, 1983; Bull, Schotter and Weigelt, 1987), (2) the political campaign expenditure literature (Snyder, 1990); and (3) the literature on rationing by waiting in line (Holt and Sherman, 1982). Presumably, given y, the probability of winning is an increasing function of x. Tullock suggested the specification

$$\pi(x,y) = \begin{cases} \dfrac{1}{2} & \text{if } x = y = 0 \\[2ex] \dfrac{x^R}{x^R + y^R} & \text{otherwise } (x \geq 0,\ y \geq 0), \end{cases} \tag{2}$$

where $R > 0$. This specification has become standard in the rent-seeking literature and other fields, see, e.g., Snyder (1990).[1] The case where $R = 1$ is studied most (Ellingsen, 1991; Nitzan, 1991a; Paul and Wilhite, 1991), but it is of interest to consider other values of R, as in Applebaum and Katz (1986) and Millner and Pratt (1989). Loosely speaking, the case $0 < R < 1$ represents decreasing returns, while $R > 1$ represents increasing returns to aggressive bidding. While the two agent pure strategy symmetric Nash equilibrium is straightforward to calculate from the first-order conditions when $0 < R \leq 2$, this is not the case when $R > 2$. Consequently Tullock (1980) devoted a large part of his discussion to these latter cases.

To date, there are only conjectures concerning the existence of a Nash equilibrium for $R > 2$ but finite. Rowley (1991), in his review of Tullock's work, lists this as one of the three important theoretical problems for a research program in the area of rent-seeking. The problem is not so much that the first-order condition for a maximum cannot be calculated; the problem is that the symmetric ($x = y$) solution to the two players' first-order conditions does not

Table 1. Millner and Pratt (1989) hypotheses and experimental results

Exponent	H_o	Experiment R = 1	H_o	Experiment R = 3
Mean individual	2	2.24	6	3.34
Expenditures		(2.42)		(−24.28)
Mean dissipation	50%	56%	150%	84%
Rates		(2.37)		(−13.37)
Number of observations		146		100

necessarily yield a global maximum (if R > 2 the symmetric solution to the first-order conditions implies a negative expected payoff, which is dominated by a zero bid). In such a case the sum of the solutions to the first-order conditions exceeds the value of the prize Q; there is the *false appearance of an over dissipation of rents*. Tullock (1980, 1984, 1985, 1987, 1989) devoted considerable attention to the case of over dissipation because of the induced excess social waste; see Dougan (1991) for a critical comment, and Laband and Sophocleus (1992) for estimates of the resource expenditures. In Tullock (1984) it was acknowledged that over dissipation may be due to a failure of the second-order conditions.[2] In the vernacular of the game theory, over dissipation is not part of a Nash equilibrium. This notwithstanding, the possibility of over dissipation is a recurrent theme in the rent-seeking literature.

In particular, Millner and Pratt (1989) examined the rent-seeking model experimentally for the cases where R = 1 and R = 3. Due to the use of laboratory dollars, the strategy space used in their experiment is discrete. For a prize worth 8 U.S. dollars they formulate two hypotheses concerning the mean of the individual expenditures and the mean dissipation rates. These hypotheses are stated in Table 1, together with their experimental results.[3] Both hypotheses are rejected for either value of R, but at markedly different p-values. The p-value for the R = 1 case is at least .015, while the p-value for R = 3 is at the most 10^{-40}. Thus, H_0 is only rejected marginally for the case R = 1, while H_0 is strongly rejected for the case R = 3. Shogren and Baik (1991) point out, however, that the null hypothesis for the case R = 3 is not the correct one. The problem, however, is that the equilibrium to the game is not known when R > 2. Our paper resolves this issue.

More specifically, for R = 1, the symmetric Nash equilibrium is known, and the associated expenditure and dissipation rates are readily verified to correspond with the hypothesized values in Table 1. This is further corroborated by a recent experiment by Millner and Pratt (1991) which shows that risk aversion can explain the discrepancies between the hypothesized and realized values in Table 1 for the case when R = 1. A major benefit of the results presented below is that we will be able to explain the discrepancy between the hypothesized values and experimental results for the case when R = 3. The punchline is that the formula based on the first-order equations (which yields a rent dissipation of 150%) is incorrect. In fact, there is not a symmetric pure-strategy equilibrium when R = 3. We characterize the "correct" Nash equilibrium, and show that the results of the Millner-Pratt experiments are in line with the theoretically correct Nash equilibrium mixed strategies. To this end we mainly focus on the two agent case in discrete strategy space. In the last section we consider a continuous strategy space by taking limits of the finite game.

Before we embark on this, we briefly review the approaches others have used to deal with the R > 2 case. The approach in the existing literature is to *modify the original game* to remove the apparent over dissipation of rents. In his original contribution Tullock (1980) suggested three modifications. The first is to let R be infinite, which turns the game into an all-pay auction. Within the rent-seeking literature this version has been studied by Hillman and Samet (1987). The complete characterization of all equilibrium strategies has been obtained by Baye, Kovenock, and de Vries (1990), and the equilibrium level of rent dissipation is derived in Baye, Kovenock and de Vries (1993). The second type of modification is to change the one shot game into a dynamic game. Tullock (1980) discusses the case of alternating bids, and this has been formalized recently by Leininger (1990) and Leininger and Yang (1990). In Corcoran (1984), Corcoran and Karels (1985), and Higgins, Shughart, and Tollison (1987) the game is changed into a two-stage game. In the first stage the number of participants is selected such that, when the rent-seeking game is played in stage two, the number of participants is consistent with (almost) complete rent dissipation. Similarly, Michaels (1988) devises a setting within which the politician has the incentive to adjust the exponent such that the first- and second-order conditions are met. The third modification deals with asymmetries between the players. This was briefly dealt with in Tullock (1980) and has been further investigated by Allard (1988). Finally Nitzan (1991b) introduces coalition behavior on the part of the contestants. *None of these contributions, though, offers a solution to the original simultaneous move rent-seeking game when R > 2.* The next section provides this solution and relates it to the experimental and theoretical literatures.

2. Solving the rent-seeking game

Consider the two-agent rent-seeking game with conditional payoffs and winning probabilities as given in equations (1) and (2). The exponent satisfies R > 0. Suppose a pure strategy equilibrium exists. Given y > 0, the first- and second-order conditions for an unconstrained (local) maximum of $U_1(x|y)$ are readily calculated as

$$Q\frac{Ry^R x^{R-1}}{(x^R + y^R)^2} - 1 = 0, \tag{3}$$

and

$$Q\frac{Ry^R x^{R-2}}{(x^R + y^R)^3} [(R-1)(x^R + y^R) - 2Rx^R] < 0. \tag{4}$$

Assuming a symmetric solution, condition (3) yields $x = y = QR/4$, for which condition (4) is readily seen to hold locally for any $R > 0$. Substituting back into equation (1) yields

$$U_i(x = y = \frac{QR}{4}) = \frac{Q}{2}(1 - \frac{R}{2}); \; i = 1, 2. \tag{5}$$

Note that in this case $U_i(.|.)$ is non-negative as long as $R \leq 2$. Moreover, for any $x, y > 0$ the factor $(R-1)(x^R + y^R) - 2R\,x^R$ in the second-order condition (4) is unambiguously negative if $R \leq 1$, while it is positive over some interval to right of $x = 0$ if $R > 1$ and becomes negative thereafter. In particular, (4) is satisfied when $x = y$. Thus for $R \leq 2$, the symmetric solution $x = y = QR/4$ constitutes a Nash Equilibrium. For $R > 2$, $U(QR/4|QR/4)$ in (5) becomes negative and hence the first-order conditions do not yield a symmetric Nash equilibrium point (because one can choose $x = 0$ given that $y = QR/4$; and earn a higher payoff. But if $x = 0$ is chosen, player two has an incentive to lower y to small $\varepsilon > 0$). Generally, the first- and second-order conditions (3) and (4) fail to characterize the global maximum when $R > 2$.[4]

In order to find a solution for the case $R > 2$, we focus on the game with a discrete strategy space. This yields a version of the game similar to that used in the laboratory experiments by Millner and Pratt (1989), 1991).[5] Due to the use of laboratory dollars, the bids are necessarily discrete, and thus the game is a so-called finite game.[6] Nash's (1951) theorem guarantees that every finite game has a mixed-strategy equilibrium.[7] It follows immediately that the Tullock rent-seeking game in discrete strategy space has a Nash equilibrium, possibly in non-degenerate mixed strategies, for any $R > 2$. While it is in general difficult to characterize the equilibria, we may be more specific in this case. Note that for any strategy pair (x,y), the payoff to the second agent is the same as the payoff to the first agent if the strategies played by the two agents are interchanged; the game is symmetric. Recalling that an equilibrium is defined to be a symmetric equilibrium if all players choose the same strategy, we may apply Dasgupta and Maskin's (1986) Lemma 6; a finite symmetric game has a symmetric mixed-strategy equilibrium.

In summary, the Tullock rent-seeking game with a discrete strategy space certainly has a symmetric Nash equilibrium, even when $R > 2$. These results immediately raise the following questions: (i) Can we characterize the equilibria for $R > 2$, even though previous authors have been unable to do so? In particular, is it possible to provide an explicit solution for the symmetric equilibria that arise for different values of R? (ii) Can the equilibria of the finite game be used to shed light on infinite game (continuous strategy space) equilibria? A derivative question is: (iii) How do the answers to these questions relate to the experimental work reported by Millner and Pratt for the case $R = 3$?

We answer question (i) by employing a device which was first used by Shilony (1985). The payoffs to the game will be written in matrix format. We then show this yields a matrix equation which can be manipulated to yield the symmetric mixed strategy solution. Some numerical examples and a special case of this procedure are provided. To answer the derivative question (iii) we manipulate the matrix equation to obtain tight bounds on the equilibrium dissipation rate. Question (ii) is answered by letting the mesh of the strategy space become small relative to the value of the prize.

Recall equation (1) which gives the conditional payoffs for agent 1. To obtain the unconditional or expected payoffs from playing x, $EU_1(x)$, the conditional payoffs are premultiplied by the (mixed-strategy) probability p_y that a particular y value is being played by player one's opponent, and subsequently these are summed over y. Thus

$$EU_1(x) = \sum_{y=0}^{Q} p_y \, \pi(x,y) \, Q - x. \tag{6}$$

Denote the expected payoffs to agents 1 and 2 in an arbitrary Nash equilibrium by v_1 and v_2 respectively. In the case of a symmetric Nash equilibrium note that the players' expected payoffs are identical, $v_1 = v_2 = v$ (however, v need not be unique). The manipulations below make repeated use of the following general result.

Theorem 1. In any equilibrium: (i) $EU_1(x) \leq v_1$, (ii) $EU_1(x) = v_1$ when $p_x > 0$, while (iii) $p_x = 0$ if $EU_1(x) < v_1$. Similar results hold for player 2.

A proof of this theorem can be found in Vorob'ev (1977, sec. 3.2.2., 3.4.2. and 3.4.3.). For a symmetric equilibrium – which we know exists by Lemma 6 in Dasgupta and Maskin (1986) – we can use equations (6) and (2) to restate the condition $EU_1(x) \leq v$ as

$$\sum_{y=0}^{Q} p_y \frac{x^R}{x^R + y^R} \leq \frac{v+x}{Q}. \tag{7}$$

Conditions (ii) and (iii) in Theorem 1 imply a complementary slackness-type condition for a symmetric equilibrium of the form

$$\forall\ x: p_x \left[\sum_{y=0}^{Q} p_y \frac{x^R}{x^R + y^R} - \frac{v + x}{Q} \right] = 0. \tag{7'}$$

Now note that $EU_1(x = Q) \leq 0$, and in fact $EU_1(x = Q) < 0$ if $p_{y=0} < 1$ (and R is finite). Thus in a symmetric equilibrium no mass will be placed at Q, i.e. $p_{x=q} = p_{y=q} = 0$. Suppose (without loss of generality but for ease of notation) that $Q \varepsilon N$, and that x and y can only take on the integer values, 0, 1, . . ., Q. Note that there are exactly Q conditions (7) for $x = 0, 1, \ldots, Q-1$. These can be conveniently expressed in matrix format:

$$\begin{bmatrix} \frac{1}{2} & 0 & 0 & \cdots & 0 \\ 1 & \frac{1}{2} & \frac{1}{1+2^R} & & \frac{1}{1+(Q-1)^R} \\ 1 & \frac{2^R}{2^R+1} & \frac{1}{2} & \cdots & \frac{2^R}{2^R+(Q-1)^R} \\ \vdots & & \vdots & & \vdots \\ 1 & \frac{(Q-1)^R}{(Q-1)^R+1} & \frac{(Q-1)^R}{(Q-1)^R+2^R} & \cdots & \frac{1}{2} \end{bmatrix} \begin{bmatrix} p_0 \\ p_1 \\ p_2 \\ \vdots \\ p_{Q-1} \end{bmatrix} \leq \begin{bmatrix} \frac{v}{Q} \\ \frac{v+1}{Q} \\ \frac{v+2}{Q} \\ \vdots \\ \frac{v+Q-1}{Q} \end{bmatrix} \tag{8}$$

In addition to this Q x Q matrix condition, the following constraints must be imposed:

$$\sum_{y=0}^{Q-1} p_y = 1;\ p_y \geq 0,\ y = 0, 1, \ldots, Q. \tag{9}$$

Condition (8), together with the constraints (9) and the complementary slackness condition (7′) provide a complete, but implicit characterization of the symmetric equilibrium, which we know exists by Dasgupta and Maskin's Lemma 6. These conditions form a linear programming problem which, at least in principle, can be solved for $(p_0, \ldots, p_{Q-1}, v)$. We have thus proved

Theorem 2. Suppose the strategy space is discrete. Then for any $R > 2$, the Tullock rent-seeking game has a symmetric mixed-strategy Nash equilibrium, defined implicitly by the solution to conditions (7′), (8) and (9).

In order to illustrate the practical utility of Theorem 2, we will investigate two special cases: $R = \infty$ and $R = 3$. The latter case is that examined in Millner and Pratt's experiments, while the former is the discrete strategy space version of the all pay auction examined in Baye, Kovenock, and de Vries (1990; 1993).

We begin with the case when the exponent $R = \infty$ and assume $Q > 1$ for simplicity. In this case the matrix expression in (8) becomes

$$\begin{bmatrix} \frac{1}{2} & 0 & 0 & \cdots & 0 \\ 1 & \frac{1}{2} & 0 & & 0 \\ 1 & 1 & \frac{1}{2} & \cdots & 0 \\ \vdots & & \vdots & & \vdots \\ 1 & 1 & 1 & \cdots & \frac{1}{2} \end{bmatrix} \begin{bmatrix} p_0 \\ p_1 \\ p_2 \\ \vdots \\ p_{Q-1} \end{bmatrix} \leq \begin{bmatrix} \frac{v}{Q} \\ \frac{v+1}{Q} \\ \frac{v+2}{Q} \\ \vdots \\ \frac{v+Q-1}{Q} \end{bmatrix} \tag{10}$$

It is straightforward to find symmetric equilibria if it is assumed that all $p_i > 0$. In this case the matrix inequality (10) becomes an equality by Theorem 1. The lower triangular matrix equation can then be solved through recursive substitution. This yields $p_0 = p_2 = p_4 = \ldots = 2v/Q$ and $p_1 = p_3 = p_5 = \ldots = 2(1-v)/Q$. In addition to (8), conditions (9) and (7′) have to hold. For even values of Q this restricts $v \in [0, 1]$, while for odd values of Q, we necessarily have $v = 1/2$ (see Bouckaert, Degrijse, and de Vries, 1992, for a proof of this claim).

Note that we may make the grid in the formulation of the game (7) finer and finer and normalize the value of the prize to be one by dividing all dollar units by Q and letting Q tend to infinity. The equilibrium distributions in this discrete game with $R = \infty$ then converge uniformly to the continuous uniform distribution, and the expected payoff v/Q converges to zero; there is full rent dissipation. Also note that equations (1) and (2) can be expressed as

$$U_1(x|y) = \begin{cases} Q - x & \text{if } x > y \\ \frac{1}{2}Q - x & \text{if } x = y \\ -x & \text{if } x < y \end{cases} \tag{11}$$

which is precisely the definition of the all-pay auction (cf. Baye, Kovenock, and de Vries, 1993). It follows that the symmetric equilibria of the discrete all-pay auction converge to the unique (see Baye et al., 1990) equilibrium of the continuous strategy space *two player* all-pay auction.

Next, consider the case of finite exponents. When $0 < R \leq 2$, the game has a symmetric pure strategy equilibrium ($x = y = QR/4$) as discussed earlier. Because $R = 3$ is used in Millner and Pratt's experimental work on the game, and as pointed out by Shogren and Baik (1991) the "solution" examined by Millner and Pratt is not really a Nash equilibrium, we will focus on this case.[8] For $R > 2$ and finite, the solutions to the game cannot be given in the same compact form as the solution for $R = \infty$, although conditions (7′), (8) and (9) still provide a complete but implicit description of the game and its solution. For any specific values of R and Q, it can be solved explicitly through linear programming. We list some examples.

(i) R = 3, Q = 1. There is one pure strategy solution: both agents bid zero and receive $v = 1/2$. Inter alia, this result holds for any finite value of R.

(ii) R = 3, Q = 2. There exist multiple pure strategy solutions: (1) both bid zero and receive $v = 1$, (2) one agent bids zero and the other bids one with respective payoffs $v_1 = 0$ and $v_2 = 1$, and (3) both agents bid one and receive $v = 0$. Mixed strategies whereby agents randomize over (some) of the pure strategy solutions exist as well.

(iii) R = 3, Q = 3. This case is still solvable by hand. In particular, condition (8) becomes

$$\begin{bmatrix} \frac{1}{2} & 0 & 0 \\ 1 & \frac{1}{2} & \frac{1}{9} \\ 1 & \frac{8}{9} & \frac{1}{2} \end{bmatrix} \begin{bmatrix} p_0 \\ p_1 \\ p_2 \end{bmatrix} \leq \begin{bmatrix} \frac{v}{3} \\ \frac{v+1}{3} \\ \frac{v+2}{3} \end{bmatrix} \tag{12}$$

It is readily verified that $(p_0, p_1, p_2) = (\frac{1}{7}, \frac{3}{7}, \frac{3}{7})$ and $v = \frac{3}{14}$ satisfy condition (12) and the other conditions of Theorem 2, and hence constitute an equilibrium to the game.

(iv) R = 3, Q = 4. This case is already too cumbersome to solve by hand, so we relied on the analytical computer program "Derive" to solve this game. It can be checked that there are two symmetric solutions: (i) $(p_0, p_1, p_2, p_3) =$

$\left(\frac{5}{14}, 0, \frac{9}{14}, 0\right)$ with $v = \frac{5}{7}$, and (ii) $(p_0, p_1, p_2, p_3) = \left(\frac{3}{38}, 0, \frac{35}{38}, 0\right)$ with $v = \frac{3}{19}$.

For R = 3 and Q > 4, one generally finds that all probability mass is loaded on the first few probabilities p_y, with most mass loaded on the higher p_y's, and $0 < v < 1$. For Q > 15 the computational burden increases rapidly and exact solutions take an excessive amount of computer time. This is a bit unfortunate because the experiment conducted by Millner and Pratt (1989) used R = 3 and a grid of Q = 80 (at the end of the experiment the laboratory dollars were converted into U.S. dollars at an exchange rate of 10. But subject payments were also rounded to the nearest 25 cents, generating a grid of 32 with unequal grid sizes). Their hypotheses and tests, however, all concern mean individual expenditures and mean dissipation rates. The question therefore is whether we have something to offer concerning these quantities, without explicitly calculating the solutions.[9]

The expected individual expenditures and the expected dissipation rates can be calculated from equation (6). Note that premultiplication of $EU_1(x)$ by p_x and summation over x gives the expected equilibrium payoff to player 1 in a symmetric equilibrium:

$$EU_1 = \sum_{x=0}^{Q} p_x EU_1(x) = \sum_{x=0}^{Q} p_x \left(\sum_{y=0}^{Q} p_y \pi(x,y)Q - x \right) = \sum_{x=0}^{Q} p_x v = v, \tag{13}$$

because player one only loads mass on those x's which generate the same (highest) expected payoff equal to v (see Theorem 1 above).

In order to dispel the claim that over dissipation of rents is expected when R > 2, first note that if agent 1 chooses x = 0 with probability 1, then

$$EU_1 = \sum_{y=0}^{Q} p_y \pi(0,y)Q = p_0 \frac{1}{2} Q \geq 0. \tag{14}$$

Hence each player can guarantee a non-negative expected payoff. Secondly, the expected dissipation rate is easily calculated from $EU_1 + EU_2$. Note that in any equilibrium,

$$v_1 = EU_1 = \text{Prob}\{\text{agent 1 wins}\}\ Q - \bar{x},$$

where $\bar{x} = \Sigma p_x x$ is the average individual expenditure. Adding up yields

$$v_1 + v_2 = [\text{Prob}\{\text{agent 1 wins}\} + \text{Prob}\{\text{agent 2 wins}\}]\, Q - \bar{x} - \bar{y}.$$

But since the prize is always awarded, there is always a winning agent and hence by (14)

$$0 \leq v_1 + v_2 = Q - \bar{x} - \bar{y}, \tag{15}$$

so that $\bar{x} + \bar{y} \leq Q$. The expected rate of rent dissipation, D, is defined as $D = (\bar{x} + \bar{y})/Q$. Thus

$$D = 1 - \frac{v_1 + v_2}{Q} \leq 1. \tag{16}$$

We have thus proved:

Theorem 3. The two player finite rent-seeking game devised by Tullock never involves over dissipation in any (possibly mixed-strategy) Nash equilibrium for any $R > 0$. That is, $D \leq 1$ always.

The dissipation rate is also bounded from below. But in contrast with the upper bound, the lower bound depends on the value of the exponent R. This can be easily seen by investigating the two limiting cases $R = 0$ and $R = \infty$. In the former case there is no dissipation, while in the latter case dissipation can be complete. Therefore, we will investigate specific values of R. To explain the Millner-Pratt experimental results for the case $R = 3$, one requires precise information about the size of D, and hence the tighter the lower bound on D the better. It is not too difficult to show for $Q > 2$, $R > 2$, that in any equilibrium the dissipation rate is at least 50%. With more effort, for $Q > 3$ a sharper lower bound for the symmetric equilibria is obtained in Theorem 4.

Theorem 4. In any symmetric Nash equilibrium of the two player Tullock rent-seeking game with $\infty > R > 2$ and $\infty > Q > 2$, the dissipation rate is bounded from below by $1 - \frac{2}{Q}$.

Proof. The proof comes in two parts. In Part 1 we assume that $p_0 > 0$, and show that this implies $v \leq 1$. Hence $D \geq 1 - 2/Q$. In Part 2 we show that $p_0 = 0$ implies $v < 1$. Some of the computations from Part 2 are relegated to the Appendix.

Part 1. Suppose that $p_0 > 0$. Then (by Theorem 1) for $x = 0$ condition (7) necessarily becomes an equality: $p_0 = 2\,v/Q$, so that $v = Qp_0/2$. Because p_0 is bounded above by 1, v is bounded above by $Q/2$. This implies $D \geq 0$. To improve the upper bound on v, i.e., to lower it from Q/2 to 1, we continue the presumption $p_0 > 0$. From condition (7), for $x = 1$ we have

$$p_0 + \alpha \leq \frac{v+1}{Q}\ ; 0 \leq \alpha < \frac{1}{2}\,.$$

To see this note that all the probabilities $\pi(1,y)$ except the first in the second row of matrix condition (8) are less than or equal to 1/2. Combine the presumption $p_0 = 2v/Q$ with the above inequality to get

$$\alpha \leq \frac{1}{Q} - \frac{v}{Q}\,. \tag{17}$$

Hence $1 - v \geq \alpha Q \geq 0$. Therefore $1 \geq v$.

Part 2. We now show that $p_0 = 0$ implies $v < 1$. Let x be the first row for which $p_x > 0$, $x \neq 0$, i.e., $p_0 = \ldots = p_{x-1} = 0$. Then condition (7) holds as an equality for this row, i.e.,

$$\frac{1}{2}\ p_x + \frac{x^R}{x^R + (x+1)^R}\ p_{x+1} + \ldots + \frac{x^R}{x^R + (Q-1)^R}\ p_{Q-1} = \frac{v+x}{Q}\,, \tag{18}$$

We will show that $v \geq 1$ and $p_0 = 0$ are incompatible. For $x + 1$, condition (7) reads as follows:

$$\frac{(x+1)^R}{(x+1)^R + x^R}\ p_x + \frac{1}{2}\ p_{x+1} + \ldots + \frac{(x+1)^R}{(x+1)^R + (Q-1)^R}\ p_{Q-1} \leq \frac{v+1+x}{Q}\,. \tag{19}$$

Compute p_x from the equality (18), and substitute this into the weak inequality (19). This yields the following weak inequality:

$$\left[\frac{1}{2} - 2\,\frac{(x+1)^R}{(x+1)^R + x^R}\ \frac{x^R}{x^R + (x+1)^R}\right] p_{x+1} + \ldots +$$

$$\left[\frac{(x+1)^R}{(x+1)^R + (Q-1)^R} - 2\,\frac{(x+1)^R}{(x+1)^R + x^R}\ \frac{x^R}{x^R + (Q-1)^R}\right] p_{Q-1}$$

$$\leq \frac{1}{Q} \{v+1+x - 2(v+x) \frac{(x+1)^R}{(x+1)^R + x^R}\}. \tag{20}$$

In the Appendix we manipulate the two sides of inequality (20) to show that if $v \geq 1$ the left-hand side is non-negative while the right-hand side is strictly negative. (Note that the proof would be particularly simple if $R = \infty$, since then (20) reduces to $0 \leq p_{x+1} \leq 2(1-v-x)/Q$.) This yields a contradiction so that the supposition $p_0 = 0$ and $v \geq 1$ are incompatible. QED

3. Millner and Pratt revisited

How do the above theoretical results compare with the experimental evidence reported by Millner and Pratt (1989)? Note that for Q large Theorems 3 and 4 provide tight bounds. In particular, given the values of $R = 3$ and $Q = 80$ used in the Millner and Pratt experiments, the symmetric (mixed-strategy) equilibrium expected outlays are $\bar{x} = \bar{y} = 3.9$ (after conversion to U.S. dollars) and the corresponding interval for the expected rent dissipation is $D \in [97.5\%, 100\%]$ – it is not the 150 percent dissipation rate used as the null hypothesis by Millner and Pratt. Using the experimental evidence reported by Millner and Pratt, we find the following t-statistics for the null hypotheses: -5.11 and -2.73 respectively.[10] Compare these to the values reported by Millner and Pratt and reproduced in Table 1 above. (If the rounding to the nearest 25 cents in the actual payout is taken into account, the mean dissipation rate is reduced to approximately 93.75, which does not differ significantly from the experimental result at the 5% level). Note that these t-statistics are of the same order of magnitude as those for the case $R = 1$. Also recall the experimental work by Millner and Pratt (1991) which relates the relatively small discrepancy for the case $R = 1$ to the existence of risk aversion.[11] Our conjecture is that the remaining discrepancy for the case $R = 3$ can be explained in a similar way. Importantly, though, the above shows that when the correct symmetric (mixed-strategy) Nash equilibrium is used as the theoretical benchmark to form the null hypothesis, Millner and Pratt's empirical results for the case $R = 3$ and $Q = 80$ accord well with state-of-the art rent-seeking theory. Individuals seem to behave quite efficiently after all.

4. Summary and results for the continuous strategy space case

In this paper we have solved the original rent-seeking game devised by Tullock for the case where the rent-seeking exponent (R) exceeds two. A constructive method was used to find the explicit solution for the finite game (i.e., the

Tullock game in discrete strategy space). Our theoretical results, which establish that rents are under dissipated when $R > 2$, accord well with the existing experimental evidence. We also provide tight bounds on the rate of dissipation as the mesh of the strategy space decreases.

Up to this point we have not addressed the solution to the infinite rent-seeking game, i.e., when the strategy space is continous and $R > 2$. It turns out the payoff functions in equation (1) satisfy the conditions of Theorem 6 in Dasgupta and Maskin (1986), guaranteeing the existence of a symmetric mixed strategy equilibrium for the rent-seeking game with a continuous strategy space. The proof of their theorem relies on finite approximation of the game and then letting the grid size become finer and finer, as we did in our example with an infinite R. Thus the construction of the equilibrium to the finite game in the previous section is driven to the limit. Under sufficient regularity conditions this method indeed yields a solution to the infinite game.

The application of Dasgupta and Maskin's Theorem 6 requires four conditions, each of which is satisfied for the Tullock game with a continuous strategy space. In particular, this theorem requires: (i) The sum of the payoffs must be upper semi-continous. From equations (1) and (2) we easily see that $U_1(x|y) + U_2(x|y) = Q - x - y$, which is continuous and therefore upper semi-continuous as well. (ii) The subset of discontinuities in the payoffs must be of a dimension lower than 2, and one must be able to express the elements of this subset as functions which relate the strategy of one player to the strategy of the other. For the Tullock game with $R < \infty$, this condition is simple to check, as $x = y = 0$ constitutes the only point of discontinuity. The condition guarantees that the discontinuities are relatively unimportant (have measure zero). (iii) The payoff $U_1(x|y)$ must be bounded. This holds evidently as $-Q \leq U_1(x|y) \leq Q$ on $[0,Q]$. (iv) Finally, $U_1(x|y)$ must be weakly lower semi-continuous. The only point where there could arise a problem is at the point of discontinuity, but as $U_1(x|y = 0)$ is lower semi-continuous, it is certainly weakly lower semi-continuous. This last condition guarantees that, loosely speaking, a player does not want to put weight on the discontinuity point even if the other player does, because payoffs may jump down but do not jump up.

Thus we conclude that a symmetric mixed strategy equilibrium exists for the continuous strategy space rent-seeking game for all $R > 2$ as well. An explicit closed form solution remains for future investigation. For the special case $R = \infty$, a full characterization of all the equilibria is available even when there are more than two players; see Baye, Kovenock, and de Vries (1990, 1993). Other interesting questions include the explicit solution to asymmetric versions of the game, as well as further experimental work along the lines suggested above. These remain the focus of our future research.

Notes

1. While our focus is on the Tullock specification in (2), several of our results are valid for other functional forms of π. In particular, so long as $0 \leq \pi(x,y) \leq 1$ and $\pi(x,y) + \pi(y,x) = 1$, any Nash equilibrium satisfies the properties stated in Theorem 1 below, and our Theorem 3 on the impossibility of overdissipation carries through. Only the tight lower bound on the dissipation rate given in Theorem 4 is dependent on the specific functional form in (2). We thank a referee for encouraging us to point this out.
2. Briefly considering the n-player variant, $n \geq 2$, the second order conditions fail if $R > n/(n-2)$, cf. Tullock (1984) (where the reverse condition is reported erroneously). Note that for the case $n = 2$ the second order conditions are always satisfied. But it is easily checked that for $R > 2$ the symmetric solution to the first-order conditions yields $U_1(.|.) < 0$, and hence is not a global maximum. Thus the two agent case is the most interesting case to consider, because with $n > 2$ the posited solutions obviously do not make sense if $R > n/(n-2)$.
3. The null hypotheses should be interpreted with caution because the experimental setup of Millner and Pratt (1989) is not entirely congruent with the simultaneous move requirement (neither does it fit the alternating move version studied in Leininger, 1990; Leininger and Yang (1990).
4. Baye, Tian, and Zhou (1993) show that one cannot generally blame the non-existence of a pure-strategy equilibrium on the failure of payoff functions to be quasi-concave or upper semi-continuous.
5. Although Millner and Pratt claim to be testing the Tullock model, the experiment actually allows the rent-seekers to expend resources continuously over a small time interval. Hence, the experiment does not formally test the original one-shot simultaneous-move Tullock game. This problem is corrected in the experiments of Shogren and Baik (1991), who do not reject the theoretical prediction when $R = 1$.
6. The continuous strategy space (infinite game) is dealt with below.
7. The mixed strategies may be degenerate, i.e., in the case of a pure strategy equilibrium.
8. Shogren and Baik (1991) state that the behavioral inconsistency reported in Millner and Pratt "... is due to the nonexistence of a Nash equilibrium. In this case there is no predictable behavioral benchmark to measure the experimental evidence against." Our Theorem 2, however, provides such a benchmark. Shogren and Baik are referring to the non-existence of a symmetric pure strategy Nash equilibrium.
9. In future work it may be of interest to repeat the experiment for $R = 3$ and Q small such that all the properties of the symmetric equilibrium can be evaluated, i.e., the values of the p_y's.
10. Calculations are based on $(3.34 - 3.9)/s_1 = -5.11$ and $(84 - 97.5)/s_2 = -2.73$, where s_1 and s_2 were calculated from Millner and Pratt (1989) using $(3.34 - 6)/s_1 = -24.28$ and $(84 - 150)/s_2 = -13.37$.
11. See also Shogren and Baik, who run a related experiment for $R = 1$ and find that the Nash equilibrium dissipation hypothesis cannot be rejected at the 90 percent level.

Appendix

In this Appendix we show that, for $v \geq 1$, the left-hand side of inequality (20) is non-negative, while the right-hand side is strictly negative.

Manipulate the right-hand side as follows:

$$v+1 + x - 2(v+x)\frac{(x+1)^R}{(x+1)^R + x^R} \lesseqgtr 0$$

$$\Leftrightarrow$$

$$(v+1+x)x^R \lesseqgtr (v-1+x)(x+1)^R$$

$$\Leftrightarrow$$

$$1 + \frac{2}{v+x-1} \lesseqgtr (1 + \frac{1}{x})^R.$$

Note that the left-hand side of this last inequality is decreasing in v. Hence, to show that the right-hand side of (20) is negative, it is sufficient to show that such is the case for $v = 1$. Assuming that $v = 1$, we can further manipulate the last inequality:

$$1 + \frac{1}{1 + x} \lesseqgtr (1 + \frac{1}{x})^{R-1}$$

$$\Leftrightarrow$$

$$1 + \frac{1}{1 + x} \lesseqgtr (1 + \frac{1}{x})(1 + \frac{1}{x})^{R-2}.$$

Evidently, for any $x > 0$

$$1 + \frac{1}{1 + x} < 1 + \frac{1}{x}.$$

Thus for any $R \geq 2$ and $x \geq 1$ the right-hand side of (20) is strictly negative for any $v \geq 1$.

To obtain the left-hand side result we need to show that for any t such that

$$Q - 1 \geq t \geq x + 1,$$

$$\frac{(x+1)^R}{(x+1)^R + t^R} \geq 2 \frac{(x+1)^R}{(x+1)^R + x^R} \frac{x^R}{x^R + t^R} .$$

Manipulation yields

$$[(x+1)^R + x^R][x^R + t^R] \lesseqgtr 2x^R[(x+1)^R + t^R]$$

$$\Leftrightarrow$$

$$x^R(x+1)^R + t^R(x+1)^R + x^{2R} + x^Rt^R \lesseqgtr 2x^R (x+1)^R + 2x^Rt^R$$

$$\Leftrightarrow$$

$$[(x+1)^R - x^R][t^R - x^R] \lesseqgtr 0.$$

Because $t \geq x+1 > x$, the left-hand side of this last inequality is unequivocally positive, and hence the left-hand side of (20) is non-negative.

The reluctant gamesperson — A comment on Baye, Kovenock and De Vries*

GORDON TULLOCK
University of Arizona, Department of Economics, Tucson, AZ 85721, U.S.A.

My role with respect to "efficient rent-seeking"[1] is an unfortunate one. Rather by accident, I discovered a new paradox in economics, something we emphatically don't need. Various people have attempted to abolish the paradox or demonstrate that it is not very severe. My unhappy role has been pushing the discussion "Back to the Bog".[2] Although I don't like paradoxes, I invented one and now I am defending it.

Further, this paradox is a fairly important one. I invented it in connection to rent-seeking, but any kind of competitive activity where differential capital investments give advantage raises the same problem. Thus it is some evidence that the competitive market doesn't work very well. Needless to say, I find this unpleasant. As a result of this long debate, I am beginning to wonder if it may not be true that the competitive market does have this previously unknown defect which will make it unlikely that it will reach the efficient equilibria even if it does approximate them.

There is another problem. I was originally an enthusiast for game theory. In fact, long ago when it was a simpler subject, I taught a course on it. Now I have begun wondering whether the mixed strategy is actually a legitimate solution.[3] Perhaps Pascal was right about games of strategy and Von Neuman and Morgenstern wrong. I regret to say that these doubts are going to be part of this comment.

Baye, Kovenock and De Vries propose mixed strategy solutions for the efficient rent-seeking paradox for those cases where the exponent is two or greater. As a matter of fact, Perez-Castrillo and Veredier, have already provided a solution for those cases where it is above two.[4] It is as it turns out, a pure strategy solution, although it is not obvious that Perez-Castrillo and Verdier realized this when they first submitted their article. I called it to their attention in the course of my comment.[5] I accepted their solution, but if there was going to be only one person playing there would of course have to be some way of deciding which one.

---

* He kindly explained his position to me both in letters and in conversation. The solution to the Tullock rent-seeking game when R > 2: Mixed strategy equiilibria and mean dissipation rates. Public Choice 81(3-4): 363-380.

The only obvious method is a preclusive bid by someone and this, although it works, leads to an unpleasant equilibrium. First, people have to move quickly without giving the matter careful thought. One would therefore assume that a lot of mistakes, like the one I mentioned in that note that cost Sony $45 million, could be expected.

In the area with an R of less than two both Perez-Castrillo and Verdier and Baye, Kovenock and De Vries have nothing very precise in the way of a solution. Above, the difference between the two solutions is that Perez-Castrillo and Verdier used a pure strategy and Baye, Kovenock and De Vries mixed strategies.

The first thing to be said here is that it is probably quite unusual in the real world where this kind of problem is approximated for R to be above two, so the solution to this particular part of the problem is not exactly of great practical importance. Still, it's a step. But in most cases in which you have competitive investments, whether it's rent-seeking or building new factories there is a sunk cost problem. Once started, you cannot get the money back, and you may be led step by step into very large investments. This is a problem which is not dealt with by either of the papers.

With regard to the first example on page 371, they solve it with the prize at $1.00. If they had been Germans, and calculated it in marks so instead of being $1.00, it was DM 1.40, the solution would have been different.

This is a question which I had never thought of before. I used the exponential form when I wrote "Efficient Rent-Seeking", because I wanted a form which showed economies of scale, and that was the standard elementary textbook method of doing it. With mixed strategies it raises very severe problems. Suppose I am playing a German who makes all of his calculations in marks, and I make them all in dollars. We could get radically differently mixed strategies. I have to apologize for starting the discussion without even thinking about this problem. As a matter of fact I think it is much more general. I believe that most functions which are not purely linear would raise this particular problem in cross currency calculation.

Turning to mixed strategies, to repeat, I originally thought these were wonderful, and I now think they are not.[6] Further, my reason is fairly simple and straight forward. Firstly, assume that the other players in any of these situations are playing the approximately calculated mixed strategies. Under these circumstances, the payoff to me for any of the pure strategies which is part of the mixed strategy, is the same. Thus there is no reason why I should go through all the trouble of rolling dice, etc., and if I have any reason at all for playing some other number, let us say I am risk averse, it would give the same results as the mixed strategy as long as my opponents continue playing the properly calculated mixed strategy.

For example, suppose we are playing the mix of strategies at the left of first line of page 372. By choosing 0 I avoid all risk and still have a good chance of making something. Of course, if my opponent suspects I am doing that, he has a good reply. What we have here is the paradox of the liar. If, it is assumed that the properly calculated mixed strategy is the right thing to do, then I can safely believe that other people will do it, and there is no reason why I should. On the other hand, if I have doubts about their playing the mixed strategy, then once again there is no reason why I should play the properly calculated mixed strategy. Over a short series of plays it is not even risk averse since the dice may tell me to take the most risky individual strategy. Guessing my opponents strategies will do better if I have even the most trivial ability to do so. In fact, the mixed strategy becomes simply one of the strategies in Pascal's infinite regress.

The particular set of solutions on the first line of page 372 raises another serious problem. There are two symmetric solutions. Which should I play? As Q gets bigger, there may be even more. If the two parties must agree not only which currency to use, but also which solution to play, we will have a great deal of cooperation in a non-cooperative game.

There is another problem which our authors have apparently not thought about at all. Their game strategies characteristically generate a positive value. This means that more people will want to play the game and some method must be devised to decide who shall do so. In other words, there is a preliminary game before we began playing the game whose strategies they have calculated.

This problem was discussed in my comment on Perez-Castrillo and Verdier,[7] so I need not go on here, but I should point out the result of the two games could easily result in either complete dissipation or even overdissipation, depending on the mechanism that is adopted to choose the people who will be actually permitted to play a profitable game. On the average, it should as least exactly dissipate because if it does not dissipate there remain motives for other people to enter the game.

This brings us to Ellsberg's "Reluctant Duelist"[8] in which he pointed out the only obvious reasons for playing the proper strategy from game theory standpoint, in the particular matrix which he presented, were pure risk aversion, or a feeling that that your opponent is smarter than you, and if you play a game of strategy you will get beaten. This is not only true of his game but of all games with a value of zero.

Hunt is playing poker always played games of strategy, and it turned out he was a good strategist, it was the foundation of his immense wealth. Sam Houston, retreating slowly across Texas, in front of Santa Ana's armies, gradually trained Santa Ana to take a siesta every noon. At San Jacinto he delivered a devastating surprise attack on the front of the Santa Ana armies across an open field in broad daylight. Neither Hunt nor Houston would have been willing to adopt the mixed strategy.

The pages referred to here as 371 and 372 appear in this volume as 299 and 300 - Ed.

There is actually little motive for even computing the properly calculated mixed strategy. There may be some potential strategies which should be totally avoided and their discovery may require calculation, but this is clearly a minor consideration. Unless you are playing a long series of games, it is not even risk averse. You may end up playing the particular strategy with the maximum risk of the whole set in any given game.

Harsanyi says in practice people normally play pure strategies rather than mixed strategies. Ex-ante neither one of the two players can ever know what pure strategy the other is playing, and must make some kind of probability judgement. Assuming that the other player is actually playing a mixed strategy over some finite set of possible pure strategies, is one way of doing that. It may be better than anything else.

Neverless, we are back to Pascal. The mixed strategy, even if properly calculated, is only one play in a strategic game. It is only if both parties are playing mixed strategies that either one can predict the outcome over a large number of games. If you want to do better than that predicted outcome you will presumably not play the mixed strategy. And remember, if the predicted outcome is better than zero, there must be a preliminary game to decide who will be permitted to play. For people who are afraid of doing worse, it is difficult to detect deviations from the appropriate mixed strategy by the other party. Thus they face a strategic calculation too. To repeat, Pascal was right.

Notes

1. Tullock, G. (1980) Efficient rent-seeking. In J.M. Buchanan, R.D. Tollison and G. Tullock (Eds.), *Toward a theory of the rent-seeking society*, 97-112. College Station:Texas A&M University Press.
2. Tullock, G. (1980) Efficient rent-seeking. In J.M. Buchanan, R.D. Tollison and G. Tullock (Eds.), *Toward a theory of the rent-seeking society*, 97-112. College Station:Texas A&M University Press.
3. See "Games and preference", *Rationality and Society*, Vol. 4, No. 1, 1992, pp. 24-32.
4. A general analysis of rent-seeking games, *Public Choice* 73(3): 335-350, 1992.
5. Tullock, G. (1993) "Still somewhat muddy: A comment". *Public Choice* Vol. 76 No. 4, pp. 365-370, 1993.
6. Op. cit. EN 4.
7. Op. cit.
8. Ellsberg, Daniel, "Theory of the Reluctant Duelist" *American Economc Review*, Vol 46, pp. 909-923, 1956.

The specification of the probability functions in Tullock's rent-seeking contest

Peter Kooreman, Lambert Schoonbeek*

Department of Econometrics, Faculty of Economics, University of Groningen, P.O. Box 800, 9700 AV Groningen, The Netherlands

Abstract

In his model of a rent-seeking contest, [Tullock, G., 1980. Efficient rent seeking. In: Buchanan, J.M., Tollison, R.D., Tullock, G. (Eds.), Toward a theory of the rent-seeking society. Texas A and M University Press, College Station, pp. 97–112] uses a simple concrete specification for the probability functions which determine the probability that a player wins the contest, given the bids made by the players. We discuss in general terms a set of conditions that can be imposed on probability functions in this game. Next, we show that the specification chosen by Tullock is the unique one that satisfies these conditions.

Keywords: Rent-seeking contest; Probability to win

JEL classification: D72; C72

1. Introduction

Tullock (1980) has introduced a well-known model of a rent-seeking contest in which two players compete for a rent of value V, say. The probability that player 1 wins the contest is given by the function $p(x_1, x_2)$, where x_i is the bid (effort) put forward by player i ($i = 1, 2$). The probability that player 2 wins equals $1 - p(x_1, x_2)$. Tullock, and a large literature following him, used a concrete (logit type) specification of the function $p(x_1, x_2)$. In this paper we will demonstrate that Tullock's concrete specification must be used if one requires that a probability function of this game has to satisfy a set of general, reasonable, conditions that will be presented below. Doing so, we provide a motivation for the use of Tullock's concrete specification. See also Skaperdas (1996).

2. The analysis

Let us define the set $S = \{(x_1, x_2) | x_1 > 0, x_2 > 0\}$ and let $p(x_1, x_2)$ be an arbitrary function, defined

*Corresponding author. Tel.: 0031 50 363 3798; fax: 0031 50 363 3720; e-mail: L.Schoonbeek@eco.rug.nl

on S, representing the probability that player 1 wins the contest. Clearly, we must have $0 \leq p(x_1, x_2) \leq 1$ for all $(x_1, x_2) \in S$. The expected payoff of player 1 equals $\pi_1(x_1, x_2) \equiv p(x_1, x_2)V - x_1$. We will consider the following conditions that can be imposed on $p(x_1, x_2)$:

(i) $p(x_1, x_2)$ is a continuously differentiable function with $[\partial p(x_1, x_2)/\partial x_1] > 0$ and $[\partial^2 p(x_1, x_2)/\partial x_1^2] < 0$ for all $(x_1, x_2) \in S$;
(ii) $p(\lambda x_1, \lambda x_2) = p(x_1, x_2)$ for all $(x_1, x_2) \in S$ and all $\lambda > 0$;
(iii) $p(x_1, ax_1) = \frac{1}{2}$ for all $x_1 > 0$ and some given $a > 0$;
(iv) $[\partial p(x_1, x_2)/\partial x_1]\ [x_1/p(x_1, x_2)] = r(1 - p(x_1, x_2))$ for all $(x_1, x_2) \in S$ and some given $r > 0$.

Let us discuss the meaning of these conditions. Condition (i) requires that $p(x_1, x_2)$ is a 'smooth' function of x_1 and x_2. It seems reasonable to require that the probability to win reacts in a 'smooth' way on the bids of both players. Further, it imposes the standard requirement that $p(x_1, x_2)$ is an increasing and strictly concave function in x_1. The strict concavity implies that the maximization problem of $\pi_1(x_1, x_2)$ with respect to x_1 (given x_2) is well defined, i.e. there exists a unique global maximum. Condition (ii) states that $p(x_1, x_2)$ is homogeneous of degree zero, i.e. if both players multiply their bids with the same factor λ, then the probability that player 1 wins the contest remains unaffected. In other words, only the relative size of the bids matters. We remark here that one might possibly argue, that the probability that player 1 wins, should be a function of the absolute size of the difference between the bids of the players. However, such an approach easily leads to problems, e.g. with the requirement that $p(x_1, x_2)$ is strictly concave in x_1 (take e.g. $p(x_1, x_2) = [1/1 + \exp(x_2 - x_1)]$).

In order to discuss condition (iii), first suppose that $a = 1$. We then see that if both players make the same bid, each one has the same probability to win the contest. In case $a > 1$, there is a bias in favor of player 1: i.e. if player 1 bids x_1, then player 2 must bid $ax_1 (> x_1)$ in order to have the same probability to win as player 1 has. Analogously, there is a bias in favor of player 2 in the case $a < 1$. Finally, condition (iv) states that the elasticity of the probability that player 1 will win the contest with respect to his own bid x_1, is proportional to $1 - p(x_1, x_2)$. This reflects the natural requirement that the elasticity must be equal to zero in the case $p(x_1, x_2) = 1$. Further, it incorporates the idea that the percentage change in $p(x_1, x_2)$ implied by, say, a one per cent change in x_1 is smaller, the closer is $p(x_1, x_2)$ to unity. We note that the magnitude of the parameter r determines the 'overall' sensitivity of $p(x_1, x_2)$ with respect to x_1.

Proceeding forward, let us suppose that our (arbitrary) probability function $p(x_1, x_2)$ satisfies the conditions (i) up to and including (iv). Using condition (i) we then can define the continuously differentiable function $\bar{p}(x)$ for all $x > 0$ according to $\bar{p}(x) \equiv (x, 1)$. Notice that $\bar{p}(x) = p([x_1/x_2], 1) = p(x_1, x_2)$ with $x = (x_1/x_2)$. Next, observe that

$$\frac{\partial p(x_1, x_2)}{\partial x_1} \frac{x_1}{p(x_1, x_2)} = \frac{\mathrm{d}\bar{p}(x)}{\mathrm{d}x} \frac{x}{\bar{p}(x)}, \tag{1}$$

with $x=(x_1/x_2)$. Combining this with condition (iv), we see that $\bar{p}(x)$ satisfies the differential equation

$$\frac{\mathrm{d}\bar{p}(x)}{\mathrm{d}x}\frac{x}{\bar{p}(x)}=r(1-\bar{p}(x)), \tag{2}$$

or, equivalently,

$$\frac{\mathrm{d}\bar{p}(x)}{\bar{p}(x)(1-\bar{p}(x))}=r\frac{\mathrm{d}x}{x}. \tag{3}$$

Integrating both sides of this equation we find that $p(x)$ must satisfy

$$\log\left(\frac{\bar{p}(x)}{1-\bar{p}(x)}\right)=r\log x+A, \tag{4}$$

where A is the integration constant. Substituting $x=(1/a)$ in the latter equation, and noting that condition (iii) implies that $\bar{p}(\frac{1}{a})=\frac{1}{2}$, we conclude that $A=-r\log(\frac{1}{a})$. Using this, we see that $\bar{p}(x)$ must equal

$$\bar{p}(x)=\frac{(ax)^r}{(ax)^r+1}. \tag{5}$$

In turn this implies that

$$p(x_1,x_2)=\frac{(ax_1)^r}{(ax_1)^r+x_2^r} \tag{6}$$

for all $(x_1, x_2)\in S$. The conclusion is that if we require that a probability function $p(x_1, x_2)$ satisfies the conditions (i) up to and including (iv), then $p(x_1, x_2)$ must be given by (6). We observe now that (6) is in fact the specification used by Tullock (1980). See also Leininger (1993), (p. 48) and Yang (1994). Finally, we remark that the requirement that $p(x_1, x_2)$ is strictly concave in x_1 holds if and only if $r\leq 1$, cf. Baye et al. (1994), (p. 367).

Tullock's rent-seeking contest with a minimum expenditure requirement

L. SCHOONBEEK & P. KOOREMAN
Faculty of Economics, University of Groningen, P.O. Box 800, 9700 AV Groningen, The Netherlands; e-mail l.schoonbeek@eco.rug.nl.

Abstract. We consider a rent-seeking contest of the kind introduced by Tullock (1980) in which two players compete for a monopoly rent. We extend the contest by requiring that if a player puts forward an effort, his expenditures must be larger than or equal to some minimum level. We show that, depending on the model parameters, the number of Nash equilibria of the extended model can be zero, one, two or four. Furthermore, it turns out that the extent of rent dissipation in a Nash equilibrium of the extended model can be larger than, equal to, or smaller than the extent of rent dissipation in the unique Nash equilibrium of the original model.

1. Introduction

Tullock (1980) has introduced a seminal game-theoretic model of a contest in which two players compete for a monopoly rent. In the basic game, the probability that a player wins the rent is given by the ratio of the expenditures of the player himself and the total expenditures of both players. Tullock focuses on the case in which both players attach the same valuation to the rent. Hillman and Riley (1989) have extended Tullock's basic model by allowing that the players might value the rent differently (see also Ellingsen, 1991; and Leininger, 1993). They show that the model thus obtained has a unique Nash equilibrium in which both players have positive expenditures. Furthermore, they demonstrate that the size of the total expenditures of both players in this Nash equilibrium is equal to one half times the harmonic mean of the two players' individual valuations of the monopoly rent. These total expenditures can be considered as a measure of the extent of rent dissipation in the contest.

In this paper we extend the model of Tullock by introducing a minimum expenditure requirement, i.e., we assume that if a player decides to put forward an effort, then his expenditures must be larger than or equal to some given minimum level. Doing so, we allow that the two players attach a different value to the monopoly rent. We demonstrate that, depending on the magnitudes of the players' valuations of the monopoly rent and the size of the minimum expenditure level, the extended model either has no Nash equilibrium at all, or has one, two or four Nash equilibria. This contrasts with the unique Nash equilibrium of the model without a minimum expenditure requirement. Moreover, we point out that the extent of rent dissipation in a Nash equilibrium of the extended model can be larger than, equal to, or smaller than the extent of rent dissipation in the unique Nash equilibrium of the original model.

The device of a minimum expenditure requirement can be relevant in practice. For instance, in the Netherlands political parties participating in an election contest for the parliament or the municipal council must pay to the government a (sizable) fixed and equal, legally determined, amount of money (entry fee). A minimum expenditure requirement has been discussed before in the rent-seeking literature by Hillman and Samet (1987). However, the contest analysed by these authors is not of the kind of Tullock (1980), but rather one in which the player with the highest expenditures wins the monopoly rent for sure. Yang (1993) employs a minimum expenditure requirement in a contest which is inspired by the model of Tullock. However, the model of Yang is a multi-period one in which the two players decide alternatingly in a sequential way about their expenditures. We investigate the impact of a minimum expenditure requirement within the original single-period model of Tullock (1980) and Hillman and Riley (1989), in which the players decide simultaneously.

The paper is further organized as follows. In Section 2 we describe the contest with a minimum expenditure requirement and derive the reaction curves of both players. In Section 3 we characterize the Nash equilibria for all feasible configurations of the model parameters. We conclude in Section 4.

2. The model and the reaction curves

Following Tullock (1980), we consider a contest in which two players compete for a monopoly rent. The probability that player i (i = 1,2) wins the contest is given by $p_i(x_1,x_2)$, where x_i denotes the expenditures of player i. Player i has two options regarding the size of his expenditures. First, he can choose $x_i = 0$. Second, he can choose some $x_i > 0$. In that case it is required that x_i is greater than or equal to some minimum level $x_0 > 0$. The size of x_0 is given to both players. The probability that player i wins the contest is given by

$$p_i(x_1,x_2) = \begin{cases} \frac{x_i}{x_1+x_2} & if\ \ x_i \geqq x_0 \ \ x_j \geqq x_0 \\ 1 & if\ \ x_i \geqq x_0,\ x_j = 0 \\ 0 & if\ \ x_i = 0,\ \ x_j \geqq x_0 \\ \frac{1}{2} & if\ \ x_i = 0,\ \ x_j = 0 \end{cases} \qquad (1)$$

with $j \neq i$. Notice that $p_1(x_1,x_2)$ and $p_2(x_1,x_2)$ are defined on the set $D = \{(x_1, x_2)|x_1 \geqq x_0\ x_1 = 0 \text{ or } x_2 \geq x_0 \text{ or } x_2 = 0\}$; cf. Baye, Kovenock, and de Vries (1994).[1]

If a player wins the contest, he obtains the monopoly rent. Otherwise, he obtains nothing. We assume that player i (i = 1,2) attaches a valuation of $v_i > 0$ to the monopoly rent, and suppose that $v_1 \leqq v_2$. The expected payoff of player i is given by

$$\pi_i(x_1, x_2) = v_i p_i(x_1, x_2) - x_i \tag{2}$$

with $(x_1,x_2) \in D$.

Now, consider the problem faced by player i. We assume that this player chooses x_i in order to maximize his own expected payoff given the expenditures, x_j ($j \neq i$), of his rival. The reaction curve $f_i(x_j)$ gives the optimal choice of player i for all feasible values of x_j. It turns out that we have to distinguish four different cases with respect to $f_i(x_j)$ (see the Appendix for the derivation). In the case $v_i < 2x_0$ we have

$$f_i(x_j) = \begin{cases} 0 \ if \ x_j = 0 \\ 0 \ if \ x_j \geqq x_0 \end{cases} . \tag{3}$$

In the case $v_i = 2x_0$ we have

$$f_i(x_j) = \begin{cases} 0 \ or \ x_0 & if \ x_j = 0 \\ 0 \ or \ x_0 & if \ x_j = x_0 \\ 0 & if \ x_j > x_0 \end{cases} \tag{4}$$

whereas in the case $2x_0 < v_i \leqq 4x_0$ we have

$$f_i(x_j) = \begin{cases} x_0 & if \ x_j = 0 \\ x_0 & if \ x_0 \leqq x_j < v_i - x_0 \\ 0 \ or \ x_0 & if \ x_j = v_i - x_0 \\ 0 & if \ x_j > v_i - x_0 \end{cases} \tag{5}$$

and, finally, in the case $4x_0 < v_i$ we have

$$f_i(x_j) = \begin{cases} x_0 & if \ x_j = 0 \\ -x_j + \sqrt{x_j v_i} & if \ x_0 \leqq x_j < x_j^* \\ x_0 & if \ x_j^* \leqq x_j < v_i - x_0 \\ 0 \ or \ x_0 & if \ x_j = v_i - x_0 \\ 0 & if \ x_j > v_i - x_0 \end{cases} \tag{6}$$

where

$$x_j^* = \frac{(v_i - 2x_0) + \sqrt{v_i(v_i - 4x_0)}}{2}. \tag{7}$$

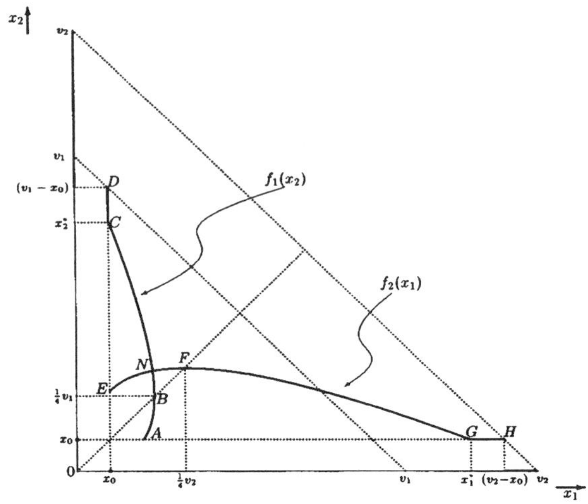

Figure 1.

Note that in case $4x_0 < v_i$, (i) x_j^* is a real number satisfying $x_0 < x_j^* < v_i - x_0$, and (ii) $f_i(x_j) > x_0$ if $x_0 \leqq x_j < x_j^*$.

Figure 1 illustrates the reaction curve of both players for a situation with $4x_0 < v_1 < v_2$ (in particular, we have used the values $v_1 = 10$, $v_2 = 14$ and $x_0 = 1$). The reaction curve of player 1 is given by the point (x_0,0), the line ABCD, and the vertical line segment along the x_2-axis with $x_2 \geqq v_1$-x_0. The reaction curve of player 2 is given by the point (0,x_0), the line EFGH, and the horizontal line segment along the x_1-axis with $x_1 \geqq v_2 - x_0$. The line through OBF is given by $x_1 = x_2$. We observe with respect to the reaction curve of player 1 that the curved part ABC corresponds to the part where $f_1(x_2) = -x_2 + \sqrt{x_2 v_1}$. Point B, with coordinates $(\frac{1}{4}v_1, \frac{1}{4}v_1)$, is the point with the maximum x_1-coordinate. Similarly, the part EFG pertains to the part where $f_2(x_1) = -x_1 + \sqrt{x_1 v_2}$. Point F, with coordinates $(\frac{1}{4}v_2, \frac{1}{4}v_2)$, is the point with the maximum x_2-coordinate.

3. The Nash equilibria

In this section we will present two propositions (one for the case with $v_1 < v_2$ and one for the case with $v_1 = v_2$) that characterize the Nash equilibria of our game: i.e., the combinations $(\hat{x}_1, \hat{x}_2) \in D$ such that $\hat{x}_1 = f_1(\hat{x}_2$ and $\hat{x}_2 = f_2(\hat{x}_1)$ (in Figure 1 the Nash equilibrium is given by point N). Before presenting the propositions, it is useful to examine briefly as a benchmark case the situation in which $x_0 = 0$. It then follows from (7) that $x_1^* = v_2$ and $x_2^* = v_1$. As a result, the reaction curve of player *i* reduces to

$$f_i(x_j) = \begin{cases} -x_j + \sqrt{x_j v_i} & if\ 0 \leqq x_j < v_i \\ 0 & if\ x_j \geqq v_i \end{cases} \tag{8}$$

Hillman and Riley (1989) (see also Ellingsen, 1991) have shown that the unique Nash equilibrium in this case is given by

$$\begin{cases} \hat{x}_1^0 &= s(1 - \frac{s}{v_1}) \\ \hat{x}_2^0 &= s(1 - \frac{s}{v_2}) \end{cases} \tag{9}$$

with $s = 1/\left(\frac{1}{v_1} + \frac{1}{v_2}\right)$. We have attached an index '0' to the Nash equilibrium of the benchmark case. Observe that (i) $\hat{x}_1^0 = \frac{s^2}{v_2} > 0$ and $\hat{x}_2^0 = \frac{s^2}{v_1} > 0$, (ii) $\hat{x}_1^0 + \hat{x}_2^0 = s = \frac{v_1 v_2}{v_1+v_2}$, (iii) if $v_1 < v_2$, than $\frac{1}{2}v_1 < s < v_1$ and $s < \frac{1}{2}v_2$, and (iv) if $v_1 = v_2 \equiv v$, then $\hat{x}_1^0 = \hat{x}_2^0 = \frac{1}{4}v$ and $s = \frac{1}{2}v < v$. We see from (i) that both players do expend in the Nash equilibrium, and from (ii), (iii) and (iv), respectively, that the total expenditures are given by s and always less than the valuation v_1.

Returning to the case with $x_0 > 0$, we first examine the situation with $v_1 < v_2$. Doing so, recall that we have distinguished four different cases for the reaction curve of player 1 – i.e., $v_1 < 2x_0, v_1 = 2x_0, 2x_0 < v_1 \leqq 4x_0$ and $4x_0 < v_1$ – as well as four different cases for player 2 – i.e., $v_2 < 2x_0, v_2 = 2x_0, 2x_0 < v_2 \leqq 4x_0$ *and* $4x_0 < v_2$. If we combine all cases for the two players together, in principle we expect to obtain sixteen different cases. However, it turns out that seven of these cases cannot occur. For instance, the combination of $v_1 = 2x_0$ with $v_2 < 2x_0$ is not feasible, since we assume now that $v_1 < v_2$. As a result, we actually end up with the following nine different possible cases: case A: $v_1 < v_2 < 2x_0$; case B: $v_1 < 2x_0 = v_2$; case C: $v_1 < 2x_0 < v_2 \leqq 4x_0$; case D: $v_1 < 2x_0 < 4x_0 < v_2$; case E: $v_1 = 2x_0 < v_2 \leqq 4x_0$; case F: $v_1 = 2x_0 < 4x_0 < v_2$; case G: $2x_0 < v_1 < v_2 \leqq 4x_0$; case H: $2x_0 < v_1 \leqq 4x_0 < v_2$; and case I: $4x_0 < v_1 < v_2$. We now present our first proposition.[2]

Proposition 1. Consider the model defined by (1) and (2). Suppose that $0 < x_0 < v_1 < v_2$, so that s = $\frac{v_1, v_2}{v_1+v_2}$. Depending on the size of the parameters v_1, v_2 and x_0, the number of Nash equilibria of the model is zero, one, or two. In particular, for the cases A to I we have the following results: In order to discuss this proposition, recall that in the benchmark case with $x_0 = 0$, there is a unique Nash equilibrium given by (9). Proposition 1 points out that the introduction of a minimum expenditure requirement may change the outcome completely. Depending on the values of v_1, v_2 and x_0, the model can have one or two Nash equilibria, or no Nash equilibrium at all.

We can use Proposition 1 to investigate what happens if we keep the values of v_1 and v_2 fixed and take increasing values of x_0 in the (feasible) region $0 < x_0 < v_1$. In particular, we can examine the development in the Nash equilibria and, in order to assess the extent of rent dissipation, the development of the size of the total expenditures in these equilibria compared with the size of the total expenditures s in the benchmark case with $x_0 = 0$. Doing so, we have to distinguish three different situations, i.e., $2v_1 < v_2, 2v_1 > v_2$ *and* $2v_1 = v_2$.

First, take the situation with $2v_1 < v_2$. If we consider now increasing values of x_0 from 0 to v_1, we pass in turn through the cases, I, H, F, D, C, B and A. We note that, depending on the numerical values of v_1, v_2 and x_0, it might happen that from a certain point onwards the last cases in this sequence cannot occur (e.g., case A, or case B and A). A typical example of the present situation is given by $v_1 = 1$ and $v_2 = 5$, which implies that $s = \frac{5}{6}$. Using Proposition 1 we can derive the following results. In this example the cases C, B and A cannot occur. There is either one Nash equilibrium or no one at all. Further, depending on the value of x_0, the size of $\hat{x}_1 + \hat{x}_2$ can be larger than, equal to, or smaller than $s = \frac{5}{6}$. Stated otherwise, the extent of rent dissipation can be larger than, equal to, or smaller than the extent of rent dissipation in the benchmark case with $x_0 = 0$.

Next, consider briefly the situations $2v_1 > v_2$ *and* $2v_1 = v_2$. If we have $2v_1 > v_2$, keep v_1 and v_2 fixed and take increasing values of x_0 from 0 to v_1, we pass through the cases I, H, G, E, C, B and A (as in the situation with $2v_1 < v_2$, possibly only up to a certain point in this sequence). Analogously, in the situation $2v_1 = v_2$, we pass through the cases I, H, E, C, B and A.[3] We remark that if $2v_1 > v_2$ or $2v_1 = v_2$, then the subcases Hii and Iβii cannot occur. This can be seen by noting that $2x_0 < v_1$ and $2v_1 \geqq v_2$ imply that $\sqrt{x_0 v_2} \leqq v_1$.[4]

Proceeding, we turn to the case in which both players have the same valuation of the monopoly rent. Using the reaction curves derived in Section 2 we can easily prove Proposition 2 for this case.

Proposition 2. Consider the model defined by (1) and (2). Suppose that $0 < x_0 < v_1 = v_2 = v$. Depending on the size of the parameters v and x_0, the number of Nash equilibria of the model is one or four. In particular, we have the following different cases: Recall that in the benchmark case with $x_0 = 0$, there is a unique Nash equilibrium with $x_1 = x_2 = \frac{1}{4}v$ *and* $s = \frac{1}{2}v$. We see from Proposition 2 that the presence of a minimum expenditure requirement implies that either there is one Nash equilibrium or there are four Nash equilibria. One can verify that in the model with $x_0 > 0$ the extent of rent dissipation in a Nash equilibrium can be larger than, equal to, or smaller than the extent of rent dissipation in the Nash equilibrium of the model with $x_0 =$

0. The size of $\hat{x}_1 + \hat{x}_2$ is largest in the Nash equilibrium (x_0, x_0) associated with the case $v = 2x_0$. In that case $\hat{x}_1 + \hat{x}_2 = v$, i.e., there is full rent dissipation.

4. Conclusion

This paper has extended Tullock's game-theoretic model of a contest for a monopoly rent, by incorporating a minimum expenditure requirement. We have shown that such a requirement may have different kinds of effects on the number of Nash equilibria and the extent of rent dissipation. Thus, one must be careful in this respect if such a minimum expenditure requirement is relevant. The precise effects depend on the value of the minimum expenditures as well as on the sizes of the players' valuations of the monopoly rent.

Notes

1. Alternatively, one might also suppose that $p_1(0,0) = p_2(0,0) = 0$, i.e., if both players decide to expend nothing, then the contest stops and nobody wins the rent. In that case we can easily modify the results of this paper. In particular, in the Propositions 1 and 2 of Section 3, the terms '$2x_0$' have to be replaced by 'x_0': e.g., the relevant condition of case C in Proposition 1 becomes $v_1 < x_0 < v_2 \leqq 4x_0$.
2. The proof of Proposition 1 is available from the authors upon request.
3. Typical examples of these two situations are given by $v_1 = 1$ and $v_2 = 1.9$, and $v_1 = 1$ and $v_2 = 2$, respectively. Analysis of these examples will be left to the reader.
4. Remark that if $2v_1 \geqq v_2$, then there exist values of x_0 falling in case C such that the size of $\hat{x}_1 + \hat{x}_2 (= x_0)$ is respectively larger than, equal to, or smaller than s. This can be understood by noting that there always holds $\frac{1}{2}v_1 < s < \frac{1}{2}v_2$, *or* $v_1 < 2s < v_2$. In combination with $2v_1 \geqq v_2$, we obtain from this that $v_1 < 2s < v_2 < 4s$. If we take $x_0 = s$, we have $v_1 < 2x_0 < v_2 < 4x_0$, i.e., case C holds. Clearly, there also exist $x_0 < s$ *and* $x_0 > s$ satisfying case C.

Appendix: The derivation of the reaction curves

In this appendix we derive the reaction curve $f_i(x_j)$ of player i. It is convenient to suppose first that $x_j \geqq x_0$ and to require that x_i must satisfy $x_i \geqq x_0$. Doing so, the optimal choice of player i can be determined by solving the Kuhn-Tucker conditions

$$\begin{cases} \frac{v_i x_j}{(x_i+x_j)^2} - 1 + \mu_i = 0 \\ \mu_i(x_i - x_0) = 0 \\ \mu_i \geqq 0,\ x_i - x_0 \geqq 0 \end{cases}$$

where μ_i is the Kuhn-Tucker multiplier associated with the constraint $x_i \geqq x_0$ (see Takayama, 1985). From these conditions it can be derived that the optimal choice of player i is given by the reaction curve

$$\tilde{f}_i(x_j) = \begin{cases} -x_j + \sqrt{x_j v_i} & if\ -x_j + \sqrt{x_j v_i} > x_0 \\ x_0 & if\ -x_j + \sqrt{x_j v_i} \leqq x_0 \end{cases} \qquad \text{(A.1)}$$

We have attached a tilde to the reaction curve to indicate that we have limited the attention here to the case $x_j \geqq x_0$ and $x_i \geqq 0$. It can be verified that there exists at least one $x_j \geqq x_0$ satisfying the first subcase of (A.1) if and only if $4x_0 < v_i$.

In case $4x_0 < v_i$, we can reformulate (A.1) as

$$\tilde{f}_i(x_j) = \begin{cases} -x_j + \sqrt{x_j v_i} & if\ x_0 \leqq x_j < x_j^* \\ x_0 & if\ x_j \geqq x_j^* \end{cases} \qquad \text{(A.2)}$$

where $x_j^* = ((v_i - 2x_0) + \sqrt{v_i(v_i - 4x_0)})/2$. In case $4x_0 \geqq v_i$, (A.1) reduces to $\tilde{f}_i(x_j) = x_0$ for all $x_j \geqq x_0$.

Next, let us introduce again the possibility that player i can decide to choose an expenditure level equal to zero. Take for instance player 1, and consider in turn case (a) in which his rival's choice satisfies $x_2 \geqq x_0$ and case (b) in which $x_2 = 0$.

In case (a), with $x_2 \geqq x_0$, we have to compare two alternatives for player 1: he can choose either $x_1 = 0$ or $x_1 = \tilde{f}_1(x_2)$. Considering the possible choice $x_1 = 0$, we notice that $\pi_1(0, x_2) = 0$ because $x_2 \geqq x_0$. Considering the alternative choice $x_1 = \tilde{f}_1(x_2)$, we derive from equation (2) of Section 2 that $\pi_1(\tilde{f}_1(x_2), x_2) > 0$ if $\tilde{f}_1(x_2)+x_2 < v_1$, whereas $\pi_1(\tilde{f}_1(x_2), x_2) = 0$ (< 0) if $\tilde{f}_1(x_2)+x_2 = v_1$ ($> v_1$). Now suppose first that $4x_0 < v_1$ and the first subcase of (A.2) holds (i.e., $x_0 \leqq x_2 < x_2^*$). As a result, $\tilde{f}_1(x_2) = -x_2 + \sqrt{x_2 v_1}$, which means that $\tilde{f}_1(x_2)+x_2 = \sqrt{x_2 v_1}$. Because $x_2 < x_2^*$ and $x_2^* < v_1$, it follows that $\pi_1(\tilde{f}_1(x_2), x_2) > 0$. Recalling that $\pi_1(0, x_2) = 0$, we conclude from a comparison of the payoffs that player 1 will prefer the choice $x_1 = \tilde{f}_1(x_2)$ now.

Second, suppose that either $4x_0 < v_1$ and the second subcase of (A.2) holds (i.e., $x_2 \geqq x_2^*$) or $4x_0 \geqq v_1$. Considering the possible choice $x_1 = \tilde{f}_1(x_2)$, we see that now $\tilde{f}_1(x_2)$

$= x_0$, and the resulting expected payoff $\pi_1(x_0, x_2)$ is positive if $x_0 + x_2 < v_1$, equal to zero if $x_0 + x_2 = v_1$, and negative if $x_0 + x_2 > v_1$. Recalling again that $\pi_1(0, x_2) = 0$, we conclude that player 1 will choose $x_1 = \tilde{f}_1(x_2) = x_0$ in case $x_2 < v_1 - x_0, x_1 = 0$ in case $x_2 > v_1 - x_0$, and either $x_1 = 0$ or $x_1 = \tilde{f}_1(x_2) = x_0$ in case $x_2 = v_1 - x_0$. (In the latter case he is indifferent between the two choices.)

Next, consider case (b), i.e., the case with $x_2 = 0$. We distinguish the following three alternative choices for player 1: $x_1 = 0$, $x_1 = x_0$, or $x_1 > x_0$. If he chooses $x_1 = 0$, then his (certain) payoff equals $\pi_1(0, 0) = \frac{1}{2}v_1$, whereas his (certain) payoff is $\pi_1(x_0, 0) = v_1 - x_0$ if he chooses $x_1 = x_0$. Finally, player 1 will never choose $x_1 > x_0$, because $\pi_1(x_1, 0) < \pi_1(x_0,0)$ for all $x_1 > x_0$. From a comparison of the payoffs, we conclude that player 1 will choose $x_1 = 0$ in case $v_1 < 2x_0$, $x_1 = x_0$ in case $v_1 > 2x_0$, and either $x_1 = 0$ or $x_1 = x_0$ in case $v_1 = 2x_0$. (In the latter case he is indifferent between the two choices.)

Concluding, we see that we have to distinguish four different cases with respect to the reaction curve $f_1(x_2)$ of player 1, i.e., $v_1 < 2x_0$, $v_1 = 2x_0$, $2x_0 < v_1 \leqq 4x_0$ and $4x_0 < v_1$. We further remark that we can derive in a completely similar way the reaction curve $f_2(x_1)$ of player 2. Combining results, we obtain the reaction curve $f_i(x_j)$ of player i as given in (3), (4), (5) and (6) in Section 2.

Case	Conditions on v_1, v_2 and x_0	Nash equilibria $(\hat{x}_1, \hat{x}_2)$
A	$v_1 < v_2 < 2x_o$	(0,0)
B	$v_1 < 2x_0 = v_2$	(0,0) and $(0,x_0)$
C	$v_1 < 2x_0 < v_2 \leqq 4x_0$	$(0,x_0)$
D	$v_1 < 2x_0 < 4x_0 < v_2$	$(0,x_0)$
E	$v_1 = 2x_0 < v_2 \leqq 4x_0$	$(0,x_0)$ and (x_0,x_0)
F	$v_1 = 2x_0 < 4x_0 < v_2$	$(0,x_0)$
G	$2x_0 < v_1 < v_2 \leqq 4x_0$	(x_0,x_0)
H	$2x_0 < v_1 \leqq 4x_0 < v_2$ *and*	
• subcase Hi	$\sqrt{x_0 v_2} \leqq v_1$	$(x_0, -x_0 + \sqrt{x_0 v_2})$
• subcase Hii	$\sqrt{x_0 v_2} > v_1$	no one
I	$4x_0 < v_1 < v_2$ *and*	
• subcase Iα	$\frac{s^2}{s-x_0} < v_1 < v_2$	$(s(1-\frac{s}{v_1}), s(1-\frac{s}{v_2}))$
• subcase Iβi	$v_1 \leqq \frac{s^2}{s-x_0} < v_2$ *and* $\sqrt{x_0 v_2} \leqq v_1$	$(x_0, -x_0 + \sqrt{x_0 v_2})$
• subcase Iβii	$v_1 \leqq \frac{s^2}{s-x_0} < v_2$ *and* $\sqrt{x_0 v_2} > v_1$	no one

Case	Condition on x_0	Nash equilibria $(\hat{x}_1, \hat{x}_2)$
subcase Iα	$0 < x_0 < \frac{5}{36}$	$(\frac{5}{36}, \frac{25}{36})$
subcase Iβi	$\frac{5}{36} \leqq x_0 < \frac{1}{5}$	$(x_0, -x_0 + \sqrt{5x_0})$
subcase Iβii	$\frac{1}{5} \leqq x_0 < \frac{1}{4}$	no one
subcase Hii	$\frac{1}{4} \leqq x_0 < \frac{1}{2}$	no one
F	$x_0 = \frac{1}{2}$	$(0, \frac{1}{2})$
D	$\frac{1}{2} < x_0 < 1$	$(0, x_0)$

Conditions on v and x_0	Nash equilibria $(\hat{x}_1, \hat{x}_2)$
$v < 2x_0$	(0,0)
$v = 2x_0$	(0,0), $(0, x_0)$, $(x_0, 0)$ and (x_0, x_0)
$2x_0 < v \leqq 4x_0$	(x_0, x_0)
$4x_0 < v$	$(\frac{1}{4}v, \frac{1}{4}v)$

Rent-seeking with asymmetric valuations

KOFI O. NTI *
Smeal College of Business Administration, Penn State University, 308 Beam BAB, University Park, PA 16802, U.S.A.

Abstract. This paper analyzes Tullock's rent-seeking game with asymmetric valuations for a variable range of the returns to scale parameter. A necessary and sufficient condition for a unique pure strategy Nash equilibrium is established. Equilibrium effort and expected profits are determined and subjected to comparative statics analysis. Increasing the underdog's valuation induces both players to increase their efforts. Increasing the favorite's valuation increases his effort but decreases the effort of the underdog. Expected profits increase with a player's valuation but decreases with the valuation of the competitor. The impact of the returns to scale parameter is also analyzed.

1. Introduction

The theory of rent-seeking has advanced considerably since Tullock (1980) proposed his well-known game theory model to explore the issue of rent dissipation. Various researchers have clarified the conditions under which partial or full rent dissipation occurs. (See Corcoran and Karels 1985, Hillman and Samet 1987, Higgins et al. 1987, Shogren and Baik 1991, Pérez-Castrillo and Verdier 1992, Baye et al. 1994; also see the recent survey by Nitzan 1994a for additional references on rent-seeking contests.) A striking feature of the majority of the existing theoretical and experimental research is the assumption that the contestants are identical or symmetrically situated.

The rent-seeking paradigm has tremendous possibilities. It can be used to illuminate issues in procurement (Rogerson 1989), lobbying for trade protection (Hillman 1989), public goods (Katz et al. 1990), market entry (Nti 1995), and others. In many of these situations, the contestants may value the prize differently. In government procurement, a previous contract holder may value the prize more because it has sunk resources or gained experience (Baik 1994); in lobbying, the imposition or removal of various taxes and subsidies may be valued differently by different pressure groups because these policies will typically impact them differently (Becker 1983);

* I thank an anonymous referee for helpful comments and suggestions.

pollution removal may be valued differently by different localities (Katz et al. 1990); and an incumbent may value a patent for a new substitute product more highly than a potential entrant because the incumbent has a monopoly position to protect (Baik 1994). These examples clearly show that asymmetric player valuations are natural and quite common in many applications of rent-seeking paradigm.

Most of the extensive literature on rent-seeking have assumed that the contestants assign a common valuation to the prize. The few exceptions include Hillman (1988), Hillman and Riley (1989), Katz et al. (1990), Ellingsen (1991), Leininger (1993), Baik (1994), and Baye et al. (1993, 1996).[1] Hillman (1988) and Hillman and Riley (1989) study a perfectly discriminating contest (i.e., a first price all-pay auction) and noted that asymmetric valuations may act as a barrier to entry and reduce rent-dissipation. They also extended their results to the Tullock contest with constant returns to scale rent-seeking technology. Ellingsen (1991) applies the results of Hillman and Riley (1989) to study the welfare implications of rent-seeking by prospective monopolists and strategic buyers. Baye et al. (1993) show that the designer of an all-pay auction may have an incentive to exclude certain high valuation lobbyist from the game. Baye et al. (1996) provide a comprehensive solution to the all-pay auction with asymmetric valuations, noting that the auctioneer's expected revenue may differ across the multiple equilibria.

Clearly, the all-pay auction with asymmetric valuations has been well-studied. In contrast, imperfectly discriminating rent-seeking contests (i.e., the lottery form) with asymmetric valuations have not been analyzed as comprehensively. Most of the analyses study asymmetric valuations for the special case of the Tullock game with constant returns to scale rent-seeking technology. Within this framework, Hillman and Riley (1989) relate total rent-seeking efforts to the harmonic mean of the players' valuations. In a study of public goods, Katz et al. (1990) discuss the impact of asymmetric valuations and population size on rent-seeking efforts in a group contest; and Leininger (1993) contains explicit expressions for the Nash equilibrium efforts and payoffs for constant returns to scale Tullock game with asymmetric valuations. Baik (1994) by-passes the Tullock game and uses a general rent-seeking technology to study the qualitative properties of player efforts in a contest with asymmetric valuations and differential abilities. But his analysis does not readily apply to the generalized Tullock game, which is the subject of this paper.

The purpose of this paper is to contribute to the theory of imperfectly discriminating rent-seeking contests with asymmetric valuations. We analyze the Tullock (1980) rent-seeking game with asymmetric valuations for a variable range of the returns to scale parameter. A necessary and sufficient condition for the existence of a unique pure strategy Nash equilibrium is established. We show that the player with the higher valuation expends more effort but both players allocate the same fraction of their valuations to rent-seeking activities. Thus the higher valuation player is favored to win the contest and the lower valuation player is the underdog. We comment on issues relating to rent dissipation; however, our primary focus is on the qualitative structure of equilibrium efforts and expected profits. We develop explicit expressions for equilibrium efforts and expected profits and subject them to comparative statics analyses. We investigate how changes in valuations affect the efforts and payoffs of the contestants. Increasing the underdog's valuation induces both players to increase their efforts. In contrast, an increase in the favorite's valuation leads him to increases his effort but induces the underdog to decrease her effort. Expected profits increase with a player's valuation but decreases with the valuation of the competitor. The impact of the returns to scale parameter is also analyzed.

This paper extends and generalizes certain results on imperfectly discriminating rent-seeking contests with asymmetric valuations. Because we consider the Tullock rent-seeking technology for a variable range of the returns to scale parameter, our analysis generalizes certain aspects of Katz et al. (1990) and Leininger (1993), both of which involve the constant returns case. The focus of our analysis is closer to Baik (1994), but he employs a more general rent-seeking technology. However, we exploit the relative simplicity of the rent-seeking technology to produce more definitive results. We should mention that we study the qualitative properties of both effort and payoffs in the generalized Tullock model; how payoffs vary with valuations are not studied in Baik (1994). Other interesting relationships and differences between Baik (1994) and this paper will be discussed after we have developed the main results. A strength of this paper is that it contains simple expressions for the efforts and payoffs of the players in the general Tullock contest with asymmetric valuations. In addition, all the results in this paper are stated explicitly in terms of the parameters of the model, namely the valuations and the returns to scale parameter.

The rest of the paper is organized as follows. The model is presented in Section 2. Section 3 provides a closed form solution and discusses conditions for the existence of a pure strategy equilibrium. Section 4 analyzes the effect of changes in player valuations on efforts and expected profits. Section 5 concludes the paper.

2. The model

We consider Tullock's (1980) model of rent-seeking where two risk neutral players compete to win a prize but we assume that players valuation of the prize may be different. Let V_1 be player 1's valuation of the prize and let V_2 be player 2's valuation, where $V_1 \leq V_2$. Suppose player i, i = 1 and 2, expends effort x_i in hopes of winning the prize, where the effort is measured in the same units as the prize. Given a profile of effort levels (x_1, x_2), we assume, as in Tullock (1980), that the probability that player i wins the prize takes the symmetric, logit form

$$P_i(x_1, x_2) = \frac{x_i^r}{x_1^r + x_2^r}, \tag{1}$$

where $r > 0$, and we may define P_i to equal $1/2$ if $x_1 = x_2 = 0$. In order words, the rent-seeking technology is $P(x) = x^r$, where r is the returns to scale parameter. There is decreasing returns to scale when $0 < r < 1$ and increasing returns to scale when $r > 1$. As noted earlier, a great deal of the rent-seeking literature has been devoted to the constant returns to scale case where $r = 1$. This paper considers returns to scale of all types.

Given the above specification of the winning probabilities, the expected profit of player i is

$$\begin{aligned} \pi_i(x_1, x_2) &= P_i(x_1, x_2)V_i - x_i, \\ &= \frac{V_i x_i^r}{x_1^r + x_2^r} - x_i. \end{aligned} \tag{2}$$

The first order conditions for an interior Nash equilibrium of the model are

$$\frac{\partial \pi_i}{\partial x_i} = \frac{rV_i x_i^{r-1} x_j^r}{(x_1^r + x_2^r)^2} - 1 = 0 \tag{3}$$

The second order sufficiency conditions are

$$\frac{\partial^2 \pi_i}{\partial x_i^2} = \frac{rV_i x_j^r}{(x_1^r + x_2^r)^3}\left[(r-1)x_i^{r-2}(x_1^r + x_2^r) - 2rx_i^{2r-2}\right] < 0. \tag{4}$$

Later we will provide a remarkably simple condition that ensures that the second order sufficiency conditions are satisfied.

We may rewrite the first order condition (3) as

$$\frac{rV_i x_i^{r-1} x_j^r}{(x_1^r + x_2^r)^2} = 1 \tag{5}$$

and take the ratio of the two first order conditions to get the following relationship between equilibrium effort levels and a player's valuation of the prize:

$$\frac{x_1}{V_1} = \frac{x_2}{V_2} \tag{6}$$

Since $V_2 \geq V_1$, the above relationship also implies that $x_2 \geq x_1$. These relationships are summarized in the next proposition.

Proposition 1

The player who values the prize more expends more effort in equilibrium but both players allocate the same fraction of their valuations to the contest, regardless of the magnitude of the returns to scale parameter r.

Proposition 1 is quite remarkable. Regardless of whether there is increasing, constant, or decreasing returns to scale, the higher valuation player expends more effort in equilibrium; however, the two players dissipate the same fraction of their values in rent-seeking activities. Katz et al. (1990) obtained Proposition 1 for the constant returns case but we have shown that it holds for all positive r that are compatible with the existence of a pure strategy equilibrium. Proposition 1 is also relevant for the two stage group contest of Katz and Tokatlidu (1996), which also employs a constant returns to scale rent-seeking technology. Under the endogenous sharing rule they employed, the value of the prize expected at the end of stage one is inversely proportional to the square of the group size. Thus the smaller group has a higher valuation for the prize. Proposition 1 implies that the smaller group should supply more aggregate effort than the larger group, which agrees with the results in Katz and Tokatlidu (1996).

Proposition 1 raises interesting questions about the structure of relative advantages and profits of the players. Obviously, the results may depend on the valuations as well as the returns to scale parameter r. To obtain insightful answers to these questions, we now proceed to provide a detailed analysis of the model.

3. Closed form solution

A closed form solution is available for the Tullock rent-seeking game with asymmetric valuations. The idea is to use the effort to value relationship (6) to eliminate x_j from the first order condition for player i and then solve the resulting equation for x_i. Substituting $x_2 = (V_2/V_1)x_1$ into the first order condition for player 1 and solving for x_1 yields

$$x_1^* = \frac{rV_1^{r+1}V_2^r}{(V_1^r + V_2^r)^2}. \tag{7}$$

Hence

$$\frac{x_1^*}{V_1} = \frac{x_2^*}{V_2} = \frac{rV_1^r V_2^r}{(V_1^r + V_2^r)^2} \tag{8}$$

and

$$x_2^* = \frac{rV_2^{r+1}V_1^r}{(V_1^r + V_2^r)^2}. \tag{9}$$

It is interesting to observe from (7) and (8) that when the players entertain a common valuation V for the prize ($V_1 = V_2 = V$) we obtain the familiar results that $x_1^* = x_2^* = rV/4$. That is, each player dissipates a fraction $r/4$ of his or her valuation in rent-seeking. Thus, in the symmetric case, the fraction of the value dissipated per player increases (linearly) in r but is independent of the common valuation. When V_1 and V_2 are different but $r = 1$, the effort levels coincide with those obtained by Leininger (1993) for the simultaneous move game with equal rent-seeking abilities. Now let us examine the issue of rent dissipation under asymmetric valuations. Let $v = V_1/V_2$, $0 < v < 1$, then

$$\frac{x_i^*}{V_i} = \frac{rv^r}{(1 + v^r)^2}$$

and

$$\frac{\partial(x_i^*/V_i)}{\partial v} = \frac{r^2 v^{r-1}}{(1 + v^r)^3}\left[1 - v^r\right] > 0.$$

Thus the fraction of a player's valuation expended in rent seeking is increasing in the valuation ratio V_1/V_2. That is, the more skewed the valuations, the smaller the fraction of the value dissipated in rent-seeking. It can also be seen from Figure 1 that the fraction of the value dissipated per player may or may not increase with r when the valuation ratio is fixed. Consider the three values of r used in Figure 1. When $v = V_1/V_2$ is small ($v < 0.1$), the fraction corresponding to $r = 0.5$ exceeds that for $r = 1.0$, which in turn exceeds the fraction for $r = 1.5$. The relationship is reversed when v is large ($v > 0.3$). The relationship is not monotonic if v lies between 0.1 and 0.3.

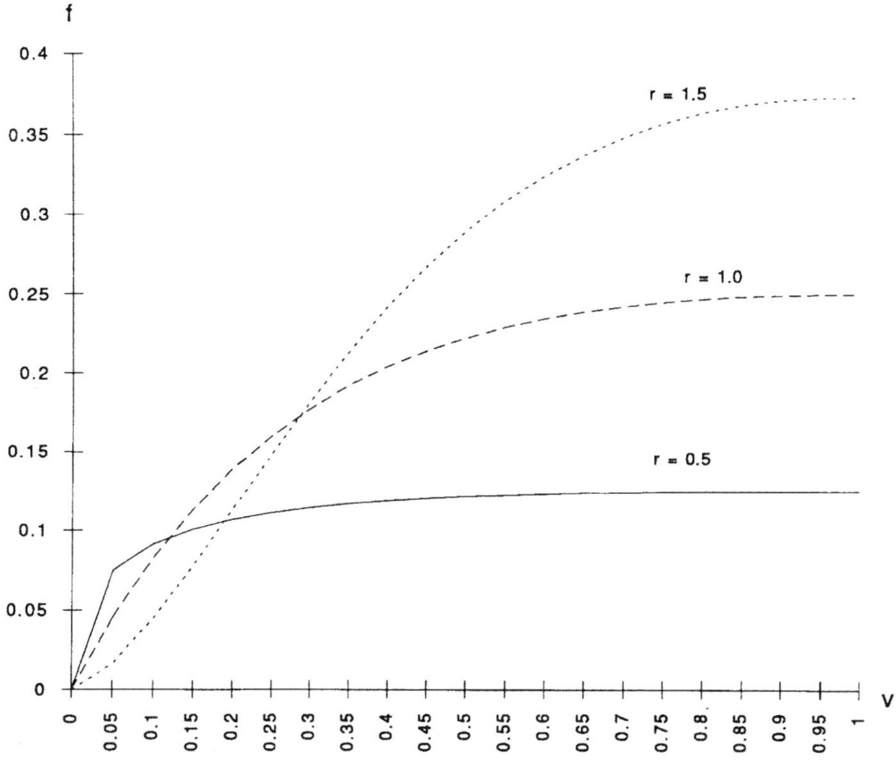

Figure 1. Fraction of player's valuation dissipated.

These insights may be usefully exploited by a contest designer to control the degree of rent-dissipation.

Proposition 2

The fraction of player valuations expended in rent-seeking increases with the valuation ratio $v = V_1/V_2$ *but is not monotonic in the returns to scale parameter* r.

We may also calculate the winning probabilities and expected payoffs for the players. The equilibrium winning probability for player i is

$$P_i^* = \frac{V_i^r}{V_1^r + V_2^r}. \tag{10}$$

And the expected payoffs are

$$\begin{aligned} \pi_1^* &= \frac{V_1^{r+1}}{V_1^r + V_2^r} - \frac{rV_1^{r+1}V_2^r}{(V_1^r + V_2^r)^2} \\ &= \frac{V_1^{r+1}}{(V_1^r + V_2^r)^2}\left[V_1^r + V_2^r - rV_2^r\right] \end{aligned} \tag{11}$$

and

$$\begin{aligned} \pi_2^* &= \frac{V_2^{r+1}}{V_1^r + V_2^r} - \frac{rV_2^{r+1}V_1^r}{(V_1^r + V_2^r)^2} \\ &= \frac{V_2^{r+1}}{(V_1^r + V_2^r)^2}\left[V_1^r + V_2^r - rV_1^r\right]. \end{aligned} \tag{12}$$

Two observations are in order. First, equilibrium winning probabilities P_i^* in (10) are computed as if the players fully dissipate their values in the rent-seeking contest. Of course, the players only dissipate a fraction of their values in equilibrium, but the winning probabilities are the same as in the non-equilibrium outcome where $x_i = V_i$. This insight can be used to develop intuition on the structure of the model. For example, the higher valuation player is favored to win the contest. Thus we may follow the terminology of Dixit (1987) and refer to the higher valuation player as the favored player or favorite and the lower valuation player as the underdog, whenever it is convenient (or less verbose). We should note that if $V_1 < V_2$ then the equilibrium probability ratio $P_1^*/P_2^* = (V_1/V_2)^r$ is increasing in the valuation ratio V_1/V_2 but decreasing in r. In the symmetric case ($V_1 = V_2 = V$) the odds are equal and independent of r or the common valuation V. The second observation is that the equilibrium expected profits in 11 and 12 are positive if and only if $V_1^r + V_2^r - rV_i^r > 0$ for $i = 1$ and 2. Since $V_1 \leq V_2$, the following assumption is sufficient for the analysis.

Assumption

The returns to scale parameter r *and the players' valuations* V_1 *and* V_2 *satisfy the relationship* $V_1^r + V_2^r > rV_2^r \geq rV_1^r$.

Proposition 3

Given $V_1 \leq V_2$, *the Tullock rent-seeking game with asymmetric valuations has a unique pure strategy Nash equilibrium if and only if* $V_1^r + V_2^r > rV_2^r$.

Proof

Since the prize is valued positively by both players, any pure strategy equilibrium involves positive effort levels by both players. The analysis has shown that there is a unique solution (x_1^*, x_2^*) to the first order conditions. In addition, the expected profit of both players is positive under the assumption. Evaluating the second order sufficiency condition for player 1, for example, and making use of $x_1/x_2 = V_1/V_2$, shows that

$$\begin{aligned}\frac{\partial^2 \pi_1}{\partial x_1^2} &= \frac{rV_1 x_2^r}{(x_1^r + x_2^r)^3}\left[(r-1)x_1^{r-2}(x_1^r + x_2^r) - 2rx_1^{2r-2}\right] \\ &= \frac{rV_1^{1-r}x_2^r x_1^{2r-2}}{(x_1^r + x_2^r)^3}\left[rV_2^r - V_2^r - V_1^r - rV_1^r\right] \\ &< 0,\end{aligned}$$

since $rV_2^r - V_2^r - V_1^r < 0$ from the assumption. Therefore player 1 is maximizing against x_2, and similarly for player 2. Thus the sufficiency condition implies a unique pure strategy equilibrium. And if the sufficiency assumption is violated, at least one player will receive a negative payoff; that player can improve by reducing his or her effort to zero, which will destroy the equilibrium. □

Let $v = V_1/V_2$, where $0 < v \leq 1$. Then we may write the sufficiency condition as $r \leq 1 + v^r$. Given v, let R(v) be the maximum value of r that solves the inequality $r \leq 1 + v^r$. Then for any v, $0 < v \leq 1$, the Tullock rent-seeking game has a pure strategy equilibrium for $0 < r \leq R(v)$. It is easy to see that $R(v) > 1$ for all $v > 0$ and that $R(1) = 2$. This shows that, in general, R depends on the valuation ratio, is greater than 1, and equals 2 only when the contest is symmetric. (See Shogren and Baik 1991 and Baye et al. 1994 for a discussion on the crucial role of $R = 2$ in the analysis of symmetrically valued contest; also see Chung 1996 for a related result where R is not a constant but depends on the players common marginal valuation.) Figure 2 illustrates the general relationship between R and v. It is interesting to observe that R is increasing from 1 to 2 within the feasible range. Thus we may conclude that the more skewed the players valuations, the smaller the range of the returns to scale parameter supporting pure strategy equilibria.

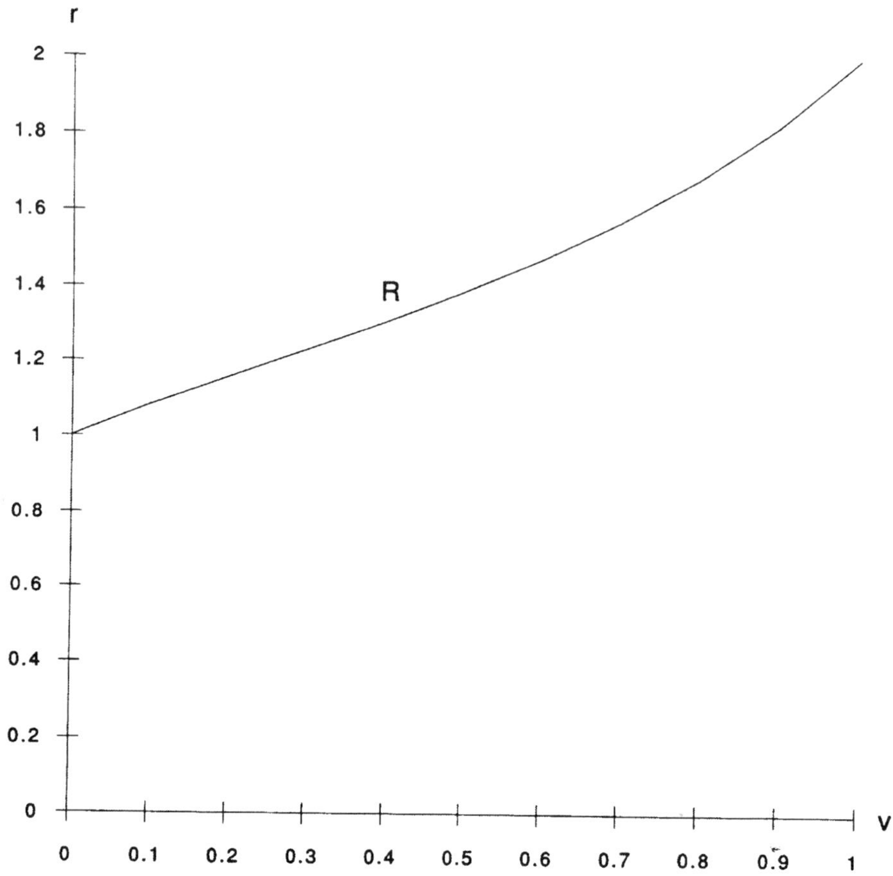

Figure 2. Dependence of R on valuation ratio v.

Evidently, the symmetric game has pure strategy equilibria for the largest possible range of the returns to scale parameter.

4. Comparative statics

The need to obtain the comparative statics properties of contests and rent-seeking games arises naturally in a variety of applications. Recently, Nti (1997) has developed comprehensive comparative statics results for symmetric contests. His analysis applies to the symmetric Tullock game with decreasing returns to scale. But his results do not readily extend to contest with asymmetric valuations or with increasing returns technology. It is also not straightforward to apply the results from the asymmetric contest model of Baik (1994), as we will explain later. Fortunately, we have obtained a closed form solution to the Tullock game. Therefore, we can use elementary methods to determine how efforts and payoffs respond to variations in the parameters defining the contest. First, we examine the response of effort levels. Performing the necessary differentiation, simplifying, and using the relationship $V_1^r + V_2^r > rV_2^r > rV_1^r$ yields[2]

$$\frac{\partial x_1^*}{\partial V_1} = \frac{rV_1^r V_2^r}{(V_1^r + V_2^r)^3}[V_1^r + V_2^r - rV_1^r + rV_2^r] > 0,$$

$$\frac{\partial x_1^*}{\partial V_2} = \frac{rV_1^{r+1} V_2^{r-1}}{(V_1^r + V_2^r)^3}[rV_1^r - rV_2^r] < 0,$$

$$\frac{\partial x_2^*}{\partial V_1} = \frac{rV_1^{r-1} V_2^{r+1}}{(V_1^r + V_2^r)^3}[rV_2^r - rV_1^r] > 0,$$

and

$$\frac{\partial x_2^*}{\partial V_2} = \frac{rV_1^r V_2^r}{(V_1^r + V_2^r)^3}[V_1^r + V_2^r - rV_1^r - rV_2^r] > 0.$$

This proves the next proposition.

Proposition 4

Effort of the favored player increases with his own valuation and with the valuation of the underdog; effort of the underdog increases with her own valuation but decreases with the valuation of the favored player.

Proposition 4 shows that an increase in the valuation of the underdog raises the effort of both players. That is, competition becomes more intense as the valuation of the underdog increases. On the other hand, an increase in the valuation of the favored player dampens the effort of the underdog and stimulates the effort of the favorite. We may say that competition becomes less intense as the valuation of the favored player increases. This is quite interesting and seems to be in agreement with casual observations. Competition becomes keener when the gap between the contestants is not too large. Sports and political elections generally attract more attention and effort when the contestants are about equally matched.

Finally, we examine the response of expected profits to parametric variations. Performing the necessary differentiation, simplifying, and making use of the relationship $V_1^r + V_2^r > rV_2^r > rV_1^r$ leads to

$$\frac{\partial \pi_1^*}{\partial V_1} = \frac{[V_1^{2r} + (r+1)V_1^r V_2^r]}{(V_1^r + V_2^r)^3}[V_1^r + V_2^r - rV_2^r] + \frac{r^2 V_1^{2r} V_2^r}{(V_1^r + V_2^r)^3} > 0,$$

$$\frac{\partial \pi_1^*}{\partial V_2} = -\frac{rV_1^{r+1} V_2^{r-1}}{(V_1^r + V_2^r)^3}[V_1^r + V_2^r - rV_2^r] - \frac{r^2 V_1^{2r+1} V_2^{r-1}}{(V_1^r + V_2^r)^3} < 0,$$

$$\frac{\partial \pi_2^*}{\partial V_1} = -\frac{rV_1^{r-1} V_2^{r+1}}{(V_1^r + V_2^r)^3}[V_1^r + V_2^r - rV_1^r] - \frac{r^2 V_1^{r-1} V_2^{2r+1}}{(V_1^r + V_2^r)^3} < 0,$$

and

$$\frac{\partial \pi_1^*}{\partial V_2} = \frac{[V_2^{2r} + (r+1)V_1^r V_2^r]}{(V_1^r + V_2^r)^3}[V_1^r + V_2^r - rV_1^r] + \frac{r^2 V_1^r V_2^{2r}}{(V_1^r + V_2^r)^3} > 0.$$

This proves the next proposition.

Proposition 5

Expected profit of a player increases with his or her own valuation but decreases with the valuation of the other player.

Proposition 5 shows that an increase in valuations have symmetrical effects on the players' expected profits. An increase in a player's valuation is beneficial to him or her but has an adverse effect on the competitor. A player benefits when he or she competes against others who have a lower valuation for the prize. This suggests that there may be incentives for sophisticated rent seekers to contest in arenas where the competition is likely to have a lower valuation. The reverse is that shrewd contest organizers may want to separate contestants with highly skewed valuations.

Finally, it is instructive to comment on the relationship between the results in this paper and those of Baik (1994). Baik formulates a two player asymmetric contest to study the response of effort levels to variations in relative valuations and relative abilities. His results for the simultaneous move game with equal abilities is relevant to this paper. Using the notation of this paper, Baik's model involves a general rent-seeking technology $P(x)$ and player valuations

$V_1 = vV$ and $V_2 = V$, where $v > 0$. Clearly, player 1 has a lower valuation for the prize when $0 < v < 1$, and has a higher valuation when $v > 1$.

Baik (1994) shows that player 1 is the favorite if the Nash equilibrium effort profile (x_1^*, x_2^*) satisfies $vP'(x_1^*) > P'(x_2^*)$; player 1 is the underdog if the inequality is reversed. (See Lemma 2 of Baik 1994.) If P is linear, Baik's condition clearly implies that player 1 is the underdog if $0 < v < 1$; player 1 is the favorite if $v > 1$. But if we consider $P(x) = x^r$, $r \neq 1$, then it is difficult to apply Baik's result to determine who the underdog is. To do so requires an explicit knowledge of the Nash equilibrium profile. Baik acknowledges that his result is conditional. We have shown in this paper (Proposition 1) that for $P(x) = x^r$ the higher valuation player is unconditionally the favorite. Applying these results to Baik's model, we can conclude that player 1 is the underdog if $0 < v < 1$; player 1 is the favorite if $v > 1$. This may also be verified by substituting our solution for x_1^* and x_2^* into Baik's condition.[3]

Baik (1994) also investigates how effort levels respond to changes in v. He showed that both players increase their efforts as v increases from zero to one, but as v increases beyond one player 1 expends more effort while player 2 expends less. (See Proposition 1 of Baik 1994, noting that with equal abilities the contest is "even" when $v = 1$.) For $P(x) = x^r$, Proposition 4 in this paper gives the same qualitative results as Baik. To see this, note that increasing v from zero to one is equivalent to increasing the valuation of the underdog; increasing v beyond one is equivalent to increasing the valuation of the favorite. We established in Proposition 4 that effort of both players increase their effort when the underdog's valuation is increased; effort of the favorite increases as his valuation is increased but effort of the underdog decreases. Although we have the same qualitative results as Baik (1994), we should mention that Baik's conclusions are conditional. Baik requires that the conditions $P''(x_1^*)(P(x_1^*) + P(x_2^*)) < 2(P'(x_1^*))^2$ and $P''(x_2^*)(P(x_1^*) + P(x_2^*)) < 2(P'(x_2^*))^2$ hold at the Nash equilibrium (x_1^*, x_2^*). For $P(x) = x^r$, these conditions are obviously satisfied when $0 < r \leq 1$, but when $r > 1$ it is difficult to determine from Baik (1994) alone whether these conditions are satisfied or not. Again, we may use our explicit expression for x_1^* and x_2^* to check his conditions but that would be laborious. We also mentioned earlier that Baik (1994) does not include a discussion of how expected profits vary with valuations. Proposition 5 in this paper addresses these issues. On the other hand, Baik (1994) contains interesting discussions on how variations in relative abilities impact effort levels. Thus this paper and Baik (1994) complement each other substantively and technically.

5. Conclusion

This paper extended the Tullock rent-seeking game to consider a situation where the players may have different valuations for the prize and for a variable range of the returns to scale parameter. It was shown that the player with the higher valuation expends more effort but both players allocate the same fraction of their valuations to rent-seeking activities. Thus the higher valuation player is favored to win the contest and the lower valuation player is the underdog. A necessary and sufficient condition for a unique pure strategy Nash equilibrium was established. Equilibrium effort levels and expected profits were subjected to various parametric variations. An increase in the valuation of the underdog induces both players to increase their efforts. In contrast, an increase in the valuation of the favored player increases his own effort but decreases the effort of the underdog. Expected profits of a player increases with his or her own valuation but decreases with the valuation of the competitor. The impact of the returns to scale parameter was also studied. Similarities and differences between the results obtained under asymmetric versus symmetric valuations were noted throughout the paper. We also discussed the relationship between the results obtained here and those in Baik (1994), which also studies a two player contest with asymmetric valuations.

This paper suggests several directions for future research. First, it contains a rich set of hypotheses that may be subjected to empirical or experimental testing. Asymmetric player valuations introduces an additional degree of freedom that can be exploited to improve experimental design and analysis of rent-seeking in actual or simulated markets. Secondly, the results and insights obtained here may be applied to illuminate issues in lobbying, public goods, procurement, and market entry where asymmetric player valuations are natural and prevalent. Finally, it would be interesting to generalize the analysis to derive analogous results for other specifications of the winning probability and also for games with sequential or dynamic structure.

Notes

1. Asymmetries in rent-seeking abilities or costs are discussed in Dixit (1987), Allard (1988), Baik and Shogren (1992), Leininger (1993), Baik (1994), and Gradstein (1995); strategic implications of introducing asymmetries in the order of moves are examined in Dixit (1987), Baik and Shogren (1992), and Leininger (1993). Group contests with asymmetric population sizes are discussed in Katz et al. (1990). Nitzan (1991) studies a group contest with asymmetric sharing rules; a two stage group contest of Katz and Tokatlidu (1996) with asymmetric population sizes also generates a contest with an asymmetrically valued prize.

2. These variations are of significant interest when $V_2 > V_1$. As noted earlier, the symmetric case where $V_1 = V_2 = V$ has effort levels $x_1^* = x_2^* = (r/4)V$, which is increasing in both V and r. Expected profits are $\pi_1^* = \pi_2^* = (1/4)(2 - r)V$, which is increasing in V and decreasing in r.
3. Nitzan (1994b) uses this approach to reconcile Baik and Shogren (1992) and Leininger (1993).

The incidence of overdissipation in rent-seeking contests *

MICHAEL R. BAYE[1,*], DAN KOVENOCK[2] & CASPER G. DE VRIES[3]
[1]*Department of Business Economics and Public Policy, Indiana University, School of Business, 1309 East Tenth Street, Bloomington, IN 47405-1701, U.S.A.;* [2]*Purdue University and Tinbergen Institute, The Netherlands;* [3]*Erasmus Universiteit Rotterdam and Tinbergen Institute, The Netherlands;* **corresponding author.*

Abstract. Tullock's analysis of rent seeking and overdissipation is reconsidered. We show that, while equilibrium strategies do not permit *overdissipation in expectation*, for particular realizations of players' mixed strategies the total amount spent competing for rents can exceed the value of the prize. We also show that the cross-sectional *incidence of overdissipation* in the perfectly discriminating contest ranges from 0.50 to 0.44 as the number of players increases from two to infinity. Thus, even though the original analysis of overdissipation is flawed, there are instances in which rent-seekers spend more than the prize is worth.

1. Introduction

Gordon Tullock's seminal contribution in the area of rent-seeking, and wasteful over-dissipation in particular, has not had the influence outside of *Public Choice* that it deserves. The purpose of this paper is to point out that even though his original analysis of overdissipation is technically flawed, the definition of overdissipation can be modified to explain instances in which rational rent-seekers spend more to win a prize than the prize is worth.

Specifically, since Tullock's seminal paper in 1967 most of the literature has focused on the degree to which the competition for rent dissipates that rent. While this literature extends across several fields,[1] it is concentrated to a large extent in the field of public choice,[2] where a standard tool in the theoretical analysis of rent-seeking is Tullock's rent-seeking game (1975, 1980). In this game, n risk-neutral players enjoy complete information and simultaneously submit nonnegative bids for a prize worth Q dollars. Letting $(x_1, \ldots, x_n) \geq 0$ denote the bids of players 1 through n, the probability player 1 wins the prize is given by

* Part of this research was completed when Kovenock was on leave at the Tinbergen Institute and when Baye was affiliated at The Pennsylvania State University. We benefitted from the suggestions of an anonymous referee, Heinrich Ursprung, and the editor's observations at the Public Choice meetings in San Francisco.

$$p_i(x_1, \ldots, x_n) = \begin{cases} 1/n & \text{if } x_1 = x_2 = \ldots = x_n = 0, \\ \frac{x_i^R}{\sum_{j=1}^n x_j^R} & \text{otherwise.} \end{cases}$$

Here R is a parameter, $R > 0$. If $R = \infty$, then the game becomes perfectly discriminating and coincides with the all-pay auction. The payoff to player i from submitting a bid of x_i when the other n-1 players submit bids of $x_{-i} \equiv (x_1, x_2, \ldots, x_{i-1}, x_{i+1}, \ldots x_n)$ is given by

$$U_i(x_i, x_{-i}) = p_i(x_i, x_{-i})Q - x_i.$$

Henceforth, we will refer to this symmetric, simultaneous-move game of complete information as the *Tullock game*.

By the end of the 1970s, two competing postulates emerged about rent-seeking games:

Posner's Rent Dissipation Postulate: In equilibrium, the total expenditures of rent-seekers equals the value of the prize.

Tullock's Rent Dissipation Postulate: In equilibrium, rent-seeking expenditures exceed the value of the prize when $R > n/(n - 1)$.

Posner's postulate (1975) relies on a strong free-entry assumption: If existing rent-seekers were in the aggregate spending less than the value of the prize, their expected profits would be positive. This would induce entry by other rent-seekers until profits are driven to zero. Tullock's postulate is based on the Tullock game and his observation that when $R > n/(n-1)$, the sum of the solutions to each player's first order conditions exceeds the value of the prize Q. Tullock (1980, 1984, 1985, 1987, 1989) devoted considerable attention to this possibility, presumably because of the strong implication for excessive social waste.[3] Indeed, as R increased, the amount of overdissipation would tend to infinity. A large literature emerged in an attempt to eliminate the apparent overdissipation of rents by altering the Tullock game.[4] Contributions in this line of research include Corcoran (1984), Corcoran and Karels (1985), Higgins, et al. (1987), Michaels (1988), Allard (1988), Leininger (1993), Leininger and Yang (1994) and Ellingsen (1991).

It is now widely recognized (Hillman and Samet (1987), Baye, et al. (1989, 1993, 1994, 1996)) that expected overdissipation is not part of a Nash equilibrium to the Tullock game for any value of R, even as R approaches infinity. The reason is that the Tullock game has a pure strategy Nash equilibrium if and only if $R \leq n/(n-1)$. For $R > n/(n-1)$ the symmetric solution to the players' first order conditions for expected payoff maximization does not yield a global maximum; at this solution players have a negative expected payoff, which is dominated by bidding zero. Thus, Tullock's postulate is based on a false premise.

In light of this, it is perhaps surprising that we demonstrate below that the *overdissipation postulate* for which Tullock is most frequently criticized can, in fact, be defended on theoretical grounds within the confines of his original model! The defense, it turns out, relies on the fact that when the Tullock parameter exceeds n/(n–1) the Nash equilibrium involves mixed-strategies. Specifically, Baye, Kovenock, and de Vries (1994) show that equilibrium mixed strategies in the Tullock game do not permit *overdissipation in expectation*: the expected total amount spent competing for rents cannot exceed the value of the prize.[5] However, since the equilibrium involves mixed-strategies, it turns out that for particular realizations of the mixed strategies the total amount spent competing for rents can exceed the value of the prize! In fact, we show below that the cross-sectional *incidence of overdissipation* may be quite high. For a symmetric perfectly discriminating contest ($R = \infty$), the probability of overdissipation in a symmetric equilibrium is roughly one-half, ranging from exactly one-half in the two player case to approximately .44 as the number of players approaches infinity.

The implication of this is straightforward: even when rent-seekers have complete information and are "perfect calculators", roughly one-half of the time they will spend more in the aggregate than the prize is worth. Roughly equally frequently they will, as a group, spend less than it is worth. This stochastic nature of the overdissipation of rents when $R > n/(n - 1)$ is the conceptual innovation that we examine in Sections 2 and 3 of this paper.

2. Defining the overdissipation of rents

For the two player case, Tullock postulated that equilibrium entails the overdissipation of rents when $R > 2$. As we noted in the introduction, in this case the only Nash equilibria to the Tullock game are in nondegenerate mixed-strategies. For this reason, it is necessary to distinguish between the expected level of rent dissipation that arises based on the ex ante strategies employed by players, and the level of rent dissipation that arises ex post (that is, for particular realizations of the strategies). In addition, it is useful to distinguish situations where the group as a whole spends more than the value of the prize (either in an ex ante or ex post sense) from those in which one or more individuals each spend more than the value of the prize. This gives rise to four alternative notions of the *overdissipation* of rents:

(EIO) **Expected Individual Overdissipation** occurs if an individual player's expected bid exceeds the value of the prize.

(EAO) **Expected Aggregate Overdissipation** occurs if the expected sum of the payments by the players exceeds the value of the prize.

(PIO) **Probabilistic Individual Overdissipation** occurs if there is a positive probability that an individual player bids more than the value of the prize.

(PAO) **Probabilistic Aggregate Overdissipation** occurs if there is a positive probability that the sum of all players' bids exceeds the value of the prize.

The following result is immediate and shows the relation among these four definitions of overdissipation.

Proposition 1: For the Tullock game,
(a) EIO $\Rightarrow$ EAO $\Rightarrow$ PAO;
(b) EIO $\Rightarrow$ PIO $\Rightarrow$ PAO.

Thus, for the Tullock game, the broadest of the definitions of overdissipation is PAO, and the most narrow is EIO. Notice that the contrapositive of Proposition 1 implies that if there is not probabilistic aggregate overdissipation, then there is not overdissipation in the other three senses either.

3. Equilibrium overdissipation in the Tullock model?

We begin with

Proposition 2: There do not exist equilibria to the Tullock game in which EAO, EIO, or PIO arise.

The formal proof of this proposition merely involves extending the results in Baye, Kovenock and de Vries (1994) from the two player case to the n-player case, and is thus omitted. The essential intuition can be seen by noting that a player can guarantee a payoff of at least zero by bidding zero. Hence, no equilibrium strategy can involve PIO, since bids above Q guarantee a negative payoff, and hence are strictly dominated. Similarly, no equilibrium can involve EIO because EIO requires PIO. Finally, since the above argument implies that $U_i(x_i, x_{-i}) \geq 0$ for every i, summing over all players and noting that the prize is awarded with probability one implies that no equilibrium can involve EAO. Furthermore, these arguments are valid for both pure and nondegenerate mixed-strategy equilibria.

Interestingly, however, the Tullock game does exhibit probabilistic aggregate overdissipation when R exceeds n/(n-1):

Proposition 3: Suppose R > n/(n-1). Then in any Nash equilibrium to the Tullock game, PAO arises.

Proposition 3 follows directly from that fact that equilibria to Tullock's original game involve non-degenerate mixed-strategies if R > n/(n-1). It indicates that an incidence of aggregate overdissipation is indeed possible in the original Tullock framework, but only in those instances where the equilibrium involves nondegenerate mixed-strategies and when one looks at *aggregate ex post* expenditures. We will illustrate that the actual incidence of overdissipation due to PAO can be quite high.

To this end we will use as a benchmark the perfectly discriminating (Hillman and Riley (1989)) or first-price all-pay auction (Baye et al. (1989, 1993, 1996)) version of the Tullock game. This game form is the limiting case of the Tullock game when R = ∞; thus, the probability that player i wins the prize is one if player i submits the highest bid and zero otherwise.[6] The R = ∞ case is a useful benchmark because Baye, Kovenock, and de Vries (1993) have shown that at this level of R the expected level of rent dissipation is maximized. Furthermore, when R = ∞ there is complete rent dissipation in the sense of EAO (the expected sum of the bids exactly equals the value of the prize).

Without loss of generality, suppose the value of the prize, Q, equals 1. Hence the payoff to player i as a function of the vector of bids of all n players is

$$U_i(x_1, x_2, \ldots, x_n) = \begin{cases} -x_i & \text{if } \exists j \text{ such that } x_j > x_i \\ \frac{1}{m} - x_i & \text{if i ties for high bid with } m-1 \text{ others} \\ 1 - x_i & \text{if } x_i > x_j \; \forall j \neq i. \end{cases}$$

For n = 2 the unique equilibrium of this game is symmetric (Hillman and Riley, 1989). For n > 2 there is a continuum of asymmetric equilibria as well as a unique symmetric equilibrium (Baye, Kovenock and de Vries, 1996). We focus here on the symmetric mixed-strategy equilibrium, which involves players randomizing according to a continuous mixed strategy with associated cumulative distribution function $F(x) \equiv x^{1/(n-1)}$ on [0,1]. This symmetric equilibrium fully dissipates rents in the sense of EAO, as do all of the asymmetric equilibria (Baye, Kovenock, and de Vries, 1996).

Since each player's bid is a random draw from F and the value of the prize is one, there cannot be overdissipation in the sense of either EAO, EIO, or PIO (this illustrates Proposition 2). However, notice that there is a positive probability that the sum of the realizations of the players' bids exceeds 1, i.e. the assumed value of the prize.

To see this, let $z = x_1 + x_2 + \ldots + x_n$ denote the sum of the bids. Notice that z is a random variable induced by the mixed strategies employed by the players, so let $G(Z) = \text{Prob}\{z \leq Z\}$ be its cumulative distribution function. The probability of overdissipation is given by the probability that the sum of the bids exceeds unity, which is $\text{Prob}\{z > 1\} = 1 - G(1)$. The symmetric Nash equilibrium mixed strategies imply that each x_i has a density $f(x_i) = a{x_i}^{a-1}$ on [0, 1], where $a = 1/(n-1)$. Hence,

$$G(1) = a^n \int_0^1 x_n^{a-1} \int_0^{1-x_n} x_{n-1}^{a-1} \cdots \int_0^{1-x_n-x_{n-1}\ldots-x_2} x_1^{a-1} dx_1 dx_2 \ldots dx_n. \quad (1)$$

We now state the following general result:

Proposition 4. Suppose $R = \infty$ and $n \geq 2$ in the original simultaneous-move Tullock game. Then in any symmetric equilibrium we have PAO $\in$ [0.44, 0.5]. More specifically:

a. The probability of aggregate overdissipation is

$$1 - G(1) = 1 - \left(\frac{n-1}{n}\right)\left[\Gamma\left(\frac{n}{n-1}\right)\right]^{n-1}. \quad (2)$$

where $\Gamma(t) = \int_0^\infty x^{t-1} e^{-x} dx$ is the *Gamma function*;

b. The probability of aggregate overdissipation is monotonically decreasing in the number of players;

c. The probability of aggregate overdissipation is maximized in the two player case in which the probability of aggregate overdissipation is exactly ½;[7]

d. In the limit as the number of players tends to infinity, the probability of aggregate overdissipation tends to $1 - e^{-\gamma} \approx .44$, where γ is Euler's constant.[8] Hence, the probability of aggregate overdissipation is bounded from below by .44.

Proof: See the Appendix.

Proposition 4 makes it clear that Tullock's postulate is, in a sense, correct: in the aggregate, rent-seekers may frequently spend more to win a prize than the prize is worth. This result helps explain why PAO is confirmed in some of the published experimental literature (cf. Millner and Pratt, 1989, 1990) as well as in the experiments we have run at the CREED laboratory, see Potters, de Vries and Van Winden (1997). The theoretical and empirical literatures can be reconciled because when $R > n/(n-1)$, equilibria of the Tullock game involve nondegenerate mixed-strategies.

It is worthwhile to provide some intuition for the contents of Proposition 4. In the two player case, it is easy to see why the incidence of aggregate overdissipation must be positive: with probability $\frac{1}{2} \cdot \frac{1}{2} = \frac{1}{4}$ both players bid more than $\frac{1}{2}$. As the number of players increases, players begin submitting low bids more frequently than higher ones. The increase in the number of players is not sufficient to offset this effect, and thus the incidence of aggregate overdissipation falls as the number of players rises. It is not too difficult to see why the incidence remains strictly within the interval (0, 1) as the number of players n increases. If the incidence of aggregate overdissipation tended to 1 as the number of players approached infinity, then in the limit the sum of the bids would exceed the value of the prize with probability one. This would violate individual rationality, since each player is guaranteed a payoff of at least zero in any Nash equilibrium. A similar arbitrage argument precludes the incidence from converging to zero as the number of players goes to infinity.

4. Other rent-seeking contests

It is of interest to apply our new definitions of overdissipation to other types of contests. This will also make it clear why it is useful to make a distinction between individual and aggregate overdissipation.

Consider, for instance, the (stationary) symmetric equilibrium of the two person symmetric war of attrition, which is equivalent to a second-price all-pay auction. Assume that the value of the prize and the cost to each player per unit of time spent fighting both equal one, and that there is no discounting. Each player's symmetric equilibrium strategy in this game is mixed and is represented by the cdf, $G(t) = 1 - e^{-t}$. This gives the probability that the player stops fighting before t. In the interpretation as a second-price all-pay auction it is the probability the player bids below t. The game ends at the minimum realized stopping time. The time elapsed equals the cost incurred by each player. Hence, the distribution of the cost incurred by each player fighting for the prize is the distribution of the minimum order statistic $G_{min}(t) = 1 - [1 - G(t)]^2 = 1 - e^{-2t}$, which also gives the distribution of the game's termination time.

The expected payoff to each player in this equilibrium is zero. Since each player incurs a cost of 1 per unit of time until the game ends, if the game stops after t = ½, the aggregate cost of the contest will exceed the value of the prize; overdissipation will arise. Hence, PAO characterizes the symmetric equilibrium. Aggregate overdissipation occurs with probability $1 - G_{min}(1/2) = e^{-1} \approx .368$, which is lower than in the first-price all-pay auction.

The war of attrition, unlike the first-price all-pay auction, also has the property that the probability of overdissipation by a *single* player is nonzero, i.e. PIO is also a property of the symmetric equilibrium. In this equilibrium, if the game ends after t = 1 *each* player's individual cost is greater than the value of the prize. This event has probability $1 - G_{min}(1) = e^{-2} \approx .135$.

This makes it clear that Tullock's original postulate is, in a way, correct; every individual player can make payments that are greater than the value of the prize. Individual overdissipation, however, cannot occur in the game Tullock examined (in which all players pay their own bids) or in the manner Tullock described (*ex ante* expectation).

Another rent-seeking contest in which it is possible for individual players to make payments greater than the value of the prize is the sad-loser auction. In this auction each player i simultaneously bids x_i. The highest bidder wins the prize (of value 1) and is refunded her bid. The remaining bidders forfeit their bids.

This type of auction might be viewed as a reduced-form for situations, such as contests for procurement contracts, in which the bids represent pre-award (prototype) development costs, and the winning bidder can recoup these costs under the terms of the contract. In the two bidder case the individual players' symmetric equilibrium bidding strategies are $G(x) = x/(1+x)$, which has an unbounded mean. Each player earns a zero payoff in expectation. The aggregate payment in the game is the minimum order statistic, which has a distribution $G_{min}(x) = 1 - [1/(1+x)]^2$. Hence the probability of aggregate overdissipation is $1 - G_{min}(1) = 1/4$. Since only the loser pays, this is also the probability that there is individual overdissipation by some player. Hence, PIO and thus also PAO characterize the symmetric equilibrium to this game.

Like the first price all-pay auction, the war of attrition and the sad loser auction are contests with complete information. Of course, if we allow for incomplete information it should not seem surprising that overdissipation is possible, and that the probability of overdissipation will depend on the distributional assumptions maintained when transforming the game to one of complete, but imperfect information in which types are chosen by nature. Due to the lack of a clear benchmark model, we omit a formal analysis at this stage.

5. Conclusion

Gordon Tullock has done the profession a great service by pointing to the need to understand how institutions affect the wasteful expenditure of resources on rent seeking. Tullock's (1980) description of rent seeking through a contest has become the industry's standard. This contest does not have a pure strategy equilibrium for a range of the exponent parameter R, but a mixed strategy solution exists. Initially, this was not well understood and led to some speculation that there might be overdissipation. As a response[9] several interesting perturbations of the game, including versions with a sequential move structure, risk aversion and entry, have been investigated. But as we have made clear (see Baye, Kovenock and de Vries (1994)), the Nash concept never leads to overdissipation in an expected sense as long as individuals have the chance to opt out of the game and receive a payoff of zero (by spending zero).

Even though the Nash concept precludes *expected* overdissipation in the Tullock game, for particular realizations of the players' mixed strategies, aggregate expenditures may exceed the value of the prize. In this paper we therefore introduced the concept of the incidence of overdissipation, and calculated this incidence for some of the standard contests used for modelling rent-seeking behavior. For the perfectly discriminating version of Tullock's original game, we showed that an increase in the number of players lowers the incidence, but it never drives it down to zero.

In light of the results in Section 3, we believe Tullock should reassess his distaste for mixed-strategy Nash equilibria. There are well-reasoned justifications of mixed-strategy Nash equilibria appearing in the literature (see, for instance, Brandenburger (1992)). For those like Tullock who are searching for a justification for overdissipation, it would seem that a powerful rationale for using mixed-strategies is that they can generate an incidence of overdissipation.[10]

Otherwise, one must not only propose an alternative solution concept for his game, but an alternative justification for the overdissipation of rents. Mixed strategies, as it turns out, provide both the needed solution concept as well as a defense for the Tullock postulate.

In concluding, we note that there are solution concepts that can rationalize overdissipation in expectation. For instance, it is possible to find rationalizable strategies that yield overdissipation in expectation. However, these strategy choices cannot constitute a Nash equilibrium and, hence, if the choices or conjectures generating them were mutual knowledge, at least one player would not be playing rationally. Likewise, overdissipation in expectation can arise in ϵ-equilibria to the Tullock game. However, when Gordon Tullock (1989) claims that the theory of efficient rent seeking is "based on the theory that people are perfect calculators", and dismisses experimental work for relying on the computational ability of MBA students who clearly "are not making correct calculations", it is clear that he has a Nash-like consistency requirement in mind. Section 3 above shows that *incidences* of aggregate overdissipation are not at odds with Nash consistency. Tullock's postulate is indeed correct: perfectly rational individuals might spend more, in the aggregate, competing for a prize than it is worth. But Tullock was right for the wrong reason.

Notes

1. See, for instance Posner (1975) and Fudenberg and Tirole (1987) in industrial organization, Krueger (1974) and Bhagwati (1982) in international trade, and Linster (1993) in the analysis of international alliances.
2. See surveys by Brooks and Heijdra (1989), Nitzan (1994), or Rowley (1991).
3. Tullock (1989) noted regarding the overdissipation result ... "when I demonstrated that perfect calculation leads to decidedly odd results even in a competitive market with free entry, I astonished myself". He went on to note that the original (1980) paper "was rejected by the *Journal of Political Economy* on the argument that it could not possibly be true that a competitive market would reach these results". In explaining why experiments run with MBA students for $n = 2$ and $R = 3$ did not yield overdissipation on average he reasoned "it is clear that the people concerned are not making correct calculations", and "it seems to me that ... these people do not understand the game".
4. In addition, numerous studies focus on the special case where $R = 1$ (see, for instance, Nitzan (1991); Paul and Wilhite (1991)). In this case, the solution to the first-order conditions do indeed yield a Nash equilibrium, but there is not overdissipation in the corresponding equilibrium.
5. Baye, Kovenock and de Vries (1994) analyze the case of $n = 2$ and $R > 2$. The method of proof is similar for $n > 2$ and $R > n/(n-1)$.
6. In the case of a tie among m players for the highest bid, each has a probability $(1/m)$ of winning the prize.
7. For $n = 3$ this probability is $1 - \pi/6 \approx 0.48$, while for $n = 4$ it is approximately 0.466.
8. See Abramovitz and Stegun (1965). Formally, γ is defined by

$$\gamma = \lim_{h\to\infty}\left[1 + \frac{1}{2} + \frac{1}{3} + \ldots + \frac{1}{h} - \log h\right].$$

9. The working paper version of this paper (Baye, Kovenock, and de Vries, 1997) contains a more detailed response to Tullock's (1995) comments.
10. Recent work by Che and Gale (1996) shows that the symmetric equilibrium mixed-strategies that we identify are identical to the pure strategy bidding functions that arise when rent-seekers face budget constraints and incomplete information about the size of rivals' budgets.

Appendix

To evaluate the multiple integral in equation (1) of the text, we use the following lemma:

Lemma A1: Let $\varphi(w) \equiv \int_0^{1-w} x^r(1-w-x)^s\,dx$. Then $\varphi(w) = (1-w)^{r+s+1}$ $\beta(r+1,\ s+1)$, where $\beta(r+1,\ s+1) \equiv \int_0^1 x^r(1-x)^s\,dx$ is the *Beta function*.
Proof:

$$\begin{aligned}\varphi(w) &\equiv \int_0^{1-w} x^r(1-w-x)^s\,dx \\ &= (1-w)^{r+s+1}\int_0^1 t^r(1-t)^s\,dt \\ &= (1-w)^{r+s+1}\beta(r+1, s+1)\end{aligned}$$

by the change of variable $t = x/(1-w)$. **Q.E.D.**

Proof of Proposition 4:

(a) Applying the Lemma (taking $w = 1 - x_n - x_{n-1} - \ldots - x_2$, $r = a-1$, $s = 0$, and $x = x_1$) gives us

$$G(1) = a^n \int_0^1 x_n^{a-1} \int_0^{1-x_n} x_{n-1}^{a-1} \cdots \int_0^{1-x_n-\ldots-x_3} x_2^{a-1}(1 - x_1 - \ldots - x_2)^a$$
$$\beta(a, 1)dx_2dx_3\ldots dx_n.$$

Again, using the Lemma (taking $w = 1 - x_1 - \ldots - x_3$, $r = a-1$, $s = a$, and $x = x_2$) gives

$$G(1) = a^n\beta(a, 1)\beta(a, a+1)\int_0^1 x_0^{a-1}\cdots\int_0^{1-x_n-\ldots-x_4}$$
$$x_3^{a-1}(1 - x_1 - \ldots - x_3)^{2a}dx_3\ldots dx_n,$$

and with $w = 1 - x_1 - \ldots - x_4$, $r = a-1$, $s = 2a$, and $x = x_3$,

$$G(1) = a^n\beta(a, 1)\beta(a, a+1)\beta(a, 2a+1)\int_0^1 x_n^{a-1}\cdots\int_0^{1-x_n-\ldots-x_3}$$
$$x_4^{a-1}(1 - x_n - \ldots - x_4)^{3a}dx_4\ldots dx_n.$$

Continuing in this fashion we obtain

$$\begin{aligned}G(1) &= a^n\beta(a, 1)\beta(a, a+1)\beta(a, 2a+1)\beta(a, 3a+1)\ldots\int_0^1 x_n^{a-1}(1-x_n)^{(n-1)a}dx_n \\ &= a^n\beta(a, 1)\beta(a, a+1)\beta(a, 2a+1)\beta(a, 3a+1)\ldots\beta(a, (n-1)a+1).\end{aligned}$$

Note that $\beta(a, b) = \frac{\Gamma(a)\Gamma(b)}{\Gamma(a+b)}$, where $\Gamma(t) = \int_0^\infty x^{t-1}e^{-x}dx$ is the *Gamma function*. Hence,[11]

$$\begin{aligned}G(1) = {}& a^n\frac{\Gamma(a)\Gamma(1)}{\Gamma(a+1)}\frac{\Gamma(a)\Gamma(a+1)}{\Gamma(2a+1)}\frac{\Gamma(a)\Gamma(2a+1)}{\Gamma(3a+1)}\cdots\frac{\Gamma(a)\Gamma((n-1)a+1)}{\Gamma(na+1)} \\ &= \frac{a^n[\Gamma(a)]^n}{\Gamma(na+1)} = \frac{[a\Gamma(a)]^n}{\Gamma(na+1)} = \frac{[\Gamma(a+1)]^n}{\Gamma(na+1)} = \left(\frac{1}{a+1}\right)[\Gamma(a+1)]^{n-1}.\end{aligned}$$

11. In these calculations we make use of the identities $\Gamma(t+1) = t\Gamma(t)$ and $\Gamma(n+1) = n!$, for t positive real and n positive integer valued.

Using the definition of a gives the form in equation (2) of the text.

(b) To establish monotonicity, let $P(a) = \frac{1}{1+a}[\Gamma(1+a)]^{1/a}$, where $a \in [0, 1]$, $a \equiv a(n) = 1/(n-1)$, and $n-1$ denotes number of opponents. It is sufficient to show that P(a) is decreasing in a, for this implies the probability of overdissipation, $1 - P(a(n))$, is increasing in n. Taking logs gives

$$\log P(a) = -\log(1+a) + \frac{1}{a}\log\Gamma(1+a).$$

Differentiating this expression yields

$$\frac{d\log P(a)}{da} = -\frac{1}{1+a} - \frac{1}{a^2}\log\Gamma(1+a) + \frac{1}{a}\Psi(a+1)$$

where Ψ is the Psi (or Digamma) function (see Abramowitz and Stegun, 1965). Limiting values are obtained by l'Hôpital's rule:

$$\frac{1}{a^2}[\log\Gamma(1+a) - a\Psi(1+a)]|_{a=0} =$$
$$\frac{\Psi(1+a)-\Psi(1+a)-a\Psi'(1+a)}{2a}|_{a=0} =$$
$$-\tfrac{1}{2}\Psi'(1+a)|_{a=0} = -\tfrac{1}{2}\Psi'(1) < 0$$

Hence

$$\frac{d\log P(a)}{da}|_{a=0} = -1 - \frac{1}{2}\Psi'(1) \approx -1.82 < 0$$

$$\frac{d\log P(a)}{da}|_{a=1} = -\frac{1}{2} - [\log\Gamma(2) - \Psi(2)] = -\frac{1}{2} - [0 - .42] = -.08 < 0.$$

To evaluate the intermediate values we write

$$\frac{d\log P(a)}{da} = \frac{1}{a^2}\left\{-\frac{a^2}{1+a} - \log\Gamma(1+a) + a\Psi(1+a)\right\} \qquad (A1)$$

and analyze the sign of the terms within the curled brackets on the interval (0,1). Differentiating the term in brackets yields

$$-\tfrac{2a}{1+a} + \tfrac{a^2}{(1+a)^2} - \Psi(1+a) + \Psi(1+a) + a\Psi'(1+a) =$$
$$a\Psi'(1+a) + \tfrac{a^2-2a-2a^2}{(1+a)^2} =$$
$$a[\Psi'(1+a) - \tfrac{2+a}{(1+a)^2}] =$$
$$a[\Psi'(1+a) - \tfrac{1}{1+a} - \tfrac{1}{(1+a)^2}]$$

We can concentrate on the term inside the last pair of square brackets, and write $y = 1 + a$, $y \in (1, 2)$, so that the derivative of the bracketed term becomes:

$$\Psi'(y) - \frac{1}{y} - \frac{1}{y^2}$$

We will show that this term does not change sign as $n \geq 2$ increases. Toward this end, note that

$$\Psi'(y) \equiv \int_0^\infty \frac{t\,e^{-yt}}{1-e^{-t}}dt$$

Now from the Taylor expansion of the exponential

$$\frac{1}{1-e^{-t}} = \frac{e^t}{e^t-1} = \frac{1+t+t^2/2+t^3/6+\dots}{t+t^2/2+t^3/6+\dots} = 1 + \frac{1}{t+t^2/2+t^3/6+\dots}$$

Hence, for $t \geq 0$:

$$\frac{t}{1-e^{-t}} = t + \frac{1}{1+t/2+t^2/6+\dots} \leq t + \frac{1}{1+t/2} \leq t + \frac{1}{1+t/2} \leq t+1$$

Thus

$$\begin{aligned}\Psi'(y) &< \textstyle\int_0^\infty (t+1)e^{-yt}dt \\ &= \textstyle\int_0^\infty te^{-yt}dt + \int_0^\infty e^{-yt}dt \\ &= \frac{1}{y}\textstyle\int_0^\infty tye^{-yt}dt + \frac{1}{y}\int_0^\infty ye^{-yt}dt \\ &= \frac{1}{y^2} + \frac{1}{y}\end{aligned}$$

and therefore

$$\Psi'(y) - \frac{1}{y} - \frac{1}{y^2} \leq 0.$$

Now the proof of monotonicity of $P(a)$ for $a \in [0, 1]$ is complete as

$$\frac{d \log P(a)}{da} = \frac{1}{a^2}\theta(a)$$

where $\theta(a)$ is the expression between curled brackets in (A1). At the end points

$$\theta(0) = 0, \theta(1) = -0.08 < 0$$

while the above analysis showed

$$\theta'(a) < 0 \text{ on } (0, 1] \text{ and } \theta'(0) = 0$$

Combining these gives

$$\theta(a) < 0 \text{ on } (0, 1]$$

Moreover,

$$1/a^2 > 0 \text{ on } (0, 1]$$

so that

$$\frac{d \log P(a)}{da} = \frac{1}{a^2}\theta(a) < 0 \text{ on } (0, 1]$$

Hence $\log P(a)$ is decreasing on $(0, 1]$. Incidently, note that

$$\log P(0) = \Psi(1) = \gamma \approx -.57$$

$$\log P(1) = -\log 2 \approx -.69$$

(c) This part follows directly from part (b).
(d) Setting h = n - 1, it follows that

$$\lim_{h\to\infty} \log\left[\Gamma\left(1+\frac{1}{h}\right)\right]^{h} = \lim_{h\to\infty}\left[\log\Gamma\left(1+\frac{1}{h}\right)\right]/(1/h),$$

which by l'Hôpital's rule equals

$$\lim_{h\to\infty}\left(\frac{\partial\Gamma(\omega)}{\partial\omega}/\,\Gamma(\omega)\right)|_{\omega=1+\frac{1}{h}}.$$

The expression $\frac{\partial\Gamma(\omega)}{\partial\omega}/\,\Gamma(\omega)$ is the Psi or Digamma function (see Abramowitz and Stegun (1965)) which, when evaluated at $\omega = 1$ is equal to $-\gamma$, where $\gamma \approx .5772$ is Euler's constant. Hence, as h (and hence n) goes to infinity

$$G(1) = \lim_{h\to\infty}\left(\frac{h}{h+1}\right)\left[\Gamma\left(\frac{h+1}{h}\right)\right]^{h} = e^{-\gamma} \approx .5615.$$

Therefore, in the limit, the probability of overdissipation is approximately 0.4385.

Abstract

By redirecting scarce resources away from socially productive employment, the pursuit of wealth transfers by special interest groups converts those transfers into social costs. In the limit, the available rents are fully dissipated and the welfare loss associated with rent seeking equals the sum of the value of the rent rectangle and the deadweight loss triangle. This article shows that by eliciting expenditures to defend existing rents, attempts to reform the rent-seeking society cannot lower the social cost bill; they can only add to it. Hence, the only way to avoid the reformer's dilemma is to not grant monopoly rights in the first place.

THE REFORMER'S DILEMMA

WILLIAM F. SHUGHART II
University of Mississippi

Tullock's (1980) concept of "efficient rent seeking" launched a literature exploring the extent to which available rents are likely to be dissipated in efforts to access them. The question of rent dissipation is a natural extension of Tullock's (1967) original insight that resources deployed in rent-seeking activities are wasted from society's point of view insofar as they are withdrawn from productive pursuits elsewhere in the economy and, hence, carry an opportunity cost denominated in units of foregone output or utility. The extent to which available rents are dissipated therefore helps determine the extent to which the welfare losses associated with tariffs, monopolies, and theft exceed the ordinary Harberger (1954) deadweight loss triangle or, to put it more simply, the extent to which wealth transfers are converted into social costs.[1]

But that is only the beginning. Efforts to privatize, deregulate, or otherwise reform the rent-seeking society can only increase the welfare costs associated with artificial output restrictions. Even if available rents are fully dissipated ex ante, expenditures to defend monop-

AUTHOR'S NOTE: I benefited from discussions with Robert Tollison.

oly rights add to the social cost bill. In the limit, the costs of rent seeking will exceed the value of the monopoly right by an amount equal to the successful rent seeker's private gains.

Consider Posner's (1975) familiar example. Ten risk-neutral bidders vie for a monopoly right known to be worth \$100,000 in present value terms. If bids are not refundable, lobbying is subject to constant cost conditions, and the selection process is unbiased, each will invest \$10,000 to capture the available rent. Rents are exactly dissipated under such conditions: \$100,000 is spent to capture \$100,000.[2] And if real resources are consumed in lobbying for the right to be the monopolist, the aggregate expenditure of \$100,000 is transformed into a Tullockian social cost.[3]

The successful rent seeker garners net proceeds of \$90,000, of course. Indeed, the prospect of capturing such gains is what motivates rent seeking in the first place.[4] This means, however, that the incumbent monopolist would be willing to spend up to \$90,000 to defend his rents against efforts to expropriate them. Hence, the reformer's dilemma: Proposals to privatize or deregulate government-created monopolies can raise the social costs of such policies considerably—in this case to as much as \$190,000.

For regulatory reform to have such socially costly effects, it must be unanticipated.[5] If rent seekers foresee the possibility that their rents will subsequently be reduced or eliminated, bids will be adjusted accordingly. But this does not resolve the reformer's dilemma. Lower bids ex ante simply mean that the successful rent seeker's private gains will be larger and his incentives to fight reform will be all the greater. Suppose, for example, that there is a 1 in 10 chance of deregulation. In present value terms, the monopoly right now has an expected value of \$90,000. Posner's 10 risk-neutral bidders will now each spend \$9,000 to capture the rent. This yields an ex post private gain of \$91,000 if deregulation does not occur, and that is the amount the incumbent monopolist would be willing to spend to prevent expropriation of the \$100,000 rent. Hence, whereas the threat of expropriation reduces the welfare costs of rent seeking (from \$100,000 to \$90,000 in our example), it raises the welfare costs of rent defending (from \$90,000 to \$91,000).[6]

Given that the possibility of reform lowers the aggregate amount invested in lobbying for monopoly rights, the politicians who grant such favors have incentives to create institutions that promote durability in legislative "contracts" (laws) that transfer wealth to favored special interests (Landes and Posner 1975). Given that successful rent seekers will spend nothing to defend their rights if deregulation is certain, the politicians who threaten to deprive special interests of their gains have, in return for appropriate compensation, incentives to exercise forbearance (McChesney 1997). Low probabilities of reform ex ante and few incidences of actual deregulation ex post maximize the political payoffs to the suppliers of monopoly rights and, pari passu, the social costs of rent seeking.

The dilemma identified herein, namely that a reformer can only increase the social costs of government-granted monopolies, adds to existing explanations for why deregulation is such a rare event.[7] Many of the costs of rent seeking are sunk and cannot be recovered even if deregulation should occur (McCormick, Shughart, and Tollison 1984). Nonprice competition within the regulated industry can cause costs to rise (Douglas and Miller 1974). Alternatively, the value of the monopoly rents can be capitalized into the prices of inputs or into the selling price of the regulated firm so that the owners earn only normal returns on their investments—creating what Tullock (1975) calls the "transitional gains trap."

Although it is of course true that reform can pay social dividends if all of the available rents have not been dissipated in rent-seeking or rent-defending activities (Crew and Rowley 1988) or if reformers are willing to impose capital losses on the "innocent" purchasers of previously granted public monopolies,[8] the moral of the story is to let sleeping monopolists lie.

NOTES

1. For a recent review of the literature on rent seeking, see Tollison (1997).

2. The exact (ex ante) dissipation result is robust under the assumption that the number of bidders is endogenous. See Corcoran (1984) and Higgins, Shughart, and Tollison (1985).

3. Bribery, which involves a simple cash transfer to the grantor of the monopoly right, consequently does not rise to the level of social cost.

4. For a discussion of the distinctions between rent seeking and profit seeking, see Buchanan (1980). Although animated by the same incentives, the key point is that output is fixed in the former case but not in the latter.

5. The reform process is itself costly; it is not modeled here. Any real resources devoted to reform must be added to the welfare costs of rent seeking.

6. Because the private gains from rent seeking increase as the number of bidders increases, a forward-looking extortionist has incentives to encourage entry into lobbying for monopoly rights.

7. A "utilitarian reformer" would devote resources to the reform effort up to the point where the anticipated social gains (the Harberger triangle plus the present value of any undissipated monopoly rents) are just equal to the anticipated social costs of deregulation or privatization, which costs include expenditures by the incumbent monopolist to defend his rents against expropriation and the costs of the reformer's own efforts. The incumbent may find it worthwhile to spend enough to make deregulation socially unprofitable in this case. On the other hand, a "factionalist reformer" who cares about wealth transfers but not about social costs and benefits may outspend the incumbent monopolist, rendering the social value of reform negative. The social costs of rent seeking will obviously be considerably higher in the latter case. See Tollison and Wagner (1991).

8. The compensation currently being paid for the "stranded costs" of regulated electric utilities suggests a political unwillingness to impose such capital losses (McChesney 1999).

ORCHESTRATING RENT SEEKING CONTESTS*

Mark Gradstein and Kai A. Konrad

Contests have different, sometimes quite complex, organisational structures. In particular, while most of the existing literature focusses on simultaneous contests, multistage contests are also quite frequently encountered. This paper seeks to provide a rationale for the latter by endogenising the choice of a contest structure, which is made by an organiser of a contest interested in maximising the efforts expended by the contenders.

Contexts as seemingly diverse as economic organisations, sport competitions, wars, competition for natural monopoly, patent races and political rent seeking can be described as contests whereby contestants expend resources to win a prize. A classical example is the natural monopoly setting. The opportunity of making monopolistic profits invites competitive rent seeking endeavors on the part of the potential monopolists each seeking to ensure the privileged position in the industry for itself by influencing the politicians. The literature on rent seeking (see Nitzan 1994 for a survey) studies these situations focusing in particular on the relationship between the outlay made in the course of such competition on the one hand and the rent at stake on the other hand.[1]

Contest design, that is the set of rules that define the victorious contestant(s), clearly has incentive effects as far as the amount of effort expended by the contestants goes. The interest in the amount expended by the rent seekers to win the rent relative to the value of the rent itself naturally begs the question of design of rent seeking contests.[2] For one thing, according to the dominant view in the rent-seeking literature, the politicians who allocate rents value high outlay and had they some freedom of choice to design a contest, they would choose the one that results in its maximisation. From a normative perspective, therefore, studying contest design may help to indicate which constraints, if any, should be imposed on the ability to design a contest – indeed, in reality such constraints are often imposed either at the constitutional or at the legislative stage of the political process. From a positive perspective, the particular contest used by a politician to allocate a rent among rent seekers is

* The authors are indebted to two referees and the editor of this JOURNAL for their valuable comments and suggestions.

[1] Being an ubiquitous social phenomenon, contests have been extensively studied in a variety of other contexts as well, including labour market reward structures (see e.g., Rosen, 1986; Glazer and Hassin, 1988), conflict theory (Hirshleifer, 1991; Skaperdas, 1992, 1995), and political competition (Hillman and Ursprung, 1988; Skaperdas and Grofman, 1995).

[2] Tullock's (1980) seminal paper that predicts the amount expended in a contest to be almost equal to the value of the rent has provoked much research interest. Different comparative statics results pertaining to the contestants' outlay have been derived in the literature since then. For instance, it turns out that the outlay is larger when the contestants are similar (with regard to their abilities, tastes, etc.) and if their number is big (Hillman and Riley 1989; Gradstein 1995). For the effect of risk aversion see Hillman and Katz (1984) and Konrad and Schlesinger (1997). Total outlay is smaller when the contestants first choose an order of play and then carry out the actual rent seeking game (see Morgan, 1998, and references therein); or when collective benefits exist (Nitzan, 1991).

itself the outcome of a political process in the course of which the bureaucrat – who will benefit from future rent seeking – would lobby for a design that leads to a larger rent-seeking effort. Our paper suggests the kind of a contest this should be.

Indeed, some work has been done on contest design in the last decade. Appelbaum and Katz (1987), Dixit (1987) and Michaels (1989) are early contributions to the issue; more recently, Baye *et al.* (1993) have studied optimal admittance to a contest; Lazear (1996, pp. 79–83) discusses the use of multiple prizes in a contest where contestants differ in their contest abilities; and Dasgupta and Nti (1998) have focused on the possibility for an organiser of a contest to retain part of the prize. All these papers, however, only study simultaneous (S-) contests letting the organiser choose different parameters within this framework. In contrast, here the structure of matches in the contest itself is the choice parameter, so that the winners from each stage of the overall contest are promoted to the next stage. In reality, contests exhibit various structures. For instance, while in some sport disciplines (formula I races, or long jump), we observe simultaneous contests, in other disciplines, such as tennis championships or soccer world cups, the contestants compete in multi-stage contests which consist of a series of pairwise contests – these will be labelled T-contests, as their structure resembles a tree.

Sometimes the contest structure is exogenously given. Our framework may then be used to predict in which type of contest efforts are larger – the examples of potential applicability include R&D contests and contests that are caused by technological change.[3] In other applications the contest structures are the outcome of a careful design with the view of attaining a variety of objectives, one of which is maximisation of efforts by contenders. This is certainly the case in sports, but also in other settings as well. Internal organisational design is one case in point.[4] Indeed, Keren and Levhari (1983) and Sah (1991), the former arguing from the information-theoretic perspective and the latter in the decision-theoretic framework, have shown that a multistage organisational structure may well be optimal. We suggest yet another view of organisations, according to which one can interpret the organisation's hierarchy in a steady state as consisting of a series of contests among the individual members of each level of the hierarchy for the promotion to an upper level.

[3] For instance, in monopolistic competition, technological change may change the equilibrium structure in an industry and in particular decrease the equilibrium number of firms. A series of such changes may cause a stepwise reduction in the equilibrium number of firms. The process of adjustment to the new equilibrium industry structure often has the feature of a contest: firms make sunk investments in R&D and/or in excess capacity (Thum, 1995) in order to increase their chances of surviving, and these costs cannot be recovered even if the firm has to exit. The contest nature of dynamic competition has been recognised in the R&D literature, and in the literature on network externalities (e.g., Besen and Farrell 1994). If the technology shocks are relatively small, we observe a series of contests with the winning firms in each stage qualifying for the next contest stage – the structure is similar to a T-contest. With drastic shocks, the number of contest stages is much smaller and, if one big shock yields the new long term industry equilibrium structure, the contest resembles an S-contest.

[4] Likewise, in political situations, multistage contests are very common, either explicitly as in the case of candidate selection in the primaries and the subsequent presidential elections, or implicitly, when only individuals elected for an office are qualified to run for a higher office.

Which hierarchical structure then is the one that induces the maximal overall effort across these contests?[5]

Structural design that maximises overall contest effort is the main focus of this paper.[6] Our results indicate that the optimal contest structure hinges on how discriminatory the contest is – that is, on the relative importance of contestants' effort to win the prize versus random factors. When the contest rules are discriminatory enough, and only then, does the S-contest elicit more effort; otherwise, the T-contest elicits more effort. An interesting corollary of our analysis implies that when contest structure can be optimally adjusted, then as the number of contenders grows large, the amount of exerted effort equals the value of the assigned prize. The rent is 'fully dissipated'. This is in stark contrast to the simultaneous contest case which has been extensively studied in the rent-seeking literature, where the sum of contest efforts is equivalent to the prize only when the contest is sufficiently discriminatory. Thus, our result that effort equal to the value of the contested rent can be elicited for any discriminatory extent of the contest technology contributes to the intense debate in the rent seeking literature on the ratio between equilibrium contest effort and the value of the rent in contests that originated with Tullock's (1980) paper.

1. Ingredients of a Contest

In the contests considered below, we assume that n players expend efforts in an attempt to win a prize of V.[7] Each player's payoff is the same: the expected value of the prize less the amount of own effort, where the winning probabilities depend on the players' efforts.[8] The contest may consist of a series of single stage contests. We assume that in a single stage of a contest with j

[5] In the related context of internal labour markets, the literature on tournaments (see e.g., Lazear and Rosen (1981) and Green and Stokey (1983)) has examined the optimal incentive schemes to ensure a maximal effort. In contrast to the rent seeking models, this literature typically invokes the assumption that the amount to be divided among the contestants is affected by their effort, which is non-observable or non-verifiable.

[6] Three other contributions belong to this research agenda. Lazear (1996, pp. 127–33) considers two-stage contests that differ with respect to the number of matches played. In particular, he compares knock-out systems and all-play-all contests. The number of contest stages is exogenous, but contestants differ with respect to ability. Gradstein (1998) compares simultaneous and pairwise multistage contests with a specific probability-of-winning function addressing the issue of timing of effort exertion which is absent in this paper, but without taking up the general problem of contest design, namely, what contest structure is optimal when the class of admissible contests contains all multistage (and single-stage) contests. Amegashie (1998) studies shortlisting of contestants, whereby a contest can only include a subset of potential candidates who compete for the right to enter the contest prior to the contest itself, focusing on the conditions under which shortlisting can reduce/increase the amount of resources spent. Thus, shortlisting constitutes a special case of our multistage contest with only two stages. This restricted framework, however, is unable to address the issue of the optimal number of stages in a contest, which is a central element of the contest design here.

[7] We assume in this paper that the contest rules, specifying in particular the winning odds, are exogenously given and focus exclusively on contest matching structure.

[8] This implicitly assumes that the marginal cost of effort is 1; the results can be easily extended, however, to allow any constant marginal cost.

contenders for a prize, these probabilities are given by the Tullock (1980) contest success function:[9]

$$p_i(b_1, \ldots b_j) = \frac{b_i^\gamma}{\sum_{h=1}^{j} b_h^\gamma}. \tag{1}$$

The parameter γ can be interpreted as a measure of how decisive relative contest effort is, or how discriminatory the contest rules are. For instance, when γ tends to zero, the probabilities in (1) tend to $1/j$, indicating that the designation of the winner is independent of effort. When γ tends to infinity, the contest becomes fully discriminatory: the prize is always awarded to the contestant who exerts the most effort, and the random elements of the outcome disappear.

Contestant i's payoff in such generic contest is

$$\frac{Mb_i^\gamma}{\sum_{h=1}^{j} b_h^\gamma} - b_i, \tag{2}$$

if M is the prize awarded in this single-stage contest. To ensure existence of pure strategy equilibria in each such contest we impose the restriction $0 < \gamma \leqslant j/(j-1)$. Then the equilibrium amount of individual effort can be directly derived:

$$b_i = b = \gamma M(j-1)/j^2. \tag{3}$$

Consider now the general (multi-stage) contest among n participants for the prize of V. In the first round, they are divided into several groups and compete within each group by expending effort. The winner in each group – who is determined according to (1) – goes up to the next round, where the contestants are again grouped into competition groups, etc. An optimal contest should determine the number of rounds and the individual grouping in each round, whereby contest structure is evaluated from the perspective of the organiser whose objective is maximisation of effort. Letting A_k denote the total effort level in the kth round, the organiser's objective, therefore, is maximisation of

$$E = A_1 + \ldots + A_L, \tag{4}$$

where L is the number of rounds.

2. Effort Maximising Contests

We start the analysis of the optimal (effort maximising) contest structure with the following observation.

LEMMA 1. *For any given number of rounds, the group size within each stage should be equal across the competing groups.*

[9] See Skaperdas (1996) for its axiomatisation.

Proof. Suppose that N individuals compete in a single round to win a prize whose value we normalise to 1. Let them be divided into r (exogenously given) groups, where g_j, $j = 1, \ldots, r$, is the size of group j. The prize is awarded with equal probabilities to the r winners of this round. Hence, the expected prize for each winning individual is $1/r$, and previous considerations allow us to establish that the amount of effort each group will expend, the probabilities of winning being as in (1), is $\gamma(1/r)(g_j - 1)/g_j$. Summing up, we obtain that total effort is $\gamma(1/r)\sum_{j=1}^{r}(g_j - 1)/g_j$ which is maximised (subject to $g_1 + \ldots + g_r = N$) when $g_1 = \ldots = g_r$. □

Let therefore g_k, $k = 1, \ldots, m$, be the size of each of the competition groups in the kth last round, and let α_k denote the dissipation rate in this round, that is, the ratio between the amount of contest effort and the size of the prize. Then total effort expended in the final is $\alpha_1 V$, leaving an undissipated rent of $(1 - \alpha_1) V$. Each of the finalists has the same chances of winning this rent, whose expected value for them is $(1 - \alpha_1) V/g_1$, implying that in all semifinals a total effort of $\alpha_2(1 - \alpha_1) V$ is expended, etc. Thus proceeding backwards we obtain that total effort is given by:

$$E = \left[\sum_{k=1}^{m} \alpha_k \prod_{i=0}^{k-1}(1 - \alpha_i)\right] V \tag{5}$$

with

$$\alpha_k = \gamma(g_k - 1)/g_k, \; k = 1, \ldots m, \; \text{and } g_0 \equiv 1, \; \text{so that } \alpha_0 = 0. \tag{6}$$

Furthermore, since in each competition group a single contestant emerges as a winner, who then proceeds to the next round, we obtain that multiplying the number of individuals in a group across rounds gives us the total number of individuals:

$$n = \prod_{k=1}^{m} g_k. \tag{7}$$

The problem now is to choose the size of a group in each round, g_k, $k = 1, \ldots, m$, so as to maximise (5) subject to (6) and (7). Note that the objective function (5) is concave with respect to α_k, $k = 1, \ldots, m$. Furthermore, the composite function

$$F(g_1, \ldots, g_m) = \left(\sum_{k=1}^{m}[\gamma(g_k - 1)/g_k] \prod_{i=0}^{k-1}\{1 - [\gamma(g_i - 1)/g_i]\}\right) V \tag{8}$$

that is obtained from (5) by substitution of (6) is continuous, whereas its domain is compact, ensuring existence of a solution to the maximisation problem. The following lemma constitutes an important step to finding the solution.

LEMMA 2. *For a given number of rounds, the optimal group size is the same across rounds.*

Proof. We form the Lagrangean:

$$L(g_1, \ldots, g_m) = F(g_1, \ldots, g_m) - \lambda\left(\prod_{j=1}^{m} g_j - n\right) =$$

$$\left(\sum_{k=1}^{m}[\gamma(g_k - 1)/g_k]\prod_{i=0}^{k-1}\{1 - [\gamma(g_i - 1)/g_i]\}\right)V - \lambda\left(\prod_{j=1}^{m} g_j - n\right). \quad (9)$$

Differentiating with respect to g_k we obtain after some manipulations the following first order conditions:

$$\gamma V \frac{\prod_{i=1}^{m}\{1 - [\gamma(g_i - 1)/g_i]\}}{g_k\{1 - [\gamma(g_k - 1)/g_k]\}} = \lambda n, \; k = 1, \ldots, m. \quad (10)$$

Inspection of the system of equations in (10) reveals the solution of $g_k = g_{k+1} = g$, implying that the group size should be the same in all rounds of the contest. □

To examine the implications of this result for the optimal number of rounds, we note that the constraint in (7) is now rewritten as follows:

$$n = g^m \quad (11)$$

and the objective function (8) has the form

$$F(g, \ldots, g) = \gamma V[(g - 1)/g] \sum_{i=0}^{m-1}[1 - \gamma(g - 1)/g]^i$$

$$= V\{1 - [1 - \gamma(g - 1)/g]^m\}. \quad (12)$$

Hence the optimal number of rounds is the solution of minimising

$$[1 - \gamma(g - 1)/g]^m \quad (13)$$

subject to (11). Substituting (11), the sign of the derivative of (13) with respect to m is the same as the sign of

$$[1 - \gamma(g - 1)/g]\ln[1 - \gamma(g - 1)/g] + \gamma \ln g/g \quad (14)$$

where g is given by (11). Note that when $\gamma = 0$ and when $\gamma = 1$, (14) equals zero irrespectively of m. Furthermore, (14) is a convex function of γ and it increases when $\gamma = 1$. Hence, when $\gamma = 1$, the different contest structures are equivalent and induce the same total effort. Also, (14) is positive when $\gamma > 1$ and is negative when $\gamma < 1$ implying that the optimal number of rounds is the smallest possible (that is, one) when $\gamma > 1$ and is the largest possible when $\gamma < 1$.

Hence, the simultaneous (S-) contest of all participants is the effort maximising contest structure in the former case, and the pairwise multistage (T-, for tree) contest is the effort maximising structure in the latter case (see Fig. 1 which depicts an S- contest and a T-contest, each with 8 contenders).

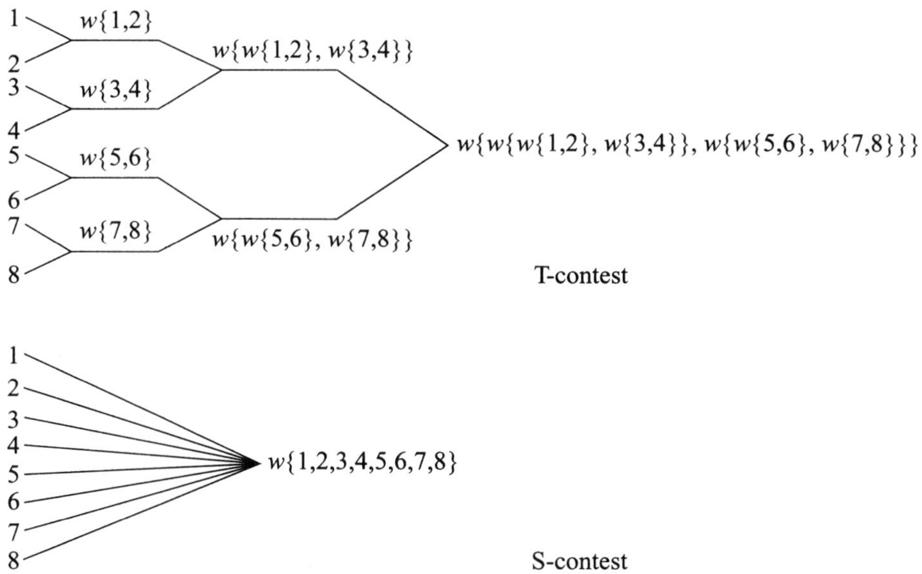

Fig. 1.

To sum up,

PROPOSITION 1. *When $\gamma = 1$, all different contest structures are equivalent provided that the group size is the same in each round of a contest; when $\gamma > 1$, the S-contest is the effort maximising contest structure; and when $\gamma < 1$, the T-contest emerges as the effort maximising structure.*

Table 1 illustrates the performance, in terms of the elicited effort, of the optimally adjusted contest structure, comparing a T-contest and an S-contest, for different values of the parameters.

In the rent seeking literature, the extent of rent dissipation – in particular,

Table 1.

Rent dissipation (the share of effort expended relatively to the prize) under a T-contest (left-hand side numbers) and an S-contest (right-hand side numbers); cells are blank whenever a pure strategy equilibrium under a S-contest is non-existent.

n	$\gamma = 0.1$	$\gamma = 0.3$	$\gamma = 0.5$	$\gamma = 0.7$	$\gamma = 0.9$	$\gamma = 1.1$
4	$0.10 > 0.09$	$0.28 > 0.23$	$0.44 > 0.38$	$0.58 > 0.53$	$0.70 > 0.68$	$0.80 < 0.83$
8	$0.14 > 0.09$	$0.39 > 0.26$	$0.59 > 0.44$	$0.73 > 0.61$	$0.83 > 0.79$	$0.91 < 0.96$
32	$0.23 > 0.10$	$0.56 > 0.29$	$0.76 > 0.48$	$0.88 > 0.68$	$0.95 > 0.87$	
128	$0.30 > 0.10$	$0.68 > 0.30$	$0.87 > 0.50$	$0.95 > 0.69$	$0.98 > 0.89$	
1,024	$0.40 > 0.10$	$0.80 > 0.30$	$0.94 > 0.50$	$0.99 > 0.70$	$1.00 > 0.90$	

the issue whether or not rent dissipation is complete for a large number of contestants – has always been a subject of intense controversy. It was argued that the answer to this question hinges on the nature of the contest success function: if it is sufficiently non-discriminatory (i.e., when $\gamma < 1$), then rent dissipation will be incomplete. Our results show that this conclusion, while correct when applied to S-contests, is incorrect when more flexibility in designing contests is allowed, because when n tends to infinity the effort level induced by the T-contest converges to V implying complete rent dissipation. This can be confirmed from (12), which tends to V as n tends to infinity. Hence, we obtain

PROPOSITION 2. *When the contest structure is optimally adjusted, then complete rent dissipation is achieved for a large number of contestants, independently of the discriminatory extent of the contest technology.*

Table 1 above illustrates the power of a T-contest for $\gamma < 1$, showing the speed of convergence to full rent dissipation for different values of n.

3. Concluding Remarks

This paper studies the issue of optimal structure of matches in contests. The significance of this study comes from the observation that contests may have multiple rounds, with winners of the rounds competing with each other. The design of a contest, therefore, should clearly address the issue of multistage contests.

While this paper focuses on certain aspects of contest design, many more issues are left for consideration in future research. For instance, we have assumed identical individuals. In the world of heterogeneous individuals differing with respect to their tastes and/or abilities, these differences should be taken into account when thinking about contest design. Risk aversion – both of the contestants and the organiser – may also be an important factor. For example, when the contestants are risk averse, big contests with a great deal of strategic uncertainty may be inferior to a series of smaller multistage contests. Finally, while the prize here has been assumed indivisible, an alternative assumption would introduce new considerations into the optimal design such as the allocation of the prize in the different rounds of the contest to the respective winners in these rounds.

We believe, however, that these extensions, while valuable and worth pursuing are unlikely to change the main messages of this paper. To sum them up in a nutshell our results indicate that the effort maximising structure of a contest hinges on the extent of the decisiveness of a contest – that is, on the relative importance of one's effort to win the prize versus random factors. If the individual effort is sufficiently important, then simultaneous contests induces the larger total effort of the participants, and if random factors dominate, then a multistage contest which consists of pairwise matches does so. These results imply in particular that when contest structure can be optimally adjusted, then full rent dissipation is attained at the limit, independently of the discriminatory nature of the contest success function. This conclusion contradicts the view derived from modelling simultaneous contests that the extent of rent dissipation hinges on the success technology as embodied in the contest success function.

Ben Gurion University

Free University of Berlin

Date of receipt of first submission: February 1998
Date of receipt of final typescript: January 1999

Gordon Tullock: Master of the Muck and Mire

ALAN LOCKARD
Center for the Study of Public Choice, George Mason University, Fairfax, VA

Some 20 years ago Gordon Tullock wrote the article on "Efficient Rent Seeking" which begins this collection. He submitted it the *Journal of Political Economy*, which rejected it. The article was eventually published in *Towards a Theory of the Rent-Seeking Society*, and spawned an enormous literature, a portion of which is reproduced in this volume. At the time we began compiling this collection, the article had been cited over 200 times, and I am sure that figure will continue to grow. The article clearly qualifies as a seminal contribution to the rent-seeking literature.

In this article, Tullock challenged the intuitively appealing proposition that in a contest for a known prize, contestants will expend resources until the sum of such expenditures is equal to the prize. He argued, instead, that rent-seeking expenditures will be set such the marginal benefit of those expenditures will equal the marginal expected return. In this model, the degree of dissipation of rents depends on the number of contestants and on whether the contest exhibits increasing, decreasing, or constant returns to rent-seeking expenditures. In the case of increasing returns, it is possible to have a contest in which the equilibrium expenditure of each of several contestants exceeds the value of the prize. The only rational strategy is to not enter the contest, unless all other potential contestants rationally stay out, in which case any single entrant would win. This is Tullock's rent-seeking paradox.

Tullock has often referred to this unsolved paradox in terms of a swamp.[1] Various theorists have attempted to resolve the paradox, and our understanding of these sorts of contests has been clearly been advanced, as this volume shows. In his comments on these articles Tullock acknowledges the advances, but continually reminds us that the underlying paradox remains. Tullock has characterized his role in the debate as an unfortunate one, which he reluctantly accepts. Don't you believe it. He likes pushing people into swamps.

Although I am sure he is sincere in his assertions that he would like this particular puzzle solved, his whole career has been dedicated to pointing out that the familiar firmament upon which we rest our assumptions is not so solid as it appears. He has challenged our dearly, and too often uncritically, held beliefs in widely diverse areas, including Law and Economics, Sociobiology and Public Choice, a discipline he founded, along with James Buchanan. His

---

[1] His comments on articles in this area have titles such as *Back to the bog*, *Another part of the swamp*, and *Still somewhat muddy: A comment.*

original thinking has not always been met with open arms. His *The Logic of the Law* was the first book published in the area of Law and Economics, but the discipline did not take off until less controversial publications emerged from such contributors as Richard Posner. It was not unusual for him to have articles rejected several times before finally finding their way into print, and being heavily cited thereafter.[2] That was the certainly the case for the lead article in this collection.

I hope I will not offend any of the authors of the fine contributions to this volume if I suggest that the most important insights in this volume remain those offered in Tullock's original article. Unless we know the degree to which marginal returns to rent-seeking are increasing, decreasing or constant, we cannot know *a priori* if the equilibrium expenditures in pursuit of a prize will be less than, equal to or greater than the prize. Total rent-seeking expenditures will be less than the prize if the marginal returns to rent-seeking are sufficiently decreasing, while if the marginal returns to rent-seeking are sufficiently increasing, equilibrium rent-seeking expenditures may be so large that entry into a multi-party contest is an inherently losing proposition. These insights can advance our understanding of rent-seeking activities under varying institutional frameworks. It seems plausible that the returns to rent-seeking expenditures in a constitutional democracy, such as the United States, would fall off sharply once lobbyists win the opportunity to make their case, face to face, with a sufficient number of legislators. This may explain why lobbying expenditures are so low relative to the size of transfers in the United States budget.[3] The model suggests that in regimes where returns to rent-seeking would presumably be increasing, such as despotic governments, the contest may incorporate efforts to preclude competition for rents, which would be self-defeating. Monopolization of rent-seeking privileges could be achieved through the establishment of cronyism. Violence may also play a part in deterring entry under such regimes. Tullock, ever eager to challenge our familiar preconceptions, even applies his model to demonstrate that nepotism and hereditary monarchy are (at least potentially) socially beneficial.[4]

The contributors to this volume have certainly advanced our understanding of the properties of contests such as those proposed by Tullock. They have described various circumstances under which the apparent paradox would be resolved, often by suggesting that the contestants could adopt a mixed strategy. Leave it to Tullock to point out that there is no mechanism by which the contestants, by responding to their individual incentives, could discover such stochastic strategies, and even if they did, no particular reason

---

[2] See Brady and Tollison, 1991, *Gordon Tullock: Creative maverick of public choice.*
[3] See Tullock, 1997, *Where's the rectangle?*
[4] See *Efficient Rent Seeking*, the lead article in this volume.

why they should adhere to them if they did. The implications of this critique extend far beyond the immediate problem at hand. Once again, the firmament recedes under Tullock's discerning gaze.

We have chosen to close this collection of articles with another of Tullock's contributions. It does not directly address the paradox which is the focus of the rest of this volume, nor is it placed in the order of publication, as the rest of our entries are. Tullock's article on the metaphysical problem of the costs of rent-seeking does serve to remind us, though, that, however deep the rent-seeking bog originally appeared based on our lead article, the swamp is actually much deeper than that. Which leaves mire-master Tullock in his preferred habitat. Despite his protestations otherwise, He seems happiest beside the muck he has revealed to us, ever ready to push back in those who think they have finally found solid ground.

The costs of rent seeking: A metaphysical problem

GORDON TULLOCK
Department of Economics, Building 23, University of Arizona, Tucson, AZ 85721

It is well known that one of the reasons that Congressmen vote for such things as protective tariffs and the farm subsidy program is that they think it will attract votes. Economists are almost always opposed to these items because they think that they injure the voters. Technically speaking, what happens is that the voters specialize their vote, i.e., concentrate their entire preference function on one particular issue (or a few issues) which has considerable importance to them. Other voters, concentrating their voting decision on other special issues, ignore the well-being of the first voter.

Economists would argue that all of the voters are worse off than if they had not so specialized their votes. On the other hand democracy is supposed to give the voter his choice, not what some economists think that they should choose. The voters vote for such things. Can we count this as a cost?

There is another problem here, which is that voters are apt to be very badly informed. Indeed any *Public Choice* scholar worth his salt at sometime during his teaching proves to his students that the rational voter who gives thought to the matter will decide not to be well informed about politics unless he happens to regard politics as a hobby.

As an example of the difficulties here, consider the following from the former Chairman of the President's Council of Economic Advisors Herbert Stein (1987:3): 'The "problem" of the deficit is to make the decisions as well informed and as responsive to the desires of the public as possible.' The problem, of course, is that if the public is systematically poorly informed, then the two criteria are inconsistent. And the public *is* systematically ill-informed.

The problem raised by individuals making choices, which from the outside seems to be unwise, is a real one. Do such choices impose a cost on the chooser? Note that in the market and in politics, this is a hard question to answer but fortunately in the market, it is rarely, if ever, an important question. If we are trying to measure the cost of rent seeking, it may be very important, indeed, because it may be the principal payoff to a Congressman for votes for, let's say the farm program, come in his reelection by voters who are voting because of the farm program. Is this a cost?

Let us digress a little bit and talk about costs in the private market in cases where information is poor. 200 years ago someone who was ill would go to a doctor and ask to be bled. Suppose the doctor bleeds him, using a knife which he has earlier that day used to bleed eight or ten people with assorted diseases. He has never sterilized the knife because he has never heard of germs. Ignoring the germ problem, bleeding is a treatment which will make the person worse almost regardless of what disease he has. Is there a cost in this? With our present scientific knowledge, this was clearly an erroneous decision by the purchaser of medical services.

To make the problem a little more difficult, let us assume it is not 200 years ago, but 130 years ago and that most doctors and most patients have realized that bleeding is not a good treatment. Suppose, however, that an old-fashioned patient and an old-fashioned doctor reach a mutually agreeable bargain under which the doctor bled the patient once again, using an unsterilized knife. Does this impose a 'cost' on the patient?

These questions are not very important for a student of the market but, once again, when we turn to rent seeking, they are significant. Let us take an example where the people are well informed but where there are externalities. Suppose a car driver is polluting the air and this is in the early 1950s, where there are no regulations on it. He would be aware of the fact that if he stopped polluting the air, it would have almost no effect on him although everyone else in the society and, for the matter, he himself would be trivially better off. Since the cost would fall entirely on him and the benefit to him would be trivial, he would choose not to do so. This would be so even if the benefit from that act, summed over the entire society, was very considerably greater than the cost to him. Economists normally say that, in this case, he would be imposing a cost on the society and would favor social institutions to compel him to either stop imposing his pollution on the society or at least to pay its full costs.

Let us go to another case which is a closer fit to what we have in mind. Suppose that the society is proposing to restrict air pollutants and that the dry-cleaning establishments organized for the purpose of being exempted from the act. They make deals with various other pressure groups agreeing to vote for Congressmen who favor restricting the import of Japanese automobiles, favor the farm program, etc. As a result they get their exemption built into the act with the result that the level of air pollution is very considerably higher than it otherwise would be. Is this a cost?

The last is particularly important because it seems very largely true that rent seeking depends on just exactly that kind of maneuvering and the question of whether it is a cost or not, is important in attempting to measure the cost of rent seeking. Suppose, for example, that we have perfect information and are able to investigate all of the influences which led to, let us say, the farm program getting through. We found that misinformation about the farm program on the part of non-farmers was important. As a result of their ignorance they did not push against it and the farmers used their influence to get it. These two factors between them are, let us say, 90% of the 'causal' factors, which led to its going through. There were, in addition to this, some campaign contributions, spectacular dinners with feminine companionship and possibly bribes, but these things added up to less than 10% of the 'causal' factors. Would we include the 90% in the cost of rent seeking or would we not?

Suppose that we have a political system like that which is sometimes seen in high school civics texts, in which the voters vote in terms of what they think is good for the country. These texts imply, probably not too inaccurately, that what is good for the country is also good for the individual voter. The voter, being systematically uninformed, would make a very bad choice of policies to benefit the country. If we turn to a realistic situation, in which at least a great many voters vote specifically to benefit themselves by such things as the farm program, the outcome would certainly be different than if they were voting in terms of the 'Public Interest', but it's not obvious that it will be inferior.

As a former Foreign Service Officer and a man much interested in foreign policy, I have paid careful attention to the development of American policies in this area. No doubt, some of them are motivated by fairly selfish drives on the part of the voters. At one time, for example, the aid program was keeping the American locomotive industry alive. On the other hand, there is equally no doubt that a number of the policies do not have any particular selfish group in the United States pushing them.

Our generally vague desire that foreign countries be democracies is an example. In this case, a great many Americans will maintain, without showing any signs of realizing how absurd it is, that such democratic governments are in the interest of the United States as well as something we think is ethically good. This is, however, pretty clearly a rationalization. Schumpeter (1942) described American policy as 'ethical imperialism', i.e., an effort to impose the American ethical system through the world. This is something that most Americans want, although most of them refuse to admit that it is their objective. It doesn't have very much in the way of selfish benefit for the average American.

The point, however, of this discussion is that, having studied the situation for a considerable number of years, it is my impression that the common good of the United States in foreign affairs is, on the whole, damaged more by the policies which aim (ignorantly) at the general public good rather than by the policies which are the result of rent seeking.

This is of course merely a subjective option and in any event, even granted the reader agrees with me about foreign policy, it would not prove the same relative damage was done by the two different criteria in domestic affairs. What we have here is a case of voters who, if they get involved in attempting to deal with the public good would do so in a very badly-informed way. If the rent seekers are pushing for some special benefit for themselves, they also will not be very well informed and not engage in a great deal of thought about the problem. But the odds are that the policy will be more likely to serve their selfish interests than 'publicly interested' policy is to serve the public good.

It is not at all obvious, even if we look at this from the standpoint of an abstract external observer who knows all, that we would object to the voters specializing their interests. It may not do as much damage as attempting to implement the public good.

Another problem is that in some cases we want the special interest to be implemented. My first article (1959) in this general area dealt with the situation in which road repairing, up to a point, benefitted people who lived on the road to be repaired more than the cost imposed on society as a whole. There are many cases of this sort, i.e., situations in which for some reason or another it is hard for a small group to provide something which is of interest to them, but where providing it would cost society less than the benefit to the small group. In these circumstances we would suggest that society provide it on the assumption that all of us will from time to time be in the same small group situation.

The problem is, of course, that the small group may push for things where the benefit to them is smaller, indeed in many cases immensely smaller, than the injury inflicted on other people. Unfortunately, these rent seekers may get their way.

Of course, our desire to impose our ethical system on other people may also have very negative effects. William Jennings Bryan was Secretary of State in the early part of the Wilson Administration. His policy towards China, which was an active one, aimed at the objective of not interfering with the rapid conversion of China to Christianity which he believed was taking place at that time. Indeed, he not only refrained from interfering with it, he was in favor of pushing it ahead. This was an ethically driven policy intended to do good and the most one can say for it is that quite possibly it did no positive harm.

In a way, the Chinese Revolution was brought on by President William Howard Taft who was making a very ill-advised[1] effort to obtain special privileges for American bankers.[2] In doing so he delayed the construction of some important railroads. The delay, through a set of devious channels, was the initiating cause of the revolution in the same sense that the assassination of Archduke Franz Ferdinand was the initiating cost of World War I.

All of this has been simply a general discussion. Let's try and do a little formal reasoning. For this purpose, let me assume someone has produced a computer which knows everybody's utility and is able to calculate those private and public decisions which will maximize that utility.[3]

Let us begin with private purchases and assume that this computer is in charge of somebody's purchases and buys the things for that person which will maximize his or her lifetime utility. In 1776 this would not have ordered a bleeding, for example. Compare this with the decision that would have been made by that person himself, assuming that he also had perfect knowledge about that nature of all products and services on the market, but not perfect knowledge about his own utility production function. The last seems a little absurd, but you do buy things which you think you'll enjoy and then discover that you don't. The computer would not make this kind of error.

Thus, the computer would do better than the purchaser would even if the purchaser devoted an infinite amount of time studying before each purchase.[4] It would, in fact, do better than any human instrumentality because it would know things that have not yet been discovered. In reality, of course, the individual does not know very much about most of the products and services he buys. Further, he in essence depends on other people to make a lot of the preliminary decisions for him.

I buy clothes from stores that specialize in producing clothing for people who, like myself, are in the upper- but a long way from the top-income brackets. In doing so, I am assuming, first that my fellow consumers from this store do at least a reasonably good job in judging price and quantity and secondly, that the store owners who want to make money by pleasing their customers do a reasonably good job at meeting those standards. I am to some extent free riding on the other customers and each of them is free riding on me. If turned to such subjects as medicine, electronic devices etc. my state of knowledge differs even farther from that of our super computer.

Bentham, as mentioned above, dealt with this problem by saying that we should let the individual make decisions not because those decisions would necessarily be right, but because they were more in accord with his utility than any other mechanism we could design. In other words, he denied the existence of my super computer. Since it is only an imaginary construct, I naturally would not disagree with him. Thus, it is probably sensible to let people make decisions of this sort and indeed we can refer to a society in which such decisions control almost everything as being optimal in what is not a nonsensical use of the word 'optimal'. Those critics of the market system who point out that customers are frequently ill-informed are quite right. But once we get out of the market, the information problem is much more severe.

It's not widely known, but one of the things that the market provides to the private citizens is an opportunity to benefit other people. They may contribute money to the American Cancer Society, George Mason University or simply give money to a beggar on the street. In all of these cases, you would say that they are purchasing a feeling of satisfaction gained by benefitting other people although, once again, information can be bad (see Tullock, 1966). Indeed, in this case the information is far more likely to be bad than in the straightforward purchase because the individual who is purchasing a feeling of satisfaction from having made the gift, will not himself directly benefit or be injured as a result of what the gift actually provides.

Once again, Bentham would say, and I do not disagree, that the individual should make this decision, seeking out whatever advice he thinks is sensible.[5]

So far we have been comparing the computer with decisions made by individuals in the market environment. Further, we have totally ignored externalities. We must now deal with externalities because we are going to turn now to talking about government, specifically democratic government. After all, externalities are the basic reason that we have governments. Hence it is sensible to leave them aside in discussing the market. The government should deal with them, although anyone who looks at actual governments realizes that they're almost as likely to generate externalities as to eliminate them.

Let us then turn, once again, to our perfect computer and assume that it is dealing with some decision which, due to externalities, must be made collectively. The computer, knowing all and making no calculating mistakes, determines whether some particular government activity should be undertaken and its scale. Of course, our perfect computer could also allocate the entire cost of the activity among the taxpayers in such a way that the cost was proportional to the benefit, but we will assume that it does not do that, it uses ordinary taxes. Thus, there will be probably some people gaining and some people losing. What the computer does, is to make certain that the total gain in utility is greater than the total loss. Once again, I would like to emphasize that the machine is a piece of science fiction designed for this article.

The actual behavior of the voters is apt to deviate sharply from this ideal pattern of behavior for two reasons, one of which is they're not perfectly informed nor prefect calculators. The other is that individuals will favor things that benefit themselves, even if the total cost is greater than the total benefit. Let us take these two problems up, one at a time, beginning with information.

As mentioned above, there is a very elderly and respectable proof in the *Public Choice* literature which demonstrates that individuals are normally badly informed in politics and this is particularly true with respect to what we might call public interest types of matters. These individual decisions are apt to deviate from the decisions of our computer in a fairly extreme way simply because of poor information.

This poor information is not just poor information in the sense of lack of calculation, however. Our computer not only makes all perfect computations, but knows what other people's utilities are. The average voter will not know other people's utility.

When it comes to matters directly affecting the voter, he is apt to be better informed than in matters of general interest. To say that he is apt to be better informed is quite different from saying he is apt to be very well informed. Here too, public good consideration means that the single person who is one of a group of one hundred thousand who will be benefited by something or other will devote not too much time to becoming well informed about it. In fact, if he is well informed it is more likely to be for other reasons. He reads farming journals for technical help in running his farm and gets political information as a by-product.

When we turn to individual's knowledge of other people's utility, the situation becomes even worse. Firstly, he may not be interested in whether they are gaining or not, but, secondly, if he is interested in helping them, and most of us are to some extent interested in helping others, he has very little information as to what actually will help them. In particular, if we look at the programs to help the poor, it is obvious that the people who design them think that the poor's judgement of what will benefit them is bad. Payments in kind are very common under such circumstances and detailed efforts to regulate the lives of the people who are being aided are also very common. In a way, the charitably inclined person is like our giant computer attempting to give people what is good for them and not what they, ill-informedly, want.

There is an area where possibly bad information benefits society when looked at in the whole matter on a large scale. The individual probably has an ill-thought-out set of principles of public behavior and morality which will effect his voting behavior when he hears that something has gone on in government which he objects to. Scandals such as misappropriation of funds are an obvious example, but there are a whole collection of others. In particular, transfers or special regulations that benefit small groups have to be to some extent presented in deceptive ways which makes them much less efficient than they otherwise would be. This lack of efficiency, however, has the positive benefit that it reduces the profit from these activities and hence reduces the amount of energy that rent seekers will put into attempting to get them.

On the other hand, there is no doubt that the fact that these are ill thought out has a major disadvantage. Anyone who is attempting to sell a significant government reform knows the normal immediate reaction of simple objection with nothing very well thought out in the way of reasons for that objection and an unwillingness to devote much time and thought to the matter. The standard approach of the average voter is moralistic and he will accept moral criticism of the government and, in fact, suggest the government become more moral. But any attempt to convince him that the structure is somehow badly designed is normally resisted and the resistance is not based upon serious thought or good information.

The second problem is that the individual, unlike our machine, is interested in himself more than in other people. To repeat, he probably has, as most of us do, at least some interest in helping the country, the poor, the people who are suffering from cancer, etc. But this is usually less intense than his desire to help himself and his family.

If it were not for the externalities problem, and in politics the externality frequently takes the form of a tax on somebody else, we could ignore that matter. We could let individuals all make their decisions in terms of what benefited them, and assume that those issues which passed by majority vote, be it directly or by logrolling, on the average will be beneficial. They would not be quite as good as our machine's calculation, but they wouldn't be very much inferior.

Unfortunately, of course, governmental activities are externality laden, and the decision of the textile workers, for example, to push for a tariff on textiles[6] will generate very decided external costs.

Suppose then that we observe a set of protective tariffs which were voted through democratically. We sometimes say they are costly because they differ from what would have been passed if the voters had all been simply interested in maximizing the public interest. But are they really costly? This is the problem that I have been leading up to in this article.

It seems possible that the principle payment that politicians in the United States receive from rent-seeking groups comes not in the form of elaborate dinners or direct cash payments, but in the form of specialized votes. The special interest group which makes it clear that it has a sizeable number of voters who will ignore all other considerations and vote solely in terms of whether their congressman has or has not backed, let us say a cotton textile tariff, inflicts an injury on the economy as a whole, but can we say that these votes are in fact costly?

In a democracy, the government is supposed to be controlled by the votes cast. If the voters vote for something which economists think is not in fact desirable, can we call it a cost? Can we follow the Benthamite assumption that their judgement is better than any other judgement here? Note that, once again, Bentham's judgement did not turn on any argument that they were right, but on the argument that individuals knew more about their own utility than anyone else. It should of course also be pointed out that Bentham would be horrified by a cotton textile tariff.

This whole problem turns on deep metaphysical views as to what the government is supposedly doing. Most economists think of government as an organization for internalizing externalities. It makes it possible for us to reach a higher level of satisfaction than we could without it. From that standpoint the cotton textile tariff clearly is undesirable. We might argue that the government as a whole is highly desirable even if it does enact tariffs on cotton textiles, but still, we can say that the cotton textile tariff is simply wrong.

If on the other hand we, and once again as most economists do, believe that the people should get what they choose, the cotton textile tariff is right and desirable. Add on the prospect that if the voters stop voting in terms of their special interest and began voting in terms of the public interest, their motives for becoming well informed would be extremely weak and hence their decisions would have almost a random relationship to that public interest. Then the problem becomes even more difficult.

Let me add on a final item of difficulty and then resign the problem to my readers. The final item concerns the fact that pressure groups very commonly deliberately spread misinformation among the voters. Thus, a regulation may be so designed that it benefits some participants in a given industry but not in others, but it would be sold on the theory that it benefits 'the industry'. To take an example, when the AAA was introduced in the 1930s it benefited the owners of agricultural land a great deal and injured hired labor in agriculture a great deal. I suspect that most hired laborers would have favored congressmen who voted for this bill, because they thought it was good for 'agriculture'. Certainly they were encouraged to do so by the farm groups' propaganda.

This, however, is within the group, outside you also have this kind of misinformation. The widespread view among the citizenry that protective tariffs are beneficial not just to the industry that is protected but to everybody, is an example. Suppose that someone votes for something which he mistakenly thinks will benefit him because he is a member of a special interest group, but it will not. Is this a 'cost'? Suppose that a citizen whose only connection with the cotton textile industry is to buy clothes, is convinced that at the very least a congressman voting for a protective tariff on textiles is doing nothing which injures him and perhaps doing something that benefits him. Once again, is this a cost?

The problem here is how much weight we should give to people's ill considered views as to what should be done. The argument for giving them overwhelming weight in private decisions is not only Benthamite, but favored by practically all other economists. For public decisions the argument is not nearly as strong.

There is another problem. We have no objection to people making their market decisions in terms of their own selfish well-being. Once again, in the case of the government it is not so obvious that we should feel that way. On the other hand, it is not at all obvious that we shouldn't.

I sub-titled this article 'A metaphysical question.' Metaphysics, in this case, is not meant in strict technical terms, but in the sense of a rather confusing problem. Further, it is a problem of great importance, particularly for the analysis of rent seeking. This essay certainly does not solve it. Can the readers do better?

Notes

1. The advice came from the Department of State which simply misunderstood economics.
2. The bankers didn't want them.
3. We need not worry about the problem of comparing utility between persons. Science-fiction, after all, is science-fiction.
4. With the infinite time somehow having zero cost to him.
5. I knew a wealthy man whose foundation provided financial support for tournaments between professional bridge players. I thought this was a total waste of money, but he didn't. The Internal Revenue Service ruled that it was a charitable contribution.
6. I've just been informed that a senior professor in one of the states which produces textiles is in the process of being driven from his university because he wrote a paper in which he said that textile tariffs were a bad idea.

Bibilography

Abramovitz, M., and I. Stegun. 1970. *Handbook of Mathematical Functions*. New York: Dover.

Alchian, A. A., and W. R. Allen. 1983. *Exchange and Production: Competition, Coordination, and Control*. 3rd ed. Belmont, CA: Wadsworth.

Alexeev, M. 1999. The effect of privatization on wealth distribution in Russia. *ECON TRANSIT* 7:449-465.

Alexeev, M., and J. Leitzel. 1996. Rent shrinking. *Southern Economic Journal* 62:620-26.

Allard, R. J. 1999. Risk Aversion and the Full Costs of Rent-Seeking. *Bulletin of economic Research* 51:95-109.

Amegashie, J. A. 1998. The Design of Rent-Seeking Competitions: Committees, Preliminary and Final Contests. *Public Choice* 99:63-76.

Anam, M. 1982. Distortion-triggered lobbying and welfare: A contribution to the theory of directly unproductive profit-seeking activities. *Journal of International Economics* 13:15-32.

Anderson, S. P., and M. Engers. 1989. Strategic investment and timing of entry. University of Virginia, Discussion Paper 203

Appelbaum, E., and E. Katz. 1986. Transfer seeking and avoidance: On the full social costs of rent-seeking. *Public Choice* 48:175-181.

Appelbaum, E., and E. Katz. 1986. Rent-seeking and entry. *Economic Letters* 20:207-12.

Appelbaum, E., and E. Katz. 1987. Seeking rents by setting rents: The political economy of rent-seeking. *Economic Journal* 97:685-689.

Aumann, R. J. 1981. Survey of repeated games. In *Essays in game theory and mathematical economics in honor of Oskar Morgenstern*. Manheim: Bibliographisches Institute.

Baik, K. H. 1993. Winner-help-loser group formation in rent-seeking contests. Paper read at 62nd Annual Conference of the Southern Economic Association, at Washington, D.C.

Baik, K. H. 1994. Effort Levels in Contests with two asymmetric players. *Southern Economic Journal* 61:367-78.

Baik, K. H., and J. F. Shogren. 1992. Strategic Behavior in Contests: Comment. *The American Economic Review* 82:359-362.

Baik, K. H., and J. F. Shogren. 1995. Competitive-share group formation in rent-seeking contests. *Public Choice* 83:113-126.

Barro, R. J., and P. M. Romer. 1987. Ski-lift pricing with applications to labor and other markets. *American Economic Review* 77:875-890.

Barzel, Y. 1968. Optimal timing of innovations. *Review of Economics and Statistics* 50:348-55.

Barzel, Y. 1974. A theory of rationing by waiting. *Journal of Law and*

Economics 17:73-95.

Baumol, W. J., J. C. Panzar, and R. D. Willig. 1972. *Contestable markets and the theory of industry structure*. New York: Harcourt Brace Jovanovich, Inc.

Baye, M. R., D. Kovenock, and C. G. deVries. 1989. The economics of all-pay, winner-take-all contests. Texas A&M University.

Baye, M. R., D. Kovenock, and C. G. deVries. 1990. The all-pay auction with complete information. Working Paper 89-21

Baye, M. R., D. Kovenock, and C. G. deVries. 1993. Rigging the lobbying process: An application of the all-pay auction. *American Economic Review* 83:289-94.

Baye, M. R., G. Tian, and J. Zhou. 1993. Characterizations of the existence of equilibria in games with discontinuous and nonquasiconcave payoffs. *Review of Economic Studies* 60:935-48.

Becker, Gary S. 1968. Crime and punishment: An economic approach. *Journal of Political Economy* 76:169-217.

Becker, Gary S. 1983. A theory of competition among pressure groups for political influence. *Quarterly Journal of Economics* 98:371-400.

Becker, Gary S. 1985. Public policies, pressure groups, and deadweight costs. *Journal of Public Economics* 28:329-47.

Becker, G. S., and G. J. Stigler. 1974. Law Enforcement, malfeasance, and compensation of enforcers. *Journal of Legal Studies* 3:1-18.

Besen, S. M., and J. Farrell. 1994. Choosing how to compete: Strategies and tactics in standardization. *Journal of Economic Perspectives* 8:117-31.

Bhagwati, J. N. 1980. Lobbying and welfare. *Journal of Public Economics* 14:355-63.

Bhagwati, J. N. 1982. Directly unproductive profit seeking (DUP) activities. *Journal of Political Economy* 90:988-1002.

Bhagwati, J. N., and T. N. Srinivasan. 1980. Revenue seeking: A generalization of the theory of tariffs. *Journal of Political Economy* 88:1069-1087.

Binmore, K. G. 1992. *Fun and games*. Lexington, MA: Heath.

Birnbaum, J. H., and A. S. Murray. 1987. *Showdown at Gucci Gulch: Lawyers, lobbyists, and the unlikely triumph of tax reform*. New York: Vantage.

Bouckaert, J., H. Degrise, and C. G. de Vries. 1992. Veilingen waarbij iedereen betaalt en toch wint. *Tijdschrift voor economie en management* 37:375-393.

Brackney, H. 1959. The dynamics of military combat. *Operations Research* 7:30-44.

Brady, G., and R. D. Tollison. 1991. Gordon Tullock: Creative maverick of public choice. *Public Choice* 71:141-148.

Brandenburger, A. 1992. Knowledge and equilibrium in games. *Journal of*

Economic Perspectives 6:83-102.
Bronsstein, I. N., and K. Semendjajew. 1981. *Tashenbuch der Mathematik.* Leipzigs Teubner.
Brooks, M., and B. Heijdra. 1989. An exploration of rent seeking. *Economic Record* 65:32-50.
Buchanan, J. M. 1980. Rent seeking and profit seeking. In *Towards a theory of the rent seeking society*, edited by J. M. Buchanan, R. D. Tollison and G. Tullock. College Station: Texas A&M University Press.
Buchanan, J. M., R. D. Tollison, and G. Tullock, eds. 1980. *Towards a theory of the rent seeking society.* College Station: Texas A&M University Press.
Buchanan, James M., and Gordon Tullock. 1965. *The Calculus of Consent: Logical Foundations of Constitutional Democracy.* Ann Arbor: University of Michigan Press.
Bull, C., A. Schotter, and K. Weigelt. 1987. Tournaments and piece rates: An experimental study. *Journal of Political Economy* 95:1-33.
Bürger, G. A. 1786. *Wunderbare Reisen zu Wasser und zu Lande, Feldzuge und lustige Abenteuer des Freyherrrn von Münchhausen*: Hannover.
C. D. Delorme, Jr., and A Snow. 1990. On the limits to rent-seeking waste. *Public Choice* 67:129-154.
Cairns, R. D. 1989. Dynamic rent-seeking. *Journal of Public Economics* 39:315-334.
Cairns, R. D., and N. V. Long. 1991. Rent-seeking with uncertain opposition. *Eurpoean Economic Review* 35:1223-1235.
Capen, E. C., R. V. Clapp, and W. M. Campbell. 1971. Competitive bidding in high-risk situations. *Journal of Petroleum Technology* (June):641-651.
Carlton, D. W. 1983. Equilibrium fluctuations when price and delivery lags clear the market. *Bell Journal of Economics* 14:562-72.
Chamberlin, E. H. 1962. *The theory of monopolistic competition: A re-orientation of the theory of value.* 8th ed. Cambridge, MA.: Harvard University Press.
Cherkes, M., J. Friedman, and A. Spivak. 1986. The disinterest in regulation: Comment. *American Economic Review* 76:559-563.
Cheung, S. N. S. 1974. A theory of price control. *Journal of Law and Economics* 17:53-71.
Chung, T.-Y. 1996. Rent-seeking contest when prize increases with aggregate efforts. *Public Choice* 87:55-66.
Comanor, W. S., and R. H. Smiley. 1975. Monopoly and the distribution of wealth. *Quarterly Journal of Economics* 89:177-194.
Congleton, R. D. 1980. Competitive process, competitive waste, and institutions. In *Toward a theory of the rent-seeking society*, edited by J. M. Buchanan, R. D. Tollison and G. Tullock. College Station: Texas A&M University Press.
Congleton, R. D. 1984. Committees and rent-seeking effort. *Journal of Public*

Economics 25:197-209.

Congleton, R. D. 1989. Efficient status seeking: Externalities, and the evolution of status games. *Journal of Economic Behavior and Organization* 11:175-90.

Crew, M. A., and C. K. Rowley. 1988. Dispelling the disinterest in deregulation. In *The politcal economy of rent seeking*, edited by C. K. Rowley, R. D. Tollison and G. Tullock. Boston, MA: Kluwer.

Dasgupta, P. 1986. The theory of technological competition. In *New developments in the analysis of market structure*, edited by J. E. Stiglitz and G. F. Mathewson. Cambridge MA: MIT Press.

Dasgupta, P., and E. Mashkin. 1986. The existence of equilibrium in discontinuous games, I: Theory. *Review of Economic Studies* 53:1-26.

Dasgupta, P., and K. O. Nti. 1998. Designing an optimal contest. *European Journal of Political Economy* 14:587-603.

Dasgupta, P., and J. E. Stiglitz. 1980. Industrial structure and the nature of innovative activity. *Economic Journal* 90:266-93.

Dasgupta, P., and J. E. Stiglitz. 1980. Uncertainty, industrial structure, and the speed of R & D. *Bell Journal of Economics* 11:1-28.

Deacon, Robert T., and Jon Sonstelie. 1991. Price controls and rent dissipation with endogenous transaction costs. *The American Economic Review* 81:1361-1373.

Debreu, G. 1952. A social equilibrium existence theorem. *Proceedings of the National Academy of Science* 38:886-893.

Demsetz, H. 1968. Why regulate utilities? *Journal of Law and Economics* 11:55-66.

Demsetz, H. 1976. Economics as a guide to antitrust legislation. *Journal of Law and Economics* 19:371-384.

Denzau, A. T., and M. C. Munger. 1986. Interest groups: How unorganized interests get represented. *American Political Science Review* 76:89-107.

Dixit, A. 1987. Strategic behavior in contests. *American Economic Review* 77:891-898.

Dixit, Avinash. 1987. Strategic Behavior in Contests. *The American Economic Review* 77:891-898.

Dougan, W. R. 1991. The cost of rent-sseking: Is GNP negative? *Journal of Political Economy* 99:660-4.

Douglas, G. W., and J. C. Miller III. 1974. Quality competition, industry equilibrium, and efficiency in the price-constrained airline market. *American Economic Review* 64:657-69.

Dupuy, T. N. 1987. *Understanding war: History and theory of combat*. New York: Paragon House Publishers.

Durden, G. D., L. V. Ellis, and S. W. Millsaps. 1991. Gordon Tullock: His journal and scholarship. *Public Choice* 71:171-96.

Eismeier, T. J., and P. H. Pollock. 1986. Strategy and choice in congressional elections: The role of political action committees. *American Journal of Political Science* 30:197-213.

Ellingsen, T. 1991. Strategic buyers and the social cost of monopoly. *American Economic Review* 81:648-657.

Ellsberg, Daniel. 1956. Theory of the reluctant duelist. *American Economic Review* 46:909-923.

Esteban, J, and D Ray. 1999. Conflict and distribution. *J ECON THEORY* 87:379-415.

Farrell, A., and E. Lander. 1989. Competition between and within teams: The lifeboat principle. *Economics Letters* 29:205-8.

Fenno, R. 1978. *Home style: House members in their districts*. Boston: Little, Brown.

Ferguson, C. E. 1969. *The neoclassical theory of production and distribution*. Cambridge: Cambridge University Press.

Fisher, F. M. 1985. The social costs of monopoly and regulation: Posner reconsidered. *Journal of Political Economy* 93:410-416.

Foster, E. 1981. The treatment of rents in cost-benefit analysis. *American Economic Review* 71:171-178.

Friedman, D. 1981. Why there are no risk preferrers. *Journal of Political Economy* 89:600.

Fudenberg, D., R. Gilbert, J. Stiglitz, and J. Tirole. 1983. Preemption, leapfrogging and competition in patent races. *European Economic Review* 22:3-31.

Fudenberg, D., and O.Tirole. 1987. Understanding rent dissipation: On the use of game theory in industrial organization. *AEA Papers and Proceedings* 77:176-183.

Gahvari, F. 1989. Licensing and non-transferable rents: Comment. *American Economic Review* 79:906-909.

Gardner, B. L. 1987. Causes of U.S. farm commodity programs. *Journal of Political Economy* 95:290-310.

Glazer, A. 1993. On the incentives to establish and play political rent-seeking games. *Public Choice* 75:139-48.

Glazer, A., and R. Hassin. 1988. Optimal contests. *Economic Inquiry* 26:133-43.

Glicksberg, I. L. 1952. A further generalization of the Kakutani Fixed Point Theorem with applications to Nash equilibrium points. *Proceedings of the AMerican Mathematical Society* 38:170-174.

Godwin, R. K. 1988. *One billion dollars of influence: The direct marketing of politics*. Chatham, N.J.: Chatham House.

Gopoian, D. 1984. What makes PACs tick? An analysis of allocation patterns of economic interest groups. *American Journal of Political Science* 28:259-281.

Gradstein, M. 1991. Intensity of competition in strategic contests: Ben-Gurian

University, Beersheva. Mimeo.

Gradstein, M. 1993. Rent-seeking and the provision of public goods. *Economic Journal* 103:1236-43.

Gradstein, Mark. 1995. Intensity of competition, entry and entry deterrence in rent seeking contests. *Economics and Politics* 7:79-91.

Gradstein, M. 1995. Intensity of competition, entry and entry deterrence in rent seeking contests. *Economics and Politics* 7:79-91.

Gradstein, Mark. 1998. Optimal contest design: Volume and timing of rent seeking in contests. *European Journal of Political Economy* 14:79-91.

Gradstein, M., and S. Nitzan. 1989. Advantageous multiple rent-seeking. *Mathematical modeling* 12:511-8.

Gradstein, M., S. Nitzan, and S. Slutsky. 1992. The Effect of Uncertainty on Interactive Behavior. *The Economic Journal* 102:554-561.

Green, J., and N. Stokey. 1983. A comparison of tournaments and contests. *Journal of Political Economy* 91:349-64.

Guttman, J. M., S. Nitzan, and U. Spiegel. 1992. Rent-seeking and social investment in taste change. *Economics and Politics* 4:31-42.

Hamilton, J. H., and S. M. Slutsky. 1990. Endogeneous timing in duopoly games: Stackleberg or Cournot-Equilibria. *Games and Economic Behavior* 2:29-46.

Harberger, A. 1954. Monopoly and resource allocation. *American Economic Review* 44:77-87.

Hardin, R. 1982. With regret. *Western Political Quarterly* 35:181-188.

Harris, C., and J. Vickers. 1985. Patent races and the persistence of monopoly. *Journal of Industrial Economics* 23:461-81.

Harris, C., and J. Vickers. 1985. Perfect equilibrium in a model of race. *Review of Economic Studies* 52:193-209.

Hausken, K. 1995. The dynamics of within-group and between group interaction. *Journal of Mathematical Economics* 24:655-687.

Hazlett, T. W., and R. J. Michaels. 1993. The cost of rent-seeking: Evidence from cellular telephone license lotteries. *Southern Economic Journal* 59:425-35.

Hicks, J. 1970. Elasticity of substitution again: Substitutes and complements. *Oxford Economic Papers* N.S. 22:289-296.

Higgins, R. S., and R. D. Tollison. 1984. Notes on the theory of rent seeking. Unpublished manuscript.

Hillman, A. L. 1982. Declining industries and political-support protectionist motives. *American Economic Review* 72:1180-7.

Hillman, A. L. 1989. *The Political Economy of Protection*. London: Harwood Academic Publishers.

Hillman, A. L., and E. Katz. 1984. Risk-averse rent seekers and the social cost of monopoly power. *Economic Journal* 94:104-110.

Hillman, A. L., and E. Katz. 1987. Hierarchical structure and the social costs of bribes and transfers. *Journal of Public Economics* 34:129-142.

Hillman, A. L., and J. G. Riley. 1989. Politically contestable rents and transfers. *Economics and Politics* 1:17-39.

Hillman, A. L., and D. Samet. 1987. Dissipation of contestable rents by small numbers of contenders. *Public Choice* 54:63-82.

Hillman, A. L., and D. Samet. 1987. Characterizing equilibrium rent-seeking behavior: A reply to Tullock. *Public Choice* 54:85-87.

Hillman, A. L., and D. Samet. 1987. Dissipation of rents and revenues in small numbers contests. *Public Choice* 54:63-82.

Hillman, A. L., and H. W. Ursprung. 1988. Domestic politics, foreign interests, and international trade policy. *American Economic Review* 78:729-45.

Hirshleifer, J. 1988. The analytics of continuing conflict. *Synthese* 76:201-233.

Hirshleifer, J. 1988. *Price Theory and Applications*. Englewood Cliffs, N.J.: Prentice-Hall.

Hirshleifer, J. 1991. The paradox of power. *Economics and Politics* 3:177-200.

Hirshleifer, J., and J. C. Riley. 1978. Auctions and Contests. UCLA. Working Paper no. 188B

Holt, C. A., and R. Sherman. 1982. Waiting-line auctions. *Journal of Political Economy* 90:280-94.

Hurley, T. M., and J. F. Shogren. 1998. Effort levels in a Cournot Nash contest with asymetric information. *Journal of Public Economics* 69:195-210.

Jadlow, J. 1985. Monopoly rent-seeking under conditions of uncertainty. *Public Choice* 45:377-96.

Johnson, P. E. 1990. Asymmetries in political entry. *European Journal of Political Economy* 6:377-396.

Kahana, N., and S. Nitzan. 1993. Credibility and duration of political contests and the extent of rent dissipation. Tilburg: CentER, Tilburg University. Working Paper 9301

Katz, E., and J. Rosenberg. 1989. Rent-seeking for budgetary allocation: Preliminary results for 20 countries. *Public Choice* 60:133-44.

Katz, E., and J. Tokatlidu. 1996. Group competition for rents. *European Journal of Political Economy* 12:599-607.

Keren, M., and D. Levhari. 1983. The internal organization of the firm and the shape of average costs. *Bell Journal of Economics* 14:474-86.

Kitch, E. W. 1977. The nature and function of the patent system. *Journal of Law and Economics* 20:265-90.

Konrad, K., and H. Schlesinger. 1997. Risk aversion in rent-seeking and rent-augmenting games. *Economic Journal* 107:1671-83.

Konrad, K. A., and H. Schlesinger. 1997. Risk aversion in rent-seeking and

rent-augmenting games. *The Economic Journal* 107:1671-1683.
Krueger, A. O. 1974. The political economy of the rent-seeking society. *American Economic Review* 64:291-303.
Laband, D. N., and J. D. Sophocleus. 1988. The social cost of rent-seeking: First estimates. *Public Choice* 58:269-75.
Laband, D. N., and J. D. Sophocleus. 1992. An estimate of resource expenditures on transfer activity in the United States. *Quarterly Journal of Economics* 107:957-983.
Lancaster, F. W. 1916. Aircraft in warfare: The dawn of the fourth arm. In *The world of mathematics*, edited by J. R. Newman. New York: Simon & Schuster.
Landes, W. M., and R. A. Posner. 1975. The independent judiciary in an interest-group perspective. *Journal of Law and Economics* 18:875-902.
Lazear, E., and S. Rosen. 1981. Rank order tournaments and optimum labor contracts. *Journal of Political Economy* 89:841-64.
Lazear, E. P. 1996. *Personel economics*. Cambridge MA: MIT Press.
Lee, S. 1992. Optimal rent-seeking group. *American Economist* 36:58-60.
Lee, S. 1993. Inter-group Competition for a Pure Private Rent. *Quarterly Review of Economics and Finance* 33:261-66.
Lee, S. 1995. Endogeneous sharing rules in collective-group rent seeking. *Public Choice* 85:31-44.
Leininger, W. 1989. Escalation and cooperation in conflict situations. *Journal of Conflict Resolution* 33:231-54.
Leininger, W. 1991. Patent competition, rent dissipation and the persistence of monopoly: The role of research budgets. *Journal of Economic Theory* 53:146-172.
Linster, B. G. 1993. Stackelberg Rent-Seeking. *Public Choice* 77:307-21.
Linster, B. G. 1993. A Generalized-Model of Rent-Seeking Behavior. *Public Choice* 77:421-35.
Linster, B. G. 1993. A generalized model of rent-seeking behavior. *Public Choice* 77:421-435.
Linster, B. G. 1993. Stackleberg rent-seeking. *Public Choice* 77:307-321.
Linster, B. G. 1993. A rent-seeking model of international competition and alliances. *Defence Economics* 4:213-226.
Long, N. V., and N. Vousden. 1987. Risk-averse rent-seeking with shared rents. *Economic Journal* 97:971-985.
Lott, J. R., and R. D. Roberts. 1989. Why comply?: One-sided enforcement of price controls and victimless crime laws. *Journal of Legal Studies* 18:403-414.
Loury, G. C. 1979. Market structure and innovation. *Quarterly Journal of Economics* 93:395-410.
Magee, S. C. 1984. Endogenous tariff theory: A survey. In *Neoclassical Political Economy*, edited by D. C. Colander. Boston: Ballinger.

Magee, S. P., W. A. Brock, and L. Young. 1989. *Black hole tariffs and endogeneous policy theory: Political economy in general equilibrium.* Cambridge: Cambridge University Press.

Mayer, W., and R. G. Riezman. 1987. Endogeneous choice of trade policy instruments. *Journal of International Economics* 23:377-81.

McChesney, Fred S. 1997. *Money for nothing: Politicians, rent extraction, and political extortion.* Cambridge MA: Harvard University Press.

McChesney, Fred S. 1999. Of stranded costs and stranded hopes: The difficulties of deregulation. *Independent Review* 3:485-509.

McCormick, Robert E., William F. Shughart II, and Robert D. Tollison. 1984. The disinterest in deregulation. *Journal of Political Economy* 83:807-27.

McNulty, D. J. 1968. Economic theory and the meaning of competition. *Quarterly Journal of Economics* 82:639-656.

Michaels, R. 1979. Long-term political agreements and the origins of bureaucratic power. In *Public Choice in New Orleans*, edited by G. Tullock. Blacksburg, VA: Center for the Study of Public Choice.

Michaels, R. 1986. Conjectural variations and the nature of equilibrium in rent-seeking models. Unpublished manuscript.

Michaels, R. 1986. Political competition as a Betrand duopoly. Unpublished manuscript.

Michaels, R. 1989. Conjectual variations and the nature of equilibrium in rent-seeking models. *Public Choice* 60:31-9.

Milgrom, P. B., and R. J. Weber. 1982. A theory of auctions and competitive bidding. *Econometrica* 50:1089-1122.

Millner, E. L., and M. D. Pratt. 1989. An experimental investigation of efficient rent-seeking. *Public Choice* 62:139-151.

Millner, E. L., and M. D. Pratt. 1991. Risk aversion and rent-seeking: An extension and some experimental evidence. *Public Choice* 69:81-92.

Moore, T. G. 1978. The beneficiaries of trucking regulation. *Journal of Law and Economics* 21:327-344.

Morgan, J. 1998. Is timing everything? A model of endogeneous sequential contests. Unpublished manuscript.

Moulin, H. 1986. *Game theory for the social sciences.* New York: New York University Press.

Nalebuff, B. J., and J. E. Stiglitz. 1983. Prizes and incentives: Toward a general theory of compensation and competition. *Bell Journal of Economics* 14:21-43.

Nash, J. 1951. Non-cooperative games. *Annals of Mathematics* 54:286-295.

Nitzan, S. 1991. Rent-seeking with non-identical sharing rules. *Public Choice* 97:43-50.

Nitzan, S. 1994. Transfers or public goods provision? A political allocation perspective. *Economics Letters* 45:451-57.

North, D. 1991. Institutions. *Journal of Economic Perspectives* 5:97-112.

Nti, K. O. 1995. Potential competition and coordination in a market entry game: Penn State University. MSIS working paper 95-9.

Nti, K. O. 1997. Comparative statics of contests and rent-seeking games. *International Economic Review* 38:43-59.

Nti, Kofi O. 1997. Comparative statics of contests and rent-seeking games. *International Economic Review* 38:43-59.

Olson, M. 1965. *The Logic of Collective Action*. Cambridge, MA: Harvard University Press.

O'Neill, B. 1986. International escalation and the dollar auction. *Journal of Conflict resolution* 31:33-50.

Paul, C., and A. Wilhite. 1994. Illegal markets and the social costs of rent-seeking. *Public Choice* 79:105-115.

Pelzman, S. 1976. Toward a more general theory of regulation. *Journal of Law and Economics* 19:807-827.

Posner, R. A. 1975. The social costs of monopoly and regulation. *Journal of Political Economy* 83:807-827.

Potters, J., C. G. de Vries, and F. van Winden. 1997. Laboratories are conducive to rational rent seeking and overdissipation.

Potters, J., and F. van Winden. 1993. Models of interest groups: Four different approaches. In *Social choice and political economy*, edited by N. Schofield. Boston MA: Kluwer.

Rama, M. 1993. Imperfect rent dissipation in the rent-seeking society. Unpublished manuscript.

Raspe, R. E. 1785. *Baron Münchhausens narractive of his marvellous travels and campaigns in Russia*: Oxford.

Reinganum, J. F. 1989. The timing of innovation: Research, devlopment, and diffusion. In *hndbook of Industrial organization*, edited by R. Schmalensee and R. D. Willig. Amsterdam: North Holland.

Riaz, K., J. F. Shogren, and S. R. Johnson. 1991. Contests with endogeneously valued prizes: The case of pure public goods. Ames, IA: Iowa State University. Unpublished manuscript.

Riaz, K., J. F. Shogren, and S. R. Johnson. 1995. A general model of rent seeking for public goods. *Public Choice* 82:243-59.

Riley, J. G., and W. F. Samuelson. 1981. Optimal auctions. *American Economic Review* 71:381-92.

Rodik, D. 1986. Tariffs, subsidies and welfare with endogeneous policy. *Journal of International Economics* 21:285-99.

Rogerson, W. P. 1982. The social costs of monopoly and regulation: A game-theoretic analysis. *Bell Journal of Economics* 13:391-401.

Rogerson, W. P. 1989. Profit regulation of defense contractors and prizes for innovation. *Journal of Political Economy* 97:1284-1305.

Rosen, S. 1986. Prizes and incentives in elimination tournaments. *American Economic Review* 76:701-15.

Rosen, S. 1988. Promotions, elections and other contests. *Journal of Institutional and Theoretical Economics* 144:73-90.

Rowley, C. K. 1991. Gordon Tullock: Entrepreneur of public choice. *Public Choice* 71:149-69.

Rowley, C. K., R. D. Tollison, and G. Tullock. 1988. *The politcal economy of rent seeking*. Boston, MA: Kluwer.

Rubenstein, A. 1991. Comments on the interpretation of game theory. *Econometrica* 59:909-24.

Sah, R. K. 1987. Queues, rations, and market: Comparisons of outcomes for the poor and the rich. *American Economic Review* 77:69-77.

Sah, R. K. 1991. Fallibility in economic organizations and political systems. *Journal of Economic perspectives* 5:67-88.

Schlozman, K. L., and J. Tierney. 1986. *Organized interests and American democracy*. New York: Harper and Row.

Schmidt, T. 1992. Rent-seeking firms and consumers: An economic analysis. *Economics and Politics* 4:137-49.

Schumpeter, A. 1942. *Capitalism, socialism and democracy*. New York: Harper.

Selby, E. B., and W. Beranek. 1981. Sweepstakes contests: Analysis, strategies, and survey. *American Economic Review* 71:189-195.

Selten, R. 1965. Spieltheoretische Behandlung eines Oligopolmodells mit Nachfrageträgheit. *Zeitschrift für die gesamten Staatswissenschaften* 121:301-324.

Selten, R. 1975. Reexamination of the perfectness concept for equilibrium points. *International Journal of Game Theory* 4:25-55.

Shilony, Y. 1985. The sequence method for finding solutions to infinite games: A first demonstrating example. *Journal of Optimization Theory and Application* 46:105-17.

Shogren, J. F., and K. H. Baik. 1991. Reexamining efficient rent-seeking in laboratory markets. *Public Choice* 69:69-79.

Shogren, J. F., and K. H. Baik. 1992. Favorites and underdogs: Strategic behavior in an experimental contest. *Public Choice* 74:191-205.

Shubik, M. 1959. *Strategy and market structure: Competition, oligopoly, and the theory of games*. New York: Wiley.

Shubik, M. 1971. The dollar auction game: A paradox for equilibrium points in extensive games. *Journal of Conflict Resolution* 15:545-7.

Shubik, M. 1971. The dollar auction game: A paradox for equilibrium points in extensive games. *Journal of Conflict Resolution* 15:545-7.

Shubik, M. 1982. *Game theory and the social sciences, concepts and solutions*. Cambridge, MA: MIT Press.

Shughart, WF. 1999. The reformer's dilemma. *PUBLIC FINANC REV* 27:561-565.

Skaperdas, S. 1992. Cooperation, conflict, and power in the absence of property rights. *American Economic Review* 82:720-39.

Skaperdas, S. 1996. Contest success functions. *Economic Theory* 7:283-290.

Skaperdas, S., and B. Grofman. 1995. Modeling negative campaigning. *American Political Science Review* 89:49-61.

Snyder, J. M. 1989. Election goals and the allocation of campaign resources. *Econometrica* 57:637-660.

Snyder, J. M. 1990. Campaign contributions as investments: The U.S. House of Representatives, 1980-1986. *Journal of Political Economy* 98:1195-1228.

Sorauf, F. 1988. *Money in congressional elections*. Glenview, IL: Scott, Foresman.

Stake, JE. 1990. Toward an economic understanding of touch and concern. *PUBLIC CHOICE* 65:157-165.

Stein, H. 1987. Balancing the budget - Compared with what? *AEI Economist* (February).

Stephen, J. 1993. Preliminary vs. final decision: Another aspect of dynamic rent seeking. Portrush, Northern Ireland: Presented at the April meeting of the European Public Choice Society.

Suen, W. 1988. Diversity in the market: A statistical approach to consumer theory. Ph.D. dissertation. University of Washington

Sun, Guang-Zhen, and Yew-Kwang Ng. 1999. The effect of number and size of interest groups on social rent. *Public Choice* 101:251-265.

Sun GZ, Ng YK. 1999. The effect of number and size of interest groups on social rent dissipation. *Public Choice* 101:251-265.

Takayama, A. 1985. *Mathematical economics*. Cambridge: Cambridge university Press.

Tirole, J. 1988. *The theory of industrial organizations*. Cambridge, MA: MIT Press.

Tobin, J. 1952. A survey of the theory of rationing. *Econometrica* 20:521-53.

Tollison, R. D. 1982. Rent-seeking: A survey. *Kyklos* 35:575-602.

Tollison, R. D. 1987. Is the theory of rent-seeking here to stay? In *Democracy and Public Choice: Essays in honor of Gordon Tullock*, edited by C. K. Rowley. Oxford: Basil Blackwell.

Tollison, R. D. 1997. Rent seeking. In *Perspectives on Public Choice: A Handbook*, edited by D. C. Mueller. Cambridge: Cambridge University Press.

Tollison, R. D., and R. E. Wagner. 1991. Romance, reality and economic reform. *Kyklos* 44:57-70.

Tullock, G. 1959. Problems of majority voting. *Journal of Political Economy* 67:571-579.

Tullock, G. 1966. Information without profit. Charlottesville, VA: Thomas Jefferson Center for Political Economy. Papers on non-market decision making.

Tullock, Gordon. 1967. The welfare cost of tariffs, monopolies, and theft. *Western Economic Journal* 5:224-232.
Tullock, G. 1974. *The social dilemma: The economics of war and revolution*. Blacksburg, VA: University Publications.
Tullock, Gordon. 1975. The transitional gains trap. *Bell Journal of Economics and Management Science* 6:671-78.
Tullock, Gordon. 1975. On the efficient organization of trials. *Kyklos* 28:745-62.
Tullock, G. 1980. Rent-seeking as a negative-sum game. In *Toward a theory of the rent-seeking society*, edited by J. M. Buchanan, R. D. Tollison and G. Tullock. College Station: Texas A&M University Press. 97-112
Tullock, Gordon. 1987. Another part of the swamp. *Public Choice* 54:83-84.
Tullock, G. 1988. Future directions for rent-seeking research. In *The Politcal Economy of Rent-Seeking*, edited by C. K. Rowley and R. D. Tollison: Kluwer.
Tullock, Gordon. 1989. Editorial comment. *Public Choice* 62:153-154.
Tullock, G. 1989. *The economics of special privilege and rent seeking*. Boston, MA: Kluwer.
Tullock, G. 1991. Hawks, doves and free riders. German translated excerpts in Wirtshaftswoche, 132-4.
Tullock, Gordon. 1992. Games and Preference. *Rationality & Society* 4:24-32.
Tullock, G. 1992. Games and preference. *Rationality and Society* 4.1:24-32.
Tullock, G. 1992. Hawks, doves and free riders. *Kyklos* 45:25-36.
Tullock, Gordon. 1997. Where is the rectangle? *Public Choice* 91:149-159.
Ursprung, H. 1990. Public Goods, Rent Dissipation, and Candidate Competition. *Economics and Politics* 2:115-32.
Vany, A. S. De. 1976. Uncertainty, waiting time, and capacity utilization: A stochastic theory of product quality. *Journal of Political Economy* 84:523-41.
Varian, H. R. 1978. *Microeconomic Analysis*. New York: Norton.
Varian, H. R. 1989. Measuring the deadweight costs of DUP and rent seeking activities. *Economics and Politics* 1:81-95.
Vorob'ev. 1977. *Game theory: Lectures for economists and system scientists*. Berlin: Springer-Verlag.
Waldow, K. H. 1989. Dynamic aspects of lobbying.
Weesie, J., and A. Verbeek. 1993. A proportional rewards game: Competition among heterogeneous actors. *Journal of Mathematical Sociology* 17:261-79.
Wenders, J. T. 1987. On perfect rent dissipation. *American Economic Review* 77:456-459.
Wilson, R. B. 1977. A bidding model of perfect competition. *Review of Economic Studies* 44:511-518.
Wirl, F. 1991. The dynamics of lobbying - a differential game. Presented at

the European Meeting of the Public Choice Society, Turin, Italy, April 1991
Wright, J. 1985. PACs, contributions, and roll calls: An organizational perspective. *American Political Science Review* 79:400-414.
Y.Che, and I. Gale. 1996. Financial constraints in auctions: Effects and antidotes. *Advances in Applied Microeconomics* 6:97-120.
Yandle, Bruce. 1986. Rentless rent-seeking and abnormal returns. *Public Choice* 48:265-270.
Yang, C.-L. 1992. Essays on the theory of rent-seeking. Ph.D. Dissertation, University of Dortmund, Dortmund.
Yang, Chun-Lei. 1994. A simple extension of the Dasgupta-Mashkin existence theorem for discontinuous games with an application to the theory of rent-seeking. *Economics Letters* 45:181-3.

Index

If including degree of dissipation, see a26:442